HOLOCAUST AND THE MOVING IMAGE

HOLOCAUST AND THE MOVING IMAGE
Representations in Film and Television Since 1933

edited by Toby Haggith & Joanna Newman

WALLFLOWER PRESS
LONDON & NEW YORK

First published in Great Britain in 2005 by
Wallflower Press
6a Middleton Place, Langham Street, London W1W 7TE
www.wallflowerpress.co.uk

In association with the European Jewish Publication Society
PO Box 19948
London N3 3ZJ
www.ejps.org.uk

The European Jewish Publication Society gives grants to support the publication of
books relevant to Jewish literature, history, religion, philosophy, politics and culture.

A catalogue for this book is available from the British Library

ISBN 1-904764-51-7 (pbk)
ISBN 1-904764-52-5 (hbk)

Book design by Elsa Mathern

Printed by Thomson Press (India) Ltd.

CONTENTS

SECTION 3 • THE HOLOCAUST DOCUMENTARY IN FILM AND TELEVISION

SECTION 4 • THE HOLOCAUST IN FEATURE FILMS

ACKNOWLEDGEMENTS

We are grateful to the authors who have written such a wide array of stimulating, moving and thought provoking chapters. We are especially grateful to those symposium speakers who were initially wary of committing themselves to paper, and who had to be coaxed and, on occasion, cajoled into producing pieces for us. We hope that the reader finds the book as engrossing to read as we did to edit it.

We would also like to thank friends and colleagues in other archives and institutions for their assistance in preparing this publication: Renata Clark (Czech Centre) for her assistance with the organisation of the symposium, the subsequent film season ('Czech Cinema and the Holocaust') and Jiří Cieslar's essay; the Czech historian Vojtech Blodig for providing figures on the Terezín ghetto; Vladimir Opela (Národní Filmový Archiv) for loaning prints for the symposium and season; Susan Reynolds (British Library) for help with the footnotes for Cieslar's essay; Monika Braid (Polish Cultural Institute), for help with the symposium, the film season ('Polish Cinema and the Holocaust') and for finding an author for the chapter on that subject; Jane Dickson and Ian Wall (Film Education); Andy Hollinger and Raye Farr (USHMM) for information on the origins of the US Holocaust Memorial Museum; Orlagh Mulcahy for her thoughts on amateur film in connection with the filming of the massacre at Liepaja, Latvia; Neil Foxlee (University of Central Lancashire) for advice on the history of the Vichy government and the Occupation; Ernst Verduin for agreeing to let us publish details of a private email to the Museum; Rajiv Narayan (Amnesty International UK) for liaising with Suh Sung (formerly Soh Sung).

We are particularly grateful for the assistance and patience of our immediate colleagues and friends during the preparation and editing of this book: the eagle-eyed John Kerr (IWMFVA), who proofread the manuscript and also prepared the filmography and bibliography; Roger Smither (Keeper, IWMFVA) has been very supportive and suggested contributors, topics and film titles, as well as giving advice on editing and other aspects of the preparation of this volume; Teresa Silk (IWMFVA) for transcribing the audio recordings of the symposium proceedings and numerous other typing and administrative tasks associated with the organisation of the symposium and the preparation of the book; Matthew Lee (IWMFVA) for help with the organisation of the symposium, compiling the speakers notes and various aspects of the preparation of the book; Jane Fish and Paul Sargent (IWMFVA) for advice on copyright, film titles and much else; Melanie Carman (IWMFVA), especially for her help with the running of the symposium. Also, thanks to all the preservation and collections team at the film vaults at Duxford who have provided access to many films and videos viewed during the book's preparation: David Walsh, Giovanni Schiano, Paul Heath, John Schlackman, Samantha Hallett, Rebecca Harding, Peter Hallinan, Andrew Bullas, Ken Ball, Sophie Seymour, David Finch, Andrew McDonald.

Thanks to Trudy Gold and Claudia Gold, who helped initiate the symposium, and to the survivors whose willingness to tell their stories makes such a difference in the LJCC schools programme, and who were such a vital part of the symposium and moving force behind the idea of publishing this book. Thanks too to Terry Charman and

James Taylor (Department of Research and Information, IWM) for invaluable historical advice during the editing of the book and for giving their time to fact-check the
manuscript; Suzanne Bardgett (Director of the Museum's Holocaust Exhibition Project
Office) for reading and giving advice on the manuscript; Steve Slack (Holocaust Exhibition Project Office) for sub-editing work and fact-finding; Jeremy Richards, Richard
Bayford, Glyn Biesty and Gordon Mcleod (Darkrooms) for helping to source, prepare
and photograph images used in the book; Dilip Banerjee and Pauline Allwright (Department of Art) for access to the image of the poster for *The Eternal Jew*; we are grateful to the publisher's reader Libby Saxton, whose constructive criticism was so valuable and for her assistance with the chapter on *Shoah*; Chris Darke for translating the
chapter on the production of *Night and Fog*; Michael Tombs for preparing the index;
Nicole Proia for supporting Toby Haggith during the preparation of the book; Deirdre
O'Day for assistance with the editing of the Introduction and the chapter on 'Filming
the Liberation of Bergen-Belsen'; Uwe Westphal for help and advice throughout the
project, from symposium to finished book. Thanks also to Alice Newman for her constant encouragement.

A big thank you to the technical team of the Museum's Film and Video Archive,
who ensured that the symposium ran smoothly and have prepared, projected and tele-
cined hundreds of film and video titles viewed by the authors and editors of this book:
Brian Mongini, Tom Adams, Lynn Chapman, Stephen Lovesay and George Smith. Also
to David Wood, the IWMFVA film librarian, who is an invaluable link in the chain that
retrieves titles from the IWM film vaults.

And finally, special thanks to Yoram Allon and his colleagues at Wallflower Press
for commissioning this book and for their support and, most of all, patience during its
protracted production.

The editors and Wallflower Press would like to thank the following for providing stills
and photographs and for permission to reproduce copyright material. While every
effort has been made to trace and acknowledge copyright holders, we would like to
apologise should there be any errors or omissions: Amnesty International UK, for providing the photo of women in Afghanistan and the rights to reproduce this image;
bfi Stills, Posters and Designs, for providing the stills for *Jud Süss/Jew Süss*, *La vita è
bella/Life is Beautiful*, *The Night Porter* and *L'Oro di Roma/The Gold of Rome*; Contemporary Films, London, for the rights to reproduce the stills from *Pasażerka/Passenger*;
Disruptive Element Films for stills from *Les Voix de la Muette/If the Walls Could Speak*;
Film Education, for providing the image of the cover of the *Schindler's List* study guide;
FreemantleMedia Ltd, for providing the production still from *The World at War* and
for the rights to reproduce this image; Mira Hamermesh, for providing the still from
Loving the Dead and for the rights to reproduce this image; colleagues at the Imperial
War Museum for providing various pictures used throughout the volume and to the
Trustees of the Imperial War Museum for the rights to reproduce these images; Peter
Morley, for providing the production still from *Kitty – Return to Auschwitz* and the
rights to reproduce this image; Národní Filmový Archiv, for providing the stills from
Daleká cesta/The Long Journey and the rights to publish these images; Suh Sung for
permission to reproduce his image; Friedrich-Wilhelm-Murnau Stiftung, for the rights
to reproduce the poster from *Jud Süss*; the Wiener Library, for providing the photos of

Terezín/Theresienstadt's ghetto; Orly Yadin and Syvlie Bringas for permission to use stills from *Silence*; and Małgorszata Szum and Małgosia Błonska at the Polish Cultural Institute in London and the Polish Ministry of Foreign Affairs for their assistance in securing the permission from Studio Filmowe "Oko" for the rights to reproduce the still from *Ostatni etap/The Last Stage* used on the front cover of this volume.

Wallflower Press would also like to thank Colin Schindler at the European Jewish Publication Society for the financial support generously offered in respect of various production issues in the preparation of this book; this is enormously appreciated.

NOTES ON CONTRIBUTORS

Suzanne Bardgett was the Project Director of the Imperial War Museum's Holocaust Exhibition from its inception in 1995 until its opening in June 2000. Prior to that she worked in the Museum's Education Department and on its Directing Staff. Her team's most recent project was the creation of the Genocides Exhibition which completes the third and final stage of the Museum's Redevelopment Plan. She continues to represent the Holocaust Exhibition and to oversee the acquisition of further material for it.

Lutz Becker studied painting, history of art and film in Berlin, Hanover and London. As producer, writer and director he has made many films (including *The Double Headed Eagle: Hitler's Rise to Power 1918–1933* (1973) and *Lion of Judah* (1975)) and television documentaries on contemporary history and the arts. He is also a painter and an independent curator and art advisor, and has collaborated with a number of museums and galleries in the UK and abroad. He is a member of the Executive Committee of the Wiener Library.

Rex Bloomstein is a co-founder and Chairman of the Trustees of the Medical Foundation, a Trustee of the Prison Reform Trust and Consultant to the London Jewish Cultural Centre. He has produced and directed many documentary films for the BBC, Channel 4, Thames Television and many other television companies which have achieved critical acclaim. His body of work on the criminal justice system was the first of its kind, exposing the realities of prison life and significantly opening up the penal system. Other films have included historical studies on the Holocaust and Martin Luther King. In 1984 he made *Human Rights*, a two-hour film for Thames Television, which explored the global struggle against the violations that afflict so many people around the world and *Torture*, an examination of how this tragic phenomenon continues in contemporary society. Other works include: *Strangeways* (1980), *Auschwitz and the Allies* (1982), *Prisoners of Conscience* (1988), *The Longest Hatred* (1993), *Liberation* (1995), *The Roots of Evil* (1997), *Understanding the Holocaust* (1997), *Human Rights, Human Wrongs, Urgent Action* (1998), *Strangeways Revisited* (2000) and *Lifer: Living With Murder* (2003).

Esther Brunstein was born in 1928 in Łódź, Poland. She was a schoolgirl when the Nazis arrived, and was taken to the Łódź Ghetto. From there she was deported to Auschwitz in August 1944. From September 1944 until January 1945 she was in Hambueren, and from there taken on a death march to Bergen-Belsen, where she was liberated, yet had typhus and was unconscious until the fourth day after liberation. The Red Cross took her to Sweden. She joined her brother in England in 1947.

Terry Charman joined the staff of the Imperial War Museum in 1974 and since 1993 has been a historian in the Research and Information Department. From 1996 to 1998 he was Senior Historical Researcher on the Imperial War Museum's Holocaust Exhibition Project. His main fields of expertise are the social, diplomatic and political aspects of the Second World War with particular reference to Nazi Germany. He is the author of *The German Home Front 1939–1945* (1989) and has contributed to many radio and television programmes on these and other aspects of twentieth-century conflict.

Jiří Cieslar is Head of the Film Science and History Department at Charles University, Prague. He is the author of a monograph on Luis Buñuel, and two collections of film essays: *Film Diary* (1993) and *Concettina's View* (1997). Recently he has focused on Czech cinema and the Holocaust, and is currently preparing a monograph on the film and theatre director Alfréd Radok (1915–75).

Elizabeth Cowie is Reader in Film Studies, University of Kent at Canterbury. One of the founding editors, in 1978, of the feminist theory journal *m/f*, she has co-edited, with Parveen Adams, *The Woman in Question* (1990) and is the author of *Representing the Woman: Cinema and Psychoanalysis* (1997). She has also published widely on documentary and film noir and is currently writing a monograph on the documentary film.

Michael Darlow has directed, written and produced award-winning documentaries, arts, music and drama programmes for the BBC, ITV and Channel 4. He has also made and supervised programmes for broadcasters in America, Canada, Australia, New Zealand and Europe. He is a Fellow of the Royal Television Society and was awarded the society's Silver Medal in 2000. His television work includes programmes dealing with historical events and people, made in styles ranging from archive films to dramatic reconstructions. In addition to his work on *The World at War* (1974), *Secretary to Hitler* (1975) and *Auschwitz: The Final Solution* (1979), his three-programme series *Cities at War* (1968) dealt with the experience of ordinary civilians during the Second World War. He has taught direction, production and other disciplines at the National Film School, the BBC, LWT and in schools. He is external assessor for the National Film and Television School's course in documentary direction and a member of the National Short Course Training Advisory Committee.

Christian Delage is a historian and *maître de conférences* at University Paris VIII and at the École polytechnique. He is also an associate fellow at the Institut d'Histoire du Temps Présent (Centre National de la Recherche Scientifique). He is the author of many books, including *La Vision nazie de l'histoire* (1989) and *Chaplin, la grande histoire* (1998). In 1998 he co-edited, with Antoine de Baecque, *De l'histoire au cinéma*. Recent research on the representation of the Holocaust in cinema (starting with the films presented as evidence during the Nuremberg Trials) appears in the book he wrote with Vincent Guigueno, *L'historien et le film* (2004). Christian has also written and directed several documentary films, including *De l'exclusion a l'extermination* (in collaboration with Henry Rousso), *La rafle des enfants d'Izieu: extraits des archives filmées du procès Barbie* (1994) and *Avec les enfants?* (in collaboration with Anne Grynberg, 1995).

Annie Dodds has been involved in documentary filmmaking for many years and was a founder member of October Films. She now works independently and also writes and lectures on film. Her recent work includes *Crimes Against Humanity* (2002), a large-screen film about global genocide for permanent exhibition at the Imperial War

Museum. She previously produced the films for the Museum's acclaimed Holocaust Exhibition. Some previous productions include *For the Sake of the Children* (1997), a controversial film about images of child nudity, for Channel 4; the award-winning *Orphans of Manchuria* (1994) and *Hidden Children* (1994), also for Channel 4; and *Forgotten Heroes* (1994), about the experiences of merchant navy men on the wartime convoys for BBC2's *Timewatch*. *Hidden Children* won Best Documentary Award at the Chicago International Film Festival, and Annie was nominated for the GEMINI Producer's Award for Best Documentary by the Canadian Academy of Film and Television for *Orphans of Manchuria*.

Zdenka Fantlova-Ehrlich was born in 1922 in Rokycany, Czechoslovakia. She attended the local high school from which in 1940 she was expelled according to new racial laws. She then attended the English Institute in Prague. In January 1942 Zdenka was deported with the rest of her family to Theresienstadt, from where, in October 1944, she was transported to Auschwitz-Birkenau, and from there to Kurzbach further east. In January 1945 she was part of a death march across the Oder river to the Gross Rosen concentration camp, and later to Mauthausen. In February 1945 she was transported to Bergen-Belsen where most of the prisoners perished during a typhoid epidemic. Zdenka was found alive amongst the heaps of corpses by a member of the British Army which liberated them on 15 April 1945. Her entire family perished in the Holocaust. She was then transferred by the International Red Cross to Sweden where she stayed and worked at the Czech Embassy. In 1949 she emigrated to Australia where she married, had a daughter and was an actress for twenty years in Melbourne. In 1969 the whole family moved to England, and since then she has lived in London.

Raye Farr joined the staff of the United States Holocaust Memorial Museum after more than twenty years in documentary television production and historical film research, much of it focused on the Second World War and twentieth-century European history. She lived in England for many years, working at Granada Television and Thames Television, where she was part of the team that produced the award-winning 26-hour series, *The World at War* (1974). Raye has worked on many other television documentary series, including: *Hollywood: The Silent Years* (1980), *Vietnam: a Television History* (1983), *The Struggles for Poland* (1987), *China in Revolution* (1989), *The Nuclear Age* (1989), *Stalin* (1990) and *Heritage: Civilization and the Jews* (1994), and has produced *Hitler's Germany* (1975) and *Poland's Jews, 1919–1943* (1987). In 1990, she became director of the Museum's Permanent Exhibition and led the team responsible for the design and production of the Museum's major exhibition area. She and her colleagues received the 1995 Presidential Design Award for the Permanent Exhibition's Excellence in Design. In 1993 she became Director of the Department of Film and Video, which included the establishment of the Steven Spielberg Film & Video Archive.

Harry Fox, originally Chaim Fuks, was born into a religious family on 15 July 1930 in Tuszyn, Poland. Of the 250 Jewish families in Tuszyn from that time just two survivors remain, Harry and his brother. The Germans entered Tuszyn at the beginning of September 1939; Harry remembers that they 'rode on motor bikes and gave us sweets'. Shortly after, they were moved into the Piotrkow Ghetto. In October 1942 all the people of the Ghetto were asked to assemble in the main square. Here the women and children were selected to one side, together with all those who did not have a job. They were all sent straight to Treblinka and their deaths. Harry and his father and brother were saved for slave labour. In 1944, as the Russians advanced, they were all moved to a camp at Czestochowa. After a few weeks, his brother and he were chosen to go to Buchenwald, and went by train in cattle trucks. After only three weeks in Buchenwald, they were sent to Dora which became overflowing with slave labour, and after some weeks were moved on to a camp at Nordhausen. After some time his brother and he were moved again, to the camp of Hertzung. As the Russians advanced the camp was closed and they were sent off by train to Theresienstadt. They arrived in Theresienstadt towards the end of April 1945. Harry was liberated by the Russians on 8 May in Theresienstadt, and arrived in Carlisle, UK, on 14 August 1945.

Kay Gladstone joined the Imperial War Museum as a film cataloguer in 1972, working on the Archive's Second World War foreign language newsreel collections, researching the history of British combat filming and curating several Imperial War Museum displays on Wartime Cinematography. Having interviewed the British cameramen who filmed the liberation of Belsen, he was invited to introduce the first public screening of *Memory of the Camps* at the Berlin Film Festival in 1984. Since 1990 he has been responsible for Acquisitions and Documentation in the Film and Video Archive and has concentrated on developing the Imperial War Museum's post-1945 holdings (for example, the NATO Film Collection, UNTV in Former Yugoslavia) and acquiring civilian and military amateur film from all periods.

Jack Gold was born in London on 28 June 1930. After completing a degree in law and economics at London University he joined the BBC in 1955 as a film editor, where he worked on the *Tonight* news programme with the reporters Alan Whicker and Fyfe Robertson. His humanistic concerns surfaced in his anti-fox hunting film for the BBC, *Death in the Morning* (1964), and his Marxist perspective was evident in his direction of Jim Allen's television play *The Lump* (1967), which harshly criticised the construction industry. Jack has directed twelve feature films, including *The Bofors Gun* (1968), *The National Health* (1973), *Aces High* (1976), *The Medusa Touch* (1978) and *The Chain* (1984). In television, he has directed hundreds of short magazine films for the *Tonight* programme, twenty documentaries and forty films both in the UK and the US. He has won numerous national and international awards including two Emmies, a Golden Globe, six BAFTAs, two ACEs and the Martin Luther King Award, the Italia, two Peabodys and two Monte Carlos for such films as *The Naked Civil Servant* (1975), *The Sailors Return* (1978), *Sakharov* (1984), *Murrow* (1986), *Escape from Sobibor* (1987) and *Goodnight Mister Tom* (1998).

Trudy Gold is Chief Executive of the London Jewish Cultural Centre (LJCC). She has over twenty years experience of teaching Jewish history, both in adult education and in schools and colleges. She specialises in teaching Jewish history through the medium of film. Trudy initiated and runs the LJCC Holocaust education programmes in the UK and abroad and is a member of the British Delegation on the Task Force for International Cooperation on Holocaust Education, Remembrance and Research.

Toby Haggith works in the Imperial War Museum's Film and Video Archive, where he is Head of the Public Services Section, and programmes the cinema. He has lectured widely on various aspects of film and social history. His doctorate, undertaken at the Centre for Social History, University of Warwick, was on British films on housing and town planning from 1939–51. He has published articles on British peace-aims films of the Second World War, official film and British national identity, the Isotype films of Otto Neurath, reconstructing the 'official' score for Battle of the Somme, and a comparison of *Saving Private Ryan* (1998) with army combat film shot on the Normandy beaches.

Mira Hamermesh was born in Łódź, Poland. In 1941 she was one of a group of Jewish youngsters who found safety in Palestine. Her passion for painting began in childhood and at the age of sixteen she had an exhibition in Jerusalem and Tel Aviv, organised by the British Council. At the end of the war an art scholarship took her to London where she studied at the Slade School of Fine Arts. A one-woman show at the Brook Street Gallery, London, was followed by exhibitions in Jerusalem, Tel Aviv and Paris. In 1961 she was awarded a scholarship to study at the celebrated Polish National Film School in Łódź. As a filmmaker she has won many international awards, amongst them the Prix Italia and the Royal Television Society Award. Her trilogy on conflict in South Africa, Israel/Palestine and India – *Maids and Madams* (1986), *Talking to the Enemy* (1988), *Caste at Birth* (1990) – and *Loving the Dead* (1991) are among her most outstanding films. She has recently published her memoirs, *The River of Angry Dogs* (2004).

David G. Harrison is a freelance documentary producer. He worked for the BBC for thirty years where he was, among other things, Deputy Editor of *Panorama*. His *Journey Into Darkness* (1994), made in collaboration with Fergal Keane, was the first of six programmes *Panorama* has produced on Rwanda.

Rudy Kennedy was born near Breslau/Wrocław. When expelled from the local high school after attempts to defend himself against regular bullying he then went to a Jewish grammar school which was closed in 1940. In 1943 at the age of 15 he and his family were deported to Auschwitz. His mother and sister were gassed on arrival. His father survived just eight weeks. It was in Buna Monowitz, Auschwitz III, that Rudy was used as a slave labourer by I. G. Farben. In 1945 shortly before the Russians liberated Auschwitz, he was forced to go on a ten-day death march to Dora. From Dora, where he was used by Werner von Braun in the manufacture of VI and V2 rockets, Rudy was moved on once again, this time to Bergen-Belsen. When Belsen was liberated by the British, Rudy was one of the living skeletons found. It then took 18 months for him to reach the UK. During this time he was one of a group of three who ran away from typhoid-infected Belsen in order to reach American-occupied Frankfurt. In Frankfurt he was arrested and imprisoned on trumped-up charges. In the UK, Rudy gained a degree in Electrical Engineering and began working on defence projects. His security clearance was high enough to grant him access to rocket facilities in the US where Werner von Braun and some of his team from Dora were now employed. Rudy is a founder member of the Association of Claims for Jewish Slave Labour Compensation, a major aim of which is to expose the complicity of German industry in the genocide of Jews working for them.

Fred Knoller was born in 1921 in Vienna, Austria. He was a 20-year-old student in France when the Nazis arrived, hiding under a false identity in Paris, taking German soldiers to nightclubs at Place Pigalle in Paris and receiving commission from the owners. In 1943 he joined a Resistance movement in the Département de Lot in France, where he was involved in partisan operations against German troop trains and learnt to handle explosives and guns. In the summer of that year he was captured in Drancy, France and deported to Buna Monowitz, Auschwitz III where he was held for almost two years. In January 1945, the camp was evacuated and Fred was brought to Nordhausen concentration camp. From there, he was deported to Bergen-Belsen where he was liberated, close to death, by British troops in 1945. Fred emigrated to America in 1947, married an English girl in 1950 and went with her to England in 1952, where he has been living since.

Matthew Lee joined the Imperial War Museum Film and Video Archive in November 2000 as a Public Services Assistant. He had previously studied film history at Exeter University. His particular areas of interest include pre-cinema history, experimental film and Second World War propaganda.

Helen Lennon obtained her M.Phil in the Department of Comparative Literature at Yale University in May 1999, where she specialised in documentary film, literary theory and feminist legal criticism. Concurrent to her ongoing doctoral studies, she obtained her Juris Doctorate at the University of California at Berkeley in May 2002, with concentrations in United States criminal law, international humanitarian law, human rights law and trial advocacy.

Trude Levi was born in Szombathely, a Hungarian town on the Austrian border. At the age of eighteen she started a nursery nurse course at a Jewish training college in Budapest. She was very proud to be chosen to be assistant at the model nursery of the college in January 1944. In March 1944 Hungary was occupied by Nazi Germany; she returned to her family home in Szombathely, and was deported to Auschwitz-Birkenau and then transferred to Hessisch-Lichtenau, an outcamp of Buchenwald. In this camp Levi became a slave labourer making munitions in the Dynamit Nobel factory. As a member of a sabotage group she damaged the grenades that they were meant to produce. In March 1945 the camp was evacuated and Levi's group was taken to Leipzig. On 23 April 1945, her twenty-first birthday, Levi collapsed on the death march. She was lucky to escape being shot: she was not considered worth the bullet required to kill her. After the war she decided not to return to Hungary and as a result lost her Hungarian nationality. As she was stateless Trude was locked up in Toulon and Marseille for four months along with members of the SS and German, French and Italian fascists. Between May 1945 and September 1958 when she became a British citizen, she lived in France, South Africa and Israel, often working illegally. She supported herself and her husband and son by doing odd jobs and teaching Hebrew. In 1959 she started work at the Wiener Library, and then worked for 22 years as an archivist and librarian at University College London. After retiring in 1988 she wrote about her experiences. Her book, *A Cat Called Adolf*, was published in January 1995 and she has been invited to speak at many schools and universities, and anti-racist societies. Trude believes that it is the duty of survivors who are able to speak, to speak out and tell their story. Her book has been published in Germany and in 1997 she received an Honorary PhD from Anglia Polytechnic University in Cambridge in recognition of her work in genocide education.

Giacomo Lichtner studied History at the University of Reading, UK, where he is currently completing a PhD on representation of the Holocaust and its reception in Italy and France between 1955 and 1998. His work focuses on a comparative analysis of the role played by film in the evolution of popular memory of the Holocaust in these two countries. Since July 2003 he has been Lecturer in Film and History at Victoria University of Wellington, New Zealand. His main research interests lie in the history of twentieth-century Europe, with a particular focus on cinema's role in the construction of national and social myths and the use of film as historical evidence.

Ruth Lingford has made a number of award-winning experimental films produced on a home Amiga computer, including *Death and the Mother* (1988), *What She Wants* (1994) and *Pleasures of War* (1998), devised in collaboration with the novelist Sara Maitland. In 2002, she made another film for the Arts Council of England's Animate! scheme, *The Old Fools*, using a poem by Philip Larkin with a reading by Bob Geldof. She has contributed to Peter Gabriel's Real World CD-ROM multimedia project *Ceremony of Innocence* (1998). Ruth is principal animator on *Silence* (1998), for Halo Productions for Channel 4, winner of a Gold Hugo at the Chicago International Film Festival and Special Prize at the Hiroshima International Animation Festival. In 2002, she co-directed a music video, *An Eye for an Eye* with Shynola for UNKLE. This won the Norman MacLaren award at the Edinburgh International Film Festival and was shown on Channel 4 to mark the first anniversary of the events of 11 September 2001.

Ewa Mazierska is Senior Lecturer in Film and Media, Department of Humanities, University of Central Lancashire. Her publications include numerous articles in Polish and English about contemporary Polish and world cinema; Ewa is the sole author of two books, on James Ivory and Wong Kar-Wai, and co-author, with Laura Rascaroli, of *From Moscow to Madrid: European Cities and Postmodern Cinema* (2003), *The Cinema of Nanni Moretti: Dreams and Diaries* (2004) and *Crossing New Europe: Postmodern Travel and European Cinema* (forthcoming from Wallflower Press).

Peter Morley was a leading member of the British post-war documentary movement, as a film editor, writer and director. His many works includes *Tyranny: The Years of Adolf Hitler* (1959), *Israel: The Birth of a Nation* (1959), *The Two Faces of Japan* (1960), *This Week* (1960–63), *A Son of Liberty* (1963), *Black Marries White: The Last Barrier* (1964), *The State Funeral of Sir Winston Churchill* (1965), *The Life and Times of Lord Mountbatten* (1965–69), *Europe: The Mighty Continent* (1971–73) and *Women of Courage* (1979–80). As freelance producer/director, he has made over 300 programmes for ITV and the BBC; these were mainly documentaries, but also included sorties into opera, music and remote-broadcasts of state occasions. Peter pioneered the first interactive videodiscs in the UK, using the now obsolete VHD and LaserVision systems. This resulted in a series of science subjects for both teachers and students in junior schools.

Much of his work in the US was sponsored by the National Science Foundation and the American Chemical Society.

Joanna Newman is Executive Director, Arts and Education at the London Jewish Cultural Centre (LJCC) where she is responsible for adult education and the centre's cultural programme. She lectures on various aspects of modern Jewish and European history, including refugee history, Western responses to Nazi Germany and European Jewry and the Holocaust. She was awarded a Parkes Studentship at the University of Southampton and her doctorate was on the British Caribbean, British Government and refugees during the Second World War. She has worked as a journalist, researcher and producer for television, print and radio in Germany and the UK and has lectured at the University of Warwick and University College London. She is an Honorary Research Fellow at the University of Southampton and a Council Member of the Anglo-Jewish Historical Society.

Anna Reading is a Principal Lecturer in Media in the Division of Arts and Media at South Bank University, London. She has published several books on the media in Eastern Europe and the UK, including *The Social Inheritance of the Holocaust: Gender, Culture and Memory* (2002) on the cultural memory of the Holocaust in three countries. She is an editor of the journal *Media, Culture and Society*, and teaches live performance scriptwriting and the reception and making of Holocaust memory and citizenship in different cultural contexts.

Laurence Rees is Creative Director, History, at the BBC and Editor, *Timewatch*. As an executive producer of historical documentaries he has won three Emmy Awards (two in 1994 and one in 1996). He has most recently written and produced a major six-part television series for the BBC, *Auschwitz: The Nazis and the Final Solution* (2005). The series is the result of three years of in-depth research, drawing on the close involvement of worldwide experts on the period. It is based on nearly a hundred interviews with survivors and perpetrators, many of whom are speaking in detail for the first time. As a writer and producer of historical documentaries he has won numerous awards including the British Academy of Film and Television Arts (BAFTA) award for best factual series, for *The Nazis: A Warning from History* (1997). Laurence was also the founder editor of *Reputations*, the BBC's Historical Biographical strand which he launched in 1994. He was also an executive producer of the BBC's *Remember* season for the fiftieth anniversary of the liberation of Auschwitz in January 1995 and was the executive producer of much of the BBC VE-day and VJ-day documentary output. He was also executive producer of the BBC TV award-winning series *The Crusades* with Terry Jones as well as the recent Michael Wood series on Alexander the Great. In 1999, Laurence wrote and produced the acclaimed BBC2 series *War of the Century* about the Hitler/Stalin war and in 2000 the equally critically-acclaimed series *Horror in the East* about the Japanese psyche at war.

Frank Reiss was born in Berlin and fled Germany with his parents in 1937, through Austria to Czechoslovakia. From there Frank's father was taken to Majdanek concentration camp where he died. His mother, a member of the underground, was caught and executed in Warsaw by the Nazis. Aged seven, Frank and his guardian, Simon Polak, escaped to the Czechoslovakian countryside where they paid local farmers to hide them. Just six months before the war ended Frank and Simon were discovered, arrested and sent to Nitra prison. As the Allies started bombing this area, Frank was moved on once more to Terezín, until the camp was liberated by the Russians. He was one of a hundred or so Jewish children to survive the war in Czechoslovakia. After the war Frank remained in Czechoslovakia, graduating from Bratislava School of Law with a Doctorate. He practised law in Prague until 1968 when he fled to the United States during the Prague Spring where he later obtained a Masters Degree in Social Work from Adelphi University. During the 1980s Frank was Director of European Affairs for the Anti-Defamation League. He has been a consultant to President Václav Havel of the Czech and Slovak Federated Republic. His involvement with the affairs of the Czech Republic has continued; he is currently the Representative for Foreign Affairs for the Václav and Dagmar Havel Foundation, working on projects which in their cultural significance exceed the boundaries of the Czech Republic. An expert in international relations, with a particular interest in human rights, Frank has lectured at several universities in the United States as well as at the Holocaust Museum in Washington, D.C. He has been involved in producing four documentary films including *The Journey of Butterfly* (1996) and *The Return of the Lost Citizens of Hechingen* (1998); these film projects are based on his personal and professional experience of the Holocaust.

Susan Tegel was until recently Head of History at the University of Hertfordshire. She has published several articles on *Jud Süss* (included in the *Historical Journal of Film, Radio and Television* and *Holocaust and Genocide Studies*) as well as a book: *Jew Süss Jud Süss* (1996). As a visiting scholar at the US Holocaust Memorial Museum in 2000, Susan participated in a workshop on Film and the Holocaust, and is at present writing a monograph entitled *The Nazis and Film*.

Stephen Tuck lectures in American History at Oxford University and specialises in race relations, racial protest and white supremacy from the Civil War to the present. His latest book, *Beyond Atlanta: The Struggle for Racial Equality in Georgia, 1940–1980* (2001), deals with the impact of the Second World War (amongst much else) in the deep south. He is presently writing an overview of the struggle for racial equality in the USA from 1861 to 2000.

Ian Wall was educated at the University of York where he studied English and Related Literatures, and went on to teach at the London Comprehensive School, Holland Park. In 1985, in collaboration with Professor Dick Ross, he constructed the education programme for British Film Year, involving writing materials for teachers and students, lecturing, market research and curriculum development. In 1986 he founded Film Education, which produces printed study materials, develops CD-ROMs, runs training for teachers, produces television programmes for the BBC Learning Zone and Channel 4 on film-related topics. Since 1995, working with the Film Education television team, he has developed over fifty television programmes, both as producer and director. In addition to this, he has written three textbooks for schools on Media Studies, helped to develop three examination syllabi (at both GCSE and A Level) on Media Studies and is currently Chief Moderator of the AQA Media Studies A Level. He was a founder member of the European Association for Audio Visual Media Educators, was a member of the Department of Culture, Media and Sport's Film Education Working Party and has served as a jury member for BAFTA Children's Drama Award.

Tim Webb completed a BA in animation at the West Surrey College of Art in Farnham, Surrey, graduating with a First Class Honours degree in 1986. He then became involved with the Arts Council of England's Animate! scheme, developing a collaborative film, with the autistic artist Stephen Wiltshire, *A is for Autism* (1992). This Channel 4-funded film won eight international awards and resulted in Tim being offered his first teaching work at his old college. His most recent film is *Mr Price* (2004). Tim is presently Senior Tutor in the Animation Department at the Royal College of Art.

Orly Yadin was born in Israel but has been living in London since 1977. She started working in television in the documentary field, especially historical documentaries. Over the past ten years she has gradually shifted to animation as a means of telling true stories. In 1995 Orly founded an independent production company, Halo Productions, with partner Sylvie Bringas. Recent productions include: *Gotta Get Out* (1995), *Touch Wood* (1995), *Silence* (1998), *Journey Through the Night* (1999) and *Treasure* (2001).

Daniela Zanzotto had started an academic career in Literature, History and Cultural Studies before starting to make films. After obtaining her MA, she took a couple of short courses in filmmaking. Daniela's first film, *Les Voix de la Muette* (*If the Walls Could Speak*) (1998), was awarded the first prize in the 'Out of that Darkness' film season and competition, First-Time Director category at the Institute of Contemporary Arts, London in 2000. Following this, *Kissed by Angels* (2001), about an actress coming to terms with an impending mastectomy, won a number of prizes including Best Documentary Short at the Cleveland International Film Festival. Daniela's latest film, *Battaglia* (2004), is about the life of the Sicilian photographer and anti-Mafia activist Letizia Battaglia.

PREFACE

In July 1986 the London Jewish Cultural Centre (formally the Spiro Institute) in London organised a season of films under the title 'The Holocaust and the Cinema' at the Everyman Cinema, Hampstead, in connection with the first *Remembering for the Future* conference. The same year saw the second Jewish Film Festival held by the National Film Theatre in collaboration with the Jewish Film Foundation. The centrepiece was a screening of *Shoah* and a personal appearance by its director, Claude Lanzmann. To accompany the event a slim booklet, *Film, History and the Jewish Experience*, was produced, edited by Jonathan Davis. I can well recall the excitement of seeing these films and for a while the booklet was my essential guide to movies about the Nazi persecution and mass murder of the Jews. It contained a short contribution by Annette Insdorf whose pioneering work *Indelible Shadows* had been published in the USA only three years earlier. Prior to this, the subject of 'film and the Holocaust' barely existed. In many ways 1986 was a watershed moment. Thereafter, film and television treatment of the subject expanded exponentially, monographs on the theme began to proliferate, it became the subject for new university courses, and as sure as day follows night textbooks appeared. Moreover, film and specifically-filmed testimony by survivors and perpetrators of Nazi mass murder assumed an increasingly central place in the museums and memorials that began to spring up around the world. So it was wholly fitting that in 2001 the Imperial War Museum in conjunction with the London Jewish Cultural Centre and Film Education held a five-day symposium on 'Holocaust, Genocide and the Moving Image' to survey and analyse the extraordinary florescence of celluloid and video representations rooted in the Nazi period itself.

This volume captures the results of the symposium and it is likely to become, like its much more modest predecessor, an essential guide for scholars, students and viewers for years to come. The editors, Toby Haggith and Joanna Newman, building on the work of the symposium organisers, have done a wonderful job of bringing together contributions that cover virtually every significant area of the field. There are scholarly studies of every genre including Nazi propaganda films, wartime and post-war newsreels, cinematic evidence in Nazi war crimes trials, feature films made in half a dozen countries, documentaries, factual and fictional television, and an exploration of complementary work on genocide since 1945. The contributors include practitioners as well as academics and critics, alongside exhibition curators who have made use of filmed testimony. Unusually for a symposium of this kind, it includes the transcript of a feedback session during which the voices of survivors are heard loudly and clearly. This innovation reflects the sensitivity of the organisers and editors, but also the way in which cinematic representations, the function of testimony and the role of survivors have all become entangled.

It is interesting to speculate on the origins of this nexus. Lanzmann's *Shoah*, more than the Eichmann trial (which has been mythologised and misconstrued), established the priority of testimony and brought the survivor to the foreground. *Shoah* exploded onto the cultural scene at approximately the same moment when representation and memory were becoming new, and not unrelated, academic subjects. The survivor-witness became both a vehicle of memory and the living incarnation of problems around representation: the dilemma, not to say impossibility, of 'speaking the unspeakable'. This development was not unprecedented. The Fortunoff Video Archive for Holocaust Testimonies housed at Yale University began life in 1979 as the 'Holocaust Survivors Film Project', impelled partly by the impact of the American television mini-series *Holocaust* that was screened the previous year. Under Geoffrey Hartman's guidance the archive has been responsible for much important recorded testimony and has provided a platform for some of the most profound reflections by and on the survivors. But this cross-fructification of fiction and factual filmmaking and analysis proved a false dawn by comparison with the immediate and long-term impact of *Schindler's List* in 1993. Steven Spielberg trumpeted the use of survivors and drew over his film their mantle of authenticity. The film was, of course, a global hit and generated vast revenue. Spielberg, in turn, pledged his support for a massive, worldwide effort to record the now rapidly diminishing number of survivors. The Spielberg video testimony project mobilised resources that were formerly undreamed of and, crucially, reached into countries that by chance had been recently freed from Soviet domination. Here untapped oral histories were to be found in abundance, but the window of opportunity for obtaining them was narrow and closing. This was an extraordinary if fortuitous concatenation of developments: the rise of the survivor as a player in the formation of memory and cultural representations, a Hollywood blockbuster and the contemporaneous collapse of the USSR.

We are now at a point when, in one form or another, testimony is a key to filmic representations. This may reflect another, more recent trend. Since the 2003 war in Iraq we have become habituated to the 'embedded' television journalist. The excitement of this fresh news genre has given way to many sober reflections on the strengths and limitations of such reportage. But it has had another, less obvious effect. Through the transmissions of the 'embed' the news viewer has, perforce, come to accept the partial, fragmentary view of the individual combatant or civilian in a widely dispersed conflict situation. While there is no comparison between the experience of war reporters and those who suffered Nazi persecution or witnessed genocide during the Second World War, it can be argued that they share a point of view. Survivors can only tell us with authority what happened to them or what they saw directly, and even then a memory can be deceptive and over time is subtly affected by the circumstances of its origin. This has often been a source of frustration and vexed exchanges when survivors and historians have combined but thanks to the much discussed paradox of the 'embeds' we can now see how it would be a mistake to expect or to claim more. Television journalists have been forced to confess that they could not accurately report more than they could see, were often misled by reports of what they could not verify themselves, and ended up transmitting partial and disconnected accounts of events that were also heavily inflected by their dependency on the military units they accompanied.

The interaction of technology, modes of representation and human agency is constantly dynamic and nowhere more so than with respect to history and the moving image. Just because visual representations are now so important to how we comprehend the past, as much as the present, it is crucial that we see with an educated eye. When approaching a subject as important, complex and sensitive as genocide it is more important than ever that we have good tools at our disposal for understanding modes of production, commercial constraints, techniques for exerting influence, aesthetic dilemmas, standards of accuracy and questions of authenticity. This book is a tool kit that no one in our recorded and screened times can afford to be without.

David Cesarani
Royal Holloway, University of London
June 2005

INTRODUCTION

Toby Haggith & Joanna Newman

Perhaps in twenty years time the film [*La vita è bella/Life is Beautiful*, 1998] is one of the Holocaust films that should not be shown. Because people might misunderstand and might misinterpret what the Holocaust was about, or what being in a concentration camp was about.

    – Trude Levi, Holocaust survivor[1]

This book is based on the proceedings of a symposium held at the Imperial War Museum (IWM) in April 2001 entitled 'Holocaust, Genocide and the Moving Image: Film and Television Representations Since 1933'.[2] This five-day symposium was organised by the staff of the Film and Video Archive of the Museum, in collaboration with the London Jewish Cultural Centre (LJCC) and Film Education. The symposium was a unique blend of talks, discussions and screenings and brought together a diverse group of speakers: archivists, curators, filmmakers, historians, journalists and Holocaust survivors.

As part of the Imperial War Museum's programme to mark the opening of its Holocaust exhibition in June 2000, the Film and Video archive planned an extended season of films and related events.[3] In January 2000, Brad King (IWM), Trudy Gold (LJCC) and Suzanne Bardgett (IWM), began to discuss the possibility of a film symposium that would explore in greater depth the role of film in the exhibition, and its place in the reception of the Holocaust in general. There was a feeling among the Museum's curators, and the staff in the organisations behind the symposium, that there was still much we had to learn about the complex relationship between film and the Holocaust. But there was also a realisation that we had knowledge and expertise about the subject, which should be shared among the burgeoning community of Holocaust film scholars.

The three organisations behind the symposium brought special knowledge and expertise to the proceedings. Curators at the Museum were fresh from wrestling with the difficulties of using film extensively in creating a permanent exhibition. They were also setting up an education project in which film would have a central role. In looking for archive film for the displays they were building on an existing fund of knowledge (particularly that held by the Museum's film curators and archivists) about non-fiction and propaganda film connected with the Holocaust.

Film Education has particular expertise in using film for educational purposes, and had produced a range of special educational materials on the subject of film and the

Holocaust.[4] The LJCC had also been involved in Holocaust education for a number of years. In particular its work in co-ordinating the Survivors Programme meant that it was in a unique position to bring survivors to the discussion, resulting in the 'right to reply' session, and one of the most fascinating, moving and often humorous sessions in the symposium. The LJCC was expert in producing educational film and materials for schools, having overseen the production of a short film by Rex Bloomstein and the publication of the Holocaust education pack, written by the historian Robert Wistrich.[5] The organisation has been using film for some years, in the context of its range of adult education courses.

A fourth organisation that has not yet been mentioned, but whose indirect influence was of great value in the organisation of the symposium and ultimately the book, is the International Federation of Film Archives (Fédération Internationale des Archives du Film, FIAF), of which the Museum is a long-standing member. It was partly through fraternal relations with our FIAF colleagues in archives in the Czech Republic and Poland, that we were able to arrange important seasons of Czech and Polish films about the Holocaust. These followed on from the symposium and helped to inform the editing and writing of this book.

There was also some urgency about the timing of the symposium. It was important that Holocaust survivors could take part and provide their unique insights into the films being discussed. It was also an opportunity for survivors to challenge filmmakers and for them to respond to this interrogation. The contribution of the survivors is thus a particular feature of this volume. As well as the formal inclusion of their voice in the transcript of the 'right to reply' session, the survivors' perspective is found in a number of other points in the text. Their interventions made a powerful impression on the other delegates present, some of whom later included thoughts and reflections from them in their own work, including one of the chapters in this collection (by Jiří Cieslar), and at least one other publication.[6]

How does this book differ and overlap with other studies?

Originating as it did in a symposium held within a museum, there is a particular focus on areas of archival, curatorial and educational interest. This also informed the structure of the book, suggesting an organisation of the chapters that followed the five days' events, and into categories of moving image that are also roughly chronological (witness, propaganda, documentary, dramatised features, legacy and other genocides), rather than thematic interpretations of the subject matter (see Avisar 1988; Insdorf 2003; Hirsch 2004), or into chronological periods of national cinema (see Colombat 1993; Doneson 2002).[7] This structure is unusual, but not completely new. Other scholars, notably Ilan Avisar and Joshua Hirsch, have applied a similar logic, but while these writers have only briefly or superficially acknowledged this categorisation, this book has stuck more rigidly to this modal typology.[8] Some may challenge this structure as there is often overlap between these fixed categories (for example *Jud Süss* (*Jew Süss*, 1940) is a propaganda film that is also a dramatised feature film), and indeed one of the features of Holocaust cinema is the creation of new forms of approach. However, this structure made sense and was attractive, as it enabled us to focus attention on areas of Holocaust cinema where the Museum's holdings were strong and we had particular expertise and knowledge to share. By 'Film as Witness', we mean unedited or contemporaneously edited actuality material relating to some aspect of the Holocaust, from amateur film recording the lives of pre-war European Jewish communities to films covering the liberation of the concentration camps. This definition also comprises video material of Holocaust survivors used in Museum displays, 'film' of witnesses as opposed to 'film' that witnessed.

Moving image genres (newsreel, liberation footage, amateur film and so on) within the witness category have heretofore been overlooked in Holocaust film studies. For example, scholars have tended to dismiss the liberation footage as 'newsreels' shot by anonymous cameramen without skill or art, only having value when the 'masters' (Alain Resnais, Alfred Hitchcock, Erwin Leiser and so on) have 'shaped the reality' in compilation or montage documentaries made many years later.[9] They have even seen it as a kind of naïve or pure form of actuality footage, 'raw film evidence, devoid of narrative framing'.[10] As Toby Haggith and Kay Gladstone show, this is a crude oversimplification that fails to do justice to the work of the military filmmakers.

This book is inclusive in scope, examining all technical categories of the moving image and in all its forums of presentation (film and video, the cinema, television, classroom, museum display). The use of moving image displays in exhibitions and memorials is discussed by a number of contributors (Suzanne Bardgett and Annie Dodds, Christian Delage, Raye Farr), and is also covered in the debate in the transcript of the 'right to reply' session.[11] The commitment in this volume to the television medium is also a special feature. With the notable exception of Annette Insdorf's *Indelible Shadows*, films made solely for broadcast do not appear in the studies by Avisar and Hirsch and with a handful of exceptions do not feature in those by André Colombat and Judith Doneson. As the IWM's Film and Video Archive has been the source for footage used in a number of the films and television programmes discussed here, it was natural that we should not only include examination of titles made primarily for television broadcast, but that we should also invite television directors and producers to contribute to these discussions. In other studies on Holocaust cinema, the reader only encounters a filmmaker in the third person when quoted or at best in a transcript of an interview with the author.[12] But in this book, the reader can study a filmmaker's personal exposition of a film production at first hand. These chapters will thus complement critiques offered by film scholars. For example four of the films examined by Annette Insdorf (*Kitty – Return to Auschwitz* (1979), *Escape From Sobibor* (1987), *Loving the Dead* (1991) and *Silence* (1998)) are discussed in this volume by their respective filmmakers.

Given the subject matter, there is often a moral dimension to the work of Holocaust film scholars. There is particular concern that the specificity of the suffering of the Jews in the Holocaust is not omitted. That the victims are treated with compassion and dignity[13] and that filmmakers adopt a cinematic form and language that is appropriate to articulate such an abhorrent episode in human experience. As Annette Insdorf explains, 'Rather than prove a thesis, I wish to explore the degree to which these films manifest artistic as well as moral integrity'.[14] This position is not shared by Judith Doneson, who makes clear her interest is less in the artistically or most critically appraised films than those which 'exert the strongest influence on the public'.[15] The corollary of this is that Doneson is willing to examine films containing antisemitic messages, such as *The House of Rothschild* (1934), as well as those which have increased public aware-ness, such as *Holocaust* (1978), even though they have upset some survivors specifically because they have been seen to trivialise the Holocaust.[16] This book takes a similar position, as we hold the view that any film relating to the Holocaust is relevant to our study, therefore we also include antisemitic propaganda films produced by the Third Reich since 1933. A notable omission from this category is *Triumph des Willens* (*Triumph of the Will*, 1935). While Leni Riefenstahl's film has undoubtedly been influential in the field of propaganda, it is not a directly antisemitic film, and besides, it has been dealt with exhaustively elsewhere.[17] More unusually, this volume also includes an ex-amination of propaganda films of the period that sought to combat racial discrimina-tion and prejudice, with Matthew Lee's study of anti-fascist films produced in Britain during the war years. We also wanted the reader to consider antisemitism within the broader context of race relations during this period, hence the inclusion of Stephen Tuck's chapter on the American propaganda film *The Negro Soldier* (1944), which was designed to generate enthusiasm for the war among black soldiers (both chapters ap-pear in section four).

Some film scholars have suggested that the moving image can assist in passing on the lessons of the Holocaust to succeeding generations, providing a metaphor or framework for the better understanding of similar events in today's world (Cambodia, Bosnia, Rwanda) and to help the watchful guard against actions by the State that might be seen as pre-cursors of modern-day Holocausts.[18] We have interpreted the logic of this assertion in the book's closing section, 'Legacy and Other Genocides', devoted to the representations of post-Holocaust genocides in the moving image. The title of this section also acknowledges a genre within 'Holocaust cinema' where individuals with a close personal connection to those who experienced the Holocaust (typically as the relatives of survivors) have made films and videos examining their traumatic legacy; here this genre is represented in the chapter by Daniela Zanzotto.[19] Some readers may feel uneasy about the decision to include titles about genocides since 1945 as they regard the Holocaust as a unique event in human history. Indeed during the discus-sions on the documentary day of the symposium, filmmakers and delegates roughly divided into two camps on this issue. One side, represented by Jeremy Isaacs (executive producer of *The World at War* television series), argued that documentaries about the Holocaust should be closed historical investigations. The counter argument was led by Michael Darlow and Martin Smith (director/producers from *The World at War*) who stated firstly, that one could not separate analysis of history from one's own experiences and secondly, it would be wrong not to use the history of the Holocaust to analyse or warn against political and social phenomenon that might seem to presage a recurrence of such events. Broadly speaking, this is the position to which the editors subscribe and one which is also shared by the filmmakers who write in section five. Thus for Rex Bloomstein it was natural to follow his films on the Holocaust with a series of cam-paigning programmes documenting the abuse of human rights around the globe. For Daniela Zanzotto it was imperative that she looked for contemporary parallels, when examining the history of the French concentration camp at Drancy. Nor, as Christian Delage reveals, is this a position peculiar to contemporary filmmakers, as it under-pinned the way that Alain Resnais chose to interpret the Holocaust during the making of *Nuit et Brouillard* (*Night and Fog*, 1955).

The moving image and history

What relevance has the moving image to the study of history and how may it assist the historian tackling the Holocaust? To the historian, 'film' possesses three important characteristics: firstly, it can be a record of real events that have taken place in the past. It is a particularly powerful and omniscient kind of record as it appears to require minimal interpretive skills for the viewer to comprehend what is being recalled on the screen. This gives it a universal accessibility not offered by other forms of primary resource, such as a historical document or oral testimony, where linguistic or calligraphic skills might be required. For this reason the moving image record is popular with the curators of historical museums or historical documentary makers, seeking to give an historical narrative to a non-specialist audience. The moving image also, as Helen Lennon explains, may be able instantly to describe a scene, such as an atrocity, with a facility and scope that would normally defy words or description. Because of its extraordinary powers to record and indeed reflect the scene in front of the lens, sometimes referred to as the mimetic quality of the moving image, it is often considered as superior to other documents or accounts of past events. It may even be accorded legal status and be admissible as evidence in trials as, for example, the films and tapes screened in various war crimes trails held since the end of the Second World War.

Secondly, partly because of these almost magical qualities inherent to the moving image, films, particularly those in the documentary, propaganda and feature categories described in this volume, have great power to influence the viewer and thus, when widely distributed, the moving image may have an impact on society that is of historical importance. However, interpreting the degree of influence of the moving image on an individual or audience is notoriously difficult. Typically there are few if any records to help evaluate viewer reception and, even when these are plentiful and systematic, the interpretive skills are often outside the training of historians.

Thirdly, moving images are historical artefacts in themselves, their significance residing not only in what they show of the past but also in the makers' interpretation, and how that is influenced by the historical context.

The moving image and the Holocaust

The moving image is particularly valuable when we seek to understand the history of the Holocaust. As the modernist technology of film matured into the mass medium of entertainment and a powerful instrument of influence and propaganda, it was exploited by Nazi propagandists to promote all aspects of their 'ideology', including race theory. It is paradoxical that film, employed in this period to pioneer new approaches to living in propaganda campaigns against disease and slum housing, should, in the hands of the Nazis, be used to facilitate a state-sponsored pogrom; at its heart the most medieval and anti-modern of 'projects'. An assessment of the role of film in the promotion of antisemitism during the Third Reich can be found in the chapters by Susan Tegel (who focuses on *Jud Süss*) and Terry Charman (who considers *Der ewige Jude/The Eternal Jew*, 1940), and in Lutz Becker's analysis of the representations of Terezín/Theresienstadt.

As well as the historical interest in the propaganda power of film, there is its possible value as a record of the Holocaust itself. While German antisemitic propaganda gave some clues or intimations as to what was intended for the Jews, these are not a record of 'the Final Solution' or even of the concentration camp system. Indeed, because the Nazis were secretive about the concentration camps and particularly careful in concealing the programme for the Final Solution, there are often few documents or artefacts extant that provide evidence of the Holocaust. Therefore it is surprising that many aspects of the process (apart from the exterminations in the death camps) are documented on film (and in photographs).[20] Some scenes, such as the attacks on Jews by local antisemites, life in the Jewish ghettos of occupied Europe, or Jews being loaded into wagons, destined for Auschwitz, were even filmed by German propaganda and military cameramen.[21] Much of this filming (for example, scenes in the ghettos) was to produce footage for the propaganda purposes described in the chapters by Terry Charman and Lutz Becker; the coverage of other events, such as the dispatch of Jews to the East, seems to have been part of a more routine project to record the operations of a particular unit. The fact that such scenes were recorded is an indication of the certainty with which Nazi policy towards the Jews was carried out in German occupied territory. But the most damning moments were recorded by amateur cameramen. Thus in one of those peculiar distortions and ironies that characterises the Holocaust, the home movie camera, traditionally used to record holidays and family celebrations (in a mode of framing described by one scholar as the 'loving gaze'),[22] has also recorded scenes of Jews being shot in the sand dunes of Latvia in 1941.[23]

The most widely known archival films associated with the Holocaust are the reels of film recording sites of atrocities and concentration camps discovered by the liberating Soviet and Western Allied armies towards the end of the war. These films have stood as a powerful reminder of the Holocaust for subsequent generations, one that has also validated the testimony of the liberators and survivors against those who have periodically sought to deny the Holocaust or its scale. A common reaction to these images was that they succeeded in articulating horrors that could not be put into words. Perhaps in this way they have taken some of the burden away from the survivors, sparing them the agonies of describing the totality of their experience?

However, actuality film is not an unimpeachable historical record of the Holocaust. The attraction and power of the moving image is its verisimilitude, the medium appears to be a transparent and a true record. But as many of the contributions to this volume demonstrate, film is a highly mediated and constructed account of the past, and its objectivity should be questioned as much as that for any other form of primary evidence, be it document, letter, oral testimony or drawing. Therefore curators and filmmakers should be cautious when presenting archive film as evidence in a historical narrative. For example, the over-reliance on a handful of films and photographic images that show killings can be problematic. Authenticity and provenance are notoriously difficult to establish for these films, because the events they record raise such damning questions about the involvement or culpability of the camera operator. There are also difficulties associated with the liberation footage, which is often mistakenly believed to be a 'witness' to the Holocaust. This is a false impression; no films were taken inside the camps when they were under Nazi control. This misleading impression has been fostered by those filmmakers (even including Alain Resnais) who have succumbed to the temptation to use liberation footage to illustrate accounts of the prisoners' existence. Exactly how the makers of feature and documentary representations of the Holocaust have tackled the absence of German archive film covering the camps, and particularly the death camps, is a key philosophical, aesthetic and ethical theme which is covered by a number of contributions to this volume, especially in sections three and four.

Despite the difficulties inherent in the use of archive film, it has proved popular with curators of Holocaust exhibitions and memorials. The extensive use of film in the IWM Holocaust exhibition (and the Bergen-Belsen Musuem which is presently in development and where film will be the central element of the displays) can partly be explained by the scarcity of other artefacts and historical records. But its importance is also due to the influence that television documentary-making has had on curatorial practise and in raising the respectability of archive film as a historical source. A trend demonstrated most clearly at the US Holocaust Memorial Museum (USHMM), where Martin Smith and Raye Farr, the television documentary makers and former members of the *World at War* team, were engaged as successive directors of the Permanent Exhibition. Martin Smith's appointment was made after one of the Museum's council members had seen an episode on Poland's Jews from Smith's documentary series *The Struggles for Poland* (1987),[24] and concluded that a filmmaker was needed to tell a complex story to a broad audience with a strong visual impact. Raye Farr, who succeeded Smith as Director in 1990, led the team responsible for the micro-design of the major exhibition area, an area in which film was an essential component. Links between film, television and the USHMM go deeper still, as the impact on mainstream American society of the airing of NBC TV's *Holocaust* mini-series in April 1978 helped the cause of those lobbying President Jimmy Carter for the creation of a national Holocaust memorial.[25]

Film as a source of memory

For those incarcerated in the camps, part of the urge to survive was in order to give their account of what had been happening, to use the memory as a weapon, to be a 're-membrancer'.[26] But even for those who managed to survive, the telling was unlikely to be straightforward. Simon Wiesenthal recalls that *Shutztaffel* ('Protecting Squad', SS) guards taunted the inmates of the camp where he was held by prophesying that any survivors would be unlikely to be believed after the war as the Nazis had so diligently destroyed the evidence, and because the event itself would be 'too monstrous to be believed'.[27] This was not helped by the understandable reluctance of many Holocaust survivors to share their experiences with others, both because they were traumatised by their recollections and doubted they would be believed.[28] In these circumstances film has proved a valuable if sometimes problematic tool for the survivors.

As explained above, Allied military film of the liberations helped provide at least partial evidence of the brutality and extent of the concentration camp system. It also helped survivors to bear witness, and even make sense of what had befallen them, particularly when this footage was incorporated into documentaries such as *Night and Fog*. A less well-known body of archive film is that which documents the lives of pre-war Jewish communities. On the first day of the symposium, Rafael Scharf and Jack Kagan showed amateur film of their home towns of Novogrudek and Kraków, pre-war Jewish communities decimated by the Holocaust.[29] Their compelling descriptions of the lives of these vibrant communities, as reflected in these films, remind us that archive film can provide an alternative memory and history of the European Jewish experience in the twentieth century, countering popular perceptions which have been dominated by the images of the liberated concentration camps, an issue explored by Elizabeth Cowie.

Perhaps even more important has been the way that film has helped create a wider awareness of the Holocaust, combating the Nazis' nihilistic intentions to erase the Jewish people and their culture from history, and to do so surrepticiously. Judith Doneson claims that film has become so effective in this regard, that the Holocaust has been fixed into the national consciousness of the United States. It is now part of the nation's cultural memory, a remarkable outcome in a country where the Holocaust is a 'refugee' event.[30] In France the cinema has not only played a major role in increasing the public's awareness of the Holocaust but, according to André Colombat, it has been an 'exceptional media to fight antisemitism and bigotry'.[31]

Paradoxically, it has been those films that have been most successful in creating a mass awareness of the Holocaust (*Holocaust* (1978), *Schindler's List* (1993)) that have caused so much pain and anger among the survivor community, as is demonstrated by the discussions in the survivors 'right to reply' session. Indeed these films have brought to wider attention a debate within artistic and literary circles about the representation of the Holocaust that pre-dates the 1970s. In the late 1960s Theodor Adorno made an influential pronouncement about the representation of the Holocaust in literature ('To write a poem after Auschwitz is an act of barbarism'),[32] which was widely taken as a blanket sanction against all forms of representation. Some ten years later, the Holocaust survivor Elie Wiesel, made a statement about Holocaust literature which echoed Adorno's sentiments, and shortly after was moved to write this scathing attack on the NBC TV mini-series *Holocaust*: 'Am I too harsh against? Too sensitive perhaps? But then this film is not sensitive enough … It transforms an ontological event onto a soap opera. Whatever the intention the result is shocking. Contrived situations, sentimental episodes, implausible coincidences: if they make you cry they make you cry for the wrong reasons.'[33] Even if many years later Adorno, in a much lesser known statement, had recanted his earlier position ('A perennial suffering has just as much right to find expression as a victim of torture has to scream.')[34] and Wiesel had cautiously modified his trenchant position on dramatised film treatments of the Holocaust, this sense of a 'sacred zone' has remained in place.[35] Clearly many filmmakers have been very affected by the essence of this debate, some of those who spoke at the symposium prefacing their discussion of the films they had produced with an often moving account of their reluctance to take on such a commission. But the struggle has not ended there; as Michael Darlow, Orly Yadin and Jack Gold here recount the difficulties they experienced in finding a cinematic method most ethically appropriate for the medium, and one that did justice to the experience and memories of Holocaust survivors. The Holocaust survivor Rudy Kennedy has said that when he looks back at his experiences during the Holocaust, 'I can't believe it really happened to me. I know it happened, but it's unbelievable.'[36] If it is hard for survivors to believe they lived through this horror, how does a filmmaker make real the unbelievable?

Similar constraints have also faced producers of documentaries, the medium often considered the only acceptable approach for the filmmaker who chooses to take on the Holocaust. Archive film of the ghettos, *Einsatzgruppen* killings and transportation to the camps taken by German cameramen raises a particular dilemma for the documentary maker (and the curator; see the chapters by Suzanne Bardgett and Annie Dodds and the comments by Christian Delage in the 'right to reply' chapter). As Elie Wiesel observes: 'The use of these faked, truncated images makes it difficult to omit the poisonous message that motivated them … will the viewer continue to remember that these films were made by the killers to show the downfall and the baseness of their so-called subhuman victims?'[37] One of the biggest difficulties documentary makers have had to overcome is how to incorporate the archive film of camp liberations and atrocities; a grotesque visual legacy that presents a new range of practical problems, not least relating to the audience. As will be seen, some have solved these problems by avoiding the use of archive images altogether, but perhaps few have had such a clear philosophical objection as Claude Lanzmann, who has said that if he found footage of the inside of a gas chamber, he would destroy it.[38]

Peter Novick has pointed out how little these fierce debates impinge on mainstream society; moreover, along with Judith Doneson, he is sympathetic to those films that are seen to 'trivialise' or 'Americanise' the Holocaust as they have proved to be so effective in keeping the memory of this event alive.[39] This argument has often persuaded filmmakers like Jack Gold who initially had reservations about taking on this subject. It also helps to explain the ambivalence expressed by many survivors, especially those involved in Holocaust education, towards films such as *Schindler's List*.

The ethical and philosophical issues concerning the representation of the Holocaust have led to two quite distinct traditions in filmmaking that can be recognised in both the non-fiction or documentary fields and in dramatised feature production. First is a realist tradition, best illustrated in feature films by the classical narrative cinema of Hollywood, a method which has often been very popular. The non-fiction version of the realist tradition can be illustrated by a didactic, chronological documentary treatment such as the Holocaust episodes in *The World at War* series. The second tradition is the non-linear or non-chronological, poetic and occasionally reflexive approach, in which there is particular concern, and often experimentation with, the cinematic form or language. In Europe, the rejection of more mainstream treatments of the Holocaust can be traced back as far as the Czechoslovakian feature film *Daleká Cesta/The Long Journey* (1949), discussed in section four, and in the documentary field to *Night and Fog*. Joshua Hirsch explains the non-realist approach as a kind of cultural manifestation of post-traumatic stress disorder: artists have responded to the trauma of the Holocaust and exposure to the atrocity footage that documented it (here categorised as 'Witness' films) by developing a form of filmmaking that conceded the impossibility of representing this event through realism.[40] French cinematic treatments of the Holocaust have been particularly innovative partly as, André Colombat notes, because of the 'post-new wave' interest in experimentation and in striving to find the best cinematic form to transcribe the philosophical aims of a particular film.[41] By contrast, Hollywood filmmakers have tended to take the cinematic form for granted when approaching this subject. This volume traces a trajectory in the development of non-linear approaches to the Holocaust, from Alain Resnais' *Night and Fog*, which combined a didactic, historically chronological approach with poetic and imaginative elements, through to Claude Lanzmann's *Shoah* (1985) which was an avowed rejection of the 'traditional' realist documentary form. Finally in Daniela Zanzotto's *Les Voix de la Muette/If the Walls Could Speak* (1998) we can see a filmmaker embracing new technologies in order to further disrupt and challenge the traditional documentary approach.

Historical events have had a profound impact on how the Holocaust has been represented in cinema. The Eichmann trial in Israel in 1961 was crucial in raising awareness of the Holocaust and most importantly focused on the Jewish victims of the Final Solution. International interest in the trial also helped individuals: suddenly survivors, many of whom had felt unable to speak of their experiences, found a voice. Then Hollywood began to take the subject more seriously, and a number of films were released about the Holocaust. In France filmmakers began to focus on the persecution of the Jews where previously this had been presented as 'one crime among many others' committed during the Occupation.[42] Other events have helped to promote discussion of the subject (the Six Day War, the trial of Klaus Barbie and so on) and have in turn led to developments in Holocaust cinema. The fall of the Berlin Wall and the implosion of the Soviet Union led to the release of new evidence about the Holocaust (see Laurence Rees's chapter in this collection), greater access to films made since the war, and the possibility for the people of former Soviet bloc nations to look at the Holocaust more objectively. There are also the personal historical factors: survivor testimonials (*Kitty – Return to Auschwitz*, *Silence*, *Loving the Dead* and so on), those in which the survivor recounts their story, were not possible until those individuals felt able to confront their own experiences and share them with others.

Often these 'testimonial' films entail a journey to the camp, or site of the camp, where the survivor was imprisoned. But the special qualities of film mean that these journeys do not always necessitate a trip to the actual site of that trauma. Fictionalised accounts and dramatised re-enactments of the experience of the Holocaust can be powerful and authentic representations of the event, as a number of survivors attest in the 'right to reply' session. Similar journeys and encounters have taken place in the Imperial War Museum, where Holocaust survivors come to search through the Museum's holdings of 'liberation footage'. Ernst Verduin, a survivor of Buchenwald, found that the films taken shortly after the liberation of the camp (where he had walked around with some visitors and Allied film crews) were more disturbing than his recollections: 'The reality has been much worse than my memory partly told me. I was in the belief that it was a rather neat and well-organised situation in the camp. The films, however, did show me that my memory has been suppressing the worst: it was a dirty mess and that there really – even in Buchenwald – were some stacks with corpses lying next to the crematorium. After having seen the films I do remember those horrors I have been pushing far back in, or nearly out of, my memory.'[43] But not all of these encounters are so distressing. Dita Kraus, a Czech woman who had come to Bergen-Belsen from Theresienstadt, was able to identify herself in a number of frames of footage shot by the Army cameramen. She found that the film re-awakened some pleasant, even fond memories of her time after the liberation, when she had been an interpreter for the British soldiers who had taken control of the camp.[44]

As well as being of some psychological benefit to the survivors who view these reels, these visits have been very important in helping the Museum to develop the documentation for the films in its holdings. While we are unlikely to be able to identify many of those who appear in the films, the fact of being able to identify some may help to counteract one of the perceived negative consequences of screening liberation footage, that it presents to the viewer a mass of anonymous, helpless victims.[45]

Films on the Holocaust have not always been received so positively. Throughout the history of Holocaust cinema, certain films have been politically controversial, in some cases resulting in official disapproval and the curtailment of distribution (*Night and Fog*) or even the removal from distribution altogether (*The Long Journey*). The potential for this subject to cause government disquiet and on occasion censorship has not diminished in the television era nor with the proliferation of channels. Marcel Ophuls' monumental documentary *Le Chagrin et la Pitié* (*The Sorrow and the Pity*, 1969) about the German occupation of France was banned from transmission for a decade because of its unflinching account of various aspects of the period, including the Holocaust, an area of French history that continues to create difficulties for filmmakers, as Daniel Zanzotto describes in this volume. Nor is this a problem only confined to countries that suffered occupation, as the Holocaust episodes of *The World at War* were initially banned from transmission by the South African Broadcasting Association.

Those familiar with the literature on this subject will be aware that the words 'Holocaust' and 'Shoah' are both used to refer to the events which comprise this twentieth-century catastrophe. These terms are not interchangeable: although the word 'Holocaust' is a generally accepted translation of the Hebrew word *sho'ah*, meaning destruction or annihilation, many scholars prefer the term 'Shoah' when they want to refer specifically to the Nazi programme to exterminate European Jewry. For the purposes of consistency, 'Holocaust' is the word used throughout this volume (except in the *verbatim* account of the 'right to reply' session). The term 'Holocaust' encompasses both the historical period leading up to the Final Solution and those non-Jewish victims who were imprisoned and perished in the concentration camps.

Our choice of contributions in this volume reflects the symposium proceedings. Regrettably, some of the speakers were unwilling or did not feel able to write up their papers for the book. However, these can still be read by consulting the transcript of the symposium proceedings, held in the Museum's Sound Archive and Film and Video Archive.[46] In some cases we have filled the gaps by commissioning new pieces about topics and films we felt were so important that they could not be left out.[47]

While reading and editing these chapters, one was occasionally stilled by an account of shocking brutality or one of those bizarre stories associated with the Holocaust that makes the whole thing often scarcely credible. Dedications and homilies seem trite and clichéd, so no dedication, only an exhortation – to read, to think, to discuss and if necessary to act.

Notes

1   The Holocaust survivor Trude Levi, speaking on the Film Education television programme *The Holocaust on Film – Part One*, broadcast on the BBC2 Learning Zone in April and May 1999.

2   It was decided to drop the word 'genocide' from the title for the book as we did not feel that we could do the subject justice with just the four chapters in section five, 'Legacy and Other Genocides'. As Suzanne Bardgett, the chair of the discussions on day five of the symposium, said in her opening remarks, genocide and film was a subject that merited a week-long symposium of its own.

3   The Imperial War Museum's Holocaust Exhibition was opened by Her Majesty Queen Elizabeth II on the 6 June 2000. Since the Exhibition opened to the public on the 7 June 2000, it has had almost 1.5 million visitors.

4   The Holocaust-related materials produced by Film Education are: Study Guides – I. Wall (1996) *Schindler's List*. London: Film Education. A copy of this can be downloaded from the Film Education website: http://www.filmeducation.org/filmlib/s.html; I. Wall (1998) *Screening Histories*. London: Film Education. CD-ROM – I. Wall (2003) *The Pianist*. London: Film Education. A study guide and extracts from Roman Polański's film, background and archive materials on the invasion of Poland and the Warsaw Ghetto. Related television programmes produced by Film Education are: *The Holocaust on Film – Part One*, 30 minutes and broadcast on the BBC2 Learning Zone in April and May 1999; *The Holocaust on Film – Part Two*, 30 minutes and broadcast on the BBC2 Learning Zone in May 1999 (both programmes were written, directed and produced by Jane Dickson and Ian Wall).

5   R. Wistrich (1997) *Lessons of the Holocaust*. London: London Jewish Cultural Centre. Included in the pack is a documentary called *Understanding the Holocaust* (1997), directed by Rex Bloomstein. The documentary runs for 50 minutes and is recorded on the tape in two forms, running continuously and then in segments so that it can be screened in module format for use in individual lessons.

6   Anna Reading's book on gender and the cultural memory of the Holocaust which was published a year after the Museum's symposium includes many quotes from the survivors who took part in the 'right to reply' session and general discussion during the proceedings. See A. Reading (2002) *The Social Inheritance of the Holocaust: Gender, Culture and Memory*. Basingstoke: Palgrave Macmillan.

7   A. Insdorf (2003) *Indelible Shadows: Film and the Holocaust*. Cambridge: Cambridge University Press; J. Hirsch (2004) *After Image: Film, Trauma, and the Holocaust*. Philadelphia: Temple University Press; I. Avisar (1988) *Screening the Holocaust: Cinema's Images of the Unimaginable*. Bloomington: Indiana University Press; A. Colombat (1993) *The Holocaust in French Film*. London: Scarecrow Press; J. Doneson (2002) *The Holocaust in American Film*. New York: Syracuse University Press.

8   Both writers begin their examination of Holocaust cinema with actuality footage (film of atrocities and liberation footage), followed by montage documentaries made in the immediate post-war years, or those released some years after which included archival material, before moving on to discuss feature film representations of the subject, and in the case of Hirsch, titles from the video age.

9   Insdorf 2003: 200–1.

10 Hirsch 2004: 33.

11 Peter Novick makes some valuable observations on the use of survivor testimony in exhibition video displays, but this is in a book which examines the Holocaust in American society in all its political, cultural and social manifestations, not one devoted to the moving image *per se*. See P. Novick (1999) *The Holocaust and Collective Memory: The American Experience*. London: Bloomsbury, 275.

12 The transcript of an interview with Alain Resnais discussing *Night and Fog* appears in R. Raskin (1987) *Nuit et Brouillard by Alain Resnais: On the Making, Reception and Functions of a Major Documentary Film: Including a New Interview with Alain Resnais and the Original Shooting Script*. Åarhus: Åarhus University Press.

13 Avisar 1988: 188.

14 Insdorf 2003: xv.

15 Doneson 2002: 6.

16 Ibid., 6–7.

17 For more on *Triumph of the Will* and Leni Riefenstahl see: B. Winston (1981) 'Was Hitler there?: Reconsidering *Triumph of the Will*', in *Sight and Sound*, 50, 2, 102–7; M. Loiperdinger and D. Culbert (1988) 'Leni Riefenstahl, the SA, and the Nazi Party Rally Films, Nuremberg 1933–34: *Sieg des Glaubens* and

Triumph des Willens', in *Historical Journal of Film, Radio and Television*, 8, 1, 3–38; T. Elsaesser (1993) 'Portrait of the Artist as a Young Woman', *Sight and Sound*, 3, 2, 15–18. Leni Riefenstahl's (1992) own account of the making of the film is dealt with in some detail in her ironically titled (given the numerous questions raised by scholars as to its reliability) *The Sieve of Time: The Memoirs of Leni Riefenstahl*. London: Quartet Books.

18 See Doneson 2002: 4, 7, 230–1; Insdorf 2003: xix; Hirsch 2004: 162.

19 Hirsch identifies a genre of films made by the children of Holocaust survivors which deal with a 'second-generation of trauma' in a postmodern fashion; for examples he cites Pier Marton's *Say I'm a Jew* (1984) and his own work *Second Generation Video* (1995). See Hirsh 2004: 149–52.

20 On the photographic coverage of the Holocaust see J. Struk (2004) *Photographing the Holocaust: Interpretations of the Evidence*. London: I. B. Tauris, in association with the European Jewish Publication Association.

21 The scenes of Jews getting into wagons heading for Auschwitz were shot at the railway sidings at Westerbork Camp in Holland in 1944.

22 The film scholar and filmmaker Orlagh Mulcahy, who has been studying amateur film and the history of the home movie 'movement' for some time, pointed out, in a conversation with the editors of this volume, that the 'loving gaze' is a term meant to cover a range of expressions of love – people, places and events. Mulcahy is particularly interested in the ethnographic role of home movies within the family structure and is exploring this whole subject as part of her doctoral research in the Department of Communications at Dublin City University.

23 Film of the *Einsatzgruppen* (mobile killing units) massacre in Liepaja, Latvia, was taken by Richard Wiener, a German naval sergeant who was on leave. Before the war, the Jewish population of Liepaja was more than 7,000. This massacre accounted for almost the entire Jewish population of the town. When the Red Army liberated the city in 1945, just twenty to thirty Jews remained. The information about the film is taken from the website of the US Holocaust Memorial Museum: www.ushmm.org/research/library/faq/right.htm

24 *Poland's Jews, 1919–1943*. This particular episode was produced by Raye Farr.

25 The nine-and-a-half hour *Holocaust* series was broadcast from 16 to 19 April 1978 and was seen by an estimated 120 million viewers; see E. Linenthal (1995) *Preserving Memory: The Struggle to Create America's Holocaust Museum*. New York: Viking Books, 12. According to Edward Linenthal, when Stuart E. Eizenstat asked President Carter to form a commission to recommend a national Holocaust memorial, he argued that, '"there was now stronger support than ever among many Americans – not just Jewish Americans – for an official US memorial." He mentioned the impact of NBC's *Holocaust* and the establishment of Holocaust memorials in many nations, and reminded the President, that unless a memorial was begun soon, many survivors would not live to see one', Linenthal 1995: 9. Andy Hollinger of the USHMM, relates that as a result of watching the series, a number of people were prompted to contact Eli Rosenbaum asking what should be done in the US to recognise the tragedy. Rosenbaum also eventually spoke to President Carter about the question of a Holocaust memorial. Partly as a result of this lobbying, on 1 November 1978, Carter set up the 'President's Commission on the Holocaust', which was tasked to issue a report on the state of Holocaust remembrance and education in the United States. One of its four main recommendations was the establishment of a living memorial to 'honor the victims and survivors of the Holocaust and to ensure that the lessons of the Holocaust will be taught in perpetuity'. This led to the creation of the Museum, dedicated on 22 April 1993. This quote and more details about the establishment of the Museum, can be found on the website of the USHMM; a fuller analysis of the reasons for the creation of the Museum, including those crucial domestic and international political factors, can be found in Linenthal's book cited above. Andrea Liss argues that the link between the Museum and the

television series is even more profound, claiming that 'the initial idea for developing some kind of memorial to the Holocaust was initiated by' President Carter in response to watching the series! See A. Liss (1998) *Trespassing Through Shadows: Memory, Photography and the Holocaust*. Minneapolis: University of Minnesota Press, xix. However, Hollinger (in an email to Toby Haggith, 13 September 2004) could not confirm if Carter had seen the series or how much it may have influenced his actions or the discussions of those examining the creation of a memorial in the US. Hollinger wisely concludes that while the series undoubtedly helped to affect the 'popular climate' that ultimately led to the creation of the USHMM, we should see it as one of the factors rather than a major influence.

26 As Primo Levi put it: 'To tell the story to bear witness was an end for which to save oneself. Not to live and to tell, but to live in order to tell. I was already aware at Auschwitz that I was living the fundamental experience of my live.' See P. Levi (1961) *Survival in Auschwitz*. Translated by Stuart Woolf. New York: Macmillan, 13.

27 Quoted in the preface of Primo Levi's (1988) *The Drowned and the Saved*. London: Michael Joseph, 1.

28 Primo Levi first encountered the disbelief of those who had not experienced the camps when, a few weeks after leaving Auschwitz, he poured out his story to a group of Poles, who melted away half-way through his account; see P. Levi (1995) *If This is a Man* and *The Truce*. Translated by Stuart Woolf. London: Abacus, 226–7.

29 Since the symposium Rafael Felix Scharf sadly passed away, in London on 16 September 2003. Rafael was the unofficial but universally recognised chief 'remembrancer' of the pre-Holocaust Polish-Jewish world and the Grand Duke of its post-war diaspora remnants. He was also a printer, writer and art dealer. Rafael was born in Kraków on 18 June 1914; married to Betty Hinchcliff in 1944, he leaves one son and two daughters.

30 Doneson 2002: 4–5; see also Hirsch 2004: 152.

31 Colombat 1993: 373–4.

32 This quote appears in E. Garrard and G. Scarre (eds) (2003) *Moral Philosophy and the Holocaust*. Aldershot: Ashgate, 247.

33 This quote appears in J. Kolbert (2001) *The Worlds of Elie Wiesel: An Overview of his Career and his Major Themes*. London: Associated University Press, 64. Elie Wiesel has talked in similar terms about literature and specifically cinematic treatments of the Holocaust. First, on literature and written by Wiesel in 1978: 'There is no such thing as Holocaust literature – there cannot be. Auschwitz negates all literature as it negates all theories and doctrines; to lock it into a philosophy is to restrict it. To substitute words, any words for it is to distort it. A Holocaust literature? The very term is a contradiction', in *A Jew Today* (1978) (translated by Marion Wiesel). New York: Vintage, 234.

34 Adorno's next sentence is, 'For this reason it may have been wrong to write that after Auschwitz no poetry could be written.' These lines were first published in 1973 in *Negative Dialectics* and have been republished in T. Adorno (2003) *Can One Live After Auschwitz?: A Philosophical Reader*. Stanford, CA: Stanford University Press, xvi.

35 Elie Wiesel moved from this position in 1989, wondering whether, in the Foreword to Annette Insdorf's third edition of *Indelible Shadows*, the image, and particularly the filmed image, might provide another language to articulate the 'unsayable', those essential aspects of the Holocaust which the survivor cannot communicate; although he was still worried about the tendency of cinema to trivialise and glamourise: 'The image perhaps? Can it be more accessible, more malleable, more expressive than the word? More true as well? Can I admit it? I am as wary of one as of the other. Even more of the image. Of the filmed image, of course. One does not imagine the unimaginable. And in particular, one does not show it on screen. Too purist an attitude, no doubt. After all, by what right would we neglect the mass media? By what right should we deny them the possibility of informing, education, sensitising the millions of men and women

who would normally say, "Hitler, who's he?" But on the other hand, if we allow total freedom to the mass media, don't we risk seeing them profane and trivialise a sacred subject?' He then goes on to explain that he prefers documentary, the 'poetic memory' of *Night and Fog*, to the Hollywood 'superproductions' of *Holocaust*; see Elie Wiesel (1989) (translated from the French by Annette Insdorf) in Insdorf 2003: xi–xii.

36   Rudy Kennedy speaking on the Film Education television programme *The Holocaust on Film – Part One*, broadcast on the BBC2 Learning Zone in April and May 1999.

37   Elie Wiesel in the Foreword to Insdorf 2003: xii.

38   In an article in *Le Monde* on 3 March 1994, called 'Holocauste, la représentation impossible', Claude Lanzmann wrote: 'Et si j'avais trouvé un film existant – un film secret parce que c'était strictement interdit – tourné par un SS et montrant comment trois mille juifs, hommes, femmes, enfants, mouraient ensemble, asphyxiés dans un chambre à gaz du crématoire II d'Auschwitz, si j'avais trouvé cela, non seulement je ne l'aurais montré, mais je l'aurais détruit. Je ne suis pas capable de dire pourquoi. Ca va de soi'. ['And if I'd found a film that existed – a secret film because it was strictly forbidden – shot by a member of the SS and showing how three thousand Jews, men, women and children died together, suffocated in a gas chamber in crematorium II at Auschwitz, if I'd found that, not only would I not have shown it but I would have destroyed it. I can't say why. It goes without saying.']

39   Novick 1999: 21–14. See also Doneson 2002: 231.

40   Hirsch 2004: 245

41   Colombat 1993: xviii.

42   Ibid., 373.

43   In an email from Ernst Verduin to Toby Haggith, 2 December 2004, held in the IWMFVA. Verduin had come to Buchenwald from Monowitz (Auschwitz III) and the concentration camp at Vught in the Netherlands.

44   Dita Kraus (née Polachova) was born in Prague and interned in Terezín's ghetto, Auschwitz and a labour camp near Hamburg, before ending up in Bergen-Belsen. After a period as an interpreter she fell ill with typhoid. She can be identified as the woman with the polka-dot scarf acting as interpreter for the Movietone film crew at Bergen-Belsen on page 53 of this volume. Kraus appears in the following film reels held in the IWM: A70 307/04 and A70 308/03. A recorded interview with Dita Kraus is held in the Museum's Sound Archive, accession no: 23090.

45   Incidentally, this process contradicts Jacques Derrida's influential view of film archives as institutions which 'incite forgetfulness' or a loss of memory, as valuable films recording aspects of the past become lost, either through bad archival practise or the inscrutable cataloguing methods of the curators. See M. Chanan (2004) 'Documentary and Social Memory' in *Journal of British Cinema and Television*, 1, 1, 68. Derrida's view accords with the popular media stereotype of film archives as 'dusty vaults' with piles of unidentified gems in 'rusty film cans', waiting to be unearthed by the heroic film researcher, historian or journalist.

46   IWM Sound Archive's accession no: 24442.

47   The newly-commissioned chapters are those by Helen Lennon, Peter Morley, Raye Farr, Ruth Lingford and Tim Webb, Mira Hamermesh, Ewa Mazierska, Giacomo Lichtner, and Suzanne Bardgett and Annie Dodds.

SECTION I

FILM AS WITNESS

Film as testament

This opening part of the symposium explored film as a record of what has been destroyed, of evidence of a past world. Two short films were shown that were shot in 1931 in Novogrudek and 1939 in Kraków respectively. Both films were made to appeal to an American-Jewish community to send money back to their brethren in Eastern Europe. They were made at a time of increasing political instability and economic uncertainty, rising nationalism and antisemitism, and general poverty among the population. Since the mid-1920s emigration from Eastern Europe had been curtailed, and the majority of Eastern European Jews were stuck within the borders of the former Russian Empire. These films recorded a vanished past and it gives one a bitter taste to watch Jewish life as if in a goldfish bowl, under the impossible view of hindsight. Neither film was able to do more than suggest the rich variety of pre-Holocaust Jewry in Eastern Europe. This was left to witnesses Jack Kagan and Rafael Scharf, whose testimony gave colour to the black-and-white grainy quality of the films:

> A man goes to Kraków and on return tells his friend, 'The Jews of Kraków are remarkable people. I saw a Jew who spends all his nights dreaming, and all his days planning the revolution. I saw a Jew who spends all his time studying the Talmud. I saw a Jew who chases every skirt he sees. I saw a Jew who didn't want anything to do with women. I saw a Jew who was full of schemes how to get rich quick.' The other man says, 'I don't know why you are astonished. Kraków is a big city, and there are many Jews, all sorts of people.' 'No', says the first, 'It was the same Jew.'[1]

There can be a danger in idealising a past that we no longer have access to, and Scharf warned against romanticising the sordid conditions, poverty, powerlessness and oppression of pre-war Jewish life in Eastern Europe. Yet there is enormous value in film as witness to a world lost forever. Despite the quality of the print on this video version and the off-putting voiceover, the original mute film recording life in Novogrudek is a unique testimony to a town where two-thirds of the population were Jewish. Since the majority were murdered during the Nazi occupation, this film immediately takes on a far more precious importance, now as a reminder of what has been lost, a window onto a lost world.[2]

The importance of survivor testimony is emphasised in both Suzanne Bardgett's and Annie Dodds' contributions here about the Holocaust Exhibition at the Imperial

War Museum. When looking for archive film for the displays, Dodds found that there was less material than they had imagined which, when assembled, could tell the story. What they had found – footage of the camp liberations, photographs, newsreels, official propaganda and amateur film – only gave a partial picture. These films were used in the Exhibition as historical records and to bear witness to historical accounts of, for example, the burning of synagogues on 9 November 1938. This is a good example of a particularly well-documented event that appeared on newsreel and led to a temporary change in British immigration policy and the admittance of children on block visas. Yet it was the newly-filmed interviews that Annie Dodds carried out with survivors that gave voice and individual experience to each stage of the Exhibition and gives meaning to the visual images.

Film as witness to atrocity

The speed with which images can be taken and broadcast into our homes today makes us all witnesses to atrocities taking place, from Bosnia to Rwanda. In an essay in section five, David Harrison writes about filming *Journey Into Darkness* for *Panorama*. The team went into Rwanda in June 1994 to report on the war there, and filmed extraordinary scenes of mass killing. At the conference, Harrison was asked why the boundaries between war and genocide were not explored in the film. What they witnessed was atrocity, later to be called genocide. It is this capacity to be a window, to witness, that the contributions in this section are concerned with.

Being there on the scene, cameramen feel a strong commitment to record evidence so it cannot be refuted. At the beginning of the American film *Die Todesmühlen/Death Mills*, voiceovers provided affidavits authenticating the film footage. The Allied cameramen who filmed the liberation of Bergen-Belsen camp in April 1945 had similar concerns to Harrison's television crew in 1994 – to use film as a witness and to provide evidential proof. The caption sheets record the conflicting emotions and imperatives that the cameramen felt during the closing months of the war: horror at the scenes of suffering that they witnessed, a desire to record for posterity and to record in such a way as to avoid accusations of faking footage or using editing tricks. There are also many rolls of film that testify to the attempts to humanise the survivors, showing them on a slow course back to normality. The rolls attest to the sensitivity of the cameramen, but Toby Haggith also hints at the excitement that some must have felt at being witnesses to the 'greatest crime' of the twentieth century.

Kay Gladstone's chapter explains how the diverging interests of Britain and the United States, and the changing realities of post-war *realpolitik*, affected the making and subsequent release of footage of the liberation of the camps. Yet the task of bearing witness that faced the camera teams was an urgent one: at the same time as they were being directed to record the sites where atrocities took place, evidence was being destroyed as the task of cleaning up the camps and restoring order became a priority. By July 1945 the Americans had pulled out of the project, begun as a joint initiative of the Supreme Headquarters Allied Expeditionary Force (SHAEF), and in 1946 released their own film *Death Mills*. The British film, today entitled *Memory of the Camps*, was not shown to the public until 1984. The American film was widely shown to German audiences. But while the film undoubtely had the power to shock,

Gladstone questions whether it made any of those watching it feel a responsibility for what had happened.

Helen Lennon's analysis on the medium of film as witness examines the power that atrocity images have on television, and the role of film as a forensic witness and its increasing use in war crime trials. Since footage was first introduced as evidence in the Nuremberg War Crime trials, we have become used to seeing violent photographic, film and video images of atrocities, broadcast to us via television and the internet. The immediacy of these images have the ability to shock and change world opinion, as was the case recently with the photographs taken inside Abu Ghraib prison of Iraqi inmates being tortured by Allied troops. In August 1992 video images of a victim standing inside a camp in Trnopolje, Bosnia, were immediately seized upon by journalists as proof that the Serbs were running a Nazi-style concentration or 'death camp', described in British newspapers as 'Belsen 92'. Months after these images were shown on television, the UN established an International Criminal Tribunal. Lennon questions how film is used as legal evidence: 'These images – and the laws they question, affirm, challenge and fortify – traverse the increasingly fragile boundaries between "proof" and "propaganda".'[3]

Can witness and film be used as interchangeable words? The following contributions show that although film is a window onto reality, it is not a transparent medium. It can be a witness to what has been lost, evidence of what has taken place, it has a forensic quality that can be admissible as legal evidence, and it has historic value as an artifact in its own right.

Notes

1   Rafael Scharf, in the transcript of the proceedings of the Holocaust Film conference, held in the Imperial War Museum's Sound Archive under accession number 24442.

2   See the Virtual Exhibition on Novogrudek, www.novogrudek.co.uk

3   See Helen Lennon's chapter, p. 66.

1   Film and the making of the Imperial War Museum's Holocaust Exhibition

Suzanne Bardgett

This chapter is written from the point of view of the initial vision for the Holocaust Exhibition and the integration of the ambitious and highly successful audio-visual element. The following chapter, by Annie Dodds, describes the more intimate perspective of having actually made the films.

Creating the Holocaust Exhibition posed a number of challenges. Now that it is built and has enjoyed both a good verdict from the press and strong attendances it is hard to recall just how much apprehension there was – back in 1995 – about how such a thing would be delivered and how it would be received. There was the depressing nature of the subject – would visitors stick with a narrative which patently had so little 'light relief'? Was there even a risk of them leaving the Exhibition early, too distressed or overwhelmed by the graphic detail of deportation and mass killing? There was a widespread feeling – particularly in the Jewish community – that the Museum's Atrium with its array of guns and tanks would provide an overly aggressive preamble to a subject for which one would want visitors to be in a quiet and contemplative frame of mind. How were we to ensure that the Exhibition was somehow sealed away from such intrusions and given its own distinctive ambience? There was also the British angle to consider. Britain's response to the news of mass killings in Poland and the Eastern Front during the war had been documented in detail in this country for two decades. But there was nonetheless concern in some quarters as to whether a national museum would be free to comment critically on British official attitudes.

But against these anxieties there were a number of definite assets to be counted. The need for the Exhibition to work within the existing framework of the Imperial War Museum gave us boundaries which were on the whole useful, rather than restrictive. In narrative terms, the end of the First World War and the origins and course of the Second would provide an anchor to the rest of the Museum, whose displays provided a useful and informative back-drop against which our Holocaust story would be told. Unlike many 'stand-alone' Holocaust museums, we had a pre-existing structure of collecting and public services departments. Their staff were able to provide the necessary expertise in conservation, documentation and eventually security, visitor care, publicity and marketing. And I had my small dedicated team of curators – most of them recruited specifically for the project and bringing enthusiasm, useful languages and boundless energy to the task. They found most of the artefacts, documented them and eventually oversaw the dressing of the showcases and production of the graphics panels. Each of them gave their all to the exhibition-making process, working unsocial hours and travelling overseas for long periods to ensure that the display was richly furnished with material.

Visits to existing Holocaust museums and related places of memory, and discussions with our Advisory Group, convinced us that the only approach to representing the Holocaust was a purist one which relied on authentic material to stimulate the visitor's imagination and curiosity. Film, we were convinced, would be essential – for its ability to convey the power of propaganda, to capture so vividly the confrontation between perpetrator and persecuted, and to show the very fabric of everyday life. We were familiar with television programmes like the *World at War* episode 'Genocide' and *The People's Century's* 'Master Race', whose use of film showed more convincingly than any written description the dehumanising way in which the Nazi persecution was carried out. I had a conviction that the moving image would play a key role in the display, and could visualise – albeit somewhat vaguely at this early stage – how monitors of various sizes carrying archive film could form powerful ingredients in our display. A strongly conceived film or set of films would surely be the ideal opener to the Exhibition, providing a space in which visitors would get some sense of the seriousness of what they were about to see. It would also provide a powerful ending.

But there was a more prosaic reason for giving film a generous proportion of the space and the budget. When we started the project back in 1996, we had virtually no artefacts for the Exhibition. Building a collection of objects was our main goal for the first two years, but what if we could not find enough? Painfully aware of the high expectations for this Exhibition from various quarters, I calculated that if our artefact collection risked seeming paltry, we could at least aim to make the films a 'must see' element, and have plenty of them. The talent was available in this country. These films, once made, would be a permanent fixture.

I was fond of the notion of long films that could absorb the visitor for several minutes; I had particularly enjoyed the *Historial* at Peronne – the sensitively executed museum of the First World War in Picardy, where several hours of 1914–18 film can be viewed on no fewer than forty tiny monitors. The US Holocaust Memorial Museum (USHMM) had likewise been generous in the amount of film it showed, with some seven hours available in total. But curators do not always get what they want. Our visitor route was much narrower than either of the above and there were worries that long films would lead to bottlenecks. We therefore kept most films to a maximum of seven minutes. It turned out to be as well that I had argued for a large amount of audio-visual material. In the event the large budget I had sought was cut back, but we did find a reasonable number of artefacts, and the number of programmes we ended up with was – fortuitously – about right.

The design of the Exhibition by Stephen Greenberg of DEGW and Bob Baxter of Amalgam was spread over a three-and-a-half-year period and involved three stages: concept design, during which the narrative – effectively a list of chapter headings – was developed as a visitor route around two floors, with the staircase providing the literal descent into the war years; scheme design, at which the audio-visual element and likely artefacts were plotted into that framework; and detailed design, at which the fine detail – graphical elements and showcase content – was finalised. This layered approach – whereby the scheme was refined and developed over the three-and-a-half-year period – gave all-important flexibility for adjustments to be made as new artefacts were found. Two key objects – for example, the dissecting table and the funeral cart – were only firmed up weeks before the opening.

October Films joined the team in late 1997 mid-way through scheme design. With their detailed knowledge of the availability of different sequences of film, Annie Dodds and her co-producer/director James Barker, helped us in our decision of where to plot the programmes into the narrative. We became alert to the likely impact of memorable audio elements – like Hitler ranting or the insistent voice of the German commentator on a Nazi propaganda piece. The BBC series *The Nazis: A Warning From History* had been screened in autumn 1997 – another major project on our theme, also four years in the making. Laurence Rees's use of screen technology had been extremely versatile. Historical documents had been brought to life with clever devices such as translations of key orders being 'floated' over the page of the original, or infamous quotes fading in and out in large capital letters. Again aware of the dryness of much of the showcase material we were sifting through, I wondered whether our screens could not be used to similar effect. However Annie – sensibly I now see – urged restraint and we resolved to keep the content of the screens as simple and straightforward as possible.

Rees's films had shown the power of testimony, but we were unsure whether it should be a prominent element in the Exhibition. Would the presence of living people give the impression that it was the norm to survive? Would the public find it hard to concentrate on what we knew would be a fairly taxing text, with sounds coming from different directions? Of course once they were told, we realised that the survivors' stories were in large part about the gradual deterioration and loss of loved ones, so that the cumulative story was definitely one of destruction rather than survival. As to the intrusion of sound, the spaciousness of the Exhibition, together with carefully chosen auditory systems which directed and controlled sound spillage, ensured that visitors have ample opportunity to concentrate on documents and texts. Having decided to use survivor testimony, the question arose 'should we not also bring visitors face to face with perpetrators?' as had been done with such effect in one episode of *The Nazis*. In the event we decided against this, partly to keep the treatment simple and straightforward, and partly because we recognised the difficulty of obtaining truthful witness testimony from former guards.

Curating a 1200m² exhibition to a tight production schedule was a fairly large task, and we adopted a system of 'section compilers' to ensure that each section was developed to the highest standards, while at the same time achieving consistency across the whole display. The staff who had from 1996 to early 1998 worked chiefly on acquiring artefacts were in mid-1998 each allocated a number of sections of the Exhibition to curate. Within these sections they were responsible for ensuring that all the composite elements worked well together, that information was reinforced but not repeated, that spellings were consistent, and that – where possible and appropriate – links were achieved between artefacts, photographs and film. The system gave a valuable sense of ownership to the curators. Thus, for example, Kathy Jones, who had researched most of the material for the 'Ghettos' section during her two-year stint in Poland, had the satisfaction of seeing it absorbed into the showcases and integrated with the surrounding photographs and films. The system also meant that each audio-visual programme was scrutinised by a curator steeped in the content of its section.

October Films had long experience of sourcing material from numerous different archives, and it soon became clear that a retinue of curators and archivists in numerous different countries was being mobilised to provide footage and important docu-

Ghettos section of the Holocaust Exhibition (© IWM)

mentation. Sometimes special leverage had to be brought to bear to secure particular pieces of film or images. I think for example of the film of the burning synagogue in Bielefeld whose rights my German colleague Sandra Nagel managed to negotiate. And the scenes of pre-war Sopot – the Baltic resort where Edyta Klein-Smith holidayed as a child – which were tracked down by October Films' researcher Tom Collinson with help from our Polish-speaking researcher Kathy Jones.

Some pieces of film in the Exhibition had never been seen before. Kay Gladstone in the Film Archive of the Imperial War Museum brought to our attention the home movie made by a Belgian banker, Carl De Brouwer, and his wife; they had taken in two Jewish children who lived with them for much of the war under assumed identities. The film was given to us by De Brouwer's daughter, Elizabeth Van der Elst. It was too complicated a story to be incorporated into the larger production, but the material was thought to provide an illuminating glimpse into the lives of this caring family who ultimately saved the lives of two children. It found an obvious location in the 'wall of hiding' – the white wall whose seven apertures reveal different ways in which Jews were hidden. Another rarely seen piece of film – distressing in the extreme – was shown to us during a research trip to the USHMM. The film purported to show an early gas van in operation. There was a certain amount of debate over this, and the questions were raised: 'was this a post-war reconstruction?'; 'what exactly was its provenance?'[1] Our caption made it clear that its provenance was uncertain, but it provided a unique visual record of the steps taken towards industrial killing.

From mid-1998 the first films began to emerge. We had stipulated that we should have ultimate control over each programme, and a certain amount of tweaking and negotiating went on before each film was ready to be pressed. We were fortunate to have on the Exhibition Advisory Group the documentary-maker, Martin Smith. Martin had in his early career produced several programmes for the *World at War* series. He later produced and directed *The Struggles for Poland* and more recently *The Cold War*. Crucially for us he had spent two years of his career developing the USHMM's Permanent Exhibition in Washington, and he was able to provide a wealth of practical advice from that experience. We asked him to act as a special adviser on the audio-visual aspects of the project, and he gave generously of his time to this, offering his thoughts on each batch of films as it was produced. 'What is the shot telling us?' he would ask. 'Is it telling us something we don't know from elsewhere? Bearing in mind the short viewing span of visitors, it's obviously important to bring the best material to the fore.' Sensitive to the amount of sound which was going into the Exhibition, he also warned us against creating an 'arcade experience'; the hard surfaces of the Exhibition rooms and in particular the ranting from Goebbels and Hitler on the Upper Floor were known to be a potential problem. Balancing the competing sound elements on the Upper Floor was not easy, and has possibly not been achieved to everyone's satisfaction – visitors very occasionally complain about the difficulty in concentrating where sound elements overlap.

I would like to mention at this point another individual: Raye Farr, Director of Film and Video in the US Holocaust Research Institute, whose advice and support was vital to our project. Raye was a fount of knowledge both of film and exhibition making – for she had succeeded Martin as Director of the Permanent Exhibition at the USHMM. Like Martin, Raye knew this Museum from her time working on the *World at War* series in the 1970s and was able to introduce us to many colleagues in Washington who had faced similar challenges to those facing us, several years earlier. She also gave an enormous amount of practical help and advice to Annie and James during the making of the audio-visual programmes.

So, with all these things in place, the Exhibition was almost ready; yet a last-minute change of plan showed that however hard you try to stick to an agreed plan, just occasionally it is worth throwing it all out and starting again. It relates to a group of programmes in the Entrance Space. This space – the oval wooden-slatted area at the start of the Exhibition – was originally conceived as having four audio-visual programmes running simultaneously, not three as at present. The fourth was to have given a kind of flash-forward to the discovery of the concentration camps in 1945, and had as a large caption underneath it a quote from one of the war correspondents of the time. The introductory text was originally affixed to the wooden wall on the left as visitors enter.

One afternoon during a final walk around with our designers we decided that the Entrance Space was too busy, with too many competing elements. We then broke the 'no changes' rules and did several unexpected things. We moved the text introducing the Exhibition from the walnut veneer wall to the massive steel wall where it sat rather well, the words 'Under the cover of the war' being suitably echoed by the montage of German troops projected onto the black steel. We swapped the two audio-visuals dealing with life before the Holocaust from their previous position so that the compilation of footage of life in pre-war Europe was seen first, while the video introducing the survivors became embedded in the frieze of family photographs – again a logical positioning. The addition of a four-word caption, 'Life before the Nazis', gave meaning to a space whose role *we* were familiar with but which, we realised, the newly-arrived visitor might want explained. It was a lesson in how – just occasionally – a complete

'Under the cover of the war' and 'Life before the Nazis'. IWM 2000-61-11 (© IWM)

change of plan, provided it involved no re-editing of films, could achieve a better all round result.

Four years is a long time to wait to see one's plans come to fruition: the Holocaust Exhibition – which could only be installed once the building was complete – went up in a matter of weeks in late 1999 and early 2000. The production of its audio-visual programmes, on the other hand, was divided into three four-month stages – at the end of each we had a batch of completed programmes. Sometimes these were no more than silent footage, but their position within the Exhibition could be appreciated. Given the long wait to find out what the built exhibition would feel like to walk through, it was encouraging to have the thirty audio-visual elements honed to perfection several months ahead of their eventual installation. Once the full complement of films was made, we held a special preview of the testimony-carrying programmes for the survivors and their husbands or wives. Sadly one of our respondents – Rudi Bamber – had died since his recording was made. Everyone was tremendously moved to see the group's wartime experiences woven into a seamless narrative, and admiring of the care and profession-alism with which each programme had been made.

The Holocaust Exhibition used film more extensively than any other Imperial War Museum exhibition had done before, and the public's reaction to it has been extremely favourable, as demonstrated by the comments offered by visitors, some of which are cited below:

'The silence and respect of the visitors to the Exhibition is in itself a tribute. There will be many thoughtful, reflective people walking away from here today.'

'What brave, courageous people who talked on the videos, how moving this was.'

'A just and fitting tribute. Sensitively done – the use of oral testimony allows the visitor to empathise. It is like listening to a friend. The world must learn from what these survivors have to tell us.'

'I have found this exhibition a most engrossing experience. I have spent far longer than I intended to – but I am very glad I did ... If one per cent of all those who pass through the doors here are made to think about what man can do to man – then that is a start...'

Note

1   The film is purported to have been shot in Mogilev, Belarus. One historian at the IWM who is suspicious as to the authenticity of the film suggests it may have been 'mocked up' or assembled after the war by the East German state-sponsored film company DEFA (Deutsche Film Aktiengesellschaft). DEFA was inaugurated in May 1946 in the former Ufa studios at Neubabelsberg, near Berlin, and thus operated in the Soviet Zone of Occupation.

2   Preparing the video displays for the Imperial War Museum's Holocaust Exhibition

Annie Dodds

As filmmakers for the Imperial War Museum's Holocaust Exhibition, our task was to present different aspects of the Holocaust throughout the Exhibition in such a way that the films, along with other display elements – artifacts, photographs, documents and text – became an integral part of how the story was told. This was achieved in close collaboration with the Museum's Exhibition team and the designers as the project progressed. Our raw materials were existing film footage and photographs of the time, including many newsreels and official propaganda films of Nazi origin, which we counterbalanced by acquiring as much material as possible from other sources, especially amateur and home movies and personal photographs. We also filmed our own interviews with survivors, most, but not all, of whom were Jewish. All this material was used in a number of different ways: to relate events, to tell personal stories, to create a sense of time and place, as historical evidence, or to provide historical context and analysis.

Although there seems to be a large quantity of film material relating to the Holocaust, it is, in fact, a very selective and incomplete record. Memory too can be selective, but the recording of many thousands of individual eye-witness accounts since the war has helped provide a truer and more complete record of events. The survivor testimony we filmed is central to the way the story is told in the Exhibition. It is used to convey with as much immediacy as possible how it felt to live through these events, from before the outbreak of war through to the liberation and ending with reflections from today's perspective. A very few people were speaking on behalf of millions, especially those who disappeared, so we had to find ways to universalise their experiences, while at the same time retaining the intimate and personal aspects. It was something of a creative challenge to weave together brief fragments from so many different stories to arrive at films that were coherent in the personal detail and yet made sense as a whole.

An important decision we made early on was that the first images and voices visitors to the Exhibition would encounter would be those of survivors as ordinary people living ordinary lives in a pre-Holocaust world – not as skeletal camp inmates or anonymous heaps of corpses. *The way we lived*, the first film people see as they enter the Exhibition, demonstrates this vividly. It is a lively montage of scenes of daily life: town and country, markets, schools, shops, family life, nightlife, travel, work and leisure, all cut to music of the period. This is followed by *Who we were*, a film introducing individual witnesses talking about their pre-war childhoods, illustrated with family photographs. Our aim, in this opening space, was to evoke a recognisable world, full of richness and diversity, that visitors could easily identify with, so that by the end of the exhibition they would have some understanding of the enormity of what was lost – that not only were millions of people murdered, but that entire cultures were wiped out. From then on the testimony films express the experiences of those individuals going through an unimaginable process of destruction on an unimaginable scale. Although we never follow one person's story through, the effect is cumulative as visitors recognise individual witnesses at different stages of the process through to the end.

Finding the right archive images to illustrate personal testimony can be a problem. There are no hard and fast rules, though one must not use misleading footage nor does one want the visuals to interfere with the story being told. It is easy enough to find general street scenes or public events of the time, but more difficult when the story unfolding is powerful and personally specific. In the film about life in the ghettos, for example, a witness movingly describes the death of his much-loved father from starvation and the lengths the family went to give him a dignified burial. The archive footage used is in total contrast to that which is heard and is shocking in its own right, so there is a danger it might undercut the personal story. Anonymous bodies of those who died from starvation or typhus, collected from the streets on makeshift carts, are shown being tipped into mass graves. In this instance, we felt the contrast worked and that, far from dominating or confusing the story, the images fill out the testimony by making the viewer acutely aware of how important it was for the father to be shown love and respect in death, in circumstances where so many died alone and unmarked.

We also use film as straightforward narrative with explanatory captions to relate or explain events, such as the desperate flight of Jews from Europe before the outbreak of war or the differences between the Nazi occupations of France and the Netherlands. Our concern here was to ensure that we had researched all the available footage, giving ourselves the greatest choice of imagery to compress such complex stories into short, visual narratives. In the film about the flight of refugees, our research uncovered footage from Hungary which had never been seen before. It was filmed by a Hungarian steamboat captain illegally carrying refugees to join a ship that would take them to Palestine. The footage is very well shot, which adds significantly to its impact. The expressive close-ups of the faces of the Jewish refugees crowded onto the steamboat decks are particularly haunting. The collectors from whom we obtained this material have gone to great lengths to document the footage, trying to find out who the people were – searching, for example, for lists of names with the shipping company or of those who arrived in Palestine.[1] Such painstaking efforts to make the historical record as full and accurate as possible are invaluable to filmmakers like us, helping to use our archive material in the most authentic and informed way.

Film is, of course, a valuable historical record in its own right and can be used as visual evidence. Apart from the widely-known footage of the liberation of the camps, we also show other pieces of film purely as evidence – for example, amateur footage taken by a German naval officer showing Jewish men being executed by firing squad in a ditch at Liepaja (Libau) in Latvia in August 1941, and another short piece of film taken by an unknown SS cameraman in autumn 1941 which shows emaciated people being led into an experimental gas chamber, a hut connected to the exhaust pipe of a car in the grounds of a psychiatric hospital in Nazi-occupied Russia (see doubts as to its authenticity in Suzanne Bardgett's chapter). This chilling material is simply shown uncut.

We also used film in a freer, more impressionistic way to create a certain atmosphere or to evoke a sense of time and place. These films are most effective when experienced almost as an element of the design within the context of the surrounding displays. Unlike the testimony or narrative films, they require less concentration from the visitor, who can simply absorb the images and sounds as background to whatever section of the exhibition they are in. For visitors who are being expected to take in an enormous amount of information, this does have some practical benefit. One example of this is the large, silent projection, 'Under the cover of the war', which looms threateningly over the first two films about pre-war life in the entrance space. This stylised montage of super-imposed images of war creates a nightmare vision of violence and brutality, directed against civilians and especially against Jews. Another example, also a large projection, is designed to convey the rise of Nazi terror in pre-war Germany. Here, much of the effect is achieved through the soundtrack which is heard all around – the stridency of Goebbels' voice threatening the Jews, the chanting of Nazi thugs in the streets, the sound of burning books and the singing of Nazi anthems.

When we came to the section dealing with the concentration camps and extermination camps, there was no film material, so we made three sound-only programmes, describing people's arrival at Auschwitz and life and death in the camps. This gave us an opportunity to weave in a variety of other voices in addition to our own witnesses. We included some from existing interviews in the Museum's Sound Archive, from the Spielberg Foundation we obtained an eye-witness account from one of the few survivors of the *Sonderkommando* who worked in the gas chambers, and we also included an English-speaking ex-Soviet POW who was interviewed for us in Russia. Listening to these sound programmes, while contemplating the huge model which shows the ramp at Auschwitz-Birkenau and the arrival of Hungarian Jews, the visitors' imagination has to take over at this crucial point in the Exhibition where there is no visual evidence of what took place. The personal recollections in these sound programmes are not only graphic and harrowing accounts of what it was like to be in the camps, most importantly they provide the only first-hand evidence of the very heart of the Nazi crimes.

Film is perceived as being the most powerfully 'realistic' medium, but we know it can also be a highly manipulative and emotive medium. The Nazis understood the value of film and were skilled in using it in a sophisticated and cynical way to persuade or to give the impression of an objective record. We know from previous experience that, in spite of its vile messages, much of this Nazi propaganda material has a seductive, lethal attraction about it. This had been a matter of great concern to Martin Smith, for example, who was Exhibition Director at the United States Holocaust Memorial Museum (USHMM), during the setting up of their exhibition. Now, as an adviser on the setting up of the IWM Holocaust Exhibition, he made the point that the floor dealing with the rise of Hitler and Nazism in Germany could have this perversely 'attractive' quality to it unless great care was taken. We were sensitive to these concerns and made sure, when using this footage in our own films, to reveal it for what it is. The surrounding exhibition context was also carefully designed to expose the nature of the material.

I have already referred to our attempts to counterbalance the availability of so much Nazi material by researching other sources of footage. One particularly rewarding find came about through a sound interview, recorded for the Museum's Sound Archive, which we hoped to use in one of our sound programmes. The man in question, a sur-

'Propaganda and race hatred'. P6-51-13 (© IWM/HEPO)

vivor of Auschwitz, is Czech and lives in France. Shortly after the interview, he phoned us to say he had a couple of small reels of film in his attic from before the war. He did not know what they contained because he could not view them, but might we be interested? Well, yes we certainly were. Two reels of 9.5mm film duly arrived. The specialist film clinic who could run this gauge of film would only agree to run it once as it was so fragile. We decided to transfer it immediately to broadcast-standard videotape, sight unseen. To our delight, we found we were looking at beautifully-filmed home movies of the Hartmann family before the war; on a seaside holiday, playing table tennis in their garden, on a cycling tour in Germany where swastikas hang outside the hotels and restaurants – and much else besides.[2] Some of this footage appears in the introductory film. What is especially gratifying about finding this kind of material is that it is so well documented – we know who everyone is and what happened to them.

As filmmakers, our relationship to our material was complicated by the unrelenting grimness of the subject matter, especially working on it over a long period of time. We found we had to operate on two different levels simultaneously. On the one hand, we had to be fully involved in the details of this huge mass of material, trying to maintain our sensitivity while viewing it many times over and listening to stories of unimaginable wickedness; fortunately, this was offset to a degree by other material which was full of life and humour and stories which revealed the very best of human nature. On the other, we needed to take our distance from it – and not just for our own sanity. Decisions about what was to be included and what omitted had to be ruthless since the films had, of necessity, to be so short. Every single image and every single word had to carry so much weight. Hours of fascinating material, some of which we had gone to great lengths to obtain, had to be dropped – and this was especially true of the interviews we

The last room in the Exhibition where the witnesses reflect on the meaning of their experiences as a whole. PS-51-10 (© IWM/HEPO)

filmed. In those cases we had also developed a relationship with the person involved and knew how important it was for them that their stories were told. However, the witnesses have the satisfaction of knowing that their complete interviews are stored in the Museum's Film Archive for future researchers.

All our interviewees knew it would not be easy to re-live their experiences on film and then have them exposed to the general public in a way over which they had no control. The standard release forms they signed gave us permission to edit and use their testimony as we saw fit. We were always conscious of the great trust they had placed in us. There was a continual critical balance between allowing the witnesses to tell their stories in their own way, while at the same time making sure we got what we needed. Above all, we felt we had to break through the time barrier. When witnesses tell you their story, protected by distance from events, informed by everything they have learned since, with dates and places in the right order, it is almost like hearing them talk about another person. This is entirely understandable, but we wanted them to try and remember what it really felt like back then, when they were young, going through these bewildering experiences. And we did try to steer them towards this, often by going back over the same events until our interviewee fell into a more direct mode of remembering, reliving the past in their head in a more immediate, and often more painful, way. We were certainly not trying to push people into breaking down or bursting into tears. In fact, they often recalled happy moments more vividly in this way, but there is no doubt that it made the whole interview process more exhausting. Our witnesses were aware of what we were trying to achieve and, I think, saw the value in it. But it often had the effect of making their testimony less coherent and more muddled in narrative terms. This did not matter to us, as the editing process would allow us to improve upon that. But some of the interviewees worried that they had not given us a clear, polished account of their story. We had to reassure them that what they had given us was of greater worth – an extraordinary insight into the extremes of human behaviour and relationships and a greater understanding of human resilience and adaptability under circumstances beyond our comprehension.

During the development of the Exhibition we carried out extensive research on a number of different aspects of the Holocaust which are not covered in the Exhibition because of practical considerations of space, design, resources, editorial decisions and so on. Within our films, for example, one does not hear the voice of the ordinary watcher or bystander to these events, or of those swept along as enthusiastic participants. We looked, for example, at many existing interviews, including the remarkable interviews in Laurence Rees' series *The Nazis: A Warning From History* (1997), including those with unrepentant Germans who supported the Nazi regime or with a Lithuanian auxiliary involved in killing Jews. However, these were all original-language interviews designed for a six-part series and to incorporate just one brief section within the tight framework of our own short testimony films in English would not work. We discussed the possibility of trying to include some of these accounts in a separate film with subtitles, but it proved unfeasible to make a short film from these disparate voices that made sense and fitted into the Exhibition narrative. It was eventually decided that we would stay with our own specially-filmed interviews, keep the eye-witness accounts in English and that it would be the survivors' voices who carried the story.

We hope that visitors to the Exhibition might occasionally imagine themselves in the position of the bystander or the participant and reflect: How would I have behaved in these circumstances? Would I really have believed all this vicious propaganda? Would I have been brave enough to speak out or to act or would I have kept my head down? Would I even have been capable of extreme cruelty? For many reasons there was a long period of silence about the Holocaust after the war, but in recent years as more survivors have spoken about their experiences and more books and films have addressed the subject, there has been a growing fascination with these events. This proliferation of material on the subject has in itself aroused controversy and not everyone thinks it is necessarily a good thing. Be that as it may, this Holocaust Exhibition has a logical and important place in a museum dedicated to recording and examining modern conflict, especially the Second World War.

Although the Exhibition goes a long way in depicting some of the reality of the Holocaust, in the end it cannot resolve the fundamental question of how something so terrible and on such a scale could happen. Considered by many as the nadir of twentieth-century civilisation, it still defies real understanding and we need to keep asking the questions – particularly as genocide has not disappeared, not even from modern Europe. Apart from the unfolding of historical facts and events, we wanted this Exhibition to take the visitor on another kind of journey – to involve them more actively by provoking an imaginative response which would encourage people to reflect on what they are seeing and hearing and above all to question. We hope visitors will respond in this way, especially the younger ones for whom none of this is within living memory – and particularly because the personal testimony films are about the experiences of young people. The Holocaust should not become a fossilised historical catastrophe to be learned about and then put aside. Questions of morality, questions about human behaviour, about how states control their citizens and the value that is put on different human lives – these are all matters of pressing contemporary and universal relevance. If a contemplation of the horrors of the Holocaust can help a new generation consider these issues in relation to themselves and the society they are helping to build, then the Exhibition will be of lasting value.

Film production team

Producer:	Annie Dodds
Director:	James Barker
Editor:	Cathy Houlihan
Assistant:	Tom Collinson
Cameraman:	Jim Howlett
Sound recordist:	Peter Eason

Notes

1   Janos Varga, Hungarian film archivist. Péter Forgács, Hungarian film historian.
2   The Hartmann films are catalogued in the IWM collection under accession no. MGH 6432.

3   Filming the liberation of Bergen-Belsen

Toby Haggith

On the evening of 15 April 1945 members of the British Army's Film and Photographic Unit (AFPU) accompanying other elements of the 11th Armoured Division entered the camp of Bergen-Belsen. The scenes filmed by the horrified and incredulous cameramen are some of the most disturbing of all those recorded at concentration camps and sites of atrocities encountered by Allied and Soviet cameramen in the closing months of the war: scores of 'paper-thin' naked corpses strewn across the camp floor or piled in grotesque heaps of twisted limbs;[1] close-ups of decaying and bruised faces; survivors dressed in rags tottering dazed and bewildered around the camp or reaching out to grasp the hand of a British soldier; corpses slung over the backs of the camp guards, nodding and bouncing like life-sized rag dolls, which are carried from trucks then tossed, without ceremony, into huge pits; a bulldozer pushing a heap of naked corpses across the camp floor. Even to those who one might expect to be used to the horrors of war, the images of Belsen were unprecedented. Ronald Tritton, who was Director of Public Relations at the War Office, recorded in his war diary, 'The Belsen pictures came in this evening – 103 of them. They are so awful that words cannot describe them. I was almost physically sickened, and felt shaky and very upset.'[2]

Used sparingly at the time to prove the existence of the camps, these images have since become so widely used in film and television programmes, that they are now familiar icons, coming to symbolise not just the Holocaust but the evils of the Nazi regime as a whole.[3] Apart from its power to shock and disturb, the footage shot at Belsen constitutes a special place within the body of film shot of camp liberations and of the war in general. Firstly, no other camp was filmed so comprehensively and over such a long period. The film is not just a record of the liberation but also a full account of the efforts of the British army to stabilise the conditions in the camp as they found them, to save lives and return the survivors to health. Secondly, the footage shot at Belsen was the first to be admitted as evidence to a war crimes trial, when it was screened at the courtroom in Lüneburg during the trial of the Belsen guards, between 17 September and 17 November 1945.

Some documentary makers have used the footage of camp liberations and German atrocities as little more than illustrative wallpaper, rarely distinguishing between the different camps and sites featured in the archive film. There has been particular concern that the promiscuous use of the Belsen footage has distorted popular understanding of the Holocaust itself. Firstly, although the film has come to symbolise the most extreme behaviour of the Germans towards the Jews, the scenes at Belsen, however appalling, do not represent the Holocaust. The corpses and spectrally-thin people that were filmed

A camp inmate grasps the hand of Lieutenant Martin Wilson, AFPU. MH 2436 (© IWM)

at Belsen were a consequence of the neglect and cruelty of the concentration camp system, not the policy of 'the Final Solution'. For Belsen was not an extermination camp; Auschwitz-Birkenau, Chelmno, Sobibor and Treblinka were and people died there because they were murdered within hours of arriving, not through disease or starvation. Secondly, it is not clear to the viewer that the majority of the dead and survivors found at Belsen were Jewish, a problem compounded by the fact that in press reports, newsreels and official films produced for the public, there was a tendency to universalise the suffering and down-play the high number of Jews in the camp.[4] The anonymous nature of the corpses seen in the Belsen footage has even led Holocaust deniers to claim that these were in fact the victims of Allied bombing.[5]

A more insidious outcome of the screening of the Belsen footage is that it tends to demean and dehumanise Holocaust survivors in the mind of the viewer.[6] The repeated images of piles of corpses and helpless survivors creates a perception of the Jews as passive victims and reinforces a common perception that they did not resist their fate. There is also a danger that the viewer becomes hardened and even brutalised by the endless views of naked, emaciated corpses, the anonymity of the bodies distancing us from what the Holocaust meant in human terms.[7] Inevitably, the cameramen have been blamed for contributing to these distortions, by concentrating on images of the dead and losing sight of the individual in the urge to prove to the viewer the grotesque scale of the suffering.[8] There is also an implied criticism that they acted callously when filming the helpless inmates, transgressing taboos about the portrayal of the dead and the human body that showed little respect for their subjects. For these reasons, many have qualms about the screening of the Belsen footage, some arguing that it so distorts our understanding of the Holocaust that it should never be shown.[9] Although these concerns are valid and such a conclusion understandable, they stem from an acquaintance with only a small number of rolls shot in the camp, and a misunderstanding of the work of the AFPU cameramen.

Bergen-Belsen concentration camp

In March 1943 Heinrich Himmler (Chief of the SS) ordered that part of the POW camp at Bergen-Belsen be turned into a special camp for prominent European Jews, or those of neutral states, who could be held and used as exchange for Germans imprisoned abroad. Initially conditions in the camp were relatively good, but they deteriorated rapidly from March 1944 when it was designated as a 'recovery' or 'recuperation' camp for prisoners from other camps who were too ill to work. Numbers swelled further as new inmates, often already extremely sick and weak, were moved to Belsen from camps in the path of the advancing Soviet, British and American armies. As a consequence of this new influx of prisoners and under the increasingly chaotic and uninterested supervision of the camp administration, the inmates' situation had descended to an unimaginable level; by the spring of 1945 food supplies dwindled and the camp's water and sanitation services collapsed under the strain. In this environment the diseases of typhus, dysentery and tuberculosis thrived. It has been estimated that by April 1945 more than 60,000 people were enduring these appalling conditions.[10]

In the spring of 1945 Bergen-Belsen lay in the path of the advancing British Second Army and specifically the 11th Armoured Division. On 12 April the local German army commander *Oberst* Harries contacted the British army and negotiated handing over control of the camp to prevent typhus spreading to the surrounding area. He described the camp as one that contained 'political prisoners'. As a result of these negotiations a neutral zone of 48km^2 was set up around the camp, open only to units involved with medical relief. The morning after reconnoitring the camp, Sergeants Haywood, Lawrie, Lewis and Oakes, under the command of Lieutenant Martin Wilson, began to film and photograph in the camp. The cine-cameramen Lewis and Lawrie stayed until 26 April, compiling most of the moving images taken at Belsen during the crucial phase when the British army struggled to stabilise the horrendous situation in the camp.[11] As a unit the AFPU continued to cover activity at the camp up until 9 June 1945, including the ceremonial burning of the camp huts from 19 to 21 May.[12]

AFPU policy of recruiting from the ranks meant that the cameramen who went into Belsen were tough and battle-hardened, but this had not prepared them for the mounds of naked corpses, the scale of dead and suffering. Moreover, the kind of dead bodies they had previously encountered, men in uniform, were an expected consequence of battle. As the photographer Sergeant Oakes recalled, 'we couldn't understand it. We had seen corpses, we had seen our own casualties, but these bloodless bodies ... they were so young some of them as well, men and women.'[13]

In common with British civilians, the soldiers and military cameramen who entered Belsen had been sceptical of previous press reports of German atrocities and the concentration camp system.[14] Dick Williams, who was with the Royal Army Serivce Corps and one of the first to enter the camp, confided to a friend, 'I never believed all the fantastic stories we've heard, read about, and the atrocities committed by the SS men and

AFPU cameramen Sergeant Harry Oakes (left) and Sergeant William Lawrie (right). BU 8368 (© IWM)

women, but after being here four days, boy, some experience'.[15] For Sergeant Lewis, who was Jewish, the discovery of Belsen was a tremendous shock: 'The terrible discovery came to me, a sort of revelation, a flash of lightning because it penetrated these terrible scenes, to make me think. All the stories I'd heard about the persecution of people from my mother and father, here they were true.'[16]

Before April 1945, the Allied armies' direct contact with the German camp system had showed that the regime included torture and mistreatment but the evidence did not suggest mass murder.[17] Once the British army moved into Germany, however, more camps were discovered and now they often contained inmates who could provide testimony to their treatment. The discovery on 12 April of Stalag XIB at Celle, a town only 13 miles from Belsen, provided a foretaste of what they were to encounter later. Here the shocked cameramen recorded scenes of a dead inmate and various other brutalised and emaciated prisoners of the camp.[18] But as Sergeant Lawrie recalled, although this was terrible, 'as we found later, this was actually a Sunday school picnic as to what was really happening once we got further up the road'.[19] One should stress that the British army was totally ignorant as to what was really happening in Belsen. Indeed the cameramen were fairly blasé about the prospect of going into the camp and accepted the German description of it as containing political and criminal prisoners. For the British the most interesting aspect of Belsen was the unique opportunity, created by the neutral zone, to observe and film the *Wehrmacht* and SS close-up and fully armed, in their 'natural habitat'.

The cameramen were professionally as well as psychologically unprepared for the scenes they found at Celle and Belsen. AFPU training was designed to equip men with 'a sound basic knowledge for battle photography' not to teach them how to cover civilian situations.[20] Surprisingly there were no official guidelines on filming military dead let alone the kind of scenes found in concentration camps. Instead AFPU cameramen imposed their own strict but straightforward set of guidelines about what they would cover – enemy dead were filmed; badly wounded or dead Allied servicemen were not. This self-censorship was also extended to the corpses of civilians or those who were in distress. These guidelines arose out of a strong sense of comradeship with the men who served alongside the cameramen, as well as certain scruples about the portrayal of the dead. This was also a practical response to the sensibilities of British newsreel editors, who had produced a sanitised account of the war; initially newsreel company heads had been reluctant to use any film of the concentration camps.[21]

Thus before examining how the cameramen filmed in the camp, it is necessary to briefly explain why they covered these scenes at all. Although members of the AFPU were encouraged and hoped to produce footage that could be suitable for public exposure via the newsreels, the primary role of the unit was to compile a historical record of Britain's armed forces. Regardless of the attitudes of the newsreels, if the AFPU decided something was important, they would cover it. The fact that so many diverse units of the Army became involved with Belsen and that the camp was under Army jurisdiction for so long was justification enough for the Unit.[22] Moreover, a precedent for this kind of filming had already been set by the advancing Red Army and scenes of German atrocities had been appearing in Russian newsreels from early in 1943; this material

A dead German officer filmed at Arnhem, probably by Sergeant 'Jock' Walker, 14 September 1944. Sergeant Mike Lewis was with Walker at this stage of the battle and filmed linking scenes in this lane. FLM 3727 (© IWM)

had even appeared in British newsreels.[23] Theoretically, AFPU cameramen would have grasped the importance of filming camp liberations, as the propaganda derived by the Soviets from footage of German atrocities, along with scenes of British soldiers helping civilians, were among the examples given in the instructors' notes at Pinewood to instil 'news sense' in the trainees.[24]

Lieutenant Colonel Hugh Stewart, who commanded No. 5 Section of the AFPU and entered the camp on the first day, immediately realised that this discovery 'was so much one of the things that the war was about'.[25] Therefore he instructed Lieutenant Wilson and the sergeants to stay in Belsen for a couple of weeks to get total coverage. The cameramen shared Stewart's belief that Belsen was important. Indeed they felt compelled to give it special coverage, despite the great emotional and psychological strain they experienced at the camp. Years later William Lawrie recalled simply, 'This had to be recorded somehow.'[26] Paul Wyand, who was asked to film some sound interviews at the camp, 'willingly accepted' the job, 'as we feel it is the duty of everybody to see it, as it is the most revolting proof of what we are fighting for'.[27]

At first the men were overwhelmed by the situation in the camp, as Sergeant Lewis explained in his dope sheet (soldiers' slang for the shotlist or 'secret caption list')[28] of 16 April: 'It is regretted that separate shots could not be mentioned in writing but so much was happening and so quickly that it was decided to dispense with the captioning of separate shots especially as the material is self-explanatory.'[29] In this regard, they were helped by Lieutenant Wilson, who ensured that the different activities in the camp were properly covered and that the cameramen did not get too close to individual inmates or situations that would have been distressing. Mike Lewis was glad that he was busy

Sergeant Mike Lewis filming a mass burial. Former guards can be seen unloading and carrying the corpses of the inmates. FLM 1232 (© IWM)

filming every day and Sergeant Oakes busied himself with the camera equipment as a distraction. The lens both limited the scenes and operated as a protective barrier for the cameramen; Oakes talked of closing one eye from the horror.[30] Preoccupation with the job in hand led to a degree of hardening in the men's attitudes; soon they were even able to joke about what they saw. Sergeant Leatherbarrow witnessed an incident when Lawrie was filming the bulldozer filling one of the mass graves, and Lawrie shouted out 'Look out Mike here comes a beauty', within ear-shot of Ellen Wilkinson MP, who was among a party of VIPs visiting the camp. But as Lawrie himself astutely observed, 'if you had become too involved, I think you would have gone mad along with the rest of the people'.[31]

Clearly under the extreme conditions at Belsen the idea that any of the scenes could have been faked or re-staged for the camera is preposterous. This was not like the picturesque liberation of the concentration camp at Cosenza near Naples, where the inmates had twice re-enacted the moment of their liberation for Sergeant Hopkinson's camera.[32] As Lawrie recalled, 'Some of them were too far gone to move. There was certainly no way we could have asked them to rehearse a piece for us.'[33] But perhaps more importantly, faking or re-staging scenes for the camera was contrary to the ethos of the AFPU and during their training the cameramen were instructed to note down in their dope sheets if scenes were staged for the camera. The cameramen claim that the unit at Belsen did not have any instructions from outside as to what or how to film in the camp. Apart from allocating filming jobs and very general directions, Lieutenant Wilson left decisions about framing to the individual cameramen's initiative. As there are few clues to the cameramen's preoccupations in the dope sheets, and they cannot recall many details, this description is based largely on my personal assessment of viewing the reels of film.

Their most obvious concern, and one found repeated in all the liberation footage, was to gather proof of the regime in the camp. In their dope sheets the cameramen frequently commented on the evidential value of the visual record they were compiling: 'It is impossible to put into writing all that was seen but these pictures should give pictorial evidence of the brutality and callousness of the "Master Race".'[34] As Lawrie's dope sheet remark of 16 April suggests, the cameramen even believed, at least to begin with, that filming was the only method capable of adequately conveying the horrors they were witnessing. Unlike other camps where instruments of torture and gas chambers were found,[35] at Belsen the evidence of mistreatment was the condition of the camp inmates, which may partly explain why the cameramen repeatedly filmed sequences documenting the human suffering: heaps of bodies on the ground or in pits; inmates sitting listlessly on the ground; studies of survivors, their faces drawn and pinched from hunger. As well as panning and shooting in long- and mid-shot to give a sense of the great numbers that had suffered, the cameramen filmed many details in forensic close-up: arms tattooed with prison numbers; portraits of dead faces, mouths gaping open.

Despite the eloquence of film to convey what could not be described in words, there was concern that the scenes in the camps were so terrible that they would not be believed by the general public in Britain and America and would be denied by the Germans.[36] To corroborate the film evidence at Belsen, it was decided to film sound interviews with various witnesses.[37] Statements from the camp's doctor Fritz Klein, SS guards, former prisoners and members of the British contingent now in charge, were

A 'corroborating' interview with *SS-Oberlieutenant* Franz Hosler, 23 April 1945. FLM 3730 (© IWM)

duly filmed all delivered with the backdrop of a mass grave or other camp scene. The AFPU practice of taking long- and wide-shots to establish a scene followed by mid-shots and close-ups of the same subject helped to deflect possible accusations that the scenes filmed at Belsen were faked. But the cameramen also took special precautionary shots, such as panning up from a mid-shot of a dead child to a general view of the camp and views of the camp from the observation towers.

Rolls from the first couple of weeks of filming are dominated by coverage of the burials, and include some of the most disturbing scenes of naked corpses being carried by the SS or being pushed in great heaps by the blade of a bulldozer. To have self-censored such scenes might have been regarded as an attempt to minimise the horrors, even to conceal the scale of the crime of the camps. They must also be seen in context, as filming members of the SS, in uniform, collecting and burying the dead was part of the strategy of corroborating the film evidence. Secondly, these were more than burial scenes, they were also a recording of the punishment meted out on the guards by the British and on behalf of the inmates, who had before liberation been compelled to carry out this ghastly task. Thus the cameramen constantly cut from scenes of the burials to the faces of the inmates who looked on, watching their former oppressors, their moods switching between angry jubilation and subdued anguish. In a remarkably powerful gesture of identity with the inmates' feelings, the cameramen also filmed the burials from the position of the onlookers, framing sequences of the bulldozer pushing corpses, with the shoulders, heads and faces of the traumatised ex-prisoners.

In line with the primary function of the AFPU, there is much coverage of the Army's efforts to bring food and succour to the camp's inmates and of course, lengthy coverage of all aspects of the medical operation. Not surprisingly, the soldiers and AFPU cameramen took a special interest in the young women at the camp, and there are a number of sequences of women chatting with British soldiers, sleeping and washing. The cameramen tried to frame the film so that the story could be told visually and be self-explanatory. A common framing devise was to film the inmates through the lattice of the camp's barbed wire fence. They also tried to portray aspects of the camp which could not be conveyed through film; for example, to give an impression of the terrible smell, they filmed the bulldozer driver grimacing and spitting and he and the onlookers holding handkerchiefs to their faces.

The cameramen were profoundly affected by the situation at Belsen and this can be discerned in the rolls they shot. The anger they felt towards the camp system, the guards and commandant spills into the shots. The camera is often very close to the faces of the guards – as if we could spit or strike a blow through the lens. The camera looks in incomprehension at the guards' impassive faces, searching for an explanation, and contrasts the arrogant, stout, well-fed guards with the hopeless, emaciated prisoners. The contrast between the conditions inside the camp and the bucolic scenes just outside was also recorded, with Sergeant Lewis filming cows in a lush meadow and a housewife sitting with her children on a sunny lawn.[38] The hostility felt by the rest of the British contingent to the guards is also expressed in the film, with shots of the SS invariably framed by rifle butts, Sten gun barrels and bayonets.

A 'cross' in the foreground of a scene filmed by Sergeant Mike Lewis, in which Father Morrison (left) and Father Kadziok (right) bless a mass grave. FLM 3719 (© IWM)

The corpse of an inmate being dragged to a mass grave. Detail of feet filmed by Sergeant Mike Lewis, 24 April 1945. FLM 3720 (© IWM)

When asked about shot composition, Harry Oakes talked of selecting angles that would deepen the horror and Mike Lewis recalled incorporating a spade that looked like a cross near a grave to give the image extra symbolic power.[39] There are also other allegorical references in the framing, notably naked male bodies splayed, martyr-like, on the ground. In striving to produce images of great power that could communicate the crime of Belsen, the cameramen were also thinking as professional cameramen. Oakes has been honest enough to admit that photographing the camp was a great opportunity, 'We felt in many ways it was a hell of a scoop, to be there at the time, when you think of the newsreel value of such a thing, and media value...'[40]

Unlike the constrained conditions of the battlefield, the camp was a relatively safe environment in which to work and the cameramen made the most of the opportunity to explore the photographic potential of this subject. As filming progresses, one notices the cameramen becoming increasingly experimental and imaginative, notably in a series of disturbing sequences taken while riding on the bulldozer and some beautifully framed studies of the women washing their bodies and clothes in the Mobile Bath Unit. This experimentation was also driven by a desire to find new methods of imparting the horrors of the camp because, as the cameramen recalled, however hard they tried to shoot, in reality things were much worse. For example, both Lawrie and Lewis filmed the zig-zag tracks in the soil at the side of a pit, made by the feet of the corpses hanging from the shoulders of the SS; a shot that is chilling in its sensuous power.

Because the majority of documentaries about the Holocaust concentrate on the most distressing and horrific scenes at Belsen, people's knowledge of the camp is skewed towards the weeks before the British had stabilised the situation. In fact a high percentage of the rolls shot at Belsen cover the scenes in and around the German army barracks, recording the efforts of the medical teams to save lives and return people to health. Not surprisingly, the cameramen were relieved to get away from the camp and 'go on to softer things'.[41] As they had been so personally affected by the condition of the inmates they were delighted by signs of the return of normal life, captioning scenes in the dope sheets of 'fraternisation', children playing or women picking out new clothes at 'Harrods', with affection and humour: 'Interior of the stable, the blouse and jumper department. Mrs H. Tanner, of Stoke Rectory, Grantham, Lincs, helps an undecided customer to make up her mind over the important problem of whether green is more becoming than speckled brown.'[42]

A particularly powerful and basic symbol of the return of people's sense of humanity was the urge to wash. Lewis remarked in the dope sheet of the film shot on 16 April, 'The degradation of men and women for years and in spite of this, they still have a spark of decency which asserts itself to wash and clean their bodies and clothes.'[43] To the casual viewer, the many scenes of naked strangers washing (or even worse *being* washed in the hospital barracks) can seem voyeuristic and rudely intrusive. This may be so and the cameramen explained that in many cases the condition of the inmates meant they were free to film as they liked. However, the reverently-framed sequences and touchingly respectful accompanying comments in the dope sheets suggest that for the cameramen such scenes were in fact a celebration of life and humanity.

Generally AFPU dope sheets are fairly impersonal accounts detailing the scenes covered on the rolls of films. But occasionally a cameraman was so struck by a particular action or episode he had covered that the writing in his dope sheets moved beyond

Former prisoners selecting clothes in 'Harrods'. Scene filmed by Sergeant Hewitt. FLM 3722 (© IWM)

Study of women showering in the Mobile Bath Unit. Filmed by Sergeant William Lawrie, 22 April 1945. FLM 3724 (© IWM)

the impersonal shot listing into the first person, giving voice to his own impressions and opinions. The dope sheets accompanying the rolls shot at Belsen are an especially powerful and rare example of this diary form. Here the cameramen recorded not only the shock they experienced on entering the camp, but their attempt to understand what had happened there. Perhaps they saw their own written accounts and observations on the illegal and immoral camp system as a witness statement to stand alongside the film.[44]

Due to the practical difficulties of filming in the camp and the enormity and intensity of the horror at Belsen, the cameramen began to realise that there was much that could not be conveyed on film, as Lawrie apologetically remarked: 'The atmosphere about the whole camp makes the job extremely difficult – it is hoped that some of this atmosphere has got into the pictures.'[45] For this reason, the dope sheets became a place where they supplemented the images on the films with descriptions of the heat, the deathly silence and, perhaps most terrible of all, the smell.

In response to those who have criticised the 'liberation films' for ignoring or overlooking the Jews, the dope sheets reveal that the cameramen were quick to realise that Jews were in the majority at Belsen – nor did they attempt to conceal this fact. Lawrie remarked on this when recording his first day's filming: 'The inmates who were called by the Germans "political prisoners" were of all religions and countries, mostly Jews whose only crime lay in the fact that they were Jews.'[46]

Some historians have argued that many of the liberators (and even some survivors), finding themselves bereft of descriptive powers in the face of the scenes at Belsen, resorted to analogy, comparing the internees to animals or the conditions as like hell.[47] It is true that the cameramen occasionally resorted to dehumanising slang when describing the survivors as 'zombies' or 'rag dolls' and alongside a partial viewing of the camp footage, typically offered by television documentaries on the Holocaust or some aspect of the Third Reich, one would conclude that the AFPU coverage of Belsen amounted to a dehumanising, diminishing and even de-Judaised account. However, as will be found by a less partial viewing of the more than forty rolls shot at the camp, this is a very superficial account of their work. Not only did the cameramen have a strong grasp of what had happened at Bergen-Belsen, but beneath a self-protective husk they showed great sensitivity to the people they were filming. Although they abandoned the usual guidelines for the portrayal of the dead and indeed the human body, this was not done out of callousness towards the camp inmates, but in order to convey the brutality of the camp system and so as to compile a dossier of evidence to indict a regime that they despised. Closer analysis of the framing and point of view adopted by the cameramen to film the burials and other scenes (combined with their notes in the dope sheets), makes it clear where their sympathies lay. With great prescience, the cameramen even seemed to have grasped that the humanity and individuality of the people they were filming could not be expressed to the viewer and as a result they frequently wrote down accounts of conversations they had with the inmates and named their subjects whenever possible.[48] Moreover these traumatic reels, filmed in the first couple of weeks after liberation, must be viewed with the less sensational work covering the months of rehabilitation at the camp. For along with the coverage of the British (and German) medical teams treating the sick and helping the survivors to convalesce, are numerous scenes which admiringly document and pay tribute to the independent efforts of the former prisoners, to restore their sense of dignity and humanity, and rebuild their communities. Viewing and screening these lesser known reels of 'recovery' at the camp may help to challenge the widely held and stereotypical impression of the inmates as helpless and anonymous victims.

Finally this study draws attention to a neglected group of cameramen and filmmakers, whose work has implications for our understanding of the Holocaust documentaries released in the years following the war. Previously, the 'liberation' footage has been regarded as undirected raw coverage, of little meaning until edited into a film by a known director. Now we can appreciate this archival footage as a highly mediated visual record of the camps, which has in turn constrained and influenced the work of those directors who have chosen to incorporate it in their films about the Holocaust.

Notes

1   Lieutenant Colonel Hugh Stewart of the AFPU recalled seeing 'mounds and mounds of paper-thin dead bodies'. From a recorded interview with Lt. Stewart held in the IWM Sound Archives, accession no. 4579/06, reel 4.

2   Ronald Tritton, 'War Diary', 19 April 1945, held in the IWM Docs, 76. Tritton joined the War Office in January 1940 where he was appointed Head of PR2. He set up the Army Film Unit, later the AFPU, and as Director of Public Relations was responsible for the output of the Unit and for 'placing it' for good army relations.

3   The most disturbing close-ups, scenes of the burials and of the bulldozer pushing corpses into mass

graves, were not used in the 'Belsen issues' of the *Gaumont British News* and *British Movietone News*, released in the week beginning 30 April 1945.

4   J. Reilly (1998) *Belsen: The Liberation of a Concentration Camp*. London: Routledge, 77. See also T. Kushner (1994) *The Holocaust and the Liberal Imagination: A Social and Cultural History*. Oxford: Blackwell, 213; 216.

5   TNA INF 1/636 'F3030 Investigation of War Atrocities. Factual Film Report of German Concentration Camps'. At the end of the war, Americans reported to the Supreme Headquarters Allied Expeditionary Force (SHAEF) that 'both Nazi and anti-Nazi POWs' were disassociating themselves 'almost unanimously from any responsibility for the atrocities depicted. Furthermore they say that many of the pictures remind them of photographs of the German victims of Allied air raids, which they have seen constantly in the German press and in the *Wochenschau*' [Third Reich newsreel] (Davidson Taylor, Chief of Film, Theatre and Music Control Section of SHAEF to Sidney Bernstein, 25 May 1945). Although Taylor does not specifically cite the Belsen footage here, images from this camp were included in all the newsreels and propaganda compilations of German atrocities shown to Germans at the end of the war. The suggestion that Allied propagandists may have misattributed images of the German victims of Allied air raids has become part of the 'evidence' marshalled by those who claim that the Holocaust is a fabrication. For example, in *The Six Million Reconsidered*, the authors attempt to debunk the significance of a photo of corpses in a mass grave at Bergen-Belsen. Within the lengthy caption to the image, the author explains: 'The joker in this stacked deck, however, is the peculiar fact that photographs of dead German citizens – such as the hundreds of thousands killed in the barbaric raid on Dresden – have been slyly "recycled" by our prolific myth-mongers as those of murdered Jews. Something like this may be the case with the photo above. Although it may not be clear in the reproduction here, it is a fact that at least one body in this widely published picture, reputedly from Belsen, is wearing a German uniform blouse, with Wehrmacht shoulder patch (see arrow, lower left quarter).' See *The Six Million Reconsidered: Is the 'Nazi Holocaust' Story a Zionist Propaganda Ploy?*, Committee for Truth in History. Southam: Historical Review Press, 1979, 71. A similar claim is made in R. Harwood (1978) *Nuremberg and Other War Crimes Trials: A New Look*. Southam: Historical Review Press, 61. Significantly in these Holocaust denial tracts, Allied cinematography is not mentioned, suggesting that the military cameramen were successful in adopting techniques that would make the evidence of the scenes hard to refute.

6   J. Reilly, D. Cesarani, T. Kushner, C. Richmond (eds) (1997) *Belsen in History and Memory*. London: Frank Cass, 15.

7   One indication of this process is that, sadly, a common follow up request by researchers examining the Belsen footage at the Museum, is for something 'worse'.

8   Reilly *et al.* 1997 13; 187. Another criticism made by Jo Reilly in an essay in *Belsen in History and Memory* entitled 'Cleaner, Carer and Occasional Dance Partner? Writing Women Back into the Liberation of Bergen-Belsen', was that the cameramen failed to record the enormous contribution made by women carers to the medical treatment and rehabilitation of the inmates.

9   For this reason atrocity images do not appear in any of the classroom resources produced by the Imperial War Museum's Education Department. Paul Salmons, Holocaust Education Co-ordinator at the IWM explains this policy in his essay 'Moral dilemmas: history, teaching and the Holocaust', which can be downloaded from the museum's website, www.iwm.org.uk. This article also appears in 'Teaching History', *The Historical Association*, 104, September 2001, 34–40.

10   For a good history of the camp, see E. Kolb (2002) *Bergen-Belsen: From 'Detention Camp' to Concentration Camp, 1943–1945*. Göttingen: Vandenhoeck & Ruprecht. For an illustrated account of the camp placed in the context of the history of the Holocaust since 1933, see W. Scheel (ed.) (2002) *Bergen-Belsen: Explanatory Notes on the Exhibition*. Hanover: Niedersächsische Landeszentrale für Politische Bildung.

11 Sergeant Lawrie filmed scenes of British Commandos crossing the Elbe on 27 April and Sergeant Lewis caught up with the 15th Scottish Division and filmed British troops crossing the Elbe on 29 April.

12 Other filming at Belsen was conducted by Lieutenant Wilson and Sergeants Haywood, Seaholme, Grant, Leatherbarrow, Hewitt and Parkinson. At the request of SHAEF, 2,000 feet of sync-sound film was also shot by Paul Wyand and Martin Gray of *British Movietone News*.

13 Sergeant Harry Oakes, AFPU, Imperial War Museum Sound Archive interview, accession no. 19888/4 reel 2.

14 The Red Army's discovery of Majdanek in July 1944 and Auschwitz in January 1945 was widely reported in the press and in the case of Majdanek supported by radio-photographs, but there was much doubt about these reports. The BBC refused to broadcast Alexander Werth's report on Majdanek in July 1944 as it was considered 'Soviet atrocity propaganda'. The report first appeared in *The Illustrated London News* on 14 October 1944.

15 Letter to Tom Williams, 18 April, read during an interview recorded with Williams, Sound Archives, accession no. 15437/5/3.

16 AFPU Sergeant Mike Lewis, recorded interview, IWM Sound Archive, accession no. 4833/9, reel 7.

17 For example, AFPU film shot by Sergeant Gordon of the deserted concentration camp of s'Hertogenbosch in southern Holland shows watchtowers, an electrified perimeter fence, a gallows, a crematorium and a heap of ashes, but there is no human evidence or witnesses to explain what had happened (A70 187/6, 31 October 1944).

18 Sergeant Lewis and Sergeant Lawrie's footage shot at Celle on 12 April 1945 appears on A70 297/3–4.

19 From a recorded interview with Sergeant William Lawrie, AFPU, held in the IWM Sound Archive, accession no. 7481/03, reel 2.

20 '*Notes for Instructors*', for the seven-week course for AFPU trainees at Pinewood. This undated document is held in the IWM Department of Documents.

21 H. Caven (2001) 'Horror in Our Time: Images of the Concentration Camps in the British Media, 1945', *The Historical Journal of Film, Radio and Television*, 21, 3, 205–53.

22 More than 37 units of the British Army became involved in the work at Belsen. This figure does not include units from voluntary organisations such as the Friends' Relief Service, UNRRA, the Red Cross and so on. Units from other Allied armies also contributed to the operation. See P. Kemp (1991) *The Relief of Belsen, April 1945: Eyewitness Accounts*. London: Imperial War Museum, 31.

23 One of the earliest examples is found in Soviet Newsreel No. 9 (February 1943, IWM catalogue no. RNC 9) which includes footage of a mass grave and various exhumed corpses of locals that were killed by the Germans at the village of Voronotsovo-Alexandrovskoe, North Caucasus. Among the bodies identified were those of Matvei Stepanovich Kip, a 'non-party activist of the local collective farm' and communist Tatiana Ivanovna Kornienko. One of the first Soviet-discovered sites of atrocity to appear in British newsreels was the massacre of 600 forced-labourers at the Lublin Castle. This item appeared in a number of newsreels including the *War Pictorial News* issue released on 25 December 1944 (IWM catalogue no. WPN 190).

24 '*Notes for Instructors*', IWM Department of Documents.

25 Lieutenant Colonel Hugh Stewart was the officer in command of No. 5 Section of the AFPU, the Unit responsible for covering the British Army's activities in the northwestern European theatre; IWM Sound Archive, accession no. 4579/06, reel 4.

26 Sergeant William Lawrie, IWM Sound Archive, accession no. 7481/03, reel 2.

27 Paul Wyand (*British Movietone News* cameraman) in a letter to Frank Chisnell (News Editor at *British Movietone News*), 22 April 1945. IWM Department of Documents.

28 The 'dope sheets', officially called 'secret caption sheets', were the descriptive shotlists written out by the

AFPU cameramen in the field and sent back with the exposed reels of film to the UK. These detailed when and where the film was exposed, the cameraman's name, basic information about what appeared in the film and technical information for the benefit of the film processors and editors.

29 Secret Caption Sheet no. A700/304/1 & 2, sheet 2. Sergeant Mike Lewis, 16 April 1945.

30 Strictly speaking, Oakes maybe talking metaphorically here, as the AFPU cameramen were trained to film with both eyes open when shooting.

31 Sergeant William Lawrie, AFPU, Imperial War Museum Sound Archive Interview, accession no. 7481/03 reel 2.

32 AFPU Secret Dope Sheet, AYY 556/1/3, Sergeant Hopkinson, 29 September 1943. This footage subsequently appeared in an issue of the *Warwork News* (IWM catalogue no. S15 33).

33 Sergeant William Lawrie, AFPU, Imperial War Museum Sound Archive Interview, accession no. 7481/03 reel 3.

34 Secret Caption Sheet no. A700 304/3, 17 April 1945.

35 Gas chambers were filmed at Auschwitz-Birkenau, Majdanek, Dachau and Mauthausen.

36 To counter these doubts camera teams filmed visits to the camps by well-known Allied political and military figures and enforced inspection of the camps by German civilians. General Eisenhower was filmed visiting Ohrdruf on 7 April 1945, along with German citizens and a Wehrmacht officer who was forced to inspect the dead (IWM film catalogue number A70 514–14). This item later appeared in issue 210 of *War Pictorial News* (IWM catalogue no. WPN 210). A British Parliamentary Delegation was filmed visiting Buchenwald (IWM film catalogue number A70 514–72). This footage was edited into the *Gaumont British News* and *British Movietone News* issues released at the end of April (IWM catalogue nos. RMY 144 & NMV 830–2).

37 As the AFPU did not routinely record sound *British Movietone News*, which had cameramen and the bulky recording equipment in Germany, was asked to go the camp to film these scenes (PRO INF 1/636). On 22 April Sidney Bernstein (SHAEF) wrote to Paul Wyand at Movietone, 'I would appreciate you taking sound interviews of the British official and German SS men etc. at the Belsen concentration camps'. He also instructed Wyand that 'Shooting you arrange should be coordinated with the work done by AFPU'. Wyand and the soundman Martin Gray filmed 'sound shots' for the 'M.O.I. SPECIAL ON BELSEN' on 23 and 24 April. The two reels of synchronously recorded film runs for 2,000 feet, about 20 minutes in running time. The AFPU cameramen shot additional mute reels of many of the scenes covered by the sound team. As an extra precaution Wyand was careful to identify and name in the shot sheet (describing the individual when necessary), all those filmed. These sound reels are held in the IWM Film and Video Archive and are numbered A70 514/97 & 98.

38 These scenes were used with devastating irony by the editors and script writers of *Memory of the Camps/ A Painful Reminder* (IWM catalogue no. MGH 3320A).

39 This sequence appears in reel A70 308/3–4. The handle of the spade is in the foreground with Father Morrison and Father Kadziok in the background standing at the edge of one of the mass graves, presumably blessing the grave.

40 Sergeant Harry Oakes, AFPU photographer, Imperial War Museum Sound Archive Interview, accession no. 19888/4, reel 3.

41 Sergeant Harry Oakes, AFPU Photographer, Imperial War Museum Sound Archive Interview, accession no. 19888/4, reel 3.

42 Sergeant Hewitt, Secret Caption Sheet A700 335/4, 15/16 May 1945.

43 Sergeant Mike Lewis, Secret Caption Sheet A700 304/1–2, 16 April 1945.

44 'I understand from the women imprisoned in the concentration camp that these SS women committed many cruelties upon them. For instance, the women could only get their very meagre portion of food if

they carried away at least one dead body a day.' Sergeant Mike Lewis, Secret Caption Sheet, A700 304/1& 2, Lewis 16 April, 1945.

45 Sergeant Lawrie, Secret Caption Sheet A700 304/4, 18 April 1945.

46 Sergeant Lawrie, Secret Caption Sheet A700/304/3, 17 April 1945.

47 Reilly 1998: 31.

48 A job that was very difficult as the cameramen's 'army French and German' did not equip them to communicate with the Poles, Czechs, Russians, Dutch and many other nationalities which populated the camp.

4 Separate intentions: the Allied screening of concentration camp documentaries in defeated Germany in 1945–46: *Death Mills* and *Memory of the Camps*

Kay Gladstone

'One day you will realise it has been worthwhile.'
– Sidney Bernstein, congratulating Peter Tanner for his editing of a section of concentration camp film[1]

This chapter examines the history of an Allied project to produce a documentary about the Nazi concentration and extermination camps for screening in defeated Germany in 1945. What started, however, as an urgent joint project ended eventually as two separate films, belatedly released in very different circumstances. The US production *Death Mills* (*Die Todesmühlen*) was first shown in the US Zone of Military Occupation in Germany in January 1946, while the uncompleted British film was not publicly screened until February 1984, when it was presented at the Berlin Film Festival under a newly allocated archive title, *Memory of the Camps*.[2]

How this single project unravelled into two differently conceived films reveals the separate intentions of the filmmakers and the changing political background against which they worked. The ultimate drivers behind the two films were the US Information Control Division (ICD) and the British cinema entrepreneur Sidney Bernstein (rather than his friend the British feature director Alfred Hitchcock, via whose name the aborted film was first misleadingly publicised).[3]

The body responsible for planning and implementing film production and exhibition in the western zones of Occupied Germany was until mid-July 1945 the Psychological Warfare Division (PWD) of the Supreme Headquarters Allied Expeditionary Force (SHAEF). The PWD, headed by Brigadier General Robert McClure, exercised political control over the local activities of its component civilian agencies, the US Office of War Information (OWI) and its British counterpart the Ministry of Information (MOI). British film interests in this Allied structure were represented by Sidney Bernstein who combined being Chief of PWD's Film Section, Liberated Areas with his existing position of Head of the Liberated Territories Section in the MOI's Films Division.

Bernstein was an ideal representative, an energetic and persuasive force who combined first-hand knowledge of film exhibition and distribution on both sides of the Atlantic with a wide range of important contacts in a variety of cultural fields. As Honorary Films Advisor to the MOI Films Division since 1940, he had successfully promoted

Sidney Bernstein (left) stands beside Lt Cdr Anthony Kimmins (Admiralty Public Relations) and Major Hugh Stewart (commander of the British Army Film and Photographic Units in North Africa and North West Europe), during a visit to North Africa when Head of the Liberated Territories Section in the British MOI Films Division, 1943. HU 38069 (© IWM)

the exhibition of British official films in the US and played a crucial part in persuading the War Office greatly to expand the Army Film Unit. From 1942 onwards he had overseen the supply of British films, both mainstream features and MOI documentaries, to cinemas in countries freed from Axis control.

Despite some similarities in the wartime careers of Bernstein and McClure, it is clear that the Englishman's passionate interest in film, and his belief in the power of the medium to improve mankind (widely shared by his friends in the British documentary movement) set him apart from the more pragmatic outlook of his American counterparts in this Allied body. When in February 1945 Bernstein, a founder member of the London Film Society twenty years previously, revealed to McClure that he had learned from the Russian authorities in London that the films which the Soviets were preparing to show in Germany were war films, 'particularly those which show the German atrocities, the damage done by Germans to Russian towns, and the general bestial attitude of the Germans', McClure, from his own account, was not impressed. He reminded his subordinate that the Anglo-American policy of the PWD was not to show any films of this type: 'In general, I should say our films all show the way of living in democratic countries. We rather carefully avoid any war films.' Although he conceded that avoiding films about war might not suit 'long range policy' he believed the policy was sound for 'short range views, particularly where we may have to use films to control the civilian population. In this latter case, if a local commander wishes cinemas open, I doubt whether you would have a very large attendance if we were showing horror films which reflected on the Germans.'[4]

Although timing was eventually to become a critical factor in the project referred to in official memos as 'the German Atrocity Film', exactly when Bernstein first considered the idea is less important than how it evolved. By 1945 Bernstein would have been as aware as most cinemagoers in the Allied countries of the Red Army footage recorded in parts of the Soviet Union and Poland already freed from Nazi terror and seen in newsreel items sourced from Moscow. It was early in January 1945 that Bernstein appears first to have enquired about what other 'shots of German atrocities' were archived in the film libraries of the MOI itself and the separate collections of the British service film units. He learned that this material was regularly viewed by staff in the Political Intelligence Department of the Foreign Office, who had lavenders (film copies) made of the appropriate shots for use as propaganda.[5]

Bernstein must then have asked Sergei Nolbandov, his very competent producer in the increasingly busy Liberated Territories Section, to trawl through the separate film archives of Russian newsreels, the US Army Pictorial Service, War Office, RAF and the British newsreel companies to identify all sequences showing the result of German atrocities.[6] There was so much atrocity material that Nolbandov was able to report late in February 1945 that it was 'being collected with a view to preparing a film which will show the German atrocities committed in many parts of the world. The basic idea of the film is to present an objective report, almost like a criminal investigation report.'[7]

During this initial film archival phase, the intended audience was that covered by the two Sections (Allied SHAEF and British MOI) headed by Bernstein, namely non-theatrical or theatrical distribution to audiences in the liberated territories who had been exposed during the preceding four or five years to Nazi propaganda.[8] This plan was suddenly transformed, however, in early April when film of the first camps liberated by US forces advancing across central Germany was screened in London to shocked officials.[9] Their determination to have this material publicly exhibited must have been strengthened by the subsequent British footage from Belsen, for on 20 April Nolbandov was requesting copies of this material from the War Office, as 'We have been instructed by the Allied Command [i.e. SHAEF] to prepare a film immediately on this subject.'[10] Any remaining doubt as to the project's principal target audience vanished when Bernstein visited Belsen on 22 April 1945.

In filming terms, this was already 'Belsen Day 7'. British forces had liberated the camp eight days previously, and the small team of cameramen and photographers of the Army Film and Photographic Unit (AFPU) were nearing the end of recording the first ten days of Belsen's freedom. Their mute film had already covered the interrogation of the commandant Josef Kramer and bulldozers burying the dead. The mass burials continued, though now the cameramen were also filming some of the survivors, bathing and delousing scenes suggesting the first steps of their slow rehabilitation.

Bernstein instantly realised the need to authenticate the date and place of these almost incredible background scenes and on the spot requested the *British Movietone News* sound cameraman Paul Wyand to film sound interviews with British officials and members of the German SS.[11] Bernstein was aware that two British newsreel editors had initially hesitated to screen the first American camp footage on the grounds that 'picto-

'Dr Fritz Klein speaking for the British Movietone News sound truck in front of the grave in which are buried some of his victims' (original caption). Photo by Sergeant Harry Oakes, 21 April 1945. The female interpreter is former prisoner Dita Kraus. BU 4262 (© IWM)

rially it was not entirely convincing', so his intervention at Belsen marks the start of his quest to prove beyond the possibility of all future denial the existence of the camps.

Bernstein's visit to Belsen transformed the 'German Atrocity Film' project. What had been initially conceived as a retrospective compilation now became a mission to make a definitive full-length documentary based not only on archived material but also on new and specially-shot sequences. Its production basis and main target audiences, as well as its Allied status, were promptly agreed. The film was to be made by the MOI as a combined Anglo-American production on German concentration camps on behalf of PWD SHAEF, with production work being carried out in conjunction with OWI Films Division. While it was primarily intended to be shown to German civilians and German prisoners of war, other versions were likely to be prepared for showing in neutral and liberated territories, as well as in Great Britain and the United States.[12]

Bernstein quickly prepared detailed instructions for the Allied cameramen on 'Material Needed for Proposed Motion Picture on German Atrocities', covering the victims and perpetrators of atrocities, their testimony, conditions in the camps and the reactions exhibited by German civilians when confronted by the evidence.[13] He defined the psychological warfare purposes of the version intended for German audiences as: 'a) by showing the German people specific crimes committed by the Nazis in their name, to arouse them against the National Socialist Party and to cause them to oppose its attempts to organise terrorist or guerrilla activity under Allied occupation; b) by reminding the German people of their past acquiescence in the perpetration of such crimes, to make them aware that they cannot escape responsibility for them, and thus to promote German acceptance of the justice of Allied occupation measures.' The document continued that it was 'essential that the film should be factual and documented to the nth degree ... It will have to be assumed ... that in several years time the Nazis will either try to disprove the evidence or suggest that only a minority was responsible.' Cameramen were specially asked to photograph any material which would show the connection between German industry and the concentration camps – for example name plates on incinerators and gas chambers – and which firms built the camps.[14]

Bernstein's warnings against future Holocaust deniers were prescient, his instructions to Allied cameramen meticulous and comprehensive. Many of the instructions were, however, too late to be acted upon. In the final days of the war in Europe British and American combat cameramen had other stories to cover and for both sanitary and humanitarian reasons the camps were being cleared as rapidly as conditions allowed. Bernstein was informed of these difficulties by John Davidson Taylor, the American official responsible for all matters concerning film production and exhibition in the western zones of Occupation.[15] Yet he remained determined to build up a quasi-legal case on film, corroborated by legal documents and sound recordings where possible, to authenticate the evidence beyond any possibility of future denial. His staff in London continued to request assistance from PWD SHAEF, seeking for example answers to 24 questions about conditions in each of the seven camps so far liberated.[16]

Meanwhile development of the film in London was being held up for a number of reasons. Chief of these was the failure of the US Army Pictorial Service to abide by an earlier agreement to give the British priority in supplying them with duplicates of US Army Signal Corps footage of the camps. The amount of material was also considerably greater than had been first anticipated and cutting could not be started until material from all the camps had been received, while factual information on life in the camps needed for an intelligent and accurate compilation did not start to come through until the end of May.[17]

During May the first efforts were made to appoint a director and to engage a writer to prepare a rough commentary. The fact that Hitchcock's name is first mentioned (although not in a specific context) at the start of the month is not surprising since Bernstein had in 1944 already used his friend to direct two short films (*Aventure Malgache* and *Bon Voyage*) to be screened in France as part of the Liberated Territories Section programme.[18] What is more surprising is that after mooting the famous director's name, Bernstein should then have approached two other Britons (the film director Sidney Gilliat and producer/writer Lieutenant Colonel Eric Ambler), although neither was able to assist owing to prior commitments.[19] One may surmise that although Hitchcock may have been Bernstein's first choice for the position of director, his participation in the project could not (whether for logistical transport reasons or because he first wished to familiarise himself with the film) be confirmed until after his eventual arrival in London, in late June.[20] So, given the pressure to nominate a production team (more keenly felt on the American than the British side), Bernstein may have felt that the immediate need was to have a production team at least nominally in place.

The shared initial aims of the project had significantly changed since its inception. The short-term psychological warfare need for the project, which had been based on fears of continuing German resistance after Germany's surrender, had proved unnecessary. The British now defined the main purpose of the film as: 'To resist any German attempt, either now or later, to deny or minimise the charge of German atrocities, or to deny that any particular section of the German population, for example the Wehrmacht, was unaware of them. It is further desired to show how ordinary men and women have been systematically brutalised so as to tolerate or take part in such activities.'[21] For the PWD, observing and questioning actual Germans, Bernstein's prime aim of proving beyond any possibility of denial the existence of camp atrocities, no longer seemed the main requirement. As Davidson Taylor informed him, describing the experimental launch of an OWI atrocity booklet on concentration camps *KZ* at a German POW camp, the PWD had discovered that 'both Nazi and anti-Nazi prisoners-of-war dissociate themselves almost unanimously from any responsibility for the atrocities depicted. Furthermore, they say that many of the pictures remind them of photographs of the German victims of allied air raids, which they have seen constantly in the German press and the [*Deutsche*] *Wochenschau*. They say "Yes it is true that many innocent people must have suffered in the concentration camps. But you must remember also that many Germans have also suffered terribly at the hands of the Nazis"'. The American head of PWD SHAEF's Film Theatre and Music Control Section (FTMCS) continued: 'It seems to me that the greatest danger in making any atrocity document for German consumption is not that the Germans will believe the atrocities were faked, but that they will steadfastly refuse to recognise that they have any responsibility for them. This is the thing I fear most in the atrocity film. I am sure it is a problem which worries you too.'

As if to assert more forcefully that the film was an official Allied project, and not Bernstein's private undertaking, Taylor gently warned that 'the film will have to be viewed before it is distributed, because the Allies simply cannot afford to neglect any effort which can be made to make the film look convincing'. He ended by asking when the film would be ready.[22] Bernstein answered Taylor briefly, stating that not even a tentative completion date could be given, and that the film so far received 'completely lacks the factual, corroborative material which is so necessary'.[23] Nothing in Bernstein's reply can have reassured the American.

The project was still being delayed by so many factors that the principal position on the film, that of supervising editor, does not appear to have been filled until early June, when the name of the very experienced Scot, Stewart McAllister, is first mentioned.[24] Labour shortages and trade union disputes in the processing laboratories, as well as fruitless searches via their American colleagues for a Moviola editing machine and an experienced cutter, complicated progress throughout the month.

Given the incomplete documentation in the National Archive's file for this production (typical moreover for most MOI films), a sound recording with one of the two editors provides the best evidence for how the film was compiled and highlights the contributions of the notably talented individuals involved. Interviewed in 1984, Peter

Tanner was not aware until then that the film had not been completed. Tanner had been editing films in the MOI's Liberated Territories Section when he was appointed to work on the German Atrocity Film, 'with every urgency', on 21 April 1945.[25] Although he and McAllister both viewed together all the rushes coming from Belsen and the many camps in the American zone, the Scot shaped the British Army Film Unit rolls, which form the first half of the film, while Tanner worked on the American material, which comprised the greater part of the second half.

The rushes were processed at Denham Laboratories, the site of Tanner's cutting room. The material was considered too horrific for any of the young workers to view, while the elderly projectionists were so horrified that they would not watch the film at all. If the reel went out of focus, or out of rack, Tanner had the greatest difficulty attracting their attention to adjust the projector. It seemed to him that 'even the film was contaminated with this terrible thing that was going on – terrible persecution of the Jewish people in these camps.' There was much discussion as to what could be released to the newsreels and even to the Allied project, although the only sequences which Tanner recalled actually being ordered deleted by the censor were of a British sergeant kicking a German guard, and American film of a guard being stabbed by an inmate with a concealed knife just after the leading vehicle had smashed open the gates of the camp.

Tanner recalled the details of Hitchcock's contribution, describing him as the adviser on the film, and certainly not the director. He considered Bernstein had made a very clever choice, to use his considerable film and technical knowledge to make the film as interesting and telling as possible, cinematically shaping the material. He clearly remembered his first meeting with Hitchcock in his suite at Claridges Hotel. Although not all the material had yet come in, 'he'd probably seen some of the material. And anyway he had Sidney Bernstein's ideas for what was wanted. And he did outline to me at considerable length the kind of form he thought the material should take.'

Hitchcock made a great point that the material would be disbelieved by many people, and that the Allies would be accused of faking a film. To minimise the risk of such reactions he asked the two editors to avoid all tricky editing and to use as far as possible long shots and panning shots with no cuts, which panned for example from the guards onto the corpses. He recommended including film of German villagers being forced to visit one of the liberated camps; this would tie the scenes together with the outside world. Tanner also recalled Hitchcock suggesting the sequence in the final reel covering the possessions of the dead at Auschwitz, the harrowing montage of hair, wedding rings, spectacles and toothbrushes.[26]

During his hurried month's stay in London, Hitchcock worked initially with the Australian-born journalist Colin Wills who prepared the first draft treatment and first commentary, then with Richard Crossman, who had been Assistant Chief of PWD of SHAEF. Both men had first-hand knowledge of the camps (which Hitchcock of course lacked). Wills had been at Belsen since the start of filming on Day 1 as war correspondent for the *News Chronicle*, and had over the next week filed daily reports to his London paper about the clearing and rehabilitation of the camp.[27] Already an experienced commentary writer and speaker for many MOI sponsored films, Wills' participation was cut short by his departure for Paris on 17 July, evidently before the final shape of the film was agreed.[28] Crossman, who was Assistant Editor (1938–55) of *New Statesman and*

Nation, was valued for 'his knowledge of German propaganda, German mentality and German language'.[29] Even before Germany's surrender, he had been directly concerned with how photographs of Belsen should be captioned and selected for publication in Germany, urging that any text be written 'as though they [OWI's German translators] were writing not a brochure, not a moving story, but an official military report'. He was alert to the risk of such photographic evidence backfiring, even warning his American colleague against including a Belsen photograph 'which gives too gypsy-like a feeling on large-scale reproduction. We don't want to give the Germans in any way the slightest excuse for saying these prisoners were gypsies anyway.'[30]

Although Tanner could vaguely recall discussing music for the film, no music had been recorded by the time he passed the film back to McAllister at the end of September 1945. One can only conclude that at this penultimate stage in the film's production, the effective postponement of the project by British officials made it pointless for Bernstein to commission a composer.[31] Had the film been completed, the credits would have noted the contribution of the British scientist Professor Solly Zuckerman, who had been attached to Deputy Supreme Commander of SHAEF, and who was commissioned early on to act as adviser to ensure its scientific and medical accuracy. After a visit to Germany in May he listed a number of points for further investigation for the 'MOI Concentration Camp Picture', but was not called upon again for advice.[32]

While progress on the Bernstein film was being held up in England between April and June 1945, PWD SHAEF was having to respond urgently to the wide range of challenges arising from the rapidly changing situation in Germany. The PWD was, of course, concerned with a greater range of activities than the narrow film-specific focus discussed here. As McClure wrote jubilantly on the day war in Europe ended: 'The shooting war is over, here! Signed yesterday. Paris is wild with excitement – with one phase over I am now up to my neck on the control phase. We will rigidly control all newspapers, films, theatre, radio, music etc, in Germany!'[33] Over the next year McClure's organisation (renamed the Information Control Division after the dissolution of SHAEF in mid-July) rapidly expanded to control the full range of news and propaganda media, but in the immediate aftermath of Germany's defeat, Allied newspapers, photographs and radio reached a far wider audience than films could.[34]

Cinemas for German audiences remained closed until late July, unless opened exceptionally by order of Army Group Commanders, who were at liberty to show special films, such as film of concentration camp atrocities.[35] As it was precisely during this period of May and June that the PWD ran a massive radio and pamphlet campaign to inform Germans about the death camps, the relative importance of death-camp film publicity should not be overstated.[36] By June, eye-witness accounts from three separate zones showed that the German civil population (as well as captive audiences of German prisoners of war) had been made fully aware of Nazi atrocities long before the date on which the film being specially prepared to educate them on the subject was likely to be completed. They also indicate that well before the reopening of the cinemas where the film could be screened, both German civilians and Occupation officials were worried by more pressing practical matters. The British documentary film director Basil Wright, in Germany to make *A Defeated People* (1946) for the MOI, could already foresee the food shortages and other domestic difficulties the Germans were likely to face later in the coming winter. Travelling on to Wesel through the ruined landscape of the British

Zone of Occupation, he described the entrance to the military government building that had 'a large panel covered with photographs from Belsen, which no German coming to the building can avoid seeing'.

Wright was noted for his sensitivity to foreign settings, so his assessment of the mood in the British Zone one month after Germany's surrender deserves special mention: 'It is quite clear the sudden removal of the Nazi machine has left the Germans dazed and stupid … The colonel told me his only object is to avoid actual starvation setting in before the harvest. In his opinion the next two months are the danger points.'[37] Writing from Berlin in June, Harry Schneiders, an American serving in the PWD noted that sentiment had started to turn against America and towards the Russians, who controlled the city's radio station: 'The average German is horrified about the bestial and sadistic crimes committed in the concentration camps but he does not feel that he is responsible, nor does he feel himself as a criminal. After Mr and Mrs Kraut have enjoyed the nice programme from Berlin, they turn the dial (to Radio Luxembourg, London or Voice of America) and what do they hear? All about concentration camp crimes, which at first they listened to attentively, but repeated every time it became nauseating.' Having highlighted the political danger of the Western Allies' policy, Schneiders ended

Citizens of Burgsteinfurt attend a screening of Belsen and Buchenwald atrocities, as required by the British Military Government. Photo by Sergeant Stiggins, 30 May 1945. BU 7016 (© IWM)

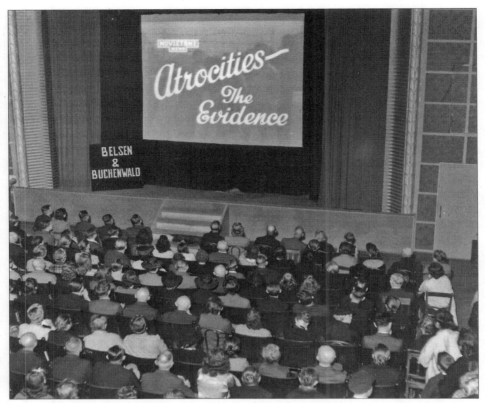

Inside the Burgsteinfurt cinema, German civilians watch the opening English title *Atrocities – The Evidence*. Photo by Sergeant Stiggins, 30 May 1945. BU 7017 (© IWM)

his Progress Report by advising the PWD not to stress hunger but to 'hold out hope of better things to come.'[38]

The most significant eyewitness report is that by Davidson Taylor, written after a week-long reconnaissance trip through the American zones in Germany and Austria in late June in the company of the film director Billy Wilder, recently arrived from OWI Films Division in London. The inhabitants of Germany's devastated cities were so stunned by the terrors they had undergone that it might 'prove difficult to move them by showing them the miseries of the concentration camps'. The relative priorities of the PWD's propaganda lines should change radically to take account of actual conditions.

At the Lichtspiele in Erlangen, he and Wilder attended a screening of one of the trial cinema programmes which had been tested on German audiences that week, in advance of the imminent reopening of cinemas in the western zones. The advertised programme comprised *Pipeline* (1944), *Welt im Film No 2* (1945), 'Duke Ellington and Orchestra' (exact title and date unknown) and 'Cowboy' (exact title and date unknown). Of particular interest to Wilder and Taylor would be the audience reaction to the last film on the programme: 'When the title *KZ* came on the screen there was a gasp throughout the audience. There were expressions of shock and horror audible throughout the picture. When the title 'Buchenwald' came on the screen, the audience spoke the word almost as one man. The atmosphere was electric throughout the exhibition of the film. There was one completely false note in the film, and a palpable feeling of incredulity ran through the audience when the narrator said that the wife of the commandant at Belsen [sic – actually Buchenwald] had made lampshades from tattooed human skin. We have footage showing this collection of tattoos and why it was not used I cannot say. After *KZ* all of the audience except three women who looked rather ill waited for the cowboy film. They were much disappointed when the manager announced that was all.'[39]

This trip marks a turning point in the history of the joint film project. Davidson Taylor was now convinced after the test screening of the OWI two-reel atrocity film that there was an urgent need for a short and accurately assembled atrocity film to be shown at once, and that 'we cannot wait from four to six months for the final perfected film before showing anything about atrocities ... Meanwhile MOI, which has not been told that we have contemplated taking the film away from them, may continue with the lengthy atrocity film. We shall give them whatever help we can, and when it is done, shall view it and decide whether it should be exhibited in the American Zone.'[40]

The American decision of 'taking the film away from' their British allies actually had no effect in the short term on Bernstein's production. By the time the Director of OWI Films Division, William Patterson, notified Bernstein that OWI was not able to provide either personnel or facilities 'for the full-length atrocity film', thus automatically making it solely a MOI venture, the letter effectively formalised a long-existing situation.[41] Crossman evidently took over from Wills, working in collaboration with Hitchcock during the brief remainder of his stay to prepare a second treatment and revised commentary. Crossman continued work through August, as McAllister and Tanner sought to finalise their respective sections. Tanner must still have been waiting for the cutting print of Russian material intended for the sixth and final reel by the time he ceased work on the production at the end of September.[42]

Long before this, however, the British project had fallen into political limbo, following the dissolution of SHAEF in mid-July, as Bernstein was sharply informed by the Foreign Office when it accidentally discovered that work had begun again on a project which clearly fell within its own territory. Commander Donald McLachlan of the German and Austrian Division of the Political Intelligence Department was aware that the Americans had backed out of the joint enterprise and wished to know who now had political responsibility for the film being made by the MOI.[43] McLachlan's opinion was that 'we need a first-class documentary record of the atrocities and that we cannot be content with the rather crude and un-thought-out newsreel [*KZ*] so far shown. On the other hand policy at the moment in Germany is entirely in the direction of encouraging, stimulating and interesting the Germans out of their apathy, and there are people round the C-in-C who will say "No atrocity film". I would say that the atrocity film, if really good and well documented, would be shown willingly and successfully in nine months' time when the difficulties of the winter have been tackled. There may therefore be no hurry for it, and raw stock and technical personnel could perhaps for the moment be spared from it for the needs which the C-in-C has stated as urgent and of which you have been informed.'[44]

The Foreign Office's intervention effectively marks the end of Bernstein's project, for although McLachlan subsequently agreed that every effort should be made to complete the work as quickly as possible, whereupon a complete rough cut would be screened for approval, this was clearly wishful thinking. Bernstein left the MOI in September 1945, leaving behind five of the six intended reels in the form of a fine-cut print, without titles, credits or sound.[45]

The Americans were apparently so frustrated by the snail's pace development of the joint venture led by Bernstein that they had already started to consider in early June 1945 (though without yet telling their British partner) the possibility of making their own short concentration camp film.[46] In Davidson Taylor's opinion, there was already sufficient material available, and he suggested Billy Wilder should oversee the production of the American film in Munich and prepare a draft treatment in consultation with FTMCS officials.[47] The Americans, anxious to get their newsreel-type treatment into circulation as quickly as possible, moved rapidly on their now independent production, in the initial stages at least.[48] In early July a proposed treatment by Lieutenant Hans Burger (rather than by Billy Wilder) was approved by the FTMCS. Burger, who had seen the two-reeler KZ with Wilder in Erlangen, had suggested the material be reworked into a three-reeler, by incorporating some of the extra material which had reached London in the meantime. The film was cut by Sam Winston, the editor of the Allied newsreel Welt im Film; he was already familiar with the material, having cut the newsreel issue KZ (which had been withdrawn as unsatisfactory in early July). By October a final treatment and cut version was ready as a two-reeler, and the commentary written by Burger's fellow émigré Lieutenant Oskar Seidlin was approved after a few changes and recorded in Munich by the German actor Anton Reimers. The changes recommended by William Patterson were to describe Auschwitz as an extermination camp and to replace the word 'Nazi' by 'German' in order to underline the responsibility and guilt of all Germans. Given the memorable title Die Todesmühlen, the 22-minute film was first released in the American Zone in the week of 25 January 1946.

Reaction to the film, which was intentionally screened without special publicity, was inevitably varied. A preliminary report to McClure from Bavaria described how audiences reacted with emotion to the scenes of horror, not doubting their authenticity, but not feeling responsibility for them. Other surveys revealed more ambiguous responses, with some people claiming the film showed only one side of history and omitted the sufferings of Germans in prisoner of war camps and the bombed cities, and the 'equally inhuman' present situation of German expellees from the Sudetenland and east of the Oder. A few people said they already had enough of this propaganda in the press and radio, while others declared they could not be held responsible for matters they had not known about.

Those social groups who thought the film credible and necessary were workers, intellectuals and soldiers who had witnessed horrors on the Eastern Front, predominantly communists and social democrats. Those who accepted the film less willingly were the lower-middle class (who had supported Nazism from the 1930s), young people and former POWs who had been badly treated. The final ICD report concluded that although few doubted the authenticity of the atrocities in the film, hardly anyone accepted responsibility for them. Even though the film had apparently succeeded better than any other attempt to make the Germans aware of the guilty nature of the Hitler regime, it had failed in its aim to awaken in Germans a consciousness of their own individual and collective guilt for the atrocities.

In retrospect this Allied joint project was probably bound to fail. Several previous Anglo-American film productions following the Second World War had ended as MOI or OWI films reflecting two separate versions of the same military campaigns. The only war documentary which overcame these divergences was *The True Glory* (1945), produced by a Joint Committee controlled by a strong chairman, governed by the strict timetable of victory celebration and expressing Eisenhower's uplifting message.

The concentration camp film was by comparison an unimaginably difficult subject. When Bernstein's initial and relatively finite project on German atrocities was transformed early in April by film from the camps in Germany, he could not have foreseen the logistical and political problems he would face in acquiring and assembling all the material within the timescale necessary for its intended message to be heard in Germany. He appears to have been so determined to make a definitive full-length work on the concentration camps that he paid no heed to the increasingly impatient requests for a completion date from his frustrated partners. By the time his production team was finally assembled in July, the original sponsor, SHAEF, had dissolved into its component parts, leaving the British to continue their film, and allowing the Americans to start their own. But the end of SHAEF left Bernstein's project directly exposed to the Foreign Office. Officials there responsible for defining policy in Germany considered press and radio the most important media for eradicating militarism and Nazism and leading Germans out of their apathy towards rebuilding Germany.[49]

Based on reported reactions to the American film, there is little reason to suppose that Bernstein's six-reel film would have succeeded any better than the two-reeler *Die Todesmühlen* in convincing Germans of their individual or collective responsibility for the atrocities of the Third Reich. The ultimate strength of Bernstein's documentary may be that although conceived in response to the immediately perceived need to educate the Germans, it gradually acquired its own momentum to become the most carefully documented and crafted film of the camps. By losing touch with the changing demands of the moment, it became a commemorative record for all time.

Notes

1   IWM Sound Archive 7379/03: Peter Tanner interview with Kay Gladstone, quoting a letter from Sidney Bernstein to Tanner, 30 September 1945.

2   The uncompleted film, previously referred to by its Ministry of Information File Number, F3080, was given this name by the author for its Berlin screening, in order to indicate the commemorative significance the film had acquired by this date. The title was translated into German as *Erinnerungen an die Lager* (*Memories of the Camps*).

3   See article in *The Times* (12 December 1983) by Caroline Moorehead, coinciding with the publication of her biography of Lord Bernstein.

4   NARA RG 331 Box 8, 062.2 Films Brigadier-General Robert McClure to Colonel Kehm and Colonel William Paley, 19 February1945.

5   IWM Documents Sidney Bernstein Collection 65/17/1–12 [9]: Miss A. Thurston to Sidney Bernstein, 7 Jan 1945.

6   Nolbandov had graduated in law from Odessa University before becoming a production manager at Ealing Studios. He joined the MOI Films Division in 1943 as a producer, and later produced the docu-

mentary series *This Modern Age* for Rank (1946–49).

7   TNA INF 1/636: Sergei Nolbandov to Mr Archibald, 22 February 1945.

8   C. Moorehead (1984) *Sidney Bernstein: A Biography*. London: Jonathan Cape, 164.

9   TNA INF 1/636: Cecil W. B. Matthews, Film Censor, to E. A. Adams (MOI), 10 April 1945.

10 TNA INF 1/636: Sergei Nolbandov to Ronald Tritton (PR1, War Office), 20 April 1945.

11 TNA INF 1/636: Sidney Bernstein to Paul Wyand, 22 April 1945.

12 TNA INF 1/636 Films for Liberated Territories. Investigation of War Atrocities. Factual Film Report on German Concentration Camps: Sidney Bernstein to Lieutenant Colonel W. A. Ulman, Army Pictorial Service, 2 May 1945.

13 Material Needed for Proposed Motion Picture on German Atrocities. Sidney Bernstein 30 April 1945. See E. Sussex (1984) 'The Fate of F3080', *Sight and Sound*, 53, 2, 92–7.

14 TNA INF 1/636: Sidney Bernstein to Lieutenant Colonel J. R. Foss, 7 May 1945.

15 TNA INF 1/636 Memo Motion Picture on German Atrocities: Davidson Taylor to Sidney Bernstein, 8 May 1945.

16 TNA INF 1/636: Gordon Taylor (PWD SHAEF Film Section) to Major Saunders-Jacobs (PWD SHAEF Intelligence Section), 10 May 1945. Attachment titled *Record of Concentration Camps: Data Required*.

17 TNA INF 1/636 Report on German Concentration Camp Material: Sergei Nolbandov to Sidney Bernstein, 29 May 1945.

18 IWM Documents Sidney Bernstein Collection 65/17/1–12 [9]: Miss A. Thurston to Jack Beddington (Director MOI Films Division): 'Mr Bernstein is agreeable to Mr Hitchcock coming over to work for him at end of May', 4 May 1945.

19 TNA INF 1/636: Sidney Gilliat to Sidney Bernstein, 25 May 1945. Draft Telegram from Sergei Nolbandov to Davidson Taylor. Undated, but c. 20 June 1945.

20 Moorehead 1984: 164. According to his biographer, Bernstein had been unable to secure Hitchcock a rapid aerial passage from the US.

21 TNA INF 1/636 Film Record of German Concentration Camps: Gordon Taylor to Major Saunders-Jacobs, 10 May 1945.

22 TNA INF 1/636: Davidson Taylor to Sidney Bernstein, 25 May 1945.

23 TNA INF 1/636 Concentration Camp Film: Sidney Bernstein to Davidson Taylor, 30 May 1945.

24 TNA INF 1/636: Gordon Taylor to Sergei Nolbandov, 7 June 1945. For an excellent analysis of McAllister's work see D. Vaughan (1983) *Portrait of an Invisible Man: The Working Life of Stewart McAllister, Film Editor*. London: British Film Institute, 153–7.

25 TNA INF 1/636 German Atrocity Film: Sergei Nolbandov to Archibald, 21 April 1945.

26 IWM Sound Archive 7379/03: Peter Tanner interview with Kay Gladstone, 23 February 1984.

27 IWM Film A700/304/1–2, shot by Sergeant Mike Lewis on 16 April 1945 shows Colin Wills speaking to a prisoner. Wills had worked in Australia as a journalist in press and radio, and also as a newsreel commentator, before moving to England in 1939. Among his other wartime credits was commentator for the MOI newsreel series *Worker and Warfront* made by Paul Rotha.

28 TNA INF 1/636: Colin Wills to Sergei Nolbandov, 16 July 1945.

29 TNA INF 1/636 German Concentration Camp Film: Sidney Bernstein to MOI Finance, 23 July 1945. Richard Grossman was elected Labour MP for Coventry East in the 1945 General Election.

30 NARA RG 331 Box 7 062 Photographs and Photography: Richard Crossman to Barney Barnes, 3 May 1945.

31 IWM Documents Sidney Bernstein Collection 65/17/1–12 [10] German Concentration Camps Factual Survey. Basic Version: German. Special Film, 17 August 1945. This final summary of credits for the MOI film, and financial commitments, makes no mention of any proposed music.

32 IWM Film and Video Archive Correspondence between Lord Zuckerman and Kay Gladstone, February–March 1984. Note headed 'MOI Concentration Camp Picture', 17 May 1945.

33 Quoted at http://www.psywarrior.com/mcclure.html, Robert McClure to Marjory McClure, 8 May 1945.

34 General Lucius D. Clay (1950) *Decision in Germany*. New York: Country Life Press, 282–3. The Deputy Military Governor notes the value of broadcasting and newspapers for communicating with the Germans in the early phase of Occupation. By contrast there were no cinemas until late July, when 15 were authorised to open, rising rapidly to a hundred by September and to over two hundred by November 1945.

35 NARA RG 331 Box No 8 062.2 Films. Film Showings by Commanders of Army Groups: Davidson Taylor to Douglas Schneider (Assistant Chief of Division for Control of German Information Services, PWD, SHAEF), 12 May 1945. IWM Film A700/347/07 and Photos BU 7013-20 ('Village of Hate' views Horror Film) show inhabitants (mostly elderly) of Burgsteinfurt forced to attend special screening in British Garrison Cinema of *Beweise der Grausamkeiten über die Konzentration Lagers Belsen & Buchenwald* (*Evidence of the Horrors at the Concentration Camps at Belsen and Buchenwald*), 30 May 1945.

36 D. Culbert (1985) 'American Film Policy in the Re-education of Germany after 1945', in N. Pronay and K. Wilson (eds) *The Political Re-education of Germany and her Allies after World War II*. London: Croom Helm, 177.

37 IWM Documents 83/10/1 Basil Wright Diary Extracts (31 May, 6 June, 8 June) for German Visit, 28 May–10 June 1945.

38 NARA RG 331 319.1 Progress Reports Box 17: Report of Harry J. Schneiders, 9 June 1945.

39 NARA RG 331 319.1 Progress Reports Box 17: Report on Trip to Munich of 20–26 June 1945: Davidson Taylor to Brigadier-General Robert McClure, 27 June 1945. Note that the film *KZ* is the same as *Welt im Film No. 5* (held by IWM FVA as WIF 5).

40 NARA RG 331 Box No 8 062.2 FILMS 27 June 1945 Atrocity Film: Davidson Taylor to Colonel W. S. Paley and Douglas Schneider (Assistant Chief of Division for Control of German Information Services).

41 TNA INF 1/636: William D. Patterson to Sidney Bernstein, 9 July 1945.

42 IWM Documents Sidney Bernstein Collection 65/17/1–12 [10]: Peter Tanner to Sidney Bernstein, 22 August 1945.

43 Donald McLachlan worked for Naval Intelligence 1940–45, and was the first editor of the *Sunday Telegraph*, 1961–66. See *Who's Who* 1969 entry.

44 IWM Documents Sidney Bernstein Collection 65/17/1–12 [9]: Donald McLachlan to Sidney Bernstein, 4 August 1945.

45 A complete version of the film (duration 55 minutes) was made by WGBH Boston for broadcasting in the US in May 1985 by assembling the last reel from existing Russian material and by recording a commentary spoken by the British actor Trevor Howard. The editing was based on a file document *Concentration Camp Film Scenes as Assembled on 7 May 1946*, while the voiceover followed another file document, *Proposed Line of Commentary for Film on Concentration Camps* (undated and unsigned, but presumed to be the revised commentary by Richard Crossman).

46 This section is mainly based on the essay by Brewster S. Chamberlin, 'Todesmühlen. Ein früher Versuch zur Massen-"Umerziehung" im besetzten Deutschland 1945-1946', *Vierteljahrheft für Zeitgeschichte XXIX Heft 3 Juli 1981*, 420–36.

47 TNA INF 1/636: Davidson Taylor to FTMCS (Rear), received 18 June 1945.

48 TNA INF 1/636: William Patterson to Sidney Bernstein, 16 July 1945.

49 TNA FO 945/905 Information Control in the British Zone of Germany – Policy Paper Draft, June 1945.

5 A witness to atrocity: film as evidence in International War Crimes Tribunals

Helen Lennon

In the twentieth century, four international war crimes tribunals were established to adjudicate crimes committed during armed conflict: the International Military Tribunal at Nuremberg (1945–46), the International Military Tribunal for the Far East (1946–48), the International Criminal Tribunal for the former Yugoslavia (established in 1993) and the International Criminal Tribunal for Rwanda (established in 1994). In every single one of these, documentary film and video has been admitted to prove such extreme forms of modern warfare as the eradication of entire populations, bureaucratised mass murder, state-sponsored rape and torture, and widespread summary executions of civilians by their own governments. Beginning with a dozen black-and-white 8mm, 16mm and 35mm exhibits at Nuremberg and expanding in the late twentieth century to the daily admission of television broadcasts, videotaped depositions and widely-distributed documentaries at the Yugoslav and Rwandan tribunals, moving images are an indispensable part of establishing the validity of events habitually denied by their perpetrators.

Indeed, film proof of wartime atrocities has exercised significant influence on the course of international law. It was film footage of Fikret Alic's emaciated body behind barbed wire at the Trnopolje camp in Prijedor, Bosnia Herzegovina, taken by British journalists in August 1992, that revitalised the aspirations for international justice first attempted at Nuremberg almost fifty years before. Broadcast on television by ITN – and subtitled as 'Belsen 92' by the *Daily Mirror* – the images immediately evoked comparisons between the Bosnian war and the Holocaust worldwide.[1] Only months after the footage was aired on 7 August, the United Nations established the International Criminal Tribunal for the former Yugoslavia (ICTY) at The Hague. Impelled by images, the dormant custom of putting war criminals on trial was resurrected. It is ironic then, and most germane to this essay, that some five years later German journalist Thomas Deichmann, examined the 'truth' of these images and the reports that were based on them, suggesting that the video coverage of Trnopolje misled the viewer about the function of the 'camp' by the simplest of 'tricks' (moving the point-of-view of the camera): it was actually the journalists and the cameraman, not the Bosnian Muslims who were encircled by a barbed wire fence.[2]

In the ever-expanding culture of transborder communications, moving images have exerted significant influence as a powerful pedagogical strategy to promote the rule of law to mitigate conflict and restore justice, rather than armed violence. Several war crimes trials have themselves been filmed and screened to communities recovering from the pandemonium of war. The trials at Nuremberg and Tokyo were ultimately screened to post-war audiences in occupied Germany and Japan as well as in certain Allied countries, the Milosevic trial is televised daily in the Balkans, and evidentiary footage from various trials is incorporated in contemporary public exhibitions. The explosion of global communications via the internet and technical advances in documentary techniques, such as the development of extremely small, lightweight, hand-held cameras, inexpensive and readily available colour recording tape and electronic transmissions, have had a tremendous impact on public response to war, human rights advocacy and other civil, political and legal discourse. As the establishment of courts to adjudicate atrocities gains rapid pace on both national and international levels (as the International Criminal Court and the tribunals in Sierra Leone, East Timor, Cambodia and Kosovo demonstrate) it is apparent that international criminal tribunals have become a permanent part of the legal and political landscape. The credibility and utility of these judicial institutions to reform and legitimise legal and political institutions in the aftermath of conflict require popular endorsement and local participation.[3] In this regard, providing verifiable proof of crimes of war to foster broad – even global – support of these proceedings is essential. As a form of proof more broadly defined, documentary images are indispensible to this task. Simply put, images do not require literacy, nor do they require linguistic translation. Images can be immediate, spontaneous and chillingly succinct. They can be circulated rapidly, viewed by many individuals at once and permanently archived in collective memory.

Even as the use of film and video as proof of war crimes increases momentum in its daily employment in contemporary war crimes trials, its potential legal and political reverberations remain unknown. One might argue that video evidence is increasingly integral to the shifting terrain of modern warfare. The taped admission of Osama bin Laden released in December 2001 is regarded as incontrovertible proof of his orchestrating the atrocities in New York City and Washington D.C. in September 2001. The beheading of *Wall Street Journal* reporter Daniel Pearl, videotaped and disseminated by his captors on the internet in February 2002, led to the attempted extradition of several individuals from Pakistan for trial in the United States. Most recently, Coalition officials protested against the broadcasting of documentary footage of American military corpses on al-Jazeera, asserting that such representations are proscribed by the Geneva Conventions. When US officials subsequently permitted news crews to film the bloated and discoloured corpses of Uday and Qusay Hussein as proof of their capture and deaths, the grisly images provoked international criticism of the barbarism of the display. The continued screening by Slobodan Milosevic of images he maintains depict NATO bombings of civilians has regenerated discussions about the use of military bombardments as a form of 'humanitarian intervention', discussions which have intensified with recent crises in Afghanistan and Iraq. These images – and the laws they question, affirm, challenge and fortify – traverse the increasingly fragile boundaries between 'proof' and 'propaganda'.

And yet, despite the stunning intersections between visual representations and international law, not a single legal rule exists that addresses the capacity of non-fiction film as a unique form of proof. Clearly, the issue of film as legally binding evidence of atrocities is a complex one, and virtually no legal scholarship yet addresses the complexities of film as a form of physical, documentary and testimonial evidence.[4] Such an endeavor must be highly interdisciplinary, drawing upon fields of international humanitarian law (the laws of war), history, visual sociology, documentary film theory, literary theory, philosophy, cultural studies, political science and anthropology. This chapter attempts to provide a concise introduction to the use of film in the four international criminal tribunals, and is by no means an exhaustive survey. Rather, several exemplary moments are introduced to bring out just a few of the issues, and elisions, that film – as a visual document, a forensic method and a mechanical witness providing a distinct kind of testimony – raises.

The uses of film and video evidence

The very term 'war crimes tribunal' evokes horrific images. The importance of film and video as evidence is in the power of moving images to concretise abstract concepts such as 'ethnic cleansing', 'military bombardments' and 'collateral damage' to audiences at a distant remove. The meanings of these concepts – and, moreover, their precise legal definitions – are by no means firmly established. Even with the very first film screened at Nuremberg, the dependency on images to fill in the fissures of legal language emerged: the American prosecutor asserted that the documentary would provide 'in a brief and unforgettable form an explanation of what the words "concentration camp" imply'.[5] This reliance on visual confirmations persists: in a recent decision in the Stakic case at The Hague, the court found that it could not determine the veracity of a witness' testimony regarding an incident of paramilitary shelling of civilians because video evidence had not been introduced that would visually corroborate the statements.[6]

The first use of film as evidence of crimes against humanity was at The Trial of the Major War Criminals before the International Military Tribunal (IMT), convened in Nuremberg, Germany in 1945 to try 22 (plus Dr Ley who committed suicide before the trial) major Nazi war criminals and six organisations. The international composition of the proceedings and the crimes the court was established to adjudicate were legally and historically unprecedented. So too was the visual documentation introduced by each of the four Allied prosecution teams – the United States, the United Kingdom, France and the Soviet Union – as proof of war crimes committed by the Nazi regime. In addition to maps, diagrams and photographs, twelve documentary films were screened in the courtroom, including a 90-second 8mm film confiscated from a German soldier depicting a 1941 Jewish pogrom, the hour-long *Kinodokumenty o Zverstrakh Nemetsko-Fashiskh Zakhvatchikov*, translated as *Cinema Documents of the Atrocities of the German Fascist Invaders* (both presented by the Soviet Union), the four-hour, 27-reel *The Nazi Plan*, a compilation of German newsreels incorporating footage of Leni Riefenstahl's *Triumph des Willens/Triumph of the Will* (1935) (admitted by the United States) and a film introduced by the French to prove crimes against humanity committed in Lidice.[7]

Despite the extreme rarity of the films – almost all were classified as 'restricted' and most have yet to be screened to the general public in the countries that produced them[8]– several images have become iconic.[9] *Nazi Concentration Camps*, six reels distilled from more than 100,000ft[10] of 35mm film shot by American and British forces when liberating the western concentration camps in April 1945, runs to 59 minutes and documents bodies stacked in piles and burned at concentration camps at Ohrdruf and

Mauthausen, the bulldozing of thousands of corpses into massive pits at Bergen-Belsen and piles of human hair at Buchenwald.[11]

It was the fear that Germans would deny the existence of concentration and extermination camps that motivated American and British military units to film the horrors of the Holocaust as they encountered them. Anticipating Nazi denials of 'the Final Solution' on the stand – subsequently borne out in Hermann Goering's testimony and the phenomenon of Holocaust revisionism surfacing several decades later – *Nazi Concentration Camps* begins with a narrated reading of filmed affidavits attesting to the authenticity of the images to follow. The Soviets also utilised this device in *Cinema Documents of the Atrocities of the German Fascist Invaders*, with a document slowly read aloud by a narrator in which the cameramen collectively attest that none of the images had been fabricated or manipulated in any way. While this was effective in fortifying the visual evidence of atrocities such as the murder of women and children, soldiers bound and gagged and the existence of mass graves, doubts about who in fact *perpetrated* the crimes persisted, especially with regard to allegations that many of the massacres in the eastern territories were in fact committed by Stalin's Red Army.

The film evidence entered against Japanese defendants accused of 'Class A' war crimes at the International Military Tribunal for the Far East is a puzzling contrast to the relatively abundant visual evidence proffered at Nuremberg. Established and presided over by United States Army General Douglas MacArthur, Supreme Commander for the Allied Powers, 28 of Japan's political, social and judicial leaders stood accused of aggressive warfare and crimes against humanity. Yet over the course of more than two-and-a-half years, only one film was admitted as evidence: *Hijoji Nippon*, translated as *Japan in Time of Emergency*, a black-and-white 35mm film produced in 1933 by the Osaka Daily Newspaper Film Department and the Ministry for the Army. The film was narrated by General Araki Sadao, Minister for the Army, in the didactic style of *benshi*, the traditional Japanese storyteller. Sadao was himself a defendant at the Tokyo tribunal, where he was found guilty and sentenced to life imprisonment for crimes of war. He was given parole in 1955.

A fast-paced montage, *Japan in Time of Emergency* incorporates natural and industrial scenes of productivity such as florid cherry trees, agricultural crops, racing trains, welding steelworkers, charging cavalry and raging seas. These moments are interspersed with maps of Japan besmirched by menacing ink stains, symbolising the threat of military invasion by the Allies as the General explains the importance of Japanese military presence in China to its national security. Other moments in the film's montage suggest that military invasion of Japan by enemy forces must be resisted through moral fortitude. In brief, contrived scenes, Japanese youth in berets and high heels succumb to vices such as alcohol, cigarettes, audacious flirting and frenzied dancing. Exemplifying what General Sadao's stentorian narration deems 'the crisis of national spirit', several youths become involved in a street skirmish, reminding the audience that military and moral strength are interdependent.

The presence of *Japan in Time of Emergency* as the only film evidence at the Tokyo tribunal signals an unsettling omission of non-fiction film images that were readily available to the prosecution, raising the question of what was *not* adjudicated at the military tribunals. For example, 16mm footage exists, captured by John Magee of the American Episcopal Mission, of gruesome incidents occurring throughout the infamous 'Rape of Nanking' – an event that took place over the course of a year during 1937–38 in which as many as 400,000 Chinese men, women and children were publicly raped, tortured, murdered and disposed of in mass graves by invading troops of the Japanese Imperial Army.[12] Non-fiction moving images of medical experiments conducted by Japanese physicians on Chinese and Korean civilians at enormous industrial facilities operated by the infamous 'Unit 731' in Manchuria were also available to the prosecution, which chose not to introduce them at trial.

At the International Military Tribunals at Nuremberg and Tokyo, the prosecution was free to consider any evidence it deemed relevant, and to disregard any it did not. The Charter for each explicitly established that their jurisdictions were strictly confined to examination of the conduct of the defendants; thus any evidence put forward by the defense discrediting the wartime conduct of the Allied Powers was steadfastly refused admission. A number of atrocities ostensibly committed by the Allies during the Second World War were also captured on film, such as the incendiary bombardments of Dresden and Tokyo, and the atomic bombing of Hiroshima and Nagasaki – the legality of which has never been determined. Despite having established other vital legal precedents, the allegation that the Nuremberg was a 'victors' trial' and Tokyo merely a 'kangaroo court' persists to this day.[13]

Attentive to the allegation that war crimes trials are the political privilege of those who ultimately prevail on the battlefield, the contemporary tribunals for Yugoslavia and Rwanda have paid considerably more attention to the due process rights of the accused, and thus video evidence has been frequently tendered by the defense. This is most obvious in the trial of Slobodan Milosevic, the first head of state to stand trial for genocide and crimes against humanity. It has been estimated that more than 600 video exhibits will have been admitted during the course of the trial, which began in February 2002 and has not yet finished. Beginning with the opening statements, both the prosecution and defense in the Milosevic trial did not waste a moment to engage in what the New York Times recounted as 'a visual tour of some of the worst atrocities in Bosnia'.[14] The prosecution's video footage was shown on small computer monitors located at each seat in the courtroom, displaying an array of images that revealed emaciated men in concentration camps, corpses concealed in military vehicles and a scene of a public rally at which Milosevic exhorted a massive crowd to purge greater Serbia of its Albanian scourge. The video footage was admitted to prove that Milosevic had administered genocide against Muslims in Bosnia Herzegovina, that Serbian military forces had followed his directives and that together they had attempted to conceal their crimes. In a four-hour retort, the defendant – representing himself as legal counsel – engaged in what the New York Times characterised as 'a duel of images, producing photographs and videos that were even more ghastly than those shown by prosecutors … of NATO air strikes. At his request, courtroom monitors flashed images of bombed sites, charred and mangled bodies, and severed human heads and limbs.'[15]

The trial transcript at the International Criminal Tribunal for the former Yugoslavia, like its precedent at Nuremberg, records every single word spoken throughout trial proceedings, also conducted and recorded simultaneously in four languages. Written transcripts for the trials conducted at Nuremberg and in The Hague exceed tens of thousands of pages, in addition to thousands of documents, still photographs and sworn affidavits.[16] Yet in describing the images used to prove systematic human extermination, these official legal records contain an elision. For every film exhibit at Nuremberg, be it 90 seconds in duration or four hours, the transcript states with startling simplicity, '[The film was then shown]'.[17] The official court transcript of the Yugoslav tribunal adheres with even greater concision to the precedent established fifty years before. The entire visual content of the footage of atrocities committed throughout Croatia, Bosnia, Serbia and Kosovo is in most instances reduced to two words: '[videotape played]'.[18]

These oversights, be they a lack of legal rules or silences within the transcript, or concepts that exceed conventional lexicons, gesture toward the fact that as a form of proof, documentary film confounds conventional categories of evidence, which distinguish between physical, documentary and testimonial evidence. Although often linked with other illustrative evidence such as maps, diagrams and computer simulations, documentary film is more than a likeness or an imitation; in a sense, it is a transparent window onto the real. Through mechanical and technical processes of light, refraction and emulsion, images imprinted on celluloid – as with their precursor, photographs – are an index of material reality, a direct transcription of the world that appears to function as a transparent window onto the real. The camera replicates what was literally physically before it, archiving the material condition of a specific time and space and as such it is an objective record. The forensic quality of documentary film reveals the 'real' in very much the same way as a fingerprint, or a strand of DNA, neither of which can be reduced to articulation through words.[19] Yet the presence of a human being 'behind' the camera, operating and positioning the focal attention of the mechanical apparatus, implicates the literal indexical representation as a personal interpretation, even an intentional statement. As such, the authority and veracity of this mechanically-mediated proof of atrocities are intertwined with the subjectivity of a human presence, and even more problematically, another's sentient experience of monstrous realities. In some instances, those filming have not survived the events they have stored on film. While film exhibits screened at Nuremberg were produced by victorious Allied military forces at the end of the war, much of the footage admitted as evidence of more recent atrocities has been filmed and transported by individuals who may not have survived the crimes they witnessed.

The ability of non-fiction moving images to turn a simple viewer into a witness lies in their appearing to convey direct referential access to the visual and aural elements of the material world, providing experiential access to an event that may have occurred decades ago, thousands of miles away. Observing the appalling conditions of the concentration camp at Dachau in 1945, corpses of Rwandan women and children murdered with machetes in 1994 or the blight left in the wake of military bombardments on Kosovo in 1999, the viewer is literally transformed into an eyewitness to atrocity, regardless of her own position in time, place or imaginative capacity.

Bridging this spatial divide is necessary. Video evidence is often utilised as a 'scene setting' device, as many of the sites that are the fundamental component to legal deliberations have been destroyed, changed dramatically over time, or are still vexed by violence. In contrast to Nuremberg and Tokyo, where the tribunals were held 'in a ruined city and among an enemy population'[20] with combat having ended, the Yugoslav tribunal is located in The Hague; armed conflict would continue to rage in the Balkans for another seven years after the court's inception. The Rwandan tribunal is located in

Arusha, in neighboring Tanzania, as the country's judicial and political infrastructure was essentially destroyed by the genocide.

The continuous succession of moving images in real time, accompanied by live recording of ambient sound, is what distinguishes film from photographs. In essence, film shows many 'photographs' in a single second. The immediacy, spontaneity and sheer power of *movement* bear a special relationship to testimonial narration as well, creating an imperceptible relationship between displaying images – showing – that in turn creates a distinct kind of telling. The delineations between showing and telling, listening and seeing, memory, visualisation and comprehension are by no means unequivocal. A human eyewitness vividly recounting an experience on the stand must recreate an event almost entirely through verbal language, enclosed by a courtroom, relying on the imaginative capacity of the listener to supplement words with images.

As a mechanical witness that testifies through moving images and sound, a number of structural forms inherent to non-fiction film are capable of being 'cross-examined' by a careful reading of the film 'text'. Shots can be 'long' and 'wide' so as to reveal a greater expanse of space to include as broad a scope and as much visual material as possible. The inverse is also true, and thus 'framing', and what is 'left on the cutting room floor', so to speak, is a vital consideration. The use of natural sound to allow the actual aural context of an event to emerge, as is often seen in contemporary video evidence, is a significant contrast to an interpretation imparted by an omnipotent narrator, as was readily practiced in the evidence at Nuremberg and Tokyo. With regard to the extremely complicated issue of 'authenticity' – a pivotal discussion beyond the necessary confines of this chapter – it must be remembered that independent of the deliberate manipulation or fabrication of images, the mechanical process of filming itself produces inevitable distortions, distortions that are only amplified with duplication to another visual format such as video and DVD. Variations in focal length, the accuracy of focus, and apertures regulating light, the angle at which the camera films its subject, and the physical position of the operator are just some of the variables at play in any moving image. For instance, film evidence has been admitted at the Rwandan tribunal that reveals several *Interhamwe* – murderous, roving youth in the service of the Hutu Militia – while they hack a woman to death with machetes as she kneels to pray for her life. Taken through some trees on a hill at some distance, the quality of the filming is poor, and the camera shakes. Was the filmmaker in fact hiding as s/he surreptitiously filmed? Was s/he sanctioned by the *Interhamwe*? The prosecution, although obtaining possession of this extraordinary footage, could not identify the operator of the camera and thus the crucial questions remain unanswered.

Questions of 'cross-examining' footage and determining 'authenticity' are absolutely essential in proceedings attempting to establish the veracity of egregious state violence. The relationship between proof and propaganda, public disclosure and calculated disinformation, security and censorship has never been more complicated than the present. As individuals continue to be indicted and tried in the Balkans and Rwanda, the proceedings of these tribunals – and the legal and historical pronouncements they make – take place in an extremely sensitive political climate. Most of the images 'captured' within the frame of documentary film and video defies the aspiration first stated at Nuremberg that images might convey 'in a brief and unforgettable form an *explanation*'[21] of atrocities that preclude logical explanation by their very existence.

The crimes this visual evidence reveals defy description and testimony by ordinary means; perhaps they resist representation at all, be it legal, linguistic, visual or otherwise. This resistance to representation does not accord well with the subtle and powerful affinity between images and proof: evolving etiologically from the Latin *videre*, 'to see', evidence innately privileges the visual, the phenomenological – that which can be observed, displayed, articulated, comprehended and thereby *known*. Accordingly, it is necessary to confront the question of what is *not* shown at these trials, asking: in what ways are these moving images directing our attention toward certain violations, and away from others? What is the law refusing to see, when '[the film was then shown]' and the '[videotape played]'?

Notes

1   On 5 August 1992, a British news team led by Penny Marshall of ITN (*News at Ten*), her cameraman Jeremy Irvin and fellow reporters Ian Williams (ITN for Channel 4), and Ed Vulliamy (*The Guardian*) visited the camp in the Serb territory of northern Bosnia. On 7 August the *Daily Mirror* front-page headline described images as 'Belsen 92' – 'THE PROOF – Behind the barbed wire, the brutal truth about the suffering in Bosnia'. Other papers saw them in similar terms: 'Belsen 92' (*Daily Star*).

2   T. Deichmann's (1997) 'The Picture that Fooled the World', *Living Marxism*, February, 24–31. The controversy following this article and further examination of the case, the reports and the handling of the story by ITN and in the British press is also covered in E. Veale (1997) 'Evading the Charges', *Living Marxism*, March, 16–20.

3   See D. Scheffer (2002) 'The Future of Atrocity Law', *Suffolk Transnational Law Review*, 25.

4   See L. Douglas, (1995) 'Film as Witness: Screening *Nazi Concentration Camps* before the Nuremberg Tribunal', *Yale Law Journal*, 105, 2, 449–81; H. Lennon (1995) 'Creating a Witness: Film as Evidence in International War Crimes Tribunals', PhD dissertation, October 2005 from the Department of Comparative Literature, Yale University.

5   T. Dodd, *Trial of the Major War Criminals Before the International Military Tribunal*, volume 2, 29 November 1945. Record Group 238: National Archives Collection of World War II War Crimes Records.

6   *Prosecutor v. Milomir Stakic, The International Tribunal for the Prosecution of Persons Responsible for Serious Violations of International Humanitarian Law Committed in the Territory of the former Yugoslavia Since 1991.*

7   *Trial of the Major War Criminals Before the International Military Tribunal*, volume 2. Record Group 238: National Archives Collection of World War II War Crimes Records.

8   In the immediate aftermath of the Second World War, Anglo-American occupation authorities considered requiring German citizens to view *Nazi Concentration Camps* and other concentration camp footage as part of the 're-education' and 'de-Nazification' of the polity. In some instances, compulsory viewing of documentary images of atrocities was a requisite to obtaining food rations and other essential, and scarce, supplies. See S. L. Carruthers, (2001) 'Compulsory Viewing: Concentration Camp Film and German Re-Education', *Millennium: Journal of International Studies*, 30, 3, 733–59.

9   Excerpts from the archival footage taken by the Supreme Headquarters Allied Expeditionary Force (SHAEF) forces was integrated into numerous documentary films, Alain Resnais' *Nuit et Brouillard/ Night and Fog* (1955) and Marcel Ophuls' *Le Chagrin et la Pitié/The Sorrow and the Pity* (1969) among them. Stanley Kramer's Oscar-winning *Judgment at Nuremberg* (1961), while a dramatic 're-enactment' of the Judges' Trial of 1946, incorporated the archival footage.

10   R. H. Jackson, 'Final Report of the Chief of Counsel for the United States, Submitted to the President, October 7 1946', Record Group 238: National Archives Collection of World War II War Crimes Records.

11   *Nazi Concentration Camps,* Record Group 238: National Archives Collection of World War II War Crimes Records, 1933–1950, Motion Picture, Sound and Video Records Collection. *Nazi Concentration Camps* was also admitted in several of the twelve war crimes trials, known as 'the Subsequent Trials', administered by the Allied Control Council for Germany in the four zones of occupation. The film was also admitted as evidence the trial of Adolf Eichmann in Israel in 1961, along with Resnais' *Night and Fog.*

12   John Magee Collection at Sterling Library, Yale University, New Haven, Connecticut.

13   *The Tokyo Major War Crimes Trial: Transcripts of the Court Proceedings of the International Military Tribunal for the Far East,* annotated, compiled and edited by R. J. Pritchard. Lewiston: Edwin Mellen Press, 1998.

14   *The New York Times,* February 13 2002, A-1.

15   Ibid.

16   Jackson, 'Final Report of the Chief of Counsel for the United States'.

17   *Trial of the Major War Criminals Before the International Military Tribunal.*

18   *Prosecutor v. Slobodan Milosevic.* http://www.icty.org

19   See P. J. Hutchings (1997) 'Modern Forensics: Photography and Other Suspects', *Cardozo Studies in Law and Literature,* 9, 2, 229–43.

20   Jackson, 'Final Report of the Chief of Counsel for the United States'.

21   T. Dodd, *Trial of the Major War Criminals Before the International Military Tribunal,* volume 2, 29 November 1945.

SECTION II

FILM AS PROPAGANDA

Have wartime propaganda films been effective weapons in the fight for public opinion? The following chapters seem to question their impact on the viewing public in both occupied Europe and Britain and the United States. What becomes apparent is that for the message to be successful, the medium must be entertaining.

Of the Nazi propaganda films with an antisemitic message, *Jud Süss* (*Jew Süss*, 1940) was without doubt the most popular and widely seen. Its portrayal of Joseph Süss Oppenheimer conventionally reinforces the image of the Jew as outsider, as a corrupting influence on the body politic. But Susan Tegel argues that the film's success was down to its popular elements rather than specifically for its anti-Jewish message. Its blend of historical melodrama and period costumes alongside good acting and a skilled producer and director meant that in wartime it served as entertainment, with or even despite its propaganda value. Between 1940 and 1943 over 20.3 million people viewed the film.

The popularity of *Jew Süss* contrasts sharply with reactions to *Der ewige Jude* (*The Eternal Jew*, 1940) despite, as Terry Charman points out, both films being confused with each other. Charman demonstrates that the grim content of the film made it deeply repellent to all but the most hardcore viewers and Nazi Party faithful. Its message – equating Jews to vermin – was underscored by film shot in the Polish ghettos of Jews in ragged and filthy circumstances. It was shown to public audiences throughout occupied Europe in at least two versions, but as Charman shows, even without the ritual slaughter scene (cut from one version) it quickly gathered a reputation as an unpleasant film, and one to avoid if possible.

Do hardcore propaganda films work? Again one could question their value after reading Lutz Becker's piece on the making of two films in the Theresienstadt ghetto, ordered by the SS commandants there. The first film, made in November/December 1942 has not survived, and Becker suggests that this may be because its actuality recorded crowded and miserable conditions, counterproductive to the SS's desire to show the ghetto in a favourable light. Indeed, Becker suggests that its disappearance was due to a decision that the film's content was too grim for mass audiences to watch. In a grotesque irony, in contrast to the message shown in *The Eternal Jew*, the next film commissioned by the SS of Theresienstadt/Terezín was to show how 'normal' and healthy Jewish life in this model town was under Nazi control. Becker describes how the SS decided to capitalise on the beautification programme that had successfully hoodwinked the Red Cross during their visit on 23 June 1944. The film would then be used to silence critics of the Nazi treatment of Jews, fuelled by rumours of atrocities carried out in Nazi concentration camps. The filming started in August 1944, and Zdenka Fantlova-

Ehrlich's account of the making of the film is a moving testimony to the brilliance of the performers and artists who lived in Terezín with the daily threat of deportation. As Fantlova-Ehrlich says, 'Theatre was not entertainment. It was more; a burning torch of hope.' Both Becker and Fantlova-Ehrlich testify to the deadly reality behind the beautification: prior to filming, 7,000 people were sent on transports to death camps so the ghetto would not look overcrowded. As soon as the filming ended, all those who took part in the film, including all the children, were sent on transports east, including Fantlova-Ehrlich, who survived Terezín, then Auschwitz and was finally liberated by the British in Bergen-Belsen.

Turning to four anti-Nazi British films made by the Films Division of the MOI, Matthew Lee describes a reluctance to include references to Nazi atrocities because of the fear that they would not be believed. Many members of the public could still recall stories about German atrocities in the First World War, since shown to be lies. The success of anti-German propaganda stories believed during the First World War thus cast a shadow over filmmakers, anxious not to alienate their audiences, and to gain their trust. In addition, it was felt that the truth would be too awful for people to believe. As Arthur Koestler noted of the British, 'this healthy lack of imagination' rendered the extraordinary truth impossible to communicate through the medium of wartime film. Lee also notes that few of the anti-fascist propaganda films were made in Britain, a result of an official British reluctance to portray the specific suffering of the Jews. Another purpose of the anti-fascist films produced by the MOI was to communicate anti-racist messages to British audiences. This was in part to counter domestic antisemitism, which saw expression in accusations of war profiteering.

Frank Capra's *The Negro Soldier* (1944) was a propaganda film made in a country that still practised segregation in its army and civil society. In his chapter, Stephen Tuck shows that the film's wide distribution (after a decision to cut its length) was so successful that it became a powerful weapon for black activists in the fight for equality in the army. One million black soldiers fought in the US Army, yet its positive message and demonstration of the black contribution to US military success could not but be controversial given widespread support of segregation throughout America. Even Prisoner of War arrangements exposed the race issue in the American and British armies: after German government complaints, black soldiers were removed from guarding German POWs for fear of German reprisals against Allied POWs. During the war years, National Association for the Advancement of Colored People (NAACP) membership grew rapidly. And four years after the film's release in 1947, the army became integrated. While the film successfully countered the propaganda of D. W. Griffiths' racist film *The Birth of a Nation* (1915), Tuck questions whether the film actually changed public opinion on race. Despite the popularity of the film, he suggests that segregation happened for pragmatic reasons and that the film's message did not pave the way for more positive portrayals of blacks in subsequent films. However, the message of *The Negro Soldier* did act as an important pre-cursor to the following generations of civil rights activists.

In occupied Europe many people felt coerced to see propaganda films such as *Jew Süss* and *The Eternal Jew*. In Britain and the United States, people went to see government-sponsored films for information, and possibly just for entertainment. While this section analyses the known factors behind the films' manufacture and known audience reactions, it cannot quantify the power that propaganda films possess to persuade.

6 Veit Harlan's *Jud Süss*

Susan Tegel

Veit Harlan's *Jud Süss* (*Jew Süss*, 1940) like D. W. Griffiths' *The Birth of a Nation* (1915) is a racist film. But Harlan's film is neither innovative nor a film classic. Its notoriety derives solely from being an antisemitic film which was a box-office success, and from the context in which it was both made and shown.

During the Third Reich just under 1,100 feature films were produced of which only 229 (just over 20 per cent) can be categorised as propaganda.[1] Of these only 96 (less than ten per cent) were *Staatsauftragsfilme* (state-commissioned films), and of them *Jew Süss* was one of the most important. The Minister of Propaganda, Joseph Goebbels, was keen that it be made. Effective propaganda, he believed, should come in the guise of entertainment: 'Even entertainment can be politically of special value', he wrote in 1942, 'because the moment a person is conscious of propaganda, propaganda becomes ineffective.'[2]

Surprisingly, few films were made on the 'Jewish question'. Despite National Socialist commitment to antisemitic policies, the German film industry was slow to produce films featuring Jewish characters.[3] It was not until 1940 that they took centre stage in two feature films and a documentary. In July 1940 *Die Rothschilds* (*The Rothschilds*) had its premiere but was not widely shown. Withdrawn after two months, possibly because it was not meant to compete with *Jew Süss* which had its premiere in late September, it was re-released in 1941 under a slightly changed title: *Die Rothschilds Aktien auf Waterloo* (*The Rothschilds' Shares at Waterloo*).[4] Its target was not just the Jews but also the British. Compared to *Jew Süss* its antisemitism was feeble. This cannot be said for the antisemitism in the documentary *Der ewige Jude* (*The Eternal Jew*) which appeared in November 1940. That was vicious, but the documentary format could not combine instruction and entertainment, for after initially good audience figures, *The Eternal Jew* did poorly at the box office (see the following chapter by Terry Charman).[5]

Jew Süss was an effective piece of antisemitic propaganda for several reasons. Aside from focusing on one target, the Jews, the story lent itself to a message that they did not belong in Germany. A lavish costume drama, on which no expense was spared, it had a number of fine actors in leading roles, excellent music by Wolfgang Zeller, and a deft and fast-moving script.[6] It met Goebbels' criteria of effective propaganda in the guise of entertainment.

The film is not only a costume drama. In taking as its subject a historic figure, it purports to be a historical drama. Joseph Süss Oppenheimer, popularly and pejoratively known as the Jew Süss, lived from 1698–1738 and acted as Court Jew to a German prince, the Duke of Württemberg. Court Jews were neither numerous nor typical. From the late seventeenth to the late eighteenth centuries they acted as agents to the German

Cinema poster for *Jud Süss* (1940). bfi-00m-zqx (© F. W. Murnau-Stiftung)

princes who ruled the numerous principalities that then constituted Germany. Enjoying privileged status, they outfitted armies or procured jewels and other luxury items.
Süss Oppenheimer engaged in all these activities.[7] He often behaved as though he were
a government minister, or 'Herr Finance Minister' as he is described at one point in the

film, though he was not in government. He was a private financial adviser, admittedly a powerful one, closely associated with harsh financial policies, the aim of which was to sort out the Duke's precarious finances. Contemporary accounts portray him as an elegant courtier, also a libertine, all of which makes him an untypical Court Jew.

After the Duke's sudden death Süss Oppenheimer was tried, convicted, sentenced to death and executed in an iron cage. To this extent the film was historically accurate. He died in the manner depicted in the film, though not for the offence of sexual relations with a Christian, but for abuse of office.[8] Otherwise, much of the film is pure invention, despite the statement following the titles – not unusual in Third Reich films – that the 'events described in this film are based on historical fact'. In a quest for historical accuracy, the film company's dramaturge in March 1939 even visited the Stuttgart archives, which held the trial proceedings.[9] Nevertheless, what emerged is pseudo-history: the occasional fact embedded in fiction with little evidence of historical research. One should not expect historical accuracy from historical films, least of all one with a specific message.

Joseph Süss Oppenheimer is also the subject of legend and literature. In the eighteenth century there was considerable media interest in his life and in the manner of his death. In 1827 a German novella by Wilhelm Hauff appeared entitled *Jud Süss* (a plagiarised English version appeared later that century).[10] But better known is the novel published in 1925 by the German Jewish writer, Lion Feuchtwanger. Also entitled *Jud Süss*, it was a bestseller, translated into many languages. In Britain it appeared as *Jew Süss*, its title literally translated. In the US it was changed to *Power* – Jew being too strong a word in the American context where antisemitism was by no means latent. The British film, *Jew Süss*, produced by Michael Balcon at Gaumont British in 1934 and starring German exile actor, Conrad Veidt, was based on Feuchtwanger.[11] The British film was no more historically accurate than the German. The Harlan script was neither based on Feuchtwanger nor on the British film, contrary to many claims,[12] nor was it based on Hauff, nor on the actual historical figure. Harlan and his predecessor, however, did watch the British film in Goebbels' special viewing studio and visual similarities are apparent in the execution scene.[13]

In October 1934 the German press gleefully reported that the British film had been banned in Vienna. The antisemitic government of the Christian-Socialist Party, later ousted by the Nazis at the time of *Anschluss*, considered it philosemitic propaganda.[14] Nevertheless, several years passed before the Germans decided to make their own version. This had more to do with the film industry's disinterest in antisemitic films than with the inappropriateness of the Feuchtwanger story which incorporated an unsubstantiated rumour that Süss was only half-Jewish.[15]

At the time of *Kristallnacht* Goebbels issued a directive for each film company to produce an antisemitic film. The Rothschild film was Ufa's contribution.[16] In January 1939 a scriptwriter at Terra, Ludwig Metzger, proposed *Jew Süss*. After a lukewarm response at Terra, he went directly to the Propaganda Ministry, and obtained a contract with Terra in February, the project having become important to the state. Metzger had not been involved in writing scripts for propaganda films; he was then at work on a musical, *Zentrale Rio* (1939). Basing his script on the Hauff novella, by the summer of 1939 a second scriptwriter was brought in, the diehard Nazi playwright, poet and SS member, Eberhard Wolfgang Möller, who had had no experience in writing film scripts. Möller's presence ensured the film met Nazi requirements. Hauff was abandoned. Though his racial credentials (unlike Feuchtwanger's) were impeccable, he was found ideologically wanting. Möller dismissed him as 'sentimental' about the 'emancipation of Jews and Poles'.[17] One would be hard put to find references to Poles in Hauff but this was the opening weeks of the war. What this suggests is confusion about what constituted an antisemitic film as well as the *ad hoc* nature of mounting this most antisemitic of films. Of those responsible for bringing the project to the screen, very few were party members, or indeed even antisemites.[18]

Not only were there difficulties with the script but also with the director. Peter-Paul Brauer had little success in finding actors: initially the fine stage and film actor, Ferdinand Marian, turned down the lead. Others also indicated reluctance. But the conquest of Poland with its large Jewish population made urgent this film on the Jewish Question, as Goebbels makes clear in his diaries. The director was sacked; Harlan was brought in from Tobis as his replacement. His reputation ensured first-class casting. Insisting on reworking the script, he nevertheless retained a great deal. His predecessors received screen credit: script by Harlan, Möller and Metzger (in that order). After the war Harlan insisted that his script was less antisemitic than his predecessors. However, he added one important sequence, which intensifies the hatred for Süss: Süss is made responsible for the execution of the blacksmith, a character not found in the previous script.[19]

After quickly completing his script in December 1939, Harlan visited Poland in January 1940 with two members of the film crew. Claiming to have consulted with a Lublin rabbi on Jewish rituals and practices, he also planned to recruit Jewish extras to add an element of authenticity. The Lublin Jews were never used. One possible explanation is Goebbels' unwillingness to allow Polish Jews into the Reich, even to participate in a film calling for their expulsion. The more plausible explanation is that the outbreak of typhus in Lublin put paid to the plan. The press in fact had been instructed not to mention the arrival of the Lublin Jews. Such an instruction indicates that they were on their way but for the outbreak of typhus.[20]

Harlan had to look elsewhere. An early sequence, set in the Frankfurt ghetto, was filmed in Berlin with non-Jewish actors. Other sequences – the entry of the Jews into Stuttgart and the synagogue scene – were filmed with Jewish extras recruited in Prague who were bussed daily to the Barrandov studios in March 1940.[21] The synagogue service is not performed correctly, but the performers were Jews, desperate in many cases for work, and it seems were even paid. Most extras were Czech Jews, but the solo singer was a German refugee. However, it is not his voice we hear on the soundtrack accompanying the film titles, despite statements from some witnesses at Harlan's trial. It most likely came from a recording.[22] Harlan wanted the Jewish extras to perform in a manner making them appear alien, what he subsequently described as the 'demonic effect' of recreating what he believed was a Hasidic service.[23]

Goebbels also intervened in casting, insisting that Ferdinand Marian and Werner Krauss accept the major Jewish roles. Krauss, who played Caligari in *The Cabinet of Dr Caligari* (1920), was a very distinguished character actor. He took on two of the major roles: Levy, the secretary to Süss and the rabbi. In addition, he also appeared in two smaller speaking parts in the early scene set in the Frankfurt ghetto: an elderly man at a window who tells his attractive daughter to cover up, and the butcher with whom he converses on the street below. Krauss clearly revels in playing Jewish roles.[24] Harlan maintained that Goebbels also insisted that his blonde Swedish wife, Kristina Söderbaum, play the female lead. Eventually, the Minister issued a disclaimer to the effect that those actors playing Jews were of pure Aryan blood.[25] This did not extend to the non-speaking Jewish parts.

The plot concerns the rise and fall of Süss. The Duke's emissary visits him in the Frankfurt ghetto. The Duke is in financial difficulties; the Württemberg Diet (not to be confused with a parliament) will not grant him funds to enable him to live in luxury – he is especially irate that they have prevented him from having a resident ballet company. Four important dissolves (the superimposition of two shots to show a link) indicate how the director employed cinematic devices to advance the film's message. They will punctuate Süss' rise and fall. To the accompaniment of ominous music the Württemberg coat of arms dissolves to the nameplate of Süss, partly in Hebrew lettering, hanging beside his door in the Frankfurt ghetto. Süss agrees to help the Duke, on condition that he is allowed entry to Stuttgart, the capital of Württemberg, where a *Judenbann* (ban on Jews) has been in existence for more than a century. His face – that of a ghetto Jew with sidelocks – then dissolves to that of an elegant eighteenth-century gentleman. He is now seated in a carriage that is hurtling towards Stuttgart. It overturns, and the blonde daughter of the leader of the Diet rescues him. Engaged to her father's assistant, the film's proto-Nazi, she has no inkling that Süss is a Jew until later, when Süss comes to pay his thanks and her fiancé exposes him. Soon Süss becomes indispensable to the Duke. Another dissolve: the gold coins, which Süss throws on a table in the Duke's presence, merge into the skirts of dancing ballerinas. The final dissolve comes towards the end of the film when the Duke dies: Süss is arrested, the face of the courtier reverts to that of a ghetto Jew. He will pay for his crimes – his criminality inherent in being a Jew – which for Fritz Hippler, who directed *The Eternal Jew* and also headed the Propaganda Ministry film department from 1939 to 1943, was a 'happy end'.[26]

The film draws on a number of negative characteristics associated with Jews, none specifically German. Jews are depicted as cut-throat capitalists: Süss the high bourgeois and ingratiating salesman; his assistant, Levy, his slippery, nasty sidekick. At the other extreme is the ragged band of Jews – poor, filthy, immigrants – who, thanks to Süss, enter Stuttgart. Blood links the Court Jew to his poor brethren. In addition, Süss poses a sexual threat: he panders to the Duke, and rapes the heroine. Missing is one negative Jewish stereotype, for obvious historical reasons: the Jew as Bolshevik. However, in encouraging and planning a coup Süss creates disorder, for the fear of Bolshevism was not merely a fear of the abolition of private property but also of breakdown. Finally, Süss appears as an effete courtier, a character found in much eighteenth-century German drama.[27] Courtiers were never Jews, but they were parasitic, an accusation levelled against Jews and emphasised in *The Eternal Jew*.

Negative Jewish stereotypes are almost always associated with a male Jew; female Jews pose less of a threat. Only in a brief early sequence, set in the Frankfurt ghetto, does one appear: a half-dressed woman at a window admonished by her father (Krauss) to cover up. This may be a Harlan touch – he liked a bit of titillation as in an early brief shot of a woman in a crowd who, for no apparent reason, other than to get a laugh from the Duke and presumably from the audience, has her bodice ripped.

Much has been said about Goebbels' interventions in this film: for example, it was claimed that rushes were sent to him on a daily basis.[28] However, it is difficult to find any evidence of significant interference in the film aside from casting and the appointment of Harlan. Certainly, Goebbels was responsible for getting the project off the ground, sacking the director and securing Marian and Krauss in the major roles. After the war it was in Harlan's interest to blame Goebbels. He claimed to have had Süss utter a curse as he was being strung up, which was cut, and the last sequence then re-filmed.[29] However, such a curse does not appear in the extant script.[30]

The film was first shown at the Venice Film Festival (6 September 1940) and opened in Berlin two weeks later to rave reviews in the censored press. Some of the SS, who had helped recruit the Jewish extras, protested at the shortage of tickets for the gala opening night with Goebbels and other Third Reich dignitaries in attendance, though not Hitler who had foresworn films for the rest of the war.[31] Given the classification *staatspolitisch* (of political importance to the state) and *besonders wertvoll* (artistically especially valuable), it was also deemed suitable for youth against some parental objections.[32] Himmler made it compulsory viewing for the SS and the police. It was shown in occupied countries as well as in pro-German countries such as Spain. Of the thirty most popular films in the period 1940–42 *Jew Süss* ranked sixth, and was one of the most popular of the state-commissioned films.[33] Viewed by 20.3 million people during the years 1940 and 1943, it grossed overall 6.2 million Reichsmarks.[34]

Its impact on audiences is harder to gauge. The Security Police recorded positive comments from audiences, but people would have been guarded in expressing negative comments.[35] That so many people saw the film still raises questions. What were they seeing? A well-made film with a racy as well as racist story could have appeared to the unpolitical viewer a heady mixture of 'sex and crime',[36] whereas to an antisemite it would have illustrated the desirability of removing the Jews from Germany. How many viewers who were not antisemitic became antisemitic as a consequence of this film is not easy to establish. Germany was at war and on numerous occasions Hitler had made the Jews responsible for its outbreak. If Germans became more antisemitic in war-time was it as a consequence of this film, or was it as a consequence of the antisemitic propaganda from other quarters?

We know why this film was made, but less about its impact. We know it boosted Harlan's career; he became the Third Reich's leading director with an appropriately large salary increase. He also went on to make other important propaganda films such as *Der Grosse König* (*The Great King*, 1942) and *Kolberg* (1945). After the war he paid for the box-office success of *Jew Süss*. He became the only Third Reich film director to face trial, though this only materialised once it seemed likely that a denazification panel would clear him. Charged with crimes against humanity, he was acquitted on the grounds that 'the Final Solution' would have taken place with or without this film, and that the decision to launch the Final Solution was taken after the premiere.[37]

How precisely does this film relate to the Holocaust? Most historians divide the persecution of the Jews into three phases: exclusion from German society up to 1938, expulsion to 1941 and finally extermination.[38] In terms of the two scripts, which justify the expulsion of the Jews from Württemberg and the restoration of the *Judenbann*, the film belongs to the second phase though it continued to be shown during the third phase. Placed chronologically, the first script was written shortly before and just after the war's outbreak. Both Harlan's appointment and reworking of the script, as well as filming, took place in the early months of the war. Completion followed the conquest of France; the premiere was one year into the war, on the eve of the Battle of Britain.

However, if we consider Goebbels' role as the film's ultimate producer there is a link to the third phase. Though most historians date the timing of the decision to launch the Final Solution to shortly before or after the invasion of the Soviet Union in June 1941, it has recently been argued that it is misleading to think in terms of a decision. Extermination was part of a process of persecution and was the final stage; genocide already began in 1939 with the uprooting of Jews and Poles from western Poland to enable the resettlement of ethnic Germans.[39] It was at this point that Goebbels intervened, just after his flying visit to Łódź in western Poland on 31 October 1939. The Jews, he recorded, were 'no longer human beings but animals', the task was not 'humanitarian' but 'surgical', and the 'cut' must be 'a very radical one', or 'Europe will perish with the Jewish disease'.[40] Shortly thereafter, impatient with the lack of progress on this important antisemitic feature film, he sacked the director and appointed Veit Harlan in his place. After this the project moved forward.

Notes

1   G. Albrecht gives the figure of 1090. See G. Albrecht (1969) *Nationalsozialistische Filmpolitik*. Stuttgart: Ferdinard Enke Verlag, 90; A. Bauer (1976) *Deutscher Spielfilmalmanach 1929–1950*, second edition, Munich: Filmladen Christoph Winterberg, gives the higher number of 1356. Albrecht excludes the 27 films which the German censor banned but includes a few made during Weimar era, while Bauer includes non-feature films, co-productions and Austrian films prior to the *Anschluss*. Robert Peck finds Albrecht too restrictive and arbitrarily splits the difference between him and Bauer, settling for a total of 1200; see R. Peck (2000) 'Misinformation, Missing Information, and Conjecture: Titanic and the Historiography of Third Reich Cinema,' *Media History*, 6, 1, 59; 71, n. 1. Eric Rentschler gives 1086 as the number of feature films which passed the censors and had their premieres in Third Reich Cinemas. In that total he includes three made during the Weimar era and the very few banned after opening but excludes the 27 that were banned prior to opening; see E. Rentschler (1996) *The Ministry of Illusion: Nazi Cinema and its Afterlife*. Cambridge, Harvard University Press, 225. If we exclude from Rentschler's figure of 1086 the three Weimar productions but include those which were banned, we get a total of 1110.
2   Goebbels' diary entry for 1 March 1942, quoted in D. Welch (1983) *Propaganda and the German Cinema, 1933–1945*. Oxford: Clarendon Press, 45.
3   D. Hollstein (1983) *Jud Süss und die Deutschen*. Frankfurt: Ullstein, 38–42.
4   Welch 1983: 262–3; Hollstein 1983: 253.
5   D. Culbert (2002) 'The Impact of Antisemitic Film Propaganda on German Audiences: *Jew Süss* and *The Wandering Jew* (1940)', in R. A. Etlin (ed.) *Art, Culture, and Media under the Third Reich*. Chicago: Chicago University Press, 151–2; E. Leiser (1974) *Nazi Cinema*, trans. G. Mander and D. Wilson. London: Secker and Warburg, 157–8; S. Hornshøy-Møller and D. Culbert (1992) '*Der ewige Jude* (1940): Joseph Goebbels' Unequaled Monument to Antisemitism', *Historical Journal of Film, Radio and Television*, 12, 1, 54, n. 21.
6   See S. Tegel (1996) *Jew Süss, Jud Süss*. Trowbridge: Flicks, 42–4.
7   See S. Stern (1929) *Jud Süss*. Berlin: Akademie Verlag; H. Haasis (1998) *Joseph Süss Oppenheimer genannt Jud Süss: Finanzier, Freidenker, Justizopfer*. Reinbek bei Hamburg: Rowolt Taschenbuch.
8   Haasis 1998: 377; 390.

9 Letter to the author from Hauptstaatsarchiv, Stuttgart, 2 February 1995 cited in S. Tegel (1996) 'Veit Harlan and the Origins of *Jud Süss* 1938–39', *Historical Journal of Film, Radio and Television*, 16, 4, 529, n. 29.

10 W. Hauff (1962) *Jud Süss*. Stuttgart: J. G. Cotta'sche Buchhandlung Nachf; A. E. Ellerman (1897) *The Prince Minister of Württemberg*. London: William Anderson.

11 S. Tegel (1995) 'The Politics of Censorship: Britain's *Jew Süss* (1934) in London, New York and Vienna', *Historical Journal of Film, Radio and Television*, 15, 2, 219–24.

12 Feuchtwanger claimed this but his widow admitted he had never viewed the Harlan film. Bundesarchiv, Koblenz (hereafter cited as BA), R109I 1568, Ufa Bestände.

13 V. Harlan (1966) *Im Schatten meiner Filme*. Gütersloh: Sigbert Mohn, 117.

14 Tegel 1995: 237.

15 Haasis 1998: 16–17. An unfounded rumour, in my view, because if true, Süss' mother would have been aged 13 at the time of his birth. Further, it is unlikely that she would have subsequently made a respectable marriage.

16 The film company, Wien, offered *Wien 1910* (*Vienna 1910*) which was not released until 1942. See R. Geehr, J. Heineman and G. Herman (1985) '*Wien 1910*: An Example of Nazi Anti-Semitism', *Film and History*, 15, 3, 50–65. Extraordinary that a recent publication should describe this film as anti-fascist: see the entry for Rudolf Forster in T. Elsaesser with M. Wedel (eds) (1999) *The BFI Companion to German Cinema*. London: British Film Institute, 105.

17 *Licht-Bild Bühne*, 25 October 1939.

18 See Tegel 1996: 527. Harlan's first wife had been Jewish.

19 Both scripts similarly entitled 'Jud Süss: ein historische Film' are at the Archiv der Stiftung Deutsche Kinemathek, Berlin.

20 See also S. Tegel (2000) '"The Demonic Effect": Veit Harlan's Use of Jewish Extras in *Jud Süss* (1940)', *Holocaust and Genocide Studies*, 14, 2, 215–41.

21 For the use of these Jewish extras see Tegel 2000: 221.

22 I am grateful to Victor Tunkel for this information.

23 Tegel 2000: 215.

24 Harlan and Krauss maintained that the latter took on these multiple roles as a ploy to avoid being in the film, as Goebbels did not like actors showing off their tricks. Harlan 1966: 103–6; 121; see W. Krauss (1958) *Das Schauspiel meines Lebens*. Stuttgart: Henry Goverts, 199–200; see also Tegel 1996: 48, n. 22.

25 See W. Boelcke (ed.) (1966) *Kriegspropaganda 1939–1941: Geheime Ministerkonferenzen im Reichspropagandaministerium*. Stuttgart: Deutsche Verlags-Anstalt, 526.

26 F. Hippler (1942) *Betrachtungen zum Filmschaffen*. Berlin: Max Hesses, 107.

27 Süss also appears this way in the Hauff novella that in itself is influenced by Schiller, another Württemberg-born writer, especially his play *Die Räuber* (*The Robbers*). See also L. Schulte-Sasse (1996) *Entertaining the Third Reich*. Durham and London: Duke University Press, 47–91.

28 Harlan 1966: 111; 120–7; Institut für Zeitgeschichte, Munich, MC31: Harlan Testimony, 8 May 1948; Hippler 1942: 211.

29 Harlan 1966 112–13; Krauss 1958: 202.

30 V. Harlan, Regisseur, 'Jud Süss: ein historische Film', Archiv der Stiftung Deutsche Kinemathek, Berlin.

31 Bundesarchiv Koblenz, RA56/132 also reproduced in J. Wulf (1983) *Theater und Film im Dritten Reich*. Gütersloh: Sigbert Mohn, 450–1; see also Tegel 2000: 215; 234, n. 1.

32 Bundesarchiv, Koblenz, R58/156 (*Sicherheitsdienst* reports: 28 November 1940).

33 The rank order of the six most popular films of the period 1940–42 are as follows: *Die grosse Liebe* (*The Great Love*, 1942); *Wunschkonzert* (*Request Concert*, 1940); *Frauen sind doch bessere Diplomaten* (*Women

Are Indeed Better Diplomats, 1940); *Wiener Blut* (*Vienna Blood*, 1942); *Annelie* (1941); *Jud Süss* (*Jew Süss*, 1940). All these films, with the exception of the third and fourth, were state commissioned; see G. Albrecht (1979) *Film im dritten Reich: Eine Dokumentation*. Karlsruhe: DOKU-Verlag, 251.

34 Ibid., 24.

35 Bundesarchiv Koblenz, R58/156.

36 F. Knilli (1983) 'Die Gemeinsamkeit von Faschisten und Antifaschisten gegenüber dem NS-Film *Jud Süss*', in F. Knilli, T. Maurer, T. Radevagen and S. Zielinski (eds) *Jud Süss. Filmprotokoll, Programmheft und Einzelanalysen*. Berlin: Volker Spiess, 67.

37 Staatsarchiv Hamburg, Misc. 6911, V. Harlan; Bundesarchiv Koblenz Z38/392; *Frankfurter Allgemeine Zeitung*, 3 April 1950.

38 See P. Burrin (1994) *Hitler and the Jews: The Genesis of the Holocaust*, trans. P. Southgate. London: Edward Arnold, 62; 88.

39 P. Longerich (1999/2000) *The Wannsee Conference in the Development of the 'Final Solution'*, trans. I. Gronbach and D. Bloxham, Holocaust Educational Trust Research Papers, I, 2, 7; See also P. Longerich (1998) *Politik der Vernichtung, Eine Gesamtdarstellung der nationalsozialistischen Judenverfolgung*. Munich: Piper, 260–3.

40 E. Fröhlich (ed.) (1987) *Die Tagebücher von Joseph Goebbels*. Munich: Saur, iii, 628 (2 November 1939).

7   Fritz Hippler's *The Eternal Jew*

Terry Charman

Dr Joseph Goebbels once remarked, 'even the most obnoxious attitude can be communicated through an outstanding work of art'. Indeed, rarely can there have been a more obnoxious attitude communicated in cinematic form than in *Der ewige Jude* (*The Eternal Jew*, 1940) which Goebbels undoubtedly saw as an outstanding film documentary, though he would have no doubt been annoyed that this 'documentary' was later to be confused with the feature film *Jud Süss* (*Jew Süss*, 1940).[1]

Post-war Swedish film historians Leif Furhammer and Folke Isaksson in their book, *Politics and Film*, describe *The Eternal Jew* as 'probably the most evil film ever made',[2] while David Stewart Hull in his 1969 study *Film in the Third Reich* describes it as 'the hate picture of all time', adding, 'the film is inaccessible beyond a few film archives where it is kept in the restricted division usually reserved for pornography, which is exactly the genre to which this film belongs'.[3] These assessments echo the contemporary judgement on the film by Derrick Sington and Arthur Weidenfeld in their 1942 book, *The Goebbels Experiment*, in which they call it an 'obscene production'.[4]

Over a year in production, *The Eternal Jew*, directed by Fritz Hippler and written by Eberhard Taubert, was premiered at the Ufa Palast am Zoo cinema on 28 November 1940 before an audience of Nazi celebrities, but not, it would appear, Dr Goebbels himself who, according to his diary, was en route for occupied Norway. Two screenings were held, for women and children the shorter version, with the full version screened at 6.30pm including the ritual slaughter scene.[5] The programme that night opened with a short documentary, *Ostraum-Deutscher Raum* (*Eastern Territory–German Territory*, 1940), the weekly newsreel was then shown before the Greater German Radio Orchestra played Beethoven's 'Egmont Overture' leading into the screening of *The Eternal Jew*. According to the *Deutsche Allgemeine Zeitung* (*DAZ*) the film received a great ovation from the VIP audience, while the *Volkischer Beobachter*, the Nazi Party newspaper, wrote of 'tremendous applause' at the film's end. For its readers, *DAZ* then went on to give a resume of the film:

> There are revealing scenes in the Polish ghettos – scenes in the synagogues where Jews are doing business; filth in the synagogues, close-ups of Jewish faces. Then the film shows by trick photography the spreading of Jews all over the world in the form of rat migration – assimilated Jews are shown – statistics of the number of Jews in the different professions – photographs of Rathenau, Police Vice President Weiss, Tauber, Lubitsch, Reinhardt, Chaplin and so on. A skilful selection of photographs of Jewish film and revues is given. The most frightful chapter comes at the end: the cruel, inhuman, barbarous slaughter of animals.

The *DAZ* correspondent 'heaved a sigh of relief when the film ended with pictures of Germans and things German'.[6] The German provincial press were equally enthusiastic; the local paper in Moers, near the Dutch border, in its review of *The Eternal Jew* stated that the film will 'clarify to the very last Germans that the Jews as a race is, and will forever remain, beneath human kind, as the rats are beneath the animals: parasites, poison carriers and subversive scroungers.'[7] Worthy of note, but not altogether surprising is the fact that Germany's last surviving semi-independent newspaper, the *Frankfurter Zeitung*, completely ignored the film; but more surprisingly so too did *Das Reich*, Dr Goebbels' new weekly, and the Wehrmacht's lavishly illustrated life-style magazine *Signal*.

After its premiere at the Ufa Palast am Zoo *The Eternal Jew* went on to be shown in every major town and city in Germany and at one time it was being screened at no less than 66 cinemas in Berlin itself.[8] The film was also shown throughout occupied Europe. In France it was given the title *Le Péril Juif* which had already been used before the war on the cover of an edition of the scurrilous forgery *The Protocols of the Elders of Zion*. In Holland a decree was issued on 22 August 1941 ordering a screening of the film in every Dutch cinema by 30 April 1942. The Dutch edition, a print of which is held today at the Netherlands Film Archive, includes 'local shots' from a 1932 Jewish documentary *Sabbath Evening*.

In January 1941 it was screened at the Casino cinema in Łódź in western Poland, re-named Litzmannstadt after the German general who had captured it during the First World War, and from where large parts of the documentary material had been collected by Hippler in October 1939. The *Film Kurier* magazine described those shots:

> The film camera walked through Litzmannstadt's ghetto before the German authorities had intervened, bringing with them some order and cleansing this Augean stable, and thus it could give an unvarnished picture of the stinking quagmire from which a steady flow seeped into world Jewry.[9]

Screenings of *The Eternal Jew* were also to take place during Alfred Rosenberg's projected massive Anti-Jewish Congress due to be held in Kraków during September 1944, but which was abandoned because of the military situation on the Eastern Front.[10]

Thanks to the surprisingly realistic and honest reports made at the time by the *Sichersheitsdienst* – the SD, the security service of the SS – it is possible to build up a nationwide picture of audience reaction to the film. Unfortunately, disappointingly few contemporary German diaries, letters or post-war memoirs mention the film. From one report dated 20 January 1941, which is now in the Bundesarchiv at Koblenz, we learn that because of the extensive publicity campaign in the press and on the radio *The Eternal Jew* had been awaited with great interest by the public and that the film had 'lived up to these high expectations', being 'more instructive, convincing and impressive than many an anti-Jewish tract'. The report goes on to say that:

> Particularly favourable comment was made – as reported from Munich, Koblenz, Schwerin, Danzig, Halle, Koenigsberg and Berlin – on the way the maps and statistics catalogued the spread of Jewry (the comparison with rats is mentioned as particularly impressive) and its expanding influence on all areas of life and in all countries of the world. The shots of Jews in America have prompted particular comment.

Collection of the Imperial War Museum PST 8327

Audiences in Schwerin and Karlsbad 'were surprised by the open revelations of the Jewish influence in and dominance of the USA'.[11] This is of course of particular interest in view of the fact that President Roosevelt had been re-elected for a third term on 5 November, only three weeks before the film's premiere. Despite the fact that the Nazi press and radio had played down the election, most Germans were fully aware of Roosevelt's antagonism towards the Hitler regime and his increasing support for the Allied cause. The report continued:

> While in Leipzig a great impression was made on the cinemagoers by the scenes in which Jews were shown 'in their original state' and in 'European fashion' as men of the world.

Throughout the Reich, the juxtapositions made by Hippler in the film – the Jewish ghetto and the parade of Hitler Youth at the 1934 Nazi Party Rally from *Triumph of the Will* (1935) – were 'thought to make an extraordinarily telling effect'.[12] In Munich, the 'capital' of the Nazi movement, audiences showed 'immediate relief' and gave 'enthusiastic' applause at the point in the film where Hitler delivers his warning to the Reichstag on 30 January 1939 that a new world war would bring about the final annihilation of European Jewry.[13]

But the SD report was not all positive from the Nazis' point of view. The remarkably high audience figures produced by the first performances of the film, encouraged by very intensive publicity, in some places had soon fallen off. This was, the report felt, because *The Eternal Jew* had followed too quickly on the feature film *Jew Süss* which had been premiered in September 1940, only two months before. The report went on:

> Since a large part of the population had already seen *Jew Süss* it was very often assumed – according to information to hand – that the documentary *The Eternal Jew* had nothing really new to say ... Statements like 'We've seen *Jew Süss* and we've had enough of Jewish filth' have been heard ... People have frequently claimed that *Jew Süss* had shown such a convincing picture of Jewry that this new and even more blatant evidence actually served no further purpose.[14]

Interestingly enough, a year later on 8 December 1941 a report from the *Kreisleitung* (circuit leadership of the Nazi Party – a *Kreis* was a small territorial sub-division within a *Gau*, or 'district') in Kiel noted that the film *Ich Klage An* (*I Accuse*), dealing with the theme of euthanasia, had been extraordinarily well-received when compared to the below-average audience attendance for *The Eternal Jew*.[15]

Reading between the lines of the SD reports it would appear that only the politically active sections of the population – Nazi Party members, in other words – deliberately sought out the film while the report concluded that, 'the typical film audience has largely avoided it, and that in some places there has been a word-of-mouth campaign against the film and its starkly realistic portrait of the Jews. The repulsive nature of the material and in particular the ritual slaughter scenes are repeatedly cited in conversation as the main reason for not seeing the film.' It was noted that in Western Germany and Breslau people were seen leaving cinemas in the middle of performances, and in some cases people actually fainted during the ritual slaughter sequence.[16]

Goebbels, as his diary entries for 1939 and 1940 show, was heavily involved in the production of *The Eternal Jew*. According to one of his biographers, Ralf Georg Reuth, he at first wanted the director of *Jew Süss*, Veit Harlan, to work the ritual slaughter scenes into his film. Harlan refused on the grounds that such cruelty would make the audience sick to their stomachs.[17] It appears that Goebbels gave orders on 8 October 1939 to Hippler, then thirty years of age and a Nazi Party member since 1925 who had taken part in the notorious book-burnings on 10 May 1933, to film scenes in the Polish ghettos. Hippler swiftly did so and produced the results for Goebbels eight days later. According to Hippler, the propaganda minister

> wanted to show me how somebody with a proper attitude to the Jewish question would react. Almost every close-up was accompanied by shouts of disgust and loathing; some scenes he criticised so strongly as if to bring a reaction from the screen itself: at the ritual slaughter scenes, he held his hands over his face.[18]

In his diary the propaganda minister wrote of 'scenes so horrific and brutal in their explicitness that one's blood runs cold. One shudders at such barbarism.'[19] Less than three months later, after intense work by Hippler and others, on 9 January 1940, Goebbels recorded that the 'Jewish film [was] in its final cut. I think we have got it now.'[20] But only three days later he wrote of having to re-work the film once again before it could be shown to Hitler. And before that happened, the film was shown to 120 so-called experts at the Ministry of Propaganda in order to assess it and to iron out any potential difficulties. Some objections were raised. For instance, Viktor Brack, of the Fuehrer's Chancellery and a man heavily involved in the euthanasia programme, thought that the singing in the synagogue scene was too close to Roman Catholic church music and could lead German Catholics to a 'wrong attitude' while Professor von Kursell of the Staatliche Kunsthochschule proposed a more positive ending with 'beautiful nordic figures'.[21]

These and other comments were passed on to Hippler and thence to Goebbels and some were incorporated into a version of the film which was shown at a private screening at the Ufa Palast am Zoo cinema to Nazi Party functionaries and others on the morning of 8 September 1940. This screening resulted in more criticism and comment particularly in relation to the ritual slaughter scenes. The minutes of the conference at the Propaganda Ministry four days later touched on this:

> Since in view of the Deputy Gauleiter, the Police President and numerous journalists the Jewish film in its present version is suitable only for people with strong nerves, two versions are to be produced, the milder one intended for women and juveniles. The version which includes the ritual slaughter scenes is to be shown by the Party in closed performances, but maybe one of the daily performances in the cinemas could show this graphic version provided the public has been accurately instructed on the subject in the press beforehand.[22]

Thus it was not until 11 October 1940 that Goebbels could eventually write in his diary: '*The Eternal Jew* is now ready at last. Now it can be released. We have worked on it for long enough.'[23] On 4 November 1940 the film, in two versions with one omitting the ritual slaughter scenes, was approved by the censor. The film begins with the rolling title and what can be seen as the keynote statement of the film:[24]

> The civilised Jews we know in Germany give but an incomplete picture of their true character. This film includes actual footage from the Polish ghettos. It shows us Jews as they really are, before they conceal themselves behind the mask of the civilised European.

First seen is footage shot in the Warsaw ghetto. Plainly visible in one sequence is a poster of Polish President Moscicki's call to arms at the time of the German invasion. It is worth recalling at this stage Hippler's claim in the magazine *Judenfrage* of 28 November 1940:

> No Jew was forced into any kind of action or position during the shooting. Moreover we let the filmed Jews be on their own and tried to shoot in moments when they were unaware of the camera's presence. Consequently we have rendered the ghetto Jews in an unprejudiced manner, real to life as they live and react in their own surroundings. All who see this film will be convinced there is never a forced or scared expression in the faces of the Jews who are filmed passing by, trading or attending ritual services. From time to time one sees a certain smugness.[25]

That is, of course, as may be, but here one recalls that the conditions were created by starving the population in the ghetto, and that by May 1942 prior to the deportations to Treblinka two months later, Jews in the Warsaw Ghetto were forced to pose by Nazi cameramen in degrading scenes.[26]

Jews are then shown at forced labour clearing away the debris of the September 1939 campaign. The film then continues with the aid of animated maps to depict the migration of Jews equating them to the mass migration of rats from Asia to Europe, Africa and America. This is followed by a listing of spurious percentage statistics of alleged Jewish involvement in world crime including drug trafficking and prostitution. The audience is then shown how Jews are supposed to transform themselves into 'Europeans' by abandoning their traditional caftans, beards and so on.

A long sequence follows purporting to illustrate how Aryan/European culture has been undermined and defiled by the Jews – decadent art and music are shown as are leading Jews in the arts and sciences including Albert Einstein, Max Reinhardt, Emil Ludwig, Curt Bois and Charlie Chaplin. Of particular interest and coincidence are the appearances in this section of film director Ernst Lubitsch and Peter Lorre in an extract from Fritz Lang's 1931 film *M*.[27] At the time *The Eternal Jew* was being shown in Germany and throughout occupied Europe, Lubitsch was making his own Hollywood film on life in Nazi-occupied Poland. This was the comedy *To Be or Not To Be* (1942) starring Jewish comedian Jack Benny – real name Josef Kubelsky – and Carole Lombard. On its release, *To Be or Not To Be* was considered to be in doubtful taste, but is now acknowledged as a classic of the cinema.

The notorious ritual slaughtering scene then soon appears, followed by footage of Hitler in the Kroll Opera House on 30 January 1939 delivering his infamous threat that a new world war unleashed by international Jewish finance would bring about the annihilation of the Jews of Europe. Some Holocaust historians have recently questioned the significance of this threat. Surely though it can be no coincidence that Hitler continued to allude to it for the next three-and-a-half years – albeit wrongly ascribing the date to 1 September 1939 – in public speeches. Hitler's 'prediction' was also used as the Nazi *'Parole der Woche'*, ('slogan of the week'), at the time of the introduction of the Yellow Star in Germany in September 1941. The film ends with Nazi-idealised Aryan types from *Triumph of the Will* and other 1930s films and newsreels.

In conclusion it is worth remembering that of the 230,000 Jews who were living in Łódź in October 1939 when Hippler set about his task and who appear in the opening shots, only 877 remained alive in the ghetto when the Red Army liberated the city on 19 January 1945.[28]

Notes

1   Viktor Reimann, for instance, in his biography of Goebbels, in giving the plot of *Jud Süss* actually describes *The Eternal Jew*; V. Reimann (1977) *The Man Who Created Hitler: Joseph Goebbels*. London: William Kimber, 187.

2   L. Furhammer and F. Isaksson (1971) *Politics and Film*. London: Studio Vista, 116.

3   D. S. Hull (1969) *Film in the Third Reich*. Berkeley: University of California Press, 173–4.

4   D. Sington and A. Weidenfeld (1942) *The Goebbels Experiment*. London: John Murray, 213.

5   S. Hornshøy-Møller and D. Culbert (1992) '*Der ewige Jude* (1940): Joseph Goebbels' Unequaled Monument to Antisemitism', *Historical Journal of Film, Radio and Television*, 12, 1, 46.

6   Quoted in Furhammer and Isaksson 1971: 116.

7   Quoted in E. A. Johnson (1999) *Nazi Terror: The Gestapo, Jews and Ordinary Germans*. London: John Murray, 385.

8   Sington and Weidenfeld 1942: 213.

9   *Film Kurier*, '*Der Ewige Jude*', c1940, quoted in Furhammer and Isaksson, 117.

10 See M. Weinrich (1999) *Hitler's Professors*. London: Yale University Press, 133; 224.

11 Cited in E. Leiser (1974) *Nazi Cinema*. London: Secker and Warburg, 157.

12 Ibid., 157–8.

13 Ibid., 158.

14 Ibid.

15 Ibid.

16 Ibid.

17 R. G. Reuth (1993) *Goebbels*. London: Constable, 261.

18 Hornshøy-Møller and Culbert 1992: 42. See also A. Tanner (2000) 'Nazi hate filmmaker looks back with some regrets'; Reuters interview with Fritz Hippler, 11 December.

19 Diary entry for 17 October 1939; translated and edited by F. Taylor (1982) *The Goebbels Diaries 1939–1941*. London: Hamish Hamilton, 23.

20 Diary entry for 9 January 1940; Taylor 1982: 90.

21 Furhammer and Isaksson 1971: 118.

22 Quoted in W. A. Boelcke (1971) *The Secret Conferences of Dr Goebbels, October 1939–March 1943*. London: Weidenfeld and Nicolson, 91.

23 Diary entry for 11 October 1940; Taylor 1982: 139.

24 Descriptions of the *The Eternal Jew* are taken from the print held by the Film and Video Archive at the Imperial War Museum, London. Film Number: GWY 522.

25 *Die Judenfrage*, 28 November 1940.

26 J. Struk (2004) *Photographing the Holocaust*. London: I. B. Tauris, 80–1.

27 Peter Lorre, a Hungarian Jew whose real name was Laszlo Lowenstein, besides his roles in *The Maltese Falcon* (1941) and *Casablanca* (1942) also appeared in the 1944 film *Hotel Berlin* based on the novel – one of Churchill's wartime favourites – by Vicki Baum. Now almost forgotten, *Hotel Berlin*, which was premiered in January 1945, was the first film, as far as I have been able to ascertain, to refer to Auschwitz, with the Peter Lorre character speaking of the ovens at Birkenau.

28 G. Reitlinger (1971) *The Final Solution*. London: Sphere Books, 325.

8   Film documents of Theresienstadt

Lutz Becker

'Forgetting extermination is part of extermination, because it is also the extermination of
memory, of history...'
    – Jean Baudrillard[1]

Theresienstadt (Terezín) is a fortified garrison town 60km north of Prague. Founded
in the eighteenth century by the Emperor Joseph II of Austria and named in memory
of his mother the Empress Maria Theresa, it was built to protect the Hapsburgs against
attacks from Prussia. It is a typical military settlement with barracks and arsenal buildings set in a geometric grid, a small urban structure surrounded by heavy ramparts. The
decision to turn this small town into a concentration camp for the Jews of the so-called
'Protectorate of Bohemia and Moravia' was made by the SS in October 1941. The deportation of the Jews to Theresienstadt started immediately.

    The first arrivals were groups of healthy young Jewish men brought to Theresien-
stadt as building workers, who under the command of the SS had to convert buildings and prepare spaces for the accommodation of the thousands of Jews who were
expected. The original population of 3,500 people was forced to leave the town between
February and June 1942, and Jews deported from all over Czechoslovakia were brought
in. These were families, who were taken away from their normal lives and had to live
from one day to the next as prisoners in the narrow spaces of that town, isolated from
the rest of the world behind mighty walls and fortifications.

    At first the SS developed Theresienstadt as a transitional camp, a station on the way
to the extermination camps of the East, particularly Auschwitz. From late 1942 onwards
the camp was turned in to an *Altersghetto* used to accommodate old age pensioners; it
became the final station for Jewish veterans of the Great War and of prominent per-
sonalities and their families. At this point the concentration camp was converted into a
ghetto. This meant that many of the prisoners were kept there longer than was normal
in labour camps. The SS then decided to develop Theresienstadt into a special ghetto for
members of the intelligentsia of Austria, Czechoslovakia and the Weimar Republic of
Germany, for personalities who had been part of the political, cultural and social life of
their countries. As a result the ghetto received a certain attention from the International
Red Cross. Limited postal contact was allowed for some people. The illusion of trans-
parency was kept up to deceive governments and concerned institutions of the neutral
countries, and support the illusion that what was happening to the Jews in Germany
and the occupied territories was legal and normal in times of war.

More than 50,000 people (reaching a peak of 58,497 on 18 September 1942) had to find space to live and to work in this over-crowded ghetto. Most families were separated, and people had to sleep in crammed rooms, attics and basements. Additional encampments made up of pre-fabricated wooden barracks were provided to house thousands of prisoners in narrow four-tier bunks. Food was scarce, the water supply and sanitation were inadequate and hygienic problems reached at times disastrous levels. Overpopulation, starvation and infectious diseases led to a daily death toll of 120 to 140 people. Regular deportations to Auschwitz reduced temporarily the population pressure, but more people came to Theresienstadt – an endless stream of new arrivals. Between 24 November 1941 and 20 April 1945 a total of 139,667 people were deported to the ghetto of whom 33,818 died. Some 86,934 were subsequently sent on, mainly to Auschwitz for extermination; only 3,586 people survived this ordeal. These figures do not include more than 15,000 who were evacuated to Theresienstadt from camps in the East after 20 April.[2]

Under the rule of the camp commandant *SS-Hauptsturmführer* Siegfried Seidl, Theresienstadt was put under a pro forma self-government, which meant that the Jewish population was made responsible for the camp conditions and its own survival. Isolated and totally dependent on every whim of the SS, the Council of Elders under the chairmanship of Dr Paul Eppstein had to manage the distribution of food, medical aid and housing.

In view of the propagandistic value of a filmed record, successive SS commandants decided to cover the life of this 'model ghetto' on film. Seidl was the first who raised funds for this purpose from the SS and the 'Zentralstelle für Jüdische Auswanderung' in Prague. His deputy *SS-Obersturmführer* Otto was put in charge of the production. The filming took place in November and December 1942.[3] Only eight-and-a-half minutes of 16mm amateur footage have survived to record the making of the film. The scenario was written by the stage director Irena Dodalová assisted by Petr Kien.[4] Kien was a gifted artist and poet who, still in his twenties, also wrote the libretto for Victor Ullman's opera *The Emperor of Atlantis*, a work that grew out of the experience of Theresienstadt.[5]

This early film, which was intended to represent the special conditions in Theresienstadt favourably, was counter-productive, as it showed the ghetto in its original, crammed, miserable state. While the film itself has disappeared, Kien's script, which is now kept in the Dutch Institute for War Studies, has remained a document of great value. In it the author describes realistically the darkness of ghetto life, the dirt, the cold, the rats, the rotten food, the terrible conditions in the sleeping quarters, the hunger and demoralised state of the inhabitants.

The first scene of the surviving footage shows the crowded interior of the ghetto café with the Ghetto Swingers playing in the background. The second scene shows the SS crew together with *Sicherheitsdienst* (SD, Security Service of the SS) cameramen filming with two Arriflex cameras the approach road to Theresienstadt. This is conclusive evidence that the film was organised by the SS as an internal production. In the third scene a Czech gendarme is guarding the town ramparts under a sign: 'Jewish settlement area – no loitering'. The fourth scene shows a cabaret performance, which includes the dancer Kamila Rosenbaumova, a barbershop act of the comedian Karel Švenk and an unidentified SS man in the audience. A scene in a puppet theatre is followed by a football game with the newly-built crematorium in the background. The final scene shows the director Irena Dodalová with SS personnel at a construction site at the Bohunice railway yards.

The film was completed, had its first screening in Prague and disappeared shortly after. Witnesses suggested that Dodalová was an inept director and that the film was fairly amateurish. Nevertheless, the disappearance of the film may have had less to do with its lack of quality than with the fact that its wider exhibition would have been damaging to the interests of the SS. The 16mm footage containing the scenes described above was discovered in 1994 and is now kept by the Polish Film Archive in Warsaw.[6]

Not deterred by the failure of this film production, a second attempt was made by *SS-Obersturmbannführer* Hans Günther, chief of the 'Zentralamt zur Regelung der Judenfrage in Böhmen und Mähren'.[7] He approached the project more efficiently than his predecessor in November 1943 and contacted the director of the Czech newsreel company Aktualita, Karel Pečený, to develop the film. The agreed budget was 35,000 Reichsmarks. The ghetto commandant *SS-Hauptsturmführer* Karl Rahm,[8] the successor of Seidl, ordered the Czech film writer Jindřich Weil, an inmate of Theresienstadt, to prepare a script for the film. By March 1944 Weil had delivered two versions. A camera team of Aktualita started filming in January a number of preliminary scenes. Shortly after his arrival at the ghetto in February 1944 the actor and director Kurt Gerron was assigned to organise the production and take over the direction of the film.

After the deportation of 450 Danish Jews to Theresienstadt in October 1943 the Danish government and the International Red Cross petitioned *SS-Obersturmbann-führer* Adolf Eichmann to allow an inspection of the ghetto. This expected exposure to the critical eye of the world was preceded by many months of a radical beautification programme, which the SS called *Stadtverschönerung*. Every inhabitant was called upon to participate in the painting of house facades, the glazing of windows and the planting of gardens. Suddenly the Market Square had a music pavilion and the Dresden Barracks had a new theatre, even a prayer room. Working to improve the ghetto gave many people new hope; it was a reminder of their self-worth. Others saw the tragic irony of what was going on and veered between disbelief and self-deception.

At the end of their toil, 7,500 people who had taken part in the beautification works were sent to Auschwitz to relieve the over-crowding of the ghetto. The Red Cross visit took place after many delays on 23 June 1944. It preceded, by one month only, the discovery by the Red Army of the horrors in the Majdanek concentration camp in Poland. Theresienstadt looked beautiful and fairly uncongested that summer's day. The SS smiled and some prisoners applauded. The deception was successful. Yet many prisoners recognised the evident success of this deception as a catastrophe, and their own failure to speak to the Commission was recognised as a missed opportunity. Leo Baeck stated after the war: 'The Commission never bothered to climb a single flight of stairs. Perhaps they knew of the real conditions – and it looked as if they did not want to know the truth. The effect on our morale was devastating, we felt forgotten and forsaken.'[9]

The Swiss member of the Red Cross Commission, Mr Rossel, was happily surprised by what he saw. He summarised his experience in a final report: 'We will say that our amazement was extraordinary, to find in the ghetto a city that was leading an almost normal existence. We told the SS officers accompanying us that the most surprising thing about our visit were the difficulties we had experienced in being allowed to make it … Our report will not change anyone's judgement; each remains free to condemn the position the Reich has taken to resolve its Jewish problem. If, however, this report dissipated a little the mystery surrounding the ghetto Theresienstadt, it will be enough.'[10]

Rossel's report was leaked to the SS almost immediately. Encouraged by the 'positive' image it presented, Günther and Rahm moved fast to exploit this opportune moment. They took the successful deception of the Red Cross Commission as a clear indication that a propaganda film could be very effective in positively influencing other critics of the Reich. They thought that the film could usefully counteract the 'horror stories' about the extermination camps that had started circulating abroad: 'We should film Theresienstadt so that the Jews will not say later we mistreated them.'[11]

The shooting of the film started seven weeks after the Red Cross visit on 21 August 1944. The ghetto population was still in a state of hopeful elation and participated willingly in the making of the film. The beautification of the ghetto had brought them some benefits and for the period of filming children were given toys and the food rations were increased. Under the controlling eyes of the SS, Gerron had to revise Weil's scripts and direct the two newsreel cameramen allocated for the production. The daily protocols, which he had to submit to Günther, dealt more with the organisation of the filming and less with the film's content. When Karel Pečený of Aktualita realised his ambition to direct the film himself Gerron was demoted to be his assistant. In October Gerron was sent to Auschwitz; he never saw a foot of the film he had shot; the film was finished by Ivan Frič, one of the two Aktualita cameramen. Under the close supervision of Günther he edited and re-edited the film during the winter of 1944–45. It is reported that the film was completed on 28 March 1945 and had its first showing a few days later at the Czernin Palace in Prague in the presence of State Secretary Karl Hermann Frank, Günther, Rahm and a number of high-ranking SS officers. On 6 April it was screened in Theresienstadt for a delegation of the International Red Cross. The film was shown to a succession of visiting commissioners and diplomats. At that time the Red Army advanced rigorously and the German hold on East Prussia and Poland was crumbling. The discovery of the concentration camps, particularly the liberation of the Auschwitz extermination camp in January 1945, had revealed for all the world to see the true nature of 'the Final Solution'. Historical facts finally defused the propagandistic power of the film and made it redundant.

In 1964 a can of film containing an unidentified fragment was discovered in a cupboard in the Prague Film School, FAMU.[12] During the years of Nazi occupation the building had housed the Czech newsreel which had been requisitioned by the Zentralfilm Gesellschäft Ost mbH (ZFO). The location of this find may be an indication that ZFO was also involved in facilitating the production of the film.[13] The fragment of 15 minutes 25 seconds in length turned out to be part of the second film made in Theresienstadt, which was presumed lost forever. Based on the title it had been given in a number of memoirs of former inmates of the ghetto the fragment was titled *Der Führer schenkt den Juden eine Stadt* (*The Führer Gives a Town to the Jews*). This title was not the correct one, as a later-discovered title sequence indicated. It was indeed much simpler and more devious: *Theresienstadt: Ein Dokumentarfilm aus dem Jüdischen Siedlungsgebiet* (*Theresienstadt: A Documentary from the Jewish Settlement Area*). The assumed title expressed the sense of bitter irony of those who were present during the filming. The original title declared the film to be an objective film document. Made within the smooth conventions of the *Kulturfilm*, this film presented the fiction of 'life in Theresienstadt' assuming the stance of truthfulness and authenticity. The use of language elevated Theresienstadt from a ghetto to a Jewish settlement. Its generalisations amplified the propaganda lie that the deported Jews were peacefully living in dedicated settlement areas.

The original duration of the film was approximately 50 to 60 minutes. It was a 35mm sound film with music, synchronised speech and a dominant commentary. The historian Karel Margry has come to the conclusion that it contained 38 scenes of which the fragment held by the Bundesarchiv covers only the latter part, scenes 26 to 37.[14]

Scenes 1 to 8 determine the general tone of the film as they represent the ghetto like a holiday camp, a place of leisure, entertainment and sport. Scenes 9 to 18 illustrate the normality of communal life in the town, the workings of the Jewish self-government and the health service. Scenes 19 to 25 introduce the viewer to maintenance work in the ghetto, to small industries, laundry, agriculture, the preparation and consumption of food. All these sections are intercut with lighter scenes of cultural activities. Scenes 26 to 31 show blacksmithing, a metal workshop and pottery production; the sculptor Rudolf Saudek from Leipzig creates a figure for a public fountain; in workshops situated in wooden huts craftsmen and women are engaged in the production of handbags, purses and shoe repair; scenes of a football game in the courtyard of the Dresden Barracks and of men and women in the central bathhouse suggesting happy sociability and health. Scene 32 shows the interior of the central library with its prominent readers Judge Heinrich Klang, Dr Desider Friedmann, both from Vienna, Prof. David Cohen from Amsterdam and Prof. Ernst Kantorowicz from Frankfurt. Scene 33 documents a

Inmates on their way from work in the ghetto's workshops. WL 5654 (© The Wiener Library)

Desider Friedmann, librarian from Vienna (right) in Theresienstadt's library. WL 5653 (© The Wiener Library)

gathering of the ghetto intelligentsia, at the occasion of a lecture given by the cultural historian Prof. Emil Utitz of Vienna. Seated in the audience are Rabbi Leo Baeck, Prof. Hermann Strauss, Dr Otto Stargardt, Dr Alexander Cohn from Berlin, Prof. Alfred Philippson from Bonn, Prof. Alfred Klein from Jena, Prof. Klang and Rabbi Benjamin Murmelstein from Vienna, Prof. Artur Stein, Prof. Leo Taussig and Prof. Maximilian Adler of Prague, Franzi Schneidhuber and Elly von Bleichröder.[15] Scenes 34 to 37 shows a concert that follows the lecture by the small ghetto orchestra, conducted by Karel Ančerl. Then we see garden allotments near the city wall, a remarkable scene that suggests that the population feed themselves through growing their own vegetables. This is followed by scenes of the evening leisure time. Groups of women meet in conversation, doing their handywork, seated between the bunk beds in huts set up to look like those used by the *Arbeitsfront* in Germany. The last scene is that of a family having dinner. It shows one of the many lies of the film; the 'family' is made up of people that did not know each other, eating food specially provided for the filming.[16]

Since its discovery this film has had a great influence on the understanding of antisemitic propaganda films made by the Nazis.[17] It gives insights into the hypocrisy of its makers and the cynicism with which the SS and its helpers viewed the destiny of the Jewish people. The staged artificiality of the fake idyll is revealed as the great lie it is: it is an inversion of reality. The truth of the film lies in all the things it does not show.

The war ended before the film could be exploited, but one can only speculate as to the damage it would have done had the war continued. It would have deflected public opinion towards a fictional version of the Final Solution. Certainly in Germany it would have replaced the reality of the extermination camps with the myth of a humane

Karel Ančerl conducting in Theresienstadt's ghetto. WL 5655 (© The Wiener Library)

Group of women inmates in their living quarters in the Theresienstadt ghetto. WL 5652 (© The Wiener Library)

resettlement policy. When we study the Theresienstadt film next to Fritz Hippler's| *The Eternal Jew*, the vilest of the antisemitic films, one can assess how Nazi propaganda would have exploited the material. One can well imagine a sequel to *The Eternal Jew*, its editing techniques, its distorted logic and the tenor of the commentator's voice, denying the Holocaust altogether.

Notes

1   J. Baudrillard (1994) *Simulacra and Simulation*. Trans. Sheila Faria Glaser. Ann Arbor: University of Michigan Press, 49.

2   These figures have been supplied by Vojtech Blodig, a historian from Terezín. A balance of prisoners who had been deported to the Terezín Ghetto by 20 April 1945, by point of departure:

Protecturate of Bohemia and Moravia	75,594
Occupied Czech borderland	612
Germany	42,219
Austria	15,274
Netherlands	4,897
Denmark	466
Slovakia	1447
Hungary	1150
Unknown	8

From 24 November 1941 to 20 April 1945, a total of 139,667 people were deported to Terezín. By 20 April 1945, 33,818 people had died in Terezín. Evacuation transports carrying 15,397 people arrived in Terezín after this date; a further 1,566 people died after 20 April. A total of 86,934 people were deported to other locations from Terezín. Of those deported from Terezín to other locations, 3,586 survived. The tally does not include some 1,260 children from Białystok that were not recorded as Ghetto prisoners. Their transport arrived in Terezín on 24 August 1943. On 5 October 1943, the 1196 still-living children were deported to their deaths in Auschwitz.

3   K. Margry (1996) 'Das Konzentrationslager als Idylle', Fritz Bauer Institut, *Auschwitz Geschichte, Rezeption und Wirkung. Jahrbuch 1996 zur Geschichte und Wirkung des Holocaust*. Frankfurt and New York: Campus, 319–52.

4   K. Margry (1999) 'The First Theresienstadt Film (1942)', *Historical Journal of Film, Radio, and Television*, 19, 3, 309–37. Irena Dodalová (born 1900 Prague, died 1989 in Buenos Aires) and her husband Karel Dodal ran a small film production company in Prague, making animation films and short documentaries. After the Nazi invasion of Czechoslovakia her husband stayed in the US where he was on business; Dodalová remained in Prague, working as a theatre director. She was deported to Theresienstadt on 20 June 1942. On her time in Theresienstadt and the making of the film, see *The Black Book: The Nazi Crime Against the Jewish People*, New York: The Jewish Black Book Committee, 1946, 291–7. She was not involved in the making of the second film; at that time she directed plays for the Yiddish theatre. Dodalová was released from Theresienstadt on 5 February 1945 and reached the USA via Switzerland. In 1948 she and her husband emigrated to Argentina. There she made a success with the production of dance and ballet films.

5   Libretto and music of the opera were hidden and only later performed. The writer Hans Georg Adler, who was a survivor of Theresienstadt, rescued this and other works of Petr Kien, which included the lost film script.

6   Wytwórnia Filmów Dokumentalnych i Fabularnych, Warsaw, WFDiF no. FM–0633.

7   Hans Günther (born 1910 in Erfurt, died c.1945) joined the *Sturmabteilung* (SA, assault troops) in 1928 and the Nationalsozialistische Deutsche Arbeiter Partei (NSDAP, National Socialist German Workers' Party) in 1929. In 1937 he joined the Gestapo and the SS. An early appointee of Eichmann he was promoted *SS-Obersturmbannführer* and became in 1939 chief of the Prague-based 'Zentralamt zur Regelung der Judenfrage in Böhmen und Mähren'. He was closely involved in the organisation of the deportation of Czech Jews to Theresienstadt and Auschwitz. It is assumed he was killed trying to escape capture.

8   Karl Rahm (born 1907, Klosterneuenburg, died 1947) became in 1934 a member of the illegal Austrian NSDAP and joined after the 'Anschluss' in 1938 the SS. In 1939 he started working for Eichmann's 'Zentralstelle' in Vienna; in 1940 he became Hans Günther's second-in-command at the Zentralamt zur Regelung der Judenfrage in Böhmen und Mähren. In 1944 he became the last camp commandant of Theresienstadt. Captured at the end of the war he was tried by a Czech court and executed.

9   Quoted in G. E. Berkley (1968) *Hitler's Gift: The Story of Theresienstadt*. Boston: Branden Books, 178.

10   Berkeley 1986, 178–9.

11   Berkeley 1986, 183.

12   This information was given to the author by the late Mirek Dohnal, who at that time was a student of FAMU.

13   The Zentralfilm Gesellsächft Ost mbH., founded in November 1941, was a subsidiary of the NS State Film Monopoly, Ufa Film GmbH (UFI) – Cautio. It was in charge of the production of propaganda films in the occupied territories of Eastern Europe.

14   K. Margry (1992) 'Theresienstadt (1944–45): The Nazi Propaganda Film Depicting the Concentration Camp as Paradise', *Historical Journal of Film, Radio, and Television*, 12, 2, 145–62.

15   Details on the personalities shown in scenes 4, 10, 22, 32 and 33 can be found in E. Makarova, S. Makarov and V. Kuperman (2000) *University over the Abyss*. Jerusalem: Verba.

16   Primary sources for the reconstruction of the complete film are the existing film fragments, frame enlargements and stills. They have been supplemented with a set of continuity drawings made during the production of the film by the Dutch artist Jo Spier, now held by Rijks Instituut voor Orlogsdokumentatie, Amsterdam.

17   The fragments were restored in 1964/65 and reconstructed in their original continuity by the Czech Filmarchive, Prague in collaboration with the Bundesarchiv (German Federal Archives), Koblenz. The film was subsequently made available as historical document for study purposes; BA no. 3372. Since then other fragments have been discovered in the archives of Yad Vashem. They have been incorporated in viewing material of some 22 minutes in length. This version is available from the National Centre for Jewish Film, Brandeis University, Waltham, MA, USA.

9   Terezín: the town Hitler gave to the Jews

Zdenka Fantlova-Ehrlich

My life in pre-war Czechoslovakia was a happy, normal, idyllic family life with my parents, brother and sister. We took it for granted that it would stay like that, forever. But it was not to be. When on 15 March 1939 the German Army marched in and occupied our country, our lives turned upside-down in a very short time. The population was quickly divided into Jews and the rest. I was 17 at that time. As a Jewish student I was expelled from my secondary school following the introduction of new racial laws, already well established in Germany. My father was arrested and sentenced to twelve years imprisonment when a neighbour denounced him for listening to the BBC Czech broadcasts from London. The rest of the family was soon evicted from our home and transported to a newly-established camp in Terezín, not far from Prague. Space was at a premium. People were put wherever they could be squeezed, even into the shop windows in the main street onto three-tiered bunks. So they actually lived in the street, except behind glass.

Since Terezín was a transit camp, not a concentration or annihilation camp (except for the veterans and elites; see the preceding chapter by Lutz Becker), transports of Jewish people were constantly coming in – but also – and what everybody dreaded – transports of thousands of people were being sent out to the East. Nobody ever knew where these transports to the East went nor what happened to the people there. It was a secret that was strictly guarded by the Germans and the biggest threat hanging over our existence. We had no choice but to wait, if and when our turn should come. In the meantime the 'community' had to function and so all the available labour was organised so that the inmates were registered, fed and housed. We lived there with the hope that we would never be sent to the East but rather stay there until the end of the war. One gets conditioned to any situation, and for us young people it was easier to cope with than for the old and sick ones who were dying there at the rate of over one hundred a day.

Thus from the unlikely but supremely fertile soil of overcrowded Terezín, amidst hunger, fear and death – but also amid hope and a refusal to succumb to pain and humiliation – there arose an unprecedented theatrical and musical culture of the highest quality. There were a lot of professional artists in the camp – musicians, conductors, writers, actors, directors, set designers. You name it they were there in abundance, all brilliant people. Concerts were arranged and plays were performed on stages built in the attics.

At that time I became an active member of the Czech Theatre. The standard of the productions at that time – as I can judge it now – was extremely high and could pass as any West End performance. The theatre there was not entertainment. It was more: a burning torch of hope, something that lifted the morale and the spirit, not only of the people on stage but also of the people in the audience. For some, a cultural experience became more important than a ration of bread.

The performances were quite different in nature than commercial enterprises elsewhere. There were no stars, nobody was paid, there was no jealousy, no names in neon lights; everybody was equal, giving the best they could. In short, the theatre represented the true essence of pure art, unrepeatable in other times.

In the spring of 1944 rumours were starting to circulate that German filmmakers were to visit Terezín to see for themselves the 'Paradise Town' that the Führer 'had given to the Jews' and make a documentary film about it. The local command ordered a campaign of embellishment. The streets and squares that the film crew would be shooting had to be spruced up. Feverish preparations were initiated. None of us knew what to make of it, what to expect; we already had the experience that change was never for the better, always for the worse. There was never any official notification for anything, only rumours, but these always had an element of truth to them. When we heard that prior to the filming the town was to be spruced up, all we were concerned about was how it was going to affect us. At such times, when you are fighting for your life you cannot afford to view any situation from a wide perspective – historical or political – but only via the narrowest perspective, how it concerns you. Our biggest fear was to be included in one of the transports to the East.

And we did not have to wait long. Prior to the filming 7,000 people were immediately sent to the East, so that the ghetto should not appear overcrowded in the film.

Women and children sitting in front of their living quarters in Terezín's ghetto. WL 5649 (© The Wiener Library)

Inmate of Terezín's ghetto in the vegetable garden of the fortress. WL 5648 (© The Wiener Library)

Everybody trembled – would it be me? The shop windows were quickly cleared of their inhabitants who were also sent to the East. The windows were then decorated with goods stolen from the luggage of the new arrivals.

People were drafted to construct a café in the main square where selected inmates would be seen 'drinking coffee and eating cakes', while a jazz orchestra, the Ghetto Swingers, played for their pleasure. Fresh grass was ordered to be sown and flowering shrubs planted around the edge of the square. Benches were set up for people to sit and make lively conversation. Others would read books, listen to the music of the orchestra in a new pavilion and give the impression of normal, happy, idyllic life. New playgrounds with swings and other delights were laid out for the children. The facades of houses were given a fresh coat of whitewash and their windows fitted with curtains. A model group of pretty young girls were ordered to cross the square carrying rakes over their shoulders, singing a happy tune, as if finishing a day's gardening. Young inmates from the children's homes – they were taken away from their parents – were to be seen crowding around *Lagerkommandant* Rahm, the German officer in charge of Terezín. He would hand out tins of sardines while they recited well-rehearsed lines: 'Oh, not sardines again, Uncle Rahm!' Now a tin of sardines was not for eating. It was a currency, unbelievably high currency. You could buy anything with it, even negotiate your life.

The day before the crew of filmmakers were due, a squad of women were assembled with brooms, cloths and pails of water, who then knelt and scrubbed the pavement until they shone like mirrors. We were not allowed to walk on them that day. Then another scene was filmed to show a group of young people enjoying a swim in the nearby river. I was chosen to be one of them. I was young and a good swimmer. In the vicinity of Terezín, not right through the town itself but outside the ghetto walls, was the Ohre River. We had to be escorted to the river and swim across it. And back, obviously. What I cannot remember is what we wore for this exercise. I know we did not pack any swimsuits before we came to Terezín, but we did not swim naked, so perhaps we were just wearing some underwear. The scene was then shown as part of the natural, free and idyllic life we were enjoying in 'Paradise Terezín'.

While the filming was in progress none of the inmates were allowed anywhere in the vicinity of the action, only those inmates who were specially chosen and directly involved in the particular scene, like film extras.

The famous German actor Kurt Gerron, now himself a prisoner in Terezín, was ordered to help with the filming. The finished document of the life in this special ghetto would now prove to the world the authenticity of the 'Paradise Terezín'. After the filming finished and the crew left, more transports were immediately sent to the East. The children who had been given the tins of sardines were the first ones to go to Auschwitz, to end their lives in the gas chambers. The fate of Kurt Gerron, a live witness to the filming, was promptly sealed when he was sent to Auschwitz where, as we learned after the war, he perished in the gas chambers.[1]

For the rest of us who had survived in Terezín for two-and-a-half years, finally the call came and we were transported to the East on 16 October 1944. This transport included all the performing artists who had created the musical and theatrical life of Terezín. Our performances were not illegal; on the contrary, the Germans encouraged them and then used them for their propaganda. We did not know then that we were sentenced to death, so we carried on and danced under the gallows. Until the last.

After Terezín, my life was teetering on the edge of death, almost daily. First the survival of Auschwitz, then the death march to Gross Rosen, the deadly transfer to Mauthausen and finally Bergen-Belsen. There, closest to death, my life was saved miraculously by the compassion and humanity of an unknown member of the liberating British Army. It was he who stretched out his hand over the abyss and pulled me back to life. I could never find out who he was and could not even thank him. But I shall forever be grateful to this country that sent him.

The end of the war also meant the end of the entire family. My mother went to the gas chambers on arrival in Auschwitz. My father died on a death march. My brother was shot dead while trying to escape from a notorious hard-labour camp. My sister died of typhus a week before the liberation of Bergen-Belsen. I was left alone as the sole survivor of the entire family, trying to find an answer to the question: what was the purpose of all this?

Note

1   Kurt Gerron (born in Berlin on 11 May 1897 – died in Auschwitz on 28 October 1944). Gerron appeared
     in over 50 films of the 1920s and 1930s including: *Der blaue Engel* (*The Blue Angel*, 1930) directed by
     Joseph Von Sternberg and *Die Drei von der Tankstelle* (*The Three from the Filling Station*, 1930), directed
     by Wilhelm Thiele. He also directed around 20 films.

10 The Ministry of Information and anti-Fascist short films of the Second World War

Matthew Lee

This chapter examines four anti-Nazi short films produced during the Second World War: *Lift Your Head, Comrade* (1942); *These are the Men* (1943); *Calling Mr Smith* (1943); and *Man – One Family* (1946). All of these films are united by their desire to either repudiate the ideology of Nazism, expose the atrocities committed in its name or attack its key proponents.

To begin, I shall summarise the nature, history and context of the British Ministry of Information (MOI) and its Films Division. Three of the above four productions can broadly be designated as 'official films' of the Second World War. That is, they were either sponsored, commissioned or distributed by the MOI and were released domestically, in neutral and Allied territories, and after hostilities had ended, in liberated countries. *Calling Mr Smith* is somewhat different as it was sponsored by the London-based Polish Ministry of Information and Documentation. However, it has been included here as it is not only an example of an overtly anti-fascist short film that was made on the margins of the official system (filling a discernible gap in the MOI's output in this area), but it also provides an opportunity to examine the film's vastly contrasting approach to its subject matter.

The MOI had a faltering start at the beginning of the war: its system of production was overly bureaucratic, the chain of command lacked co-ordination, unhelpful personality clashes developed, the press were less than enthusiastic, and distribution problems limited the number of screenings. It was this initial malaise that earned the MOI the monikers – the 'Ministry of Muddle' and the 'Ministry for Dis-Information'.[1] The Films Division came under particularly fierce attack and was criticised on a number of fronts: for fighting the last war, poor planning, amateurishness, and not fully taking advantage of the development of sound.[2] This led to two-thirds of MOI films being withdrawn in the first six months of the war. These weekly 'five-minuters' as they were commonly referred to were felt by a number of people to be too short for propaganda purposes. It was not until 1942, when a shortfall in film stock (and concern from the cinema exhibitors that the brevity of the films meant they could easily be omitted from the programme)[3] led to 'five-minuters' giving way to longer, once-monthly films, usually around the 15-minute mark.

After a number of changes in senior personnel in the Films Division (which included, in 1940, the influential appointment of Jack Beddington who had previously headed the Shell publicity department and had effectively utilised its Film Unit), a new non-theatrical Distribution Department was set-up – in the classic spirit of John Grierson.

Customised vans were soon touring the country with a portable projector, screen and 35mm films. These mobile units were able to reach venues and communities previously beyond the reach of the MOI's theatrical distribution network: canteens, institutes, factories, church halls and so on. That said, the majority of the British public would still be far more likely to come into contact with MOI shorts at their local cinema (shorts were screened before the main feature as a result of an agreement brokered between the Ministry and the Cinematograph Exhibitors' Association). By the end of the war the MOI had approved nearly 2000 short films for release and around 400 features.

Whilst *Lift Your Head, Comrade*, *These are the Men*, *Man – One Family* and *Calling Mr Smith* were not the only MOI films made during the war that were avowedly anti-fascist, the number of similarly-themed productions is relatively small. This is surprising as one of the principal aims of the Films Division was to dramatise the national case both home and abroad – thus one would think that exposing and decrying the horrors of the Third Reich would have been a subject that would have commanded considerably more attention. That is not to say that other films did not touch on the issue (*The Silent Village* (1943) was Humphrey Jennings' affecting, geographically-displaced tribute to the victims of Lidice who had been killed or sent to concentration camps as a reprisal for the assassination of Reinhard Heydrich), but very few other titles examined Jewish persecution or dealt with atrocities in any depth. Clive Coultass contends that this reticence was the result of 'a certain caution following the admitted excesses of First World War propaganda, and there was indeed a general reluctance to come to terms in official films with the precepts and effects of Nazi ideology'.[4]

Lift Your Head, Comrade

Lift Your Head, Comrade (the title's inspiration derives from a song sung by an Austrian concentration camp prisoner who was killed by the SS) was one of the first 15-minute MOI productions and provided cinema audiences of 1942 with an introduction to one of the 15 Alien Companies of the Pioneer Corps in the British Army. The film was directed by Michael Hankinson and scripted by the Hungarian-born British novelist, journalist and critic Arthur Koestler (author of *Darkness at Noon* (1940) and *Scum of the Earth* (1941)) who had recently joined the MOI. His background made him a particularly suitable scriptwriter for the film as he too had been detained in Pentonville prison and had served in the Pioneer Corps after fleeing from France.

Lift Your Head, Comrade introduces us to a band of German and Austrian anti-fascists who, by various and sometimes ingenious means, had escaped from Hitler's tyrannical regime. Although we are told that collectively the soldiers have served over 125 years in prisons and camps between them, and their number includes men from many walks of life – craftsmen, barristers, miners, doctors and so on, the film is keen to stress that they are all united in their desire to fight against Hitler, even if it means facing torture and certain death if captured.

One particularly well-handled scene focuses on Bobby Spooner's torture at Dachau. Before the war he was the amateur bantamweight champion of Europe but after being tortured in the camp, he was not able to box again. With the help of Sergeant Baer, an Austrian doctor who was with him at Dachau, they reconstruct how he and countless others were abused. Whilst this is the only graphic retelling of the suffering inflicted on former prisoners in the film, Koestler, in a sound interview with the Imperial War Museum in 1981, recalled that he was originally going to include additional stories of abuse in *Lift Your Head, Comrade* but these were left out of the final cut as the producers convinced him that 'the public wasn't prepared to accept the concentration camps at that time'. Koestler felt that this had ultimately 'castrated the film'.[5]

Although the film's most powerful scene stresses Nazi brutality, *Lift Your Head, Comrade* also successfully conveys the Pioneer Corps' sense of optimism, industry and the loyalty of its men. The soldiers may look a little awkward under the camera's gaze, but it is their earnestness and enthusiasm that give the film its emotional depth. Unfortunately, the same cannot be said for the hectoring and clichéd performances of the British Officer and NCO who introduce the troops. As a result, *Lift Your Head, Comrade* is at its most engaging and persuasive when the anti-fascist recruits are allowed to tell their own stories.

Critical opinion at the time was divided. The *Motion Picture Herald* felt it was 'a vivid human document, with flashes of humour, not without its faults, but doing what it sets to do with competence and wit'.[6] Whilst the reviewer in the *Documentary News Letter* compared the Major's role to 'between that of a circus ringmaster and a Victorian head of a reformatory'.[7]

Writing for the *New York Times* after the film had been released and after a stint of lecturing to troops about the consequences of totalitarianism, Koestler was sceptical about the value of atrocity propaganda:

> For the common people of Britain, the Gestapo and concentration camps have approximately the same degree of reality as the monster of Loch Ness. Atrocity propaganda is helpless against this healthy lack of imagination. I have tried my hand at it. Whenever I have lectured to the troops on fascist concentration camps I have had the distinct feeling that as long as I had a grip on the audience they believed me, but then as soon as I had gone they did not believe me any more than one believes in yesterday's nightmare and starts happily to sing 'Who's Afraid of the Big Bad Wolf?'[8]

These are the Men

Unlike *Lift Your Head, Comrade*, which is rather conventional in style and tone, *These are the Men* is an altogether more daring, technically accomplished and imaginative production. It was devised and compiled by Alan Osbiston and Dylan Thomas from an idea by Robert Neumann in 1943.

Thomas' passion for the cinema and his contribution to documentary film during the Second World War is not widely known, but whilst contracted to Strand Films he scripted over 10 shorts. As you might expect from a man of Thomas' political leanings and poetic talent, the film has empathy for 'the makers, the workers, the farmers, the sailors, the tailors...'[9] and its language is both lyrical and emotive (this contrasts with the often stilted and starchy scripts of many other MOI films).

Like a number of shorts from the time, *These are the Men* appropriates footage from Leni Riefenstahl's *Triumph of the Will* (1935). Film directors and newsreel editors often interpolated sequences of senior Nazis and most regular cinema-goers would be well-acquainted with the images and characters on display. For example, in 1941 *Germany*

Calling (aka *Panzer Ballet* and *Lambeth Walk*) similarly employed sequences from *Triumph of the Will* and deftly edited them to the tune of 'The Lambeth Walk'. Interestingly, *Germany Calling* was also an 'official' production, but the MOI deliberately chose to distribute the film through newsreels, masking its 'official' origins.

The structure and editing of *These are the Men*, with its often repetitive and carefully calibrated use of German propaganda, cleverly undermines the original filmmakers' intent. This includes the fastidiously composed, iconic and insidiously seductive imagery of Riefenstahl's *Triumph of the Will*, which has been adroitly subverted in a manner that newsreels often failed to do. When this is combined with Dylan's faux-confessional commentary, which has the likes of Hitler, Hess, Goering and Goebbels seemingly laying bare their personal inadequacies, stressing their hypocrisy and voicing their antisemitism, the film is at its most scathingly satirical. Goebbels, for example, mouths the following autobiography:

> 'After Heidelberg University, I became a writer of plays, a poet, a journalist. None of my work was accepted. And this was because the editors and publishers were Jews. Unemployed, Jew-hating, crippled, frustrated and bitter, I joined the Nazi Party...'[10]

The melding of Osbiston's editorial dexterity and Thomas' vituperative script have produced a film of dark, blunt and astringent humour that powerfully denounces the Nazi leadership. Although the reaction to the film at the time was mixed, the *Documentary*

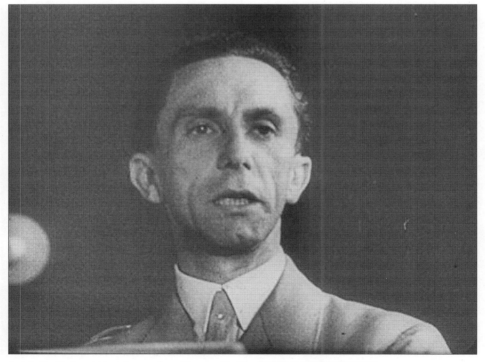

Joseph Goebbels – mid-sentence – from *These are the Men* (1943). FLM 3729 (© IWM)

News Letter rated its propaganda value as 'excellent', but felt that the pitch of the narrator's voice had the 'suspicion of hysteria' and remarked that: 'Most ordinary people have no intention of forgiving Hitler, Hess, etc, and they will be somewhat bewildered to find the government regarding it as a matter worth announcing so excitedly.'[11] A reviewer of *These are the Men* in the *Motion Picture Herald* felt the picture had been 'muffed' and would not travel well over the Atlantic: 'The messages are too obscure for American audiences, not as politically erudite as those of an England close to the Continent and long at total war.'[12]

This critical perspective from the United States is instructive as it goes some way to highlight the difficulties of making films for domestic and international audiences (it was often the case that films would have to be re-cut or renamed when they were exhibited overseas). A pointed but understandable criticism of the film came from Edgar Anstey (a producer and director of MOI shorts himself) who liked the film, but felt it should have been made earlier: 'Before the war was the time when propagandists needed freedom to expose the Nazi leaders. It is of little consolation to hear that the government is now in agreement with the man in the street.'[13]

Calling Mr Smith

Calling Mr Smith was made by the husband-and-wife team of Stefan and Franciszka Themerson in conjunction with the Polish Film Unit and the production company Concanen. During the 1930s the Themersons were key figures in the Polish avant-garde. Not only did they make experimental films and publish a periodical entitled *f.a. – the artistic film*, they also founded one of the first filmmakers' co-operatives – 'S.A.F.', in Warsaw, 1935.

The Themersons had moved to Paris a year before the outbreak of the Second World War. They subsequently found their separate ways to London; Franciszka in 1940, Stefan in 1942. Franciszka was working as a cartographer for the Polish Ministry of Information and Documentation, and Stefan was soon seconded to join the Polish Film Unit. *Calling Mr Smith* was the first film they made in England, and in keeping with their earlier work, the Themersons assumed control of all key elements of the film's production: shooting, editing and direction.

The film's central aims were to expose the 'New German Order' that had enveloped Poland and other occupied countries, and to lament the loss of Europe's cultural heritage under the Third Reich. That said, *Calling Mr Smith* is far from being a tedious work of didacticism in the early MOI mould; its humour is often sardonic (at one stage Hitler is referred to the as the 'Leonardo de Vinci of German art'), it is impassioned but not overbearing, and it boldly attempts to re-conceptualise traditional modes of film propaganda.

The Themersons' film contrasted with its MOI stable-mates in a number of ways: firstly, it was one of only a handful of colour shorts (Dufaycolor); secondly, it was shot almost entirely in their London flat; and thirdly, *Calling Mr Smith* owes a creative debt to the Dadaist movement. Although the film's structure is fragmented and the juxtaposition of archive film, photomontage, double-exposure, animation, photograms, colour filters and solarised images clashes with the conventional presentation of film propaganda, its experimental form in no way dilutes its strident anti-Nazi message.

Calling Mr Smith also experiments with sound – the acoustic distortion of the Nazi hymn, the 'Horst Wessel Lied', that accompanies images of Nazi pageantry is used to evoke the warping of German ideals. The opening strains of Bach are used to stress the betrayal of Germany's proud musical heritage. And finally, compositions by Karol Szymanowski and Chopin not only complement the mournful tone of the film but also remind audiences that the music of these composers was banned in their native Poland.

The Themersons' film is much more than a collage of eye-catching effects and classical music. It is also a self-reflexive work, drawing attention to its own means of enunciation and to the relationship between film and its audience. The clearest example of this interest occurs when it appears that the film has become entangled in the projector gate and the 35mm stock spools across the screen and languishes helplessly before our eyes. At the same time, the eponymous 'Mr Smith' (the archetypal Englishman) protests that he is 'fed up to the teeth with all this horror stuff'. This Brechtian contrivance reveals more than just the inner-workings of cinema projection: the medium of film, the role of propaganda and the nature of spectatorship are questioned and challenged from within.

An experimental sequence from *Calling Mr Smith* (1943). FLM 3731 (© IWM)

The shot from *Calling Mr Smith* that the British Board of Film Censors took exception to. FLM 3716 (© IWM)

The film's candid account of the suffering of the Polish people, which includes an accompanying pan over a chapter in *The New German Order in Poland* headed 'The Persecution of the Jews and the Ghettos', is unusually explicit for a short of this period. However, it was an uncompromising image of a woman hanging from a gallows that brought the film into conflict with the British Board of Film Censors (BBFC). According to the BBFC report received by the Themersons, dated 25 January 1944, an 'exception' to the aforementioned image was raised (although the BBFC referred to it as a 'man hanging on gallows') and this usually meant that the offending frames would have to be cut before the film was released with the 'U' certificate (more suitable for children) that was generally granted to shorts.[14] However, according to the entry in the BBFC ledger, dated 2 February 1944, the film was passed with 'no cuts made' and given an 'A' certificate (more suitable for adults). The earlier exception was 'waived' by the BBFC (possibly after discussions with the Polish Ministry of Information) in order for the film to receive a certificate without being censored. As the Themersons maintained after the war that the censor had suppressed the film, it is not clear if they were informed of the BBFC's later decision. If the MOI tried to stifle the distribution of the film, it has not been possible to find evidence to corroborate this theory.

The confusion surrounding *Calling Mr Smith*'s certification and distribution meant that it was not available for public viewing. Fortunately, two preview screenings were arranged towards the end of 1943. Unsurprisingly, the critical reception was mixed: '*Calling Mr Smith* is a somewhat confused indictment of German barbarism in perfectly horrible attempts at colour,'[15] and yet an unnamed reviewer writing in *The Tablet* praised the film for both its style and content, reporting that it was: 'full of ingenuity and technical skill [and] ambitious because it boldly tackles not only the atrocities of the German attempt to destroy Polish national life, but the reluctance of the ordinary film-goer, who wants to enjoy himself at the pictures, to be confronted with horrors.'[16]

It is regrettable that this idiosyncratic film was not able to reach the British public at the time of its release. Its robust, daring and poignant treatment of Nazi occupation and its innovative, visually arresting approach would have made it an extraordinary experience for cinema-goers of the 1940s.

Man – One Family

Man – One Family was scripted and directed by Ivor Montagu in 1945/46. This 16-minute production was the first real attempt by the MOI to debunk Nazi and, to a lesser extent, Japanese master-race theories. A number of German propaganda films such as *Erbkrank* (1936) had powerfully encapsulated Nazi beliefs on race and the need for Aryan purity, and later films such as *Der ewige Jude* (*The Eternal Jew*, 1940) were produced to reinforce the lies promulgated by the Reich Ministry of Propaganda and Public Enlightenment. In *Man – One Family*, Professor J. B. S. Haldane and Dr Julian Huxley, two well-known popularisers of science from the period, acted as script advisers to Montagu. It was this trio that provided the overdue scientific rebuttal to the theory of Aryan superiority.

The film uses animation, newsreel footage, a questioning everyman (reminiscent of *Calling Mr Smith*) and even a biblical re-enactment to deconstruct and refute the notions of 'superior' and 'inferior' races. The straightforward presentations, easy to follow arguments and lucid commentary made it popular with the critics. The *Monthly Film Bulletin* considered it 'a clear exposition of the fallacies of Hitler's racial theory', adding that the film 'cannot fail to make an impression upon every type of audience.'[17] The *Documentary News Letter* was also appreciative: 'It is a shrewd, hard-hitting, very popular-styled anti-fascist essay.'[18]

The praise for the film in the press is perhaps surprising, as correspondence between Huxley and Sidney Bernstein (head of the Granada Group and honorary advisor to the MOI) highlights the former's initial misgivings about Ivor Montagu's script: 'I must confess that when I first saw the proposed script, I didn't like it very much, and also wondered whether it would really make a satisfactory film.'[19] However, after viewing *Man – One Family*, he was impressed: 'In its final form, the film seems to me to be very successful, in putting across to the layman in dramatic but scientifically correct ways, the essence of the Nazi race-theory, and its scientific and factual baselessness.'[20]

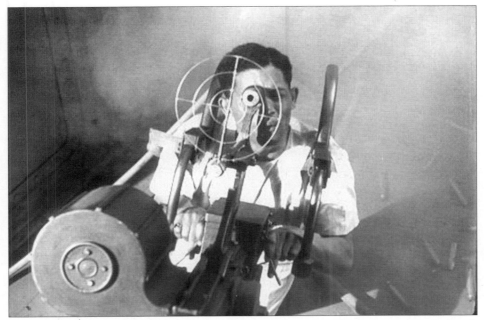

A reconstruction of Doris (Dorie) Miller's heroics on the USS West Virginia when the Japanese attacked Pearl Harbour on 7 December 1941, from *Man – One Family* (1945/46). FLM 3728 (© IWM)

After the war the film was shown non-theatrically in the UK and also in liberated countries, but when it was mooted that the film should be shown in Germany and Austria the script was closely scrutinised by G. R. Halkett of the Films Section, Political Intelligence Department of the Foreign Office. He felt that *Man – One Family* would not be well-received by German audiences, as it would be like 'Goebbels in reverse'.[21] He suggested many alterations to make it more factual in tone and less of a 'Propaganda film, with a capital P'.[22] His numerous recommendations included cutting some of the cartoons (featuring clumsy Welsh, Scottish and English stereotypes) and altering the curious biblical prologue.

Finally, it is notable that in a film that attempts to stress racial equality, highlighting as it does the bravery of Dorie Miller, the issue of segregation in the United States is ignored.

Conclusion

Although the BBFC had lifted its pre-war policy of attempting to suppress anti-Nazi films and sentiments ('the cinemagoing public in England seek amusement, not political guidance from the screen')[23] the amount of MOI shorts that dealt with atrocities or Jewish persecution from 1942 onwards were disproportionately small. This can be attributed to a number of factors. An MOI memorandum stated that, 'sheer "horror" stuff such as concentration camp torture stories … repel the normal mind' and 'horror' coverage, 'must be used very sparingly and must deal always with treatment of indisputably innocent people. Not with violent political opponents. And not with Jews.'[24]

Another justification for the paucity of anti-fascist film was that the British public would not believe that Germans were responsible for such acts. However, it was the very lack of newsreels and shorts that tackled this subject that contributed to a widespread level of disbelief. This was borne out by a Mass-Observation questionnaire that found on 1 December 1944 only 37 per cent of people believed the atrocity stories surrounding the Nazi regime were true, but by 18 April 1945 (after much press and newsreel coverage of the liberation of the camps), the number had risen to 81 per cent.[25]

It was also suggested that repeated press coverage of Nazi persecution of European Jewry might actually increase incidents of antisemitism in the United Kingdom. It is true that when a number of anti-fascist feature films such as *Pastor Hall* (1940), *The Great Dictator* (1940) and *Mr Emmanuel* (1944) were released, 'scenes of persecution, especially of Jews, were not always greeted with enthusiasm by the audience',[26] but later, when newsreel footage of the concentration camps was screened, the fires of British antisemitism were not fanned, even though the material was far more graphic than anything that had been seen before.

Notes

1   See J. Chapman (1998) *The British at War: Cinema, State and Propaganda, 1939–1945*. London: I. B. Tauris, 13.

2   For a more comprehensive review of the difficulties that beset the Ministry of Information and particularly the Films Division see F. Thorpe and N. Pronay (1980) *British Official Films in the Second World War: A Descriptive Catalogue*. Oxford: Clio Press, 14–40 and C. Coultass (1989) 'The Ministry of Information and documentary film, 1939–45', *Imperial War Museum Review*, 4, 103–11.

3   The *Documentary News Letter*, 3, 5, May 1942, noted that reports had been received that some cinemas were dropping the five-minute short from their last performance.

4   C. Coultass (1989) *Images for Battle: British Film and the Second World War, 1939–1945*. London: Associated University Press, 134.

5   IWM Sound Archive: 5393–03 Arthur Koestler Transcript, 30 November 1981, 13.

6   *Motion Picture Herald*, 150, 2 January, 1943, 1.

7   *Documentary News Letter*, 4, 3, March 1943, 195–6.

8   A. Koestler (1943) 'A Challenge to "Knights in Rusty Armor"', 14 February, *New York Times*. On-line. Available at http://partners.nytimes.com/books/00/01/02/specials/koestler-challenge.html

9   Quoted in J. Ackerman (ed.) (1995) *Dylan Thomas: The Film Scripts*. London: J. M. Dent, 40.

10 Ibid., 42.

11 *Documentary News Letter*, 4, 3, March 1943, 195–6.

12 *Motion Picture Herald*, 150, 1, 2 January 1943, 1.

13 E. Anstey (1943) 'These are the Men', *The Spectator*, 9 April, 338.

14 The BBFC report for *Calling Mr Smith* is held at the Themerson Archive, London; www.themersonarchive.com

15 P. Tabori (1943) *Daily Mail*, 15 October, 2.

16 *The Tablet*, 9 October 1943, 178.

17 *Monthly Film Bulletin*, 13, 152, 31 August 1946, 119.

18 *Documentary News Letter*, 6, 2, March/April 1946, 24.

19 IWM DOCS: 'The Sidney Bernstein Collection' 65/17/1–12: Julian Huxley's letter to Sidney Bernstein, 27

September 1945.

20 Ibid.

21 IWM DOCS: 'The Sidney Bernstein Collection' 65/17/1–12: G R Halkett's letter to Sidney Cole, 21 September 1945.

22 IWM DOCS: 'The Sidney Bernstein Collection' 65/17/1–12: G. R. Halkett's suggested alterations to *Man – One Family*. Undated.

23 Quote from the report of Colonel J. C. Hanna (the BBFC's senior script examiner throughout the 1930s) on the *March of Time* film *Inside Nazi Germany*, in J. Richards (1982) 'British Board of Film Censors and Content Control in the 1930s: Foreign Affairs', *Historical Journal of Film, Radio and Television*, 2, 1, 40.

24 The National Archives, INF 1/251 (2/2) HPC Executive Sub-Committee: 1940–42, Memorandum, 25 July 1941.

25 Mass-Observation Archive, FR 2228, 'Pre-Peace Questionnaire', 18 April 1945.

26 T. Kushner (1989) *The Persistence of Prejudice: Antisemitism in British Society During the Second World War*. Manchester: Manchester University Press, 130.

11 Fighting the government with its own propaganda: the struggle for racial equality in the USA during the Second World War

Stephen Tuck

Frank Capra's *The Negro Soldier* (1944) was commissioned by the United States War Department, Office of War Information (OWI) in 1943. Ostensibly, the film 'aimed to convey to Negro soldiers a realisation of their stake in democracy – and, more particularly, an enthusiasm for their part in the war'.[1] Of course, the very fact that the OWI felt compelled to produce a special film for black soldiers was a reminder of the extent of America's race problem during the twentieth century. In reality, *The Negro Soldier* was produced because the War Department had become increasingly aware that many real-life 'Negro soldiers' did not believe that the Second World War was their war, and that some were in violent revolt.

What the War Department had not intended, however, was for *The Negro Soldier* to become a weapon used by black activists in their campaign for racial change during the turmoil of the war years. By painting an extremely positive image of both black citizens and black troops, *The Negro Soldier* challenged assumptions of black cultural inferiority and by implication the moral legitimacy of segregation in the army and the American South. Moreover, by the end of 1945, the film had been shown to all soldiers, both black and white, and a shortened version of the film had been screened in some 5,000 commercial theatres around the country. The propaganda aimed at 'Negro soldiers' was instead used as propaganda by black Americans to force military leaders to integrate 'Negro soldiers' fully into the army.

The Negro Soldier was shot as part of Capra's *Why We Fight* series, a series that combined military efforts to bolster the war effort with Hollywood expertise. For America's one million black soldiers, however, it was clear that a specialised and sensitive form of indoctrination was required. In one OWI poll, only a narrow majority of black residents in Harlem believed that beating Germany and Japan took priority over making democracy work at home. The efforts of a coloured nation, Japan, against the white imperialist allies held particular appeal. One black soldier told an interviewer, 'I ain't fixin' to fight no Japanese. These Japanese fighting for me. I'm gonna fight myself some crackers' [cracker – southern white supremacist].[2]

On the face of it, the 43-minute film itself did not appear particularly radical. On army instructions, *The Negro Soldier* avoided the highly sensitive and embarrassing subjects of slavery and segregation. Nor did it refer to black agitators or grievances. The *New York Times* review of the film thought 'it very discreetly avoids the more realistic race problems which are generally recognised today. It definitely sugarcoats an issue which is broader than the Negro's part in the war.'[3]

Instead, the film was set in a neutral venue, a black church, and tackled seemingly uncontroversial themes – the role of black Americans in establishing democracy and the importance of liberty triumphing over the evil of fascism. Through the measured narration of the church's pastor, *The Negro Soldier* traces the history of warfare in America, highlighting the heroic role of black Americans, from the Boston Massacre to the First World War. The opportunities for blacks in democracy are also made manifest, as the preacher celebrates various black high achievers and (segregated) educational institutions. The preacher also impresses upon a slightly shocked congregation the extreme racism of the Axis powers, contrasting it with the freedom (particularly of religion) available to black Americans. The film then follows the progress of two black recruits in the army (one the son of a lady in the congregation). By following their swift and trouble-free progress to the rank of officer in the infantry, *The Negro Soldier* extols the opportunities for black soldiers in the army, implying that racial advancement was inextricably linked with true patriotism. As with many war films, *The Negro Soldier* also paints an idyllic view of army life with plenty of baseball, girls, church, guns and fun exercises on the assault course.

In the context of black aspirations and racial unrest across America, however, it was impossible for a widely-shown film celebrating black achievement to have anything less than a significant effect on American race relations. The background of the race problem and racial division in America underlined the difficulty of uniting black and white troops in the war effort. Indeed, the Second World War itself vividly exposed the underlying problems of racism and racial discrimination. For example, during the war a group of American soldiers were ordered to transport some German prisoners-of-war across Mississippi, and they stopped at a restaurant for lunch. True to Southern custom, the Nazi prisoners, who were white, were allowed to sit in the restaurant but the American soldiers, who were black, were forced to sit out in the backyard and wait to be served a basic meal. On army bases especially, problems abounded. In 1943 the War Department reported that there was 'general unrest' and even a danger of outright revolt among America's black troops.

America's war aims exacerbated grievances among black Americans. The Second World War was justified as an attempt to export democracy, oppose oppression and defeat a racist demagogue. The problem was, of course, that America had a sham democracy, experienced racial oppression and had plenty of racist demagogues of its own. Although Americans held up the Bill of Rights as an example to the world, the men who were created equal did not include black men. It was well-known that Thomas Jefferson had owned slaves. The US creed of democracy – government of the people, by the people, for the people – was simply not true in America's southern states during the 1940s, which had in place the 'Jim Crow' system of racial segregation. In practice, segregation meant harsh discrimination and at times violent oppression. Over 3,000 black Southerners were lynched during the first half of the twentieth century, and southern policeman and politicians were often members of the Ku Klux Klan. Black New York Senator Adam Clayton Powell Jr commented that the lack of enthusiasm of black Americans for the War was, 'not because we don't recognise the monster Hitler ... We recognised him immediately, because he is like minor Hitlers here.'[4]

However, if the issues at stake during the Second World War underscored racial grievances, the war also prompted a heightened challenge to Jim Crow by black Americans. Across the country black Americans used the V for Victory symbol to launch a Double-V campaign for the victory of democracy abroad and at home. The National Association for the Advancement of Colored People (NAACP) flourished, as membership increased from less than 50,000 members to almost half a million in the years 1940–46, with a third of the members from the South. At a local level, it was often black soldiers who led the way in racial protest. In Savannah, Georgia, in 1943, a black soldier from a nearby base intervened in what he considered an unfair arrest of a local black woman. The soldier then vigorously defended himself by seizing the onrushing policeman's baton and, according to witnesses, 'beat him to a pulp'. The struggle escalated as both the policeman and the soldier were joined by colleagues. By the evening, in a quite remarkable city scene, a large detachment of black soldiers, armed with guns mounted on trucks, confronted the full quota of Savannah's riot policemen. After the war, many black veterans 'returned fighting'. As one Colonel from Alabama remarked, 'I spent four years in the Army to free a bunch of Dutchmen and Frenchmen, and I'm hanged if I'm going to let the Alabama version of the Germans kick me around when I get home. No sirree-bob! I went into the Army a nigger; I'm coming out a man.'[5] The war had an impact on mainstream white opinion too. Although most white Americans had traditionally accepted the idea of a racial hierarchy, with whites at the head of the racial order, the Second World War led to an outcry against racial domination. As various contemporaries put it, 'Hitler gave racism a bad name'.

Black activists also used the war to force the first, albeit gradual, changes in the portrayal of blacks in Hollywood. Famously, NAACP leader Walter White toured some of the studios in 1942. The 'restriction of Negroes to roles with rolling eyes, chattering teeth, always scared of ghosts, or to portrayals of none-too-bright servants,' White argued in one speech to seventy top executives of the screen, 'perpetuates a stereotype which is doing the Negro infinite harm.'[6] As with much black protest of this period, however, some of the most effective pressure for change came at the local and state level. For example, across the South black leaders lambasted the release of *Gone with the Wind* in 1939 for its disingenuous depiction of harmonious race relations in antebellum days. In his Emancipation address shortly after the film's premiere at Fox's theatre in Atlanta, local NAACP leader T. M. Alexander scoffed at the 'recent premiere when we went mad with the wind.'

For all the efforts of the NAACP and local activists, however, only minimal progress was made in changing the image of blacks in Hollywood before the Second World War, just as only minimal gains were made for black Americans nationwide. Leon Washington, editor of the *Los Angeles Sentinel* and an outspoken critic of Hollywood's negative stereotyping of black characters, commented in 1942: 'Hollywood is the most vicious race-baiting, propaganda-disseminating agency in America … every theatregoer is acquainted with the Hollywood version of the Negro as shiftless, carefree, crapshooting, boisterous, gin-drinking, ante-bellum, clowning Uncle Toms and Aunt Dinahs.'[7]

It was this context of 'Jim Crow' segregation, changing public opinion, simmering racial resentment and heightened black aspirations and activism that explains the impact of *The Negro Soldier* on American race relations and the role of blacks in the army. The film's far-reaching impact was certainly nothing to do with the aims of the OWI.

Formed in 1942, the OWI's solution to the race problem was not to change the rights of black Americans but to use propaganda to change their views. For example, *The Negro Soldier* noted that during the Second World War there were three times as many serving black officers as during the First World War – an accurate statistic but hardly an impressive one given the paucity of officers during the First World War. In any case, even the OWI's limited attempts to change black opinion and avoid unduly-negative portrayals of black Americans proved singularly ineffective. In 1942, the OWI published 2.5 million copies of Chandler Owen's pamphlet *Negroes and the War*, contrasting the progress of black Americans with the record of fascism. But as one black soldier commented, it was clearly 'just a bunch of baloney'. Although the OWI set up a branch in Hollywood, a Columbia University study in 1945 found that of 100 black appearances in wartime films, only 12 were positive.

Yet the consequence of *The Negro Soldier* was a widespread publicity coup for black Americans and the army was integrated four years later – almost entirely due to the production and distribution of the film. Capra was the designated producer, but he was not involved in the production at all, leaving it ultimately to his so-called 'negro consultant' Carlton Moss, who wrote the script. Nonetheless it suited the government to have Capra's name attached to the film, and when it was clear it was going to be successful it certainly suited Capra to take the credit. As Moss reflected, somewhat ruefully, 'when the praise started coming in, he lapped it up.'[8]

The director, Carlton Moss, also played the role of the Negro Preacher who tells his congregation that the fascists are racist but the American Negro Soldier has great opportunity. FLM 3718 (© IWM)

Soldiers at a poetry reading; by representing the Negro Soldier as respectable and cultured, the movie served to counter the negative stereotype of African Americans. FLM 3717 (© IWM)

It was Moss who proved to be the key to the film's propaganda value on behalf of black soldiers. Moss was chosen, primarily, because he had already been involved in federal programmes and was well-known in government circles as a loyal, patriotic black director. Moss had been drama director of the Harlem YMCA in 1934 and subsequently one of the chief black consultants to the New Deal's Federal Theater Program. Far from being an apologist for the federal government, however, Moss believed that the way to remedy black disgruntlement was not through propaganda but by concerted action to remedy grievances. He also brought to the project a strong conviction that to destroy the negative stereotyping of black Americans would undermine the foundations of Jim Crow segregation that was predicated on the belief of black racial inferiority. As Moss told the press in 1944, the film was designed to 'ignore what's wrong with the Army and tell what's right with my people'.[9] Moss himself told 'what's right with my people' by playing the role of the preacher who narrates the involvement of black Americans in the history of American warfare. In addition, by following the progress of two diligent, clean-cut, civil, well-read young black recruits, *The Negro Soldier* countered the prevailing stereotype of young black men as lazy, unhygienic, lascivious and ignorant that was portrayed so powerfully in D. W. Griffith's *The Birth of a Nation* (1915).

In the context of race relations in the army and in America, telling what 'was right with my people' had immediate racial implications. By painting a positive view of black Americans, Moss felt sure that whites would have to ask, 'what right [do we have] to hold back people of that calibre?' The Army's own Research Branch poll showed that 67 per cent of white soldiers had a highly favourable reaction to the film, and that 90 per cent of black soldiers and 80 per cent of white soldiers thought that the film should be shown to rookies of both races.

But the key to the impact of the film was not simply its production but its distribution and publicity. Although army officials were worried about a negative reaction to the film's support of racial tolerance, the increasing unrest among black soldiers meant that officials were even more concerned that the film would be acceptable to black opinion makers. Consequently army leaders screened the first draft to 200 black journalists at the Army's public relations office in New York in January 1944. They need not have worried. Black leaders and organisations acclaimed *The Negro Soldier* as a success. Unbeknown to the Army, Moss had already shown the film to black leaders in Harlem to prepare the black community for the opportunity presented by the film. At this point black leaders seized the opportunity to put pressure on the War Department to show it widely. In a sense the army was caught in a trap. The War Department's initial intention had been to show *The Negro Soldier* only to its own black troops, but it was made compulsory viewing for soldiers of both races and was put on general release.

Black activists recognised that the film had its limitations. Walter White commented to colleagues that the film 'does not tell the truth' about the plight of black soldiers, but the key was that 'it is significant and a mark of progress that the War Department has gone as far as it has'.[10] Therefore black opinion-makers led the way in securing its wide distribution. NAACP leaders used their contacts in Hollywood, especially the Jewish owners of Hollywood studios, to endorse the film. Harry Cohn, the President of Columbia Pictures, described *The Negro Soldier* as 'the greatest War Department picture ever made'. By publicising such comments widely, the NAACP built up momentum for the widespread screening of the film. This was made even more explicit when they sent telegrams to sympathetic journalists with news of a petition of some 200 people 'who work in the motion picture industry' calling for audiences to ask for *The Negro Soldier* to be shown at neighbourhood theatres. In Syracuse, New York, in April 1944, a 'Committee for the Showing of the Film *The Negro Soldier*' consisted of 59 leading citizens and agencies, including the city mayor. The committee sought to pressurise the local chain to show the film, and when that initially proved unsuccessful the committee arranged a preview for some 400 people in a local boys' club using the 16mm version. Using their organisation's magazine, *The Crisis*, the NAACP instructed thousands of readers 'to write or telephone leading theatre managers in their cities urging them to book this film'.[11]

Ironically, part of the difficulty in persuading theatres to show the film was simply practical rather than to do with race or army politics. Fewer than 2,000 theatres took the film initially, compared with a typical showing in at least 12,000 theatres for hit movies. As Carolyn Davenport, the executive secretary of the Philadelphia branch of the NAACP, explained in a letter to Walter White in early May 1944, it is 'quite apparent that the length of the film makes it nearly prohibitive to many managers ... the picture should be reduced to about 25 minutes in order that more people will be able to see it'. When it was re-released in a shortened form of 20 minutes, it certainly received a much wider audience. Some 5,000 theatres took the film, with over 80 per cent catering to whites. In Brandt's theatres in New York, *The Negro Soldier* played with *Snow White* (1937) in Manhattan and *Address Unknown* (1944) at the Globe.

Undoubtedly the Army had unwittingly commissioned a propaganda film that by 1944 had become powerful propaganda against military segregation. Less than four years later, on 26 July 1948, President Harry Truman issued Executive Order 9981, stating that it was 'essential that there be maintained in the armed services of the United States the highest standards of democracy, with equality of treatment and opportunity for all those who serve in our country's defense ... the policy of the President that there shall be equality of treatment and opportunity in the armed services without regard to race, colour, religion or national origin'.

However, for all the unexpected success of *The Negro Soldier*, the integration of the army resulted from a wide range of other causes in addition to the film, not least the military's realisation that the segregation and under-utilisation of black troops severely undermined military efficiency. Indeed, a close reading of post-war evaluations suggest that the film had little immediate impact on individual soldiers' opinions about race relations. Also, *The Negro Soldier* did not act as the catalyst for a dramatically improved presentation of blacks on film in Hollywood. Neither Moss nor any other African-American filmmakers were able to break through the entrenched racial barriers in Hollywood, and the McCarthyite era ensured that Hollywood remained conservative during the post-war years. Ironically, Moss himself was denounced as an alleged communist in 1951. In the longer-term, though, Moss' work in education sped the development of a generation of black filmmakers.[12]

Nevertheless, by commissioning *The Negro Soldier*, the Army showed its willingness to at least confront the race problem in the face of black unrest and military necessity. Undoubtedly too, the film helped play a significant if unquantifiable role in creating an atmosphere in which a peaceful integration of the army was possible. Above all, though, the production and distribution of *The Negro Soldier* demonstrated the ability of black leaders to force the army into positive action on behalf of Negro soldiers. In this way, *The Negro Soldier* exploited the rhetoric of democracy and liberty on behalf of the black Americans in the same way that civil rights leaders were later to do so effectively. Towards the end of his famous speech at the March on Washington in 1963, Martin Luther King cited the hymn, 'my country 'tis of thee ... of thee I sing ... Let Freedom Ring' – the same hymn chosen by Carlton Moss to conclude *The Negro Soldier*.

Notes

1   *New York Times*, 22 April 1944.

2   C. R. Koppes and G. D. Black (1986) 'Blacks, Loyalty, and Motion-Picture Propaganda in World War II', *Journal of American History*, 73, 2, 386.

3   *New York Times*, 22 April 1944.

4   Koppes and Black 1986: 385.

5   J. T. Patterson (1996) *Grand Expectations: The United States, 1945–74*. New York: Oxford University Press, 23.

6   Press Release, 31 July 1942, General Office File: Films, Newspaper Clippings and Press Releases 1942, NAACP Papers, NAACP Microfilm, Cambridge University Library (hereafter NAACP microfilm).

7   *The People* (New York), 12 September 1942.

8   J. McBride (1992) *Frank Capra: The Catastrophe of Success*. London and Boston: Faber and Faber, 493.

9   McBride 1992: 492.
10   Letter, Walter White to Marshall, 4 May 1944, NAACP 1940–55, General Office Film, Films: *The Negro Soldier*, 1944–45, NAACP microfilm.
11   *Friends Intelligencer*, 101, Fourth Month 8, 1944, Number 15 (*Quaker Weekly*), 226.
12   Carlton Moss later taught black film history projects.

SECTION III

THE HOLOCAUST DOCUMENTARY
IN FILM AND TELEVISION

The chapters in this section are arranged in order of the release of the works each discusses, as we wanted to examine the degree to which filmmakers had been influenced by existing films made on the subject, and to trace how archival footage had been incorporated into subsequent generations of films. Yet this section covers such a range of documentary treatments of the Holocaust that the reader might challenge the use of this label altogether; indeed Claude Lanzmann and Alain Resnais have explicitly rejected the term 'documentary' to describe their films. How do we justify using this description when 'non-fiction' might be a better term? Firstly, 'documentary' has always been a broad umbrella term and one that has grown to cover an increasing variety of approaches. Secondly, all the films discussed here share key elements of the documentary that mean they can be examined together: they are factual films, exploring actual historical events, and featuring real people as opposed to performers.

To many readers, the Thames series *The World at War* and the BBC series *The Nazis: A Warning from History* may be regarded as archetypal examples of the historical television documentary, as they employ a range of familiar techniques to carefully guide the viewer through a historical narrative: an explanatory voiceover commentary, a linear, chronological narrative, 'talking head' interviews, the use of archive film and photographs. All these techniques are based on a faith in the ability of the documentary to uncover the past. Thus when Michael Darlow, (director of the Holocaust episodes in *The World at War* series) and Laurence Rees (the producer and writer of *The Nazis: A Warning from History*) approached their films on the Holocaust, they wanted to know how it happened and why it happened, questions born out of a belief in the power of reasoning and rational investigation to seek answers and explanations. Thus, both filmmakers seek to de-mythologise the Holocaust. It should be added that such an approach reflects a commitment to the public service role of the broadcaster that underpins British television. As Christian Delage reveals, this didactic purpose and sense of public service also underpinned the work of the producers of *Nuit et Brouillard* (*Night and Fog*), even though the film is often remembered mostly for its emotional impact and poetic use of commentary and music, for which the film was both praised and reviled by the members of *The World at War* production team present when the film was screened during the symposium. This points to the duality within the film, on the one hand a relatively straightforward historical narrative alongside an artistic and poetic meditation on the concentration camps and memory. In fact, as Christian Delage explains, the historical aims for the film were not simple as it seemed to be trying to cover too many areas – the history of the deportations and the concentration camps, the genesis of 'the Final Solution', honouring the memory of the Jewish victims of the Holocaust. But the film's director, Alain Resnais, was also concerned with the cinematic form, in particular that the archive footage was not used in a voyeuristic manner.

Claude Lanzmann and Orly Yadin reveal disillusionment with the whole rational approach to historical documentary. This questioning is underscored by the Auschwitz survivor, Primo Levi, who warns against 'understanding' the Final Solution.[1] Lanzmann has explained the particular approach he took in *Shoah* in very similar terms: 'there is an absolute obscenity in the project of understanding … there is something that is for me an intellectual scandal: the attempt to understand, historically, as if there were some sort of a genesis of death.'[2] Disillusioned or sceptical of the old certainties and conceit of documentary, these filmmakers adopted and experimented with poetic, non-linear, non-chronological and open-ended approaches to the subject. Lanzmann did not use archival images or a voiceover commentary for his Holocaust films. Orly Yadin has chosen animation as she felt it a more honest confrontation with the difficulties associated with the Holocaust (for example, the lack of archival images). She also favoured animation for her story of a Holocaust survivor because she felt it less exploitative of the witness, less voyeuristic. In two short companion pieces to Yadin's chapter on *Silence* (1998), Ruth Lingford and Tim Webb, the animators on the film, explain how animation's access to 'metaphor and transformation' can articulate trauma without recourse to horror. They also share Yadin's preoccupations with finding an ethically appropriate visual style to evoke a survivors' tale.

The titles in our third grouping, *Kitty – Return to Auschwitz* (1979), *Silence* and *Loving the Dead* (1991), are less about history than memory and trauma, about an individual coming to terms with the past. The filmmaking process for the Holocaust survivors Kitty Hart-Moxon and Tana Ross was for them a therapeutic journey. Kitty and Tana also saw the films as an opportunity to bear witness, to speak for those who did not survive. For Kitty, the film she made with Peter Morley and the experience of revisiting Auschwitz was a cathartic experience as she can now share her past with others, and since the making of the film she has become active in Holocaust education. A central element of Lanzmann's *Shoah* is also to take the survivors on a journey back to the site of their trauma (even if it is not the exact location) and to use this suggestive environment to enable them to recall deeply buried accounts of their experiences during the Holocaust. But Lanzmann is not interested in the therapeutic value of this encounter with the past, but how this may facilitate the testimony of a witness to the atrocity of the Final solution, so powerful that the gap in time is conflated. We must also think of the dramatic power that the witness brings to the screen. The Holocaust survivor has become more and more central to the whole documentary enterprise, with films often being structured around the account of a single person. In these biographical pieces, the role of the witness has gone beyond the prosaic function of proving or describing events, the survivors are now held up as models of resilience, even as moral ambassadors.

For the filmmaker and painter Mira Hamermesh, the two films she made about the Holocaust, *Take a Deep Breath* (1962), a student film based on the story of a Kapo, and *Loving the Dead*, an autobiographical film made many years later, were deeply personal experiences as her parents had perished in the Holocaust. During the shooting of the first film, she stayed at Auschwitz where her father had died and in the second, she filmed her own journey to Poland to search for her mother's grave. In *Loving the Dead* Mira confronts not just the ghosts of her parents but also the ghost of the Jewish community in Poland.

A common approach is to incorporate often lengthy sequences of the landscape in which the Holocaust took place, even when, as is often the case with the extermination camps, there is no physical evidence left at the sites. For Laurence Rees, location shooting at Treblinka helped to create atmosphere and continuity in the gaps created by the absence of archive film. Claude Lanzmann, on the other hand, would not have considered using archive film of the death camps, even if it existed. Remarkably, even when the land is bare of physical evidence it can provide information for the viewer. For example, the scale of the camp sites at Auschwitz and Treblinka impressed Peter Morley and Laurence Rees respectively; Morley gaining an understanding of the story of Auschwitz from its enormous size; Rees conversely realising how little land one really needs for an extermination camp if it is well planned and organised.

Expanding on the theoretical and philosophical issues examined in this section Elizabeth Cowie asks how a documentary film may facilitate a recollection of the Holocaust. To do this she gives an overview of a number of relevant aspects of documentary history: developments in camera technology and in filming techniques; the film of atrocities recorded by Allied military cameramen at the end of the war; and the edited documentaries *Night and Fog*, *The World at War*, *Shoah* and *Silence*. She closes this exploration by describing a new development in documentary, which commemorates the lives of those lost, by using home movie footage of Jewish families before the Holocaust.

Of all the forms of representation of the Holocaust, the documentary claims to carry the greatest authenticity. This section thus demonstrates both the limits to this claim and the lengths to which filmmakers have tested the flexibility of the form.

Notes

1   Primo Levi: '"understanding" a proposal of human behaviour means to "contain" it, containing its author, put oneself in his place, identify with him. Now no normal person will ever be able to identify with Hitler, Himmler, Eichmann and endless others … But there is no rationality in the Nazi hatred: it is a hate that is not in us; it is outside us, it is a poisonous fruit springing from the deadly trunk of fascism.' P. Levi (1995) *If This is a Man* and *The Truce*. Translated by Stuart Woolf. London: Abacus, 395.

2   Claude Lanzmann quoted in A. Colombat (1993) *The Holocaust in French Film*. London: The Scarecrow Press, 303.

12   *Nuit et Brouillard*: a turning point in the history and memory of the Holocaust

Christian Delage

Nuit et Brouillard (*Night and Fog*) was the first major French film to deal with the Nazi concentration camps.[1] Since its release in December 1955, the career of the film has been as much commercial as artistic, its relatively brief running time of 32 minutes allowing it to be shown just as easily in commercial cinemas as on art-house screens. A few rigorous teachers, such as Henri Agel, brought the film to the attention of generations of students before the public authorities imposed regular screenings in schools in order to combat the resurgence of antisemitism in French society.[2] Following the desecration of the Jewish cemetery in Carpentras in 1990, the film was programmed on all French television channels. Such official recognition might lead one to believe that the film, made by Alain Resnais and Jean Cayrol and produced by Anatole Dauman, had been received favourably from the outset or, at least, that its reputation had since become a matter of consensus due to the gravity of its subject and the ethical and aesthetic approach of the filmmakers. In fact, this was not the case on its release and its reputation remains complicated half a century later.

Despite having been well received by the critics owing to its award of the Prix Jean Vigo,[3] no sooner was *Night and Fog* completed than it had to come to terms with several types of censorship. The first of these originated in the French Commission for the Classification of Films which insisted that Resnais remove shots of corpses which were judged to be too shocking and, above all, that he excise a photograph showing a French gendarme guarding the camp at Pithiviers.[4] Then, just as it was announced that *Night and Fog* had joined the shortlist of French films to be screened at the Cannes Film Festival, it was implicated in a political and diplomatic imbroglio: the German Embassy in France attempted to have the film withdrawn, provoking a polemic whose scope rapidly became international.[5] Following its initially turbulent reception, the career of *Night and Fog* was characterised by a form of institutionalisation that brought with it a second wave of criticism questioning how apposite its status was as a key work about the history of the genocide of the Jews. Serge Klarsfeld reports that while, at the time of its release, the film had

> … greatly moved me, it can be seen differently today since it is a film whose major flaw is not to convey the singularity of the fate of the Jews. What has emerged since 1975 is the difference between those who were deported because they were political opponents of Nazism and those who were deported because they were born Jews.[6]

In the 1990s, Georges Bensoussan emphasised that 'the genocide of the Jews is almost absent from the film',[7] while Annette Wieviorka went further, saying that 'this film has nothing to say regarding the genocide of the Jews'.[8]

By reconstructing the genesis of the film, I will endeavour to show how the film-makers tried constantly to convey and interweave heterogeneous elements of the Nazi concentration camp system. However, my working hypothesis is that, far from having only been subject to the context in which it was deployed, the collective experience of *Night and Fog* can be seen today as an essential stage in the work of remembering *les années noires* (the years of Occupation) and the Final Solution.

When and why was Night and Fog made?

During 1954 a certain number of initiatives were taken that marked an inflection in French policy regarding the memory of the camps. On 14 April a law was passed inaugurating a National Day of Remembrance for the Victims and Heroes of the Deportation. On 10 November, an exhibition opened at the Pedagogical Museum at 29 rue d'Ulm entitled *Résistance-Libération-Déportation*. Inaugurated by the Minister of Education, the exhibition received almost 60,000 visitors including 30,000 students from educational establishments in Paris. Conceived by the Committee for the History of the Second World War (Comité d'Histoire de la Deuxième Guerre Mondiale, CHGM), the exhibition played no small part in transmitting the memory of the war and deportations.

One of the outcomes of the exhibition was the concern expressed by the Municipal Council of Paris about the fate of the documents assembled for the occasion and this launched the idea of 'the creation in Paris of a Municipal Museum of the Resistance, Liberation and Deportation in which the first elements will be made up of the documents above'.[9] This proposal would also be taken up in the Assemblée Nationale by Madame de Lipovsky who would present a 'proposal' with a similar outcome in mind. If 1954 marked the tenth anniversary of the Liberation of France, the following year would commemorate the opening of the camps. To allow for the two events to overlap, the exhibition, scheduled to close on 9 January, was extended until 23 January 1955 at the request of Pierre Mendès-France, the Président du Conseil.

The exhibition was acclaimed by the press both nationally and internationally for the importance of its subject. If the *New York Times* straightforwardly stated that 'the visitor learns how the occupier behaved and rediscovers the spirit behind the struggle for the Liberation',[10] the *Times* lauded the 'objectivity' of the perspective adopted:[11] 'beyond the homage to the Resistance, this exhibition offers an objective commentary on Nazi methods in occupied France and in the concentration camps'.[12] In this regard, *Déportation et Liberté* emphasised that 'it was a good thing that such an exhibition attempted to show a large audience what the concentration camps were, using images to explain how what happened in them was a deliberate execution of a plan that, fortunately, had been stopped'.[13]

As well as photographic images, there were daily projections of films about the war, the resistance and the deportations. The deportations were recalled thanks to a montage of French newsreels screened in 1945, *Les Camps de la mort*,[14] and a Polish fiction film, *Ostatni etap* (*The Last Stage*),[15] directed by Wanda Jakubowska in 1948. These would be among the first documents watched by the producers of *Night and Fog* while preparing the film and would bring together the principal partners who would get the project underway: on the French side, CHGM (the French Ministry of War Veterans) and ZBoWid (the Union of War Veterans for Liberty and Democracy) on the Polish side. In fact, at the beginning of January, Henri Michel, the organiser of the exhibition, had announced that the project of 'a film about the concentration camp system' was being considered. He had been in agreement about the project with the producer Anatole Dauman and his colleagues Philippe Lifchitz and Sylvain Halfon when he welcomed them to the exhibition.

During their visit they would have noticed that admission to the room dedicated to the Deportation – in which 'the fate of those who, imprisoned for political or racial reasons or for acts of resistance, suffered torture or death or were sent from French prisons to camps in the Greater Reich' was recounted – was prohibited to those under 17 years of age 'because of the tragic aspect of many of the documents exhibited'.[16] The problem of such images of atrocity was immediately uppermost in the minds of the film's producers. In one of the first descriptions of the project, written on 3 March 1955, Michel noted:

The subject matter and the nature of the material collected guarantees this film great dramatic intensity but the filmmakers are aware that the pitfall that needs to be avoided is that of subjecting the spectator to excessive horror. It is therefore important not to emphasis the 'sadistic', 'war crime', 'inhuman atrocity' aspect of the concentration camps but to relate, via image and commentary, a sociological explanation. In watching this film, former inmates must be able to recognise their ordeals but ordinary spectators must also understand how systematic, in its combination of cruel barbarity and scientific experiment, the phenomenon of the concentration camps was.[17]

Two requirements had to be satisfied: firstly, the quasi-pedagogic requirement to disseminate knowledge of how the concentration camps worked and secondly, relating to the issue of memory, the requirement that the experiences of surviving deportees be faithfully recounted.[18] In so doing, it was equally crucial to take account of the generation gap within the audience as it was a public of young spectators that was conceived as the film's principal target.[19]

To realise their plans, the producers invited Alain Resnais to direct the film. Resnais had already made several short films, mainly about painters (*Van Gogh* (1948), *Gauguin* (1950), *Guernica* (1950)), but he had no personal experience of the camps nor had he been deported. He was therefore initially unwilling to take on the project, accepting only when the producers agreed to also employ the poet Jean Cayrol, who had been interned at Gusen camp (a satellite of Mauthausen). Although Cayrol was eventually to write the commentary, during most of the production the team consisted of Resnais, Dauman and the two historical advisers, Michel and Wormser.

Returning to the issue of how to utilise the atrocity images, in an interview recorded in 1986, Resnais explained that, at the time,

People saw the film in private screenings and many said to me 'You're frightened of the violence, you've suppressed the terrible images we saw during the Liberation, etc.' Which is utterly wrong. I had at my disposal all the French films which had been screened at the time of the Liberation and I didn't suppress any violence. They simply imagined that they saw things in 1944 and 1945 that made an impression on them.[20]

The fear of complacently recapitulating the violence of the images of the camps would thus have led Resnais to tone them down, at least to those who remembered seeing them. It is clear that, ten years after the screenings of the newsreel images of the camps, shot at the precise moment they were liberated by the Allies, the memory of the event has become denser still, nourished as it was by the thousands of written testimonies published since as well as by exhibitions and reconsructions.[21] The reconstruction of the fate of the deportees, rather than creating a sort of critical distance, would have reinforced the initial shock experienced in 1945, in delivering, after the event, a consistency, continuity and identity to images some of whose visual elements – barbed wire, corpses, the skeletal bodies of the survivors – had acquired a dimension that was as much factual as symbolic.[22]

The archival research

Which images had Resnais actually found during the preparation of the film in 1955? There were those from the Auschwitz museum, seen on a visit with Henri Michel and Olga Wormser in September; those found by Michel in Holland at the Rijksinstituut voor Oorlogsdokumentatie (RIOD); those available in Paris from French television, Gaumont or the associations of former deportees. But according to Resnais, quite a number of archives had not been visited: the Imperial War Museum in London ('we were told that they would not make any documents available');[23] the National Archives in Washington D.C. ('I think they would have been too costly'. André Heinrich: 'Was it a question of the price or did they not wish to make anything available to you?' Resnais: 'I don't recall any such refusal');[24] the Film Service of the French Army (Service Cinématographique des Armées, SCA) which 'didn't hold anything of note. All the same, I'd requested a shot of an inauguration of a monument to the dead, something of that nature which I thought might be useful but I never received it. I got a letter instead, stating that *given the character of the film* they were not able to make any documents available to us.'[25] Besides Resnais' choice of image, a choice that seems largely to have been one made out of lack of choice, it is worth drawing attention to the censorship imposed by the SCA ('given the character of the film'). This attitude might appear surprising, since the film was still only at the writing stage and had already received the moral and financial support of, among others, the Minister of Former Servicemen. In reality, Resnais, who had only recently denounced French colonialism in *Les Statues meurent aussi* (*Statues Also Die*, 1953), undertook the film with the same political intention as his producers: the film was conceived as 'a warning' in contemporary France which was engaged in a colonial war in Algeria. When the film was first screened, Jean Cayrol would write:

> In the indifferent sky of these dry images are menacing, ever-moving clouds of racism. They roll and break over certain places, cutting down those underneath. Memory endures only as long as it is illuminated by the present. Though the crematoria are now nothing more than sorry skeletons, and silence falls like a shroud over the sites of former

camps now eaten by weeds, let us not forget that our own country is not exempt from the scandal of racism.[26]

Despite the relative paucity of material held by the SCA, Argos Productions tried in vain to get the organisation to go back on its decision.[27] Finally, Resnais, who had discovered images of Buchenwald at the SCA, obtained them from Gaumont where he would even have access to 'Unused' material ('sujets "Non Utilisés"') while editing newsreel footage.[28]

The historiographic situation

What role did historical advisors play in the making of the film and what was the state of historiographical study of the Nazi genocide in 1955?

In October 1944, and on the model established after the First World War, the provisional government of the French Republic set up the Commission of the History of the Occupation and Liberation of France (Commission d'histoire de l'Occupation et de la libération de la France) which was attached to the Ministry of Education and was directed to study the Resistance, while the Committee of the History of the War, created in 1945, under the auspices of the Presidency of the Conseil was specifically charged with gathering the stocks of documents mostly from ministries and administrations.[29] The amalgamation of the two bodies in 1951 saw the foundation of the CHGM within which a Committee for the History of the Deportation (Comité d'histoire de la Déportation) was created. In 1950, Henri Michel, director of CHGM, produced the first volume of the publication *Que sais-je?* devoted to the history of the French Resistance. This was followed, in 1954, by a collection of 190 texts, edited in collaboration with Olga Wormser, entitled *Tragedy of the Deportation 1940–1945: Testimonies of Survivors of the German Concentration Camps* (*Tragédie de la déportation 1940–1945. Témoignages de survivants des camps de concentration allemands*). In their introduction, Michel and Wormser appear to approach the history of the deportations in keeping with a context where, as Henry Rousso recalls it, 'historical research didn't much concern itself with the Vichy regime and barely at all with its anti-Jewish policies, concentrating greatly on the history of the Resistance, on deportation (but not in its racial sense) and on German repression.'[30] In fact, the editors explain that they wished to preserve 'the memory of those millions of martyrs belonging to every social class and every denomination and among whose number were citizens of 22 nations'.[31] Yet, in a circumlocutory introduction to one of the texts in the anthology, Michel and Wormser write:

> Individual executions would only deliver 'derisory' numerical results, owing to the size of the camps and the goal set by the SS, the extermination of inferior races (Jews and Gyspies) and the enemies of the Reich. The disguising of murder is one of the most striking aspects of the organisation of the camps. In no other historical circumstance and in no other country has there ever existed a means of dispensing death as 'perfected' and as prolific as in the crematoria of Auschwitz. No need, there, for the pretext of deficiency, age or disobedience. The deportees in Auschwitz (with the exception of several hundred 'Ayran politicals' who would, nevertheless, die there in great number) had to die because they were Jews.[32]

One could hardly be any clearer in presenting the specificity of the genocide of the Jews and the dedicated role that Auschwitz played in it. For that matter, it was not Resnais who decided to film footage of Majdanek and Auschwitz – even though he proposed to differentiate them from the archive images by filming them in colour – but Henri Michel. One of the film's producers sent a note to Resnais dated 3 May 1955, albeit three weeks before the director signed his contract: 'We have been visited by Monsieur Henri Michel who has shared with us his positive outlook for our film following his recent trip to Poland', wrote Philippe Lifchitz. 'He is deeply affected by the emotion of this visit to the camps which he made in the company of former deportees. He thinks that the sight of the empty camps and the museums where the personal effects and relics of the former prisoners are preserved could only impress you and may even have an influence on your conception of the film…'. One notices, however, that this thinking about the camps oscillated between emphasising the specificity of the Jewish genocide and presenting all deportees as a single community united by a tragic fate. One comes across a similar oscillation in the two special issues of the CHGM publication published before and after the making of the film.

The first, published in 1954, is devoted to the study of the German camp system[33] and focuses mainly on the concentration camps: 'Nearly ten years have passed since the deportations ended and the survivors returned. Memories are being steadily erased; documents that weren't recovered immediately are at risk of disappearing. Every effort must be made in order to gather them together.' One of the contributors to the issue is introduced as describing life in the Mauthausen camp with 'objectivity and precision', no doubt because of his own experiences as a 'NN' prisoner (Nacht und Nebel Schutzhäftling 63.584 K.L.M). Among the texts in Michel and Wormser's anthology is an extract by Jean Cayrol, in which the writer also emphasises the particularity of this identity:[34] 'I speak here only about a category of prisoner which I know well, those who were "Nacht und Nebel", that's to say, who received no parcels, no news and who were completely cut off from the outside world.'[35] These two publications informed the choices made in writing the synopsis of the film, even in the evolving titles given to the film: 'Film about Deportation' (1 March 1955); 'Film on the Concentration Camps' (3 March); 'Resistance and Deportation' (20 May); 'Night and Fog' (24 May). Elsewhere, in their first description of the project, Michel and Wormser take up the idea already developed in their anthology, to follow 'in its stations and its trials, the Way of the Cross engraved by the deportees: internment, transportation, arrival, absorption into the world of the camp, daily life, work, illness and death'. However, even with the Christian overtones of the deportees' Calvary, mention of the particular fate of the Jews is not omitted. In the preamble to the synopsis, it is, at first, associated explicitly with the presence of the Germans in France: 'the fate of the Jews (census, yellow star, despoilment, internment camps, the round-up)', then, implicitly, with Nazi ideology: 'Flashback: Nazi parade at Nuremberg, Hitler, Himmler, Goering. Phrases from *Mein Kampf* about the extermination of adversaries and inferior races.' Henri Michel presents this in paying tribute to the work undertaken by the Jewish Centre of Contemporary Documentation (le Centre de Documentation Juive Contemporaine) and explains:

Since the Nuremberg trials, the proof has been supplied and convictions secured for the unprecedented crime committed against the Jews by the Third Reich. However, discussion over its exact magnitude has not ended and controversy ignites when the number of victims is evaluated.[36] To fix the figure precisely has been the work of Léon Poliakov. In the absence of any certainty other than it being a matter of *millions* of human beings, at least the converging testimonies and the statistical evaluations allow for a realistic minimum of *six million* dead. It is the monstrosity of this figure that makes the crime of the Nazis something new ... 'The Final Solution' of 'the Jewish Problem' put in process by Himmler can only be understood as part of the ideology of Nazism from which it directly issued.

Not only is the specificity of the genocide of the Jews clearly presented, with the figures to hand, but the responsibility of the Vichy regime is sharply emphasised:

> Could one make out, in Vichy, the flames of Auschwitz? The skill of the Nazis, or their historical stroke of luck, was to have involved in their work of annihilation the govern-ments, free to a greater or lesser extent, of peoples momentarily subjugated. That this collaboration did not take place without shame, remorse, conflict or opposition is clearly shown by the way the wheels of the French state turned, as Joseph Billig has studied. This sharing of responsibilities was not easy. But the deliberate choice of collaboration – whether it resulted from a tragic error of judgement or from day-to-day opportunism – constrained those who made it to take part in the crime, implying their complicity, even when their presence meant that the severity of the crime was, for the time being, watered down. The clinching fact: the very affirmation of their independence led the Vichy governments to anticipate and outstrip the Occupation authorities in the measures taken against the Jews.[37]

The final self-censorship of Night and Fog

One can therefore propose that, far from marking a fallow period in the conjoined evo-lution of the history and memory of the Jewish genocide and the role of Vichy in the Final Solution, the years 1954–56 constitute a crucial link in the chain. In this context, Alain Resnais' film is not the simple 'representation of' something which preceded it or which overwhelmed it in terms of the event's intelligibility. Resnais accompanies the movement I have just described, being without doubt the only one able to unite per-sonalities with different experiences of the war around a common task. Aged only 33, Resnais involved himself with great humility in the ethical and aesthetic adventure that made *Night and Fog* an inaugural film in many respects. One of the film's major contri-butions lies in its anguished reflection on the trap of taking the visible as evidence and, *a fortiori*, on voyeurism as the common means of confronting history. This approach led, three years later, to Resnais meeting Marguerite Duras and to the writing of *Hiroshima mon amour*. If the filmmaker, like the historian, assumes the task of reconstructing the past it is through explicitly accepting a relationship with the present in which the past evolves. He can also go further and continue, whatever the subject addressed, to ask himself general questions about the compression of time and levels of the perception of temporality.[38] One of Resnais' responses to such questions had already been tried out in his earlier short films: the use of the travelling shot.[39] In writing the screenplay, he therefore started by foregrounding the time-lag between the progression of historical knowledge or memory of the Nazi death camps and the ineluctable decay of the visible traces of their existence:

> *Night and Fog.* Colour. A landscape: calm, neutral, banal. The camera tracks back. We are inside a concentration camp, closed down and deserted. The camera pans, disclosing the entrance to the camp in the distance flanked by a watchtower. (We can perhaps even see a group of tourists dressed in bright colours entering the camp led by a guide. The weather can be bright but, subsequently, the sky must always remain cloudy and grey). A series of very slow pans, each starting from an 'exterior' element and coming to rest on an 'interior' element. (Ideally, each of these pans should have been shot in a different camps: Struthoff, Mauthausen, Auschwitz-Birkenau, Majdanek.)

Here, a little further on in the synopsis, is what Resnais wrote regarding 1942:

> Black-and-white. Himmler's second visit in 1942. The German war effort. The multiplication of the camps after this visit. The variety of human material transported. Twenty-two countries. '10,000 Russian women to dig anti-tank ditches' etc. The 'definitive solution to the Jewish problem', decided upon in 1942. 'Inferior races must work for us. The Jews, Poles, Gypsies and Russians must be eliminated, but productively. Elimination by work is the most productive', etc…

The historians of the CHGM, who gave their agreement to the synopsis with a highly official stamp on the first page, imposed a few modifications to the first three lines:

> Black-and-white. Himmler's second visit in 1942 ['to Auschwitz']. The German war effort. The multiplication of the camps ['the camps' removed and replaced by 'Kommandos and crematoria'] after this visit ['The Pohl Law'].

Then, after shooting, came the moment for Jean Cayrol's commentary to be edited. On this final phase of the production, however crucial, we are unfortunately unable to rely on any written documentation.[40] This is the passage devoted to the year 1942 in its final version:

> 1942. Himmler visits the sites. It is necessary to exterminate, but this must be done productively. Leaving productivity to the technicians, Himmler turns to the problem of elimination. Plans and models are studied. The deportees themselves will participate in the work of execution. A crematoria can, at times, have a touch of the picture postcard about it. Later on – today – tourists will photograph each other in front of it. The deportations spread throughout Europe.

The reference which Resnais himself had put in inverted commas, as if it were a historical fact external to any literary or cinematic treatment ('The "definitive solution to the Jewish problem", decided upon in 1942') has disappeared. This last cut was made without any modification to the images and on the sole initiative of Cayrol, who was the final arbiter in the chain of collective decisions in the making of the film. The historians, moreover, started to express their displeasure at feeling excluded from control over the editing. This cut must, no doubt, be understood in relation to Cayrol's style of writing, more literary than historical. His own experience of the war should also be borne in mind: having known deportation as a resistance fighter he was anxious principally to evoke daily life in the camps and to situate the film in the contemporary reality of militancy regarding the Algerian War. Furthermore, Anatole Dauman, who was born in the Russian-Polish Jewish community of Warsaw in 1925, had also been involved in the battles for the Liberation of France and preferred to emphasise his identity as a resistance fighter over his Jewish identity.[41] This is according to the CHGM historians Henri Michel and Olga Wormser who, as we have already seen from their publications, were at the forefront of historical research in the 1950s and, it should be emphasised, confident in the power of cinema. These two were beginning to merely introduce into the historiography of the time, dominated as it was by work on the Resistance, analysis of the genesis of the extermination of the European Jews.

This period of the 1950s is, therefore, far more complicated than certain periodisations of the history of the Holocaust in France would lead one to believe. The multiple experiences brought together in the birth of the film have had simultaneously dynamic and constraining effects. Nevertheless, we are faced with a work that is utterly apart, sufficiently achieved and personal to have withstood the ravages of time even while having been part of this key moment in French historiography that saw the beginning of scholarly writing on the history of the Jewish genocide. This scholarship was not yet animating the historical community or the public memory to the extent we know today. We should not regard *Night and Fog* with suspicion from an anachronistic perspective – ignoring similar unsuccessful attempts in other post-war countries – while taking advantage of the fact that the director never attempted to make a monument of his film that would prove intimidating to spectators. Thanks to the desolate gentleness of his film, Resnais will allow many generations to be able to behold the filmed images and the material traces of the Nazi death camps.

Translated by Chris Darke.

Notes

1   This article could not have been written without the opportunity to have access to the archives of Argos Films, of Jean Cayrol and of the Committee of the History of the Second World War (Comité de l'histoire de la Deuxième Guerre Mondiale, CHGM). My particular thanks go to Florence Dauman (Argos Films), Thierry Frémaux and Nicolas Riedel (Institut Lumière), Albert Dichy (IMEC) and Jean Astruc (IHTP-CNRS), as well as to those institutions who allowed me to present this paper and to make corrections to it afterwards: The Imperial War Museum (London), The University of Paris I (Seminar on the History of the Holocaust), the University of Pennsylvania (Philadelphia), New York University and the Holocaust Educational Foundation (Lessons and Legacies VII, University of Minnesota, Minneapolis).

2   As Serge Daney recalls, 'Henri Agel – *professeur de lettres* at the lycée Voltaire – was one of the most singular communicators ("*passeurs*"). In order that he, as much as we, could skip Latin classes he put the following choice to the vote: to spend an hour studying a text by Livy or to go to the cinema. The class, which voted for the cinema, regularly left the dilapidated old ciné-club feeling pensive. Out of sadism, and probably because he had copies of them, Agel would show films that were ideal for teaching

adolescents a thing or two. These were *Le Sang des bêtes* by Franu and *Nuit et Brouillard* by Resnais.' S. Daney (1992) 'Le Travelling de *Kapo*', *Trafic*, 4, 7. Henri Agel (born in 1911) has taught film history for many years and is the author of, among other works, *Le cinéma et le Sacre* (Paris: Cerf, 1961), *Cinéma et nouvelle naissance* (Paris: Albin Michel, 1981) and *Un art de la Célébration: le cinéma de Flaherty à Rouch* (Paris: Cerf, 1987).

3   The Prix Jean Vigo was awarded on 31 January 1956. Resnais had already won the prize two years earlier for *Les Statues meurent aussi*, which did not prevent the film from remaining banned from 1956.

4   Henry Rousso recalls that Resnais was 'obliged to efface the telltale *kepi* of a gendarme spotted during a scene in the Pithiviers internment camp (created by the Germans but administered by the French). This was a strange stroke of the censor's brush, for what was suppressed was not a product of the director's imagination or his emphasis but an image from the period, hence a patent fact.' H. Rousso (1987) *Le Syndrome de Vichy, 1944–198....* Paris: Éditions du Seuil, 144–5.

5   The French Minister of Foreign Affairs, Christian Pineau, had in fact received a letter from the German Federal Republic demanding that *Night and Fog* be withdrawn from the official selection, invoking article 5 of the Festival rules which stipulated that a film could be excluded from competition if it attacked the reputation of a participating country. For the *Berliner Zeitung*, 'the scandal of Cannes is of German making, not French. Our representatives have neither the breadth of intellect nor the maturity necessary to accept a film showing German faults.' The Swiss refused to show the film, citing their neutrality as the reason. The French did not have much to be proud of, however: beside the censoring of the shot of the gendarme at Pithiviers, the French Minister of Foreign Affairs, Christian Pineau, broke ranks with the Secretary of State of Industry and Commerce, Maurice Lemaire, who decided the list of films to be retained in the official selection at Cannes. Lemaire considered that 'the very special character of the film is such that it could not compete with fiction films or even films of historical reconstruction...'. See R. Raskin (ed.) (1987) *Nuit et Brouillard by Alain Resnais: On the Making, Reception and Functions of a Major Documentary Film: Including a New Interview with Alain Resnais and the Original Shooting Script.* Åarhus: Åarhus University Press, 33–45.

6   Interview given to André Heinrich for the radio programme '*Nuit et Brouillard* au-delà de la censure', broadcast 6 August 1994 on France Culture.

7   G. Bensoussan (1998) *Auschwitz en heritage? D'un bon usage de la mémoire.* Paris: Éditions des Mille et une Nuits, 44.

8   A. Wieviorka (1992) *Déportation et genocide. Entre la mémoire et l'oubli.* Paris: Plon, 223.

9   In 1952, the City of Paris had already allotted a site at the corner of rue Geoffroy L'Asnier and the rue du Grenier-sur-l'Eau and contributed one million francs to erecting a 'Tomb for the Unknown Jewish Martyr', the first stone of which was laid on 17 May 1953. See A. Wieviorka (1987) 'Un lieu de mémoire et d'histoire: le Mémorial du martyr juif inconnu', *Revue de l'Université de Bruxelles*, 1–2, 107–32.

10   Edition of 24 November 1954, cited in the Committee for the Two Anniversaries (Comité national des deux anniversaires); Committee for the History of the Second World War (1955) *Résistance-Libération-Déportation* Exhibition, 10 November 1954–23 January 1955. Paris: Musée pédagogique, 7 (IHTP-CNRS archives, RF. 527, 1).

11   The organisers were very concerned with their scientific legitimacy. They were keen to emphasise that the exhibition was 'strictly historical, without any aspect of polemic or propaganda' (Ibid., 3) (IHTP-CNRS archives, RF. 527, 3).

12   Edition of 11 November 1954 (Ibid., 7).

13   Edition of October–December 1954 (Ibid., 8).

14   On this document, see C. Drame (1996) 'Representer l'irreprésentable: les camps nazis dans les actualités francaises de 1945', *Cinémathèque*, 10, Autumn, 12–27.

15   On this film, see Wieviorka 1987: 293–312 and S. Liebman (1988) 'Les Premières constellations du dis-
cours sur l'Holocauste dans le cinéma polonais', in A. de Baecque and C. Delage (eds) *De l'Histoire au*
cinéma. Paris and Brussels: Éditions Complexe, collection: 'Histoires du temps présent', 193–216.

16   Exhibition catalogue p. 3. In *Le Monde* a capsule review of the exhibition explained: 'Visitors under 17 years
of age are not allowed access to the room devoted to the deportation, which is as it should be. Far from
drawing from the material the lessons available to adults, they would only encounter visions of an inconceivable nightmare. Nothing of the tragedy of the concentration camps has been left in the dark: a bathtub
used by the Gestapo in Avenue Foch, deportees' personal effects, a desk blotter made of human skin, the
apparatus of a gas chamber, photographs of living dead and mass graves…' cited in Raskin 1987: 27.

17   'Documentary film on the "German concentration camp system"' 2ps. Argos Films Archives, Institut
Lumière, Lyons (Argos Archives hereafter).

18   On which subject, the principal criticism of the film made (after the fact) by Claude Lanzmann: 'The
subject of Resnais' film is what happened to those who weren't killed immediately which is to say that it
is, in a way, a film if not about the survivors, then about those who had the chance of survival and not
at all about those who were killed straight away because, in their case, there was nothing to film as there
was no trace left … It's a film that produces catharsis. In a way, people leave it feeling relieved.' Interview
with André Heinrich, broadcast cited.

19   An agreement was made with the Minister of National Education granting him non-commercial and
non-exclusive rights to screen the film in an educational context.

20   Interview with Raskin 1987: 57–8.

21   On this subject, see P. Lagrou (2000) *The Legacy of Nazi Occupation: Patriotic Memory and National Re-*
covery in Western Europe, 1945–1965. Cambridge: Cambridge University Press, in particular the chapter
'National Martyrdom', pp. 210–50.

22   On the problem of the attestation and perception of violence in the camps in 1945, see C. Delage (2001)
'L'image comme preuve. L'expérience du procés de Nuremberg', *Vingtième siècle. Revue d'histoire*, 72,
October–December, 63–78.

23   Interview with Raskin 1987: 53. It should be noted that there was nothing sinister about the fact that
Resnais was denied access to the Imperial War Museum's collection; this was probably for reasons of
logistics rather than censorship. At this stage in the archive's history, there were no viewing facilities at
the Museum for the public (the cinema was not built until the 1960s) and in fact the film storage and
preservation facilities at Hayes had not yet been constructed.

24   Interview with André Heinrich, programme cited.

25   Ibid.

26   J. Cayrol (1956) 'We conceived *Night and Fog* as a warning', *Les Lettres Françaises*, 606, 9 February 1956.
For the producer Anatole Dauman, the film had a precise political objective, which cannot have been
displeasing to the Polish communist organisations who were partners in the project: 'to explain clearly
how the system of the concentration camps (and its economic aspect) flowed automatically from Fascism
and to recall the birth of the camps at the same time as the victory of the Nazis in 1933 … Be Alert: "fascism is always possible".' ('Note on the Saturday 28 May, 1955 meeting', Argos Films Archives).

27   A hastily written note, of October 1955, indicates 'SCA: approaches ongoing' (Argos Films).

28   The two subjects to which Resnais had access were: 'Buchenwald and Dachau Trials' (1947-NU-301) and
'Buchenwald Tribunal' (1947-NU-578).

29   In an interview, Henri Michel was keen to clarify that 'the time is past when private companies undertook large contemporary historical studies, as was the case for the First World War. Today, historical
research, as with the scientific research of which it is only a part, cannot be done without public institutions. But this support, or higher patronage, does not come accompanied by directives or prohibitions.

The facilities put at the disposal of historians carry no restrictions as regards the mastery of their work.' *Tendances*, 56, December 1968, 645.

30 H. Rousso (1998) *La Hantisse du passé*. Paris: Textuel, 72–3.

31 H. Michel and O. Wormser (1954) *Tragédie de la déportation 1940–1945. Témoignages de survivants des camps de concentration allemands*. Paris: Hachette, 10.

32 Ibid., 401–2.

33 'The German Concentration Camp System (1940–1944)', *Revue d'histoire de la deuxième guerre mondiale*, 15–16, July–September 1954, with contributions by J. Cain, 'Foreword'; G. Tillion, 'Reflections on Studying the Deportation'; M. de Bouard, 'Mauthausen'; O. Wormser, 'Concentration camp labour in the German War Economy'; M. Granet, 'The Deportation at the Nuremberg International Trial'; H. Michel, 'The Work of the Commission for the History of the Deportation'; R. Vivier, 'The Deportation in Indre-et-Loire (Statistical Study)'.

34 Born in 1911, Cayrol was deported to Mauthausen for his role in the Resistance. He is the author of *Poems of Night and Fog* (*Poèmes de la nuit et brouillard*) Paris: Éditions Pierre Seghers, 1946. This was re-published in 1995 as *Poèmes de la Nuit et du Brouillard; Suivis de Larmes Publiques* (Paris: Éditions du Seuil) for which he received the Renaudot Prize. After *Night and Fog* Cayrol wrote with Resnais the script for *Muriel ou le Temp d'un Retour* (1963). Jean Cayrol died on 10 February 2005.

35 J. Cayrol (1950) *Lazare parmi nous*. Neuchatel: Éditions de la Baconnière, cited by Michel & Wormser 1954: 136–7. As Annette Wieviorka (1987: 229) recalls, 'neither a badge of resistance, nor a designation for extermination as is commonly believed, the expression "Nacht und Nebel" has, however, become a symbol with a double meaning. If we have insisted on this decree it is in as much that it has seemed to illustrate the extreme complexity of the deportation in France ... In order to symbolise the system of the concentration camps and, increasingly, the extermination of the Jews, we use the name of a decree concocted by the Wehrmacht at Hitler's initiative attempting to preserve judicial measures leading first to deportation, certainly in Germany, in prisons outside the camp system, before it later replaced the RSHA.'

36 In a note at the foot of the page, Henri Michel adds: 'As we have seen recently, with the screening in Germany of a work by the Committee of the History of the Second World War, the film *Night and Fog*.' H. Michel (1956), preface to the special issue on 'The Condition of the Jews', *Revue of the History of the Second World War*, 24 October, 2–3.

37 H. Michel (1956) preface to the special issue on 'The Condition of the Jews', *Revue of the History of the Second World War*, 24, October, 2–3. With contributions by E. Vermeil, 'Antisemitism in Nazi Ideology'; J. Billig, 'The Condition of Jews in France'; M. Borwicz, '"Final Solutions" in the light of Auschwitz-Birkenau'; L. Poliakov, 'How many victims?'; M. Mazor, 'Documents'.

38 'History is time', Alain Resnais explained recently. 'Cinema too. But time constructs memories and it's not always easy to be confronted by them ... We all have need of imagination. But this is not incompatible with history, nor with dealing rigorously with archival documents. I try to show this in my films. Imagination is not the reconstruction of the camps "for real" but rather an ability to step back from archival imagery.' Interview with A. de Baecque and C. Vassé (2000) 'The Century of Cinema' hors série, *Cahiers du cinéma*, November, 73–4.

39 In 1955 Resnais continued to experiment with this technique not only in *Night and Fog* but also in the film about the Bibliothèque nationale *Toute la mémoire du monde*. On this subject, see L. Liotard (2001) 'Le Travelling est-il une affaire de morale? Le cinéma d'Alain Resnais de *Van Gogh* à *Hiroshima mon amour* (1948–1959)', Masters thesis, University of Paris 8.

40 What we know is that Jean Cayrol, who had already discussed the writing of the synopsis with Resnais at length, had been overwhelmed by the film's first edited version and had preferred to re-work his text

without 'attaching' it to the images. It was Chris Marker, the person who had first introduced Resnais and Cayrol, who took charge of adapting text to image, before finally submitting this version to Cayrol.

41   Agent P2 in the French Combat Forces, no. 43.884, Anatole Dauman was a member of the National Union of Escaped Prisoners of War, no. 4,048, Honorary Candidate of the Croix de guerre medal 1939–45.

13   Baggage and Responsibility: *The World at War* and the Holocaust

Michael Darlow

We are told that television history programmes are the new rock 'n' roll. History channels proliferate and the punters can't get enough of it. They particularly seem to go for programmes about the Second World War. The series *The World at War* (1974) was made thirty years ago, but it comes round again and again on channel after channel.

Audiences seem to believe that television programmes are real history. Sadly, even some of those responsible for the programmes seem to think so too. In saying this I am not suggesting that presenters like Simon Schama and David Starkey are not real historians, but I am saying that claims made by some history programmes and those who make them need to be treated with a certain amount of scepticism. What, for instance, is one to make of the recent series in which a group of young men from Hull was made to go through a cod re-enactment of life in the Flanders trenches (*The Trench*, 2002)? Or of the legion of soft-focus re-enactments of men galloping endlessly towards some vague horizon, or galloping towards us through a smoke-machine-generated mist as in a bad western or a re-make of *Ivanhoe*? This sort of thing should be left to the likes of Mel Gibson or dismissed as what it is – 'visual musak' which is neither evidence nor a realistic re-enactment of historic events.

We programme makers are essentially popularisers – those who give the mass of people who do not read serious history their idea of what happened in the past. As a result, we play an important role in forming their idea of present reality – of why things are as they are. This may be an obvious thought, but it lands us programme makers with an awesome responsibility.

In examining how, as the person selected to make the programme for *The World at War* which dealt with the Holocaust, I tried to discharge that responsibility, it is first necessary to address the baggage which I brought to the programme. All programme makers bring baggage to any programme which they make, to history programmes as much as to any other kind of programme. That baggage is of a number of kinds. The first load of baggage for *The World at War* was Thames Television, the company which produced the series, and its corporate goals. When we started work in 1971, Thames was leading a campaign aimed at demonstrating that ITV was worthy of being awarded a second commercial channel. We therefore worked in the potentially schizophrenic context of an organisation simultaneously dedicated to maximising its profits and to drawing attention to the quality of its programmes.

The second element in our baggage was the period in which we were making the series: 1971–74. By the early 1970s the Second World War was far enough away to have taken on some of the character of the great justification – a justification for Britain and the British. It had come to be seen as *the* moral war, fought for moral reasons; Britain's enduring heroic legacy to a world and a new generation which should be grateful. To many British people at that time the war seemed to be about the last of those 'Good Brave causes' which, as Jimmy Porter had lamented in *Look Back in Anger*, seemed not to exist any more. Hitler and the Nazis were evil and Britain, which had 'stood alone', was good – and if you needed proof you only had to look at what the Nazis had done to the Jews!

There was also the baggage of the films that had been made before. There had been a number of histories – one series called *Victory at Sea* (1952), I vaguely remember from the 1950s – American in origin and all dark mahogany narration and heroic martial music. There had been Alain Resnais' brilliant *Nuit et Brouillard* (*Night and Fog*, 1955) – to me in 1971 that was still *the* film about the Holocaust. And then, crucially, there was the BBC's monumental series *The Great War* (1964), which had set new standards for television history programmes. That was a huge influence and something which, as professionals, we wanted to emulate or even surpass.

Finally, there was my own baggage, both professional and personal. On my tenth birthday, one week after D-Day, the first Doodlebug fell on London. I was, and am, very much a product of my generation. In 1956, when Jimmy Porter denounced the whole repressed, class-ridden horde of old farts who seemed to have run things for what seemed like the whole of my life up until then, I, with many of my contemporaries, had stood up at the back at the Royal Court Theatre and cheered him on. He was saying it for all of us too! On top of that there was additional emotional baggage. I am married to a Slav. Her father was killed fighting with Tito's partisans and her stepmother was Volksdeutsch. She is also part Jewish. At the end of the war she had wound up in Germany as one of the millions of hungry 'displaced persons' with no home to return to.

The original intention had been that Jeremy Isaacs would make the programme about the Holocaust, but quite early on he had asked me if I would do it. Being Jewish, and having lost relatives during the war, Jeremy said that he felt he had too much emotional involvement in the subject to be the right person to tackle it. I was, of course, honoured to be entrusted with such a responsibility. But I too was hesitant. The cause of my hesitation was not so much the awesome responsibility nor my own emotional involvement in the subject as the question of what film to make. What film could be made? I think I said to Jeremy (if I didn't actually say it I certainly thought it) – Why not simply show Alain Resnais' film? Anything we do must fail beside that. But clearly that was not a real option.

The first thing that I did was a great deal of reading. Many books influenced me, but above all Gerald Reitlinger's pioneering work *The Final Solution*, and Raul Hilberg's *The Destruction of the European Jews*.[1] Then, in August 1972, I wrote an essay, some 25,000 words long, far longer and more detailed than anything that could conceivably be contained in one 52-minute programme – a one-hour programme is generally considered to be worth no more than an article of about 6,000 words. To achieve more depth than that you have to use other means. There is simply no space for more argument or detail. That is one of the irresolvable problems of the medium for those who wish to use it seriously.

The World at War crew inside the perimeter at Birkenau. Left to right: Michael Darlow, Frank Hodge (camera), Sue McConachy, Polish interpreter, Ted Adcock (assistant). (© FreemantleMedia)

My essay was not a programme outline, nor even a proposal. I called it an *Argument for a film about Nazi concentration camps*. Almost the first thing I wrote was this: 'It is essential that we are clear about one point from the very outset – this is not primarily a film about the suffering of the people in the camps. It is an attempt to set down what happened and above all, why. So it is above all a film about the organisation, and people behind the organisation, of a calculated act of genocide.' I finished by describing how, when one stands in the orchard behind the ruins of the gas chambers at Birkenau, and is surrounded by the fertile, blossoming trees growing out of the ashes of millions of cremated people, one is overwhelmed with a powerless, helpless misery, and wants to turn away. 'Yet', I said, 'in this film we have got to try to face up honestly to those fields of human ashes in Poland. We have got to look at what happened there fearlessly, and in context. We must not slide out of it on a wave of easy emotion or take refuge in a wave of mystical, philosophical hand-wringing. It happened on our continent, in our generation, for perfectly ordinary and explicable reasons. It will probably happen again – and we shall be even more guilty than last time.'

So, in a sense, I wanted to de-mythologise events which, because of their unique horror, had taken on the aura of the inexplicable. I believed that upon examination even the Holocaust, supremely evil and terrible though it was, must have been just as much the product of mundane, confused, but in themselves recognisable, human actions as other atrocities in history. This meant that I would need to include not only the stories and experiences of the people who had suffered, the victims – vitally important though they were – but also, perhaps more importantly, the stories and explanations of the perpetrators. What had become clear from my reading was a kind of awful inevitability to what had happened. This, therefore, had to be the backbone of the film.

There was going to be precious little archive film. So we would have to pursue the progression of a logical nightmare through the experiences and stories of those involved. But could we find the witnesses, particularly among the perpetrators? If they agreed to talk, would they tell the truth? In the search for witnesses and such archive film as existed, I had one enormous advantage over others who had previously made films on the subject. I was part of a large team making a series that covered all parts of the globe. As a result I could draw on researchers and experts in many countries.

I did not want out-and-out baddies – the psychopaths and low-IQ bully boys who do every tyrant's dirty work and enjoy it. I was offered a number of those and rejected them. They were not interesting because they were not what made the Holocaust unique. They are everywhere when wanted – the misfit kids of whatever age, the psychopaths: go down to any National Front march, to Kosovo, to Rwanda, to Zimbabwe. There is never trouble recruiting them. No, my target was the cogs in the machine, the railway signal man, the administrator, the member of the detail that carried the tins of Zyklon B, a senior SS officer in Himmler's entourage like SS General Karl Wolff.

Wolff was an army officer with a genuine hard-luck story. He had lost his job in the demilitarisation of Germany after the First World War but risen through the SS to be an important cog in the machine of the Holocaust. Yet he still felt himself part of an honourable, military tradition. He could rationalise, even justify to his own nightmarish satisfaction, the absolutely unjustifiable. Finding him took the best part of three years. We first got on to Wolff in Holland as a result of my writer and researcher Charles Bloomberg's conversations with Mrs Rost von Tonnigen, the widow of the leader of the Dutch SS. These led from one contact to another, and via one member after another of *The World at War* team, taking in cross-checks with Simon Wiesenthal and his Vienna office, the Frankfurt and Hamburg prosecutors' offices, and Lohamei Hagetaot in Israel, to Susan McConachy, our researcher in Germany. She tracked his post-war history through a succession of small German villages. She encountered face after face that was just too blank and door after door that slammed shut in her face – 'Never heard of him here!' Then one day Wolff walked unannounced into our hotel in Berlin and said, 'I hear you've been looking for me.' Even after that there were rides in darkened cars, guard dogs, small villages in the Rhineland and days of talking to him, cooking for him – and letting him talk endlessly to us.

Finally, when we interviewed Wolff on camera we took a whole day over it. Talking at such length people frequently reveal themselves in ways that are as telling for the way in which they say things as for the actual content. Talking about the change of policy towards the Jews after Hitler invaded the Soviet Union in 1941, Wolff said:

We found a round figure of three million Jews in Poland, and then immediately after that came the Russian campaign and we found another five million Jews in Russia. How on earth could we manage to emigrate this eight million by using long and tiresome official methods if we could not, as was planned somehow or other after the war organise a general and mass-protected and organised emigration to Madagascar? We had conquered France, after all, and we could have compensated France adequately from our other colonial possessions so we could have used Madagascar – the island was big enough to accommodate such a number of Jews – but in the war we were cut off. We had no other choice.

We were working at the right moment. The Eichmann trial, ten years earlier, had brought to light a great deal of important evidence and many vital witnesses. It had led to a renewed hunt for the killers and the establishment in a number of German cities of prosecutors' offices that gave us enormous assistance. At the same time the events were now long enough ago for a number of people – victims and members of the Nazi machine – to want to talk, to put their own account on record. Revealingly, perhaps, one of our greatest difficulties was getting people on the Allied side to explain honestly their lack of effective action even after they knew exactly what was happening in Eastern Europe. Lord Avon (Sir Anthony Eden), for instance, flatly refused to talk during an interview about advice he had given to the Americans in 1943 in which he had said that they should act 'very cautiously' over the problem of the Jews. When I reminded him of papers that had already been published he simply denied that they were part of the official record.

As the series started to near completion and members of the team prepared to go off in search of other work, it seemed more and more important to those of us who had been working on 'Genocide' to use this unique opportunity to bring together all the material that we had gathered into some kind of a single coherent whole.[2] This should be left on record for future generations. We did not think of it as necessarily being a completed film. Perhaps an assembly in a logical order, ideally with a draft narration as a navigation chart through it, which in years to come could be brought out to give the lie to those who might come after and attempt to re-write history, play down or even deny that the Holocaust had ever happened.

Initially we started to work for nothing in the cutting room in the evenings. We did not see our assembly as a film for popular audiences, or as an extension of the series. However that changed once the *World at War* series became a popular success. Suddenly there were demands from Thames' sales department for more that they could sell. The opportunity now arose to finish a longer film – although still with the material we had, not by going out and getting more to fill in the gaps. This was a great opportunity, but also a problem. By this time we had a reasonable rough cut for our original purposes, running about six and a half hours. But this was too long for commercial television and unsuitable for showing to general audiences. After much effort we wrestled the film (given the title *The Final Solution – Auschwitz*) down to three hours and 15 minutes and it went out on ITV and in a number of other countries in that form.[3] It was put on sale in shops as a video (although at least one retail video version which is still available chops it off halfway through and runs eye-witness descriptions of mass shootings straight into the action of a film about American soldiers fighting in Italy, thus reducing these witnesses' testimony to a mere commercial product. This is insulting to its subject as well as being a travesty of our intentions).

If I were setting out again today I would start with a different set of considerations and baggage. Many more films have been made about the Holocaust. More footage has become available, from Russia in particular. However, more of it has been seen and fewer witnesses now survive. As a result I suspect that today I would find my task even more difficult than I did thirty years ago.

I would like to end with the words of one of our witnesses. Dov Paisikowicz was a Czech Jew who was detailed to work as a member of the *Sonderkommando* at Auschwitz, assisting people before they were gassed, removing bodies from the gas chambers and burning them in open pits or the specially constructed crematoria. He describes not only what happened to the victims but the anguish of those forced to work as he did. Paisikowicz was one of the interviewees we were able to play at greater length in the long version of the film, allowing the tragic ambiguity of his situation to emerge even more clearly. Towards the end of my interview with him he said this: 'No one who hasn't undergone such a thing can imagine what the will to live is, what a moment of life is. Every person, without exception, is capable of doing the worst thing just to live another minute.' A little later he added, 'The cries in the bunker, in the crematorium, in the gas chamber, were horrible. I wonder today why God didn't hear these cries. It's a wonder to me, that He didn't hear such a thing. They were horrible – the cries to the sky.'

Notes

1   G. R. Reitlinger (1971) *The Final Solution: The Attempt to Exterminate the Jews of Europe, 1939–1945* (second edition). London: Sphere; R. Hilberg (1961) *The Destruction of the European Jews.* London: W. H. Allen.

2   'Genocide' was the title given to episode 20 of *The World at War* series. It was first transmitted on the ITV network at 9pm on Wednesday 28 March 1974.

3   *The Final Solution – Auschwitz* was first transmitted in two parts on the ITV network on consecutive nights at 10.30pm on Tuesday 12 and Wednesday 13 August 1975. Both 'Genocide' and *The Final Solu-tion – Auschwitz* programmes were subsequently transmitted in the USA. The 'Genocide' episode on its own and as part of the series has been shown in almost every country and repeatedly ever since it was released. Both programmes have also been released on video and DVD. The films have won prizes in Is-rael, USA and Britain and *The Final Solution – Auschwitz* was nominated for the BAFTA as 'Best Factual Programme' in 1975.

14   *The Nazis: A Warning From History*

Laurence Rees

There are few subjects in history more important for study and for the attention of film-makers than the Holocaust. This area of history and the Second World War in general has been an obsession of mine for as long as I can remember: what concerns me is that future generations may not feel quite the same way about it as I do. As a child my interest was stimulated because my father fought in the war and my uncle died on the Atlantic convoys. When I was growing up the *World at War* television series was also hugely influential for me, and watching these programmes fired my interest in this area of television making; it really is a truly extraordinary achievement and we are all walking somewhat in its shadow. I think it is also particularly important to remember that this symposium is held on the sixtieth anniversary of the final stages of the planning for the invasion of the Soviet Union, which was the event that was to precipitate the systematic killings that led to the extermination that we now describe as the Holocaust.

I am going to discuss some extracts from a series I wrote and produced called *The Nazis: A Warning from History* (1997) with the brilliant academic Ian Kershaw acting as the chief historical consultant. But I trace the moment that I first wanted to make this series back to 1990, long before I met Ian, when I was making a film about Joseph Goebbels (*Goebbels: Master of Propaganda*, 1992); someone who had always interested me because of his skill with film. I remember we had interviewed his personal attaché, Wilfred von Oven, who was an extraordinarily charming, incredibly ironic, intelligent man. Von Oven was talking about working alongside Goebbels and recalling the problems he had with him going off sleeping with actresses and that he could never find him and so on. At the end of the interview we were having a cup of tea and I asked, 'If you could sum up your experience of the Third Reich for me in one word, what would it be?' And he looked back and said, 'Paradise'. I remember thinking, there's something going on here that we need to get to the bottom of. For these words could never have been said by, for example, a Stalinist apparatchik. When I subsequently went and talked to people who had worked for Stalin, none of them described the experience as 'paradise'. I believe passionately that there is something conceptually different about Nazism from, say, Stalinism. I know there are all these arguments about how many people were killed: 'Did Stalin kill more?' 'Did Hitler kill more?' But having made some films about Stalinism, and met many of those who survived Stalin's rule and those who were perpetrators of atrocities and cruelties during this time; I am still of the opinion that there is something different about the mentalities of those within the Nazi regime.

Since going to Treblinka for our series on the Nazis I have been to many other places where terrible suffering took place: I filmed in some of the gulags in Siberia, I have investigated the POW camps and the locations of the death marches in the jungle of Borneo, and I have been to Dachau and other concentration camps. But absolutely nowhere I have ever been in the world has had an effect on me like going to Treblinka and meeting Samuel Willenberg, one of only sixty survivors of that place.

Most people in this country know very little about Treblinka, as most of the focus is on Auschwitz. And they are not that clear about Auschwitz either. A common misconception about the Holocaust is the lack of differentiation between a concentration camp and an extermination camp. The reason that Auschwitz is the cause of confusion is that it was both. If you go to Auschwitz now, there are disused barracks everywhere; it was a huge operation because of course it was servicing the factories and the construction sites. There was a strong element of human selection at Auschwitz and people talk about this selection very movingly, but of course, Treblinka was completely different – 99 per cent of people on arrival at Treblinka were dead within an hour and a half. Part of the reason for this widespread misunderstanding is that we in television tend not to focus on places like Treblinka. Because, simply put, there is nothing there. The camp was in operation from the summer of 1942 to the autumn of 1943 when, its murderous job completed, the Nazis shut it down and ploughed it over. If you visit the camp now it is just a field – there is a small monument, but it is basically a field. It is also tiny. I would guess that it covers an area smaller than the Imperial War Museum. Because no records were kept, we do not know how many died there: some people say 800,000, some say it is closer to a million. People arrived at the railway station – which was designed to look like a normal station – and were taken off the train, shaved, run along into the gas chambers and killed. No selection, nothing. So for those who did survive like Samuel Willenberg it was, essentially, the result of a most enormous piece of good fortune. He knew someone who was working there already. They needed a builder, so he told Samuel, 'Say you're a builder'. So they yanked him out of the line. Treblinka, Sorbibor and Belzec have not penetrated the public consciousness as much as they should, and this is because there are images of Auschwitz and there are, by definition, more survivors of Auschwitz. This is something I feel passionately about, and it is why we called that episode *Road to Treblinka*, and not 'Road to Auschwitz'.

Most investigations and films about the Holocaust tend to concentrate on the survivors and survivor-based testimony. But for the *Nazis* series, we tried to do something that we hoped was slightly different, and central to that was perpetrator-based testimony. We wanted to find people who were committed Nazis, who believed in what was going on, and then to question them about why they did what they did. That was the overwhelming *raison d'être* of the series. If the series had one aim, it was to find out how it was possible for a man such as Wilfred von Oven to describe the Nazi regime as 'paradise' – even knowing as he did the horrors of Treblinka. And in order to answer that question it is crucial to talk to perpetrators, not just survivors.

We also interviewed those who were not perpetrators, but were committed Nazis and antisemites. One in particular was used in the series – Bruno Hähnel, a Hitler Youth leader. He did not go on to commit any war crimes, but he absolutely believed in Nazism. Moreover, he was someone who, we felt, was honest in his explanation of why he hated the Jews.

Pursuing this line of questioning a little further, does that person still hold these opinions today? I suspect he does. He certainly believed it then, and his is the absolutely standard, common line you encounter. He actually had Jewish relatives. People like him tend to give you the standard response – individually the Jews were no problem whatsoever, but taken as a whole they are part of a world conspiracy. Again, making a comparison with Stalinist Russia, I rarely came across anybody I actually thought genuinely swallowed a lot of the Stalinist ideology and propaganda. I thought they were trying to get on at the time, they were doing their best and so on, but I am not sure they really believed it. By comparison I think people like Hähnel really did believe and internalise the Nazi propaganda about the Jews.

We were very concerned about putting certain people on television. On the one hand we thought that the only way we were going to learn anything was by listening to people like this. But on the other hand, because of what they were saying, we felt they were quite dangerous people. We tried a number of methods to demonstrate that our moral position was not analogous to theirs. An obvious approach was to interview survivors and cut them in straight after the testimony from 'perpetrators'. But that just looked pusillanimous and as if we did not have the courage of our own convictions. So in the end we resolved forcefully to ask these people questions that stated our moral position. We also thought that these would be the kind of questions that the viewer watching would want to ask. And what we subsequently discovered was that we also got the best answers that way as well. The kind of question this approach produced, 'Isn't this morally disgraceful?', was one that a lot of these people were already familiar with as it had often been posed, for example, by their grandchildren. So it was actually serendipitous that the questions we wanted to put were the ones they wanted, and may have even been waiting, to answer.

Our BBC producer guidelines, quite rightly, require us to be open about the nature of the interview, we cannot say 'We want to talk to you for this series on gardening', and then spring questions about war crimes. However, we are not so naïve as to open our questioning with a 'big moral question', but we move gradually and only over time probe more deeply into controversial aspects of their former lives. And to allay the fears of those who are concerned that killers and war criminals may be benefiting financially from our interviews, again BBC guidelines prevent us from paying witnesses more than a standard flat fee, to cover costs incurred to them while an interview is taking place (electricity used by the camera team, phone calls and so on). We are also bound to pay a fee for borrowing photographs used in a programme. But apart from these tiny amounts of money to cover their legitimate expenses, these people get nothing – we would never pay for an interview with a perpetrator. I have always refused to interview any potential interviewee who has demanded a fee up front. Apart from the fact that we do not want war criminals to become rich as a result of our work, generally, such witnesses cannot be relied upon to give an honest account and may even be lying about their real identity (the 'I was Hitler's personal driver/I was a mass murderer' tendency).

In one respect Hähnel is unusual in that he was a member of the Nazi Party during the 1920s when relatively few were. In the 1928 elections for the Reichstag, the Nazi Party only secured a 2.6 per cent share of the vote, but within five years Hitler was the Chancellor. I am particularly fond of the archive film in that sequence, which shows a group of drunk Nazis on a child's swing. I do not think you need to know very much more about the kind of mentality of the people who were joining the Nazi Party at that time. To many Germans I have met, the Nazis of the 1920s were a complete joke. And in response to all those stories of Hitler's mesmeric, extraordinary powers, for every person who has said that he was mesmeric and fantastic I have spoken to another five who have said, 'I saw him speak, and I thought, "what a joke, why doesn't he do something about his voice? Oh, it gives you a headache". If Hitler was hypnotic, how does one explain what happened in the 1928 German election, when 97 per cent of the population were not hypnotised?

But what is significant about Hähnel is that he became committed to the Nazis earlier on, at a time when the vast majority of people did not buy into the Nazi idea. But then they suddenly began to around 1931 and, crucially, March 1933 saw a massive increase in applications to join the Nazi Party. This is no accident as it is exactly the time the Nazis consolidated power with Hitler as Chancellor. In fact, the people who joined in March were known as March Violets and those who had joined in the 1920s were looked on as the true Nazis. I think that was the root of Hitler's obsession with people who were with him at the Beer Hall Putsch. They were the people he could really trust, and he stood by them and protected them, even though some of them from that early period were outright liabilities.

Something happened to the mass of Germany's population in the early 1930s that led them to change their attitude to the Nazis. Indeed from our interviews and Ian Kershaw's research we were satisfied that had free elections been held in 1936 or 1937, Hitler would have got back in with a fairly substantial majority. Partly I believe that one can explain this change with the rather prosaic observation that the vast majority of people just want to get on with their lives and make the most of their situation. And it was comparatively easy in Nazi Germany to make the best of it, unlike Stalinist Russia, because what Hitler did was to isolate specific, named risk groups: work-shy people, homosexuals, those on the political left, and Jews, particularly Jews. So if you were not in one of those risk groups, and kept your nose clean, you could have a relatively positive time, and a lot of people's memories of this time are very good. That is the difference with the Stalinist experience, because practically anyone could have had the 'knock on the door' in Stalin's Russia, and being a high-ranking Communist Party member was no protection.

To illustrate this point, below is a report that influenced my thinking and approach to the making of this series. It was written in 1936 by a member of the Sozialdemokratische Partei Deutchlands (SPD) (German Social Democratic Party), one of the outlawed opposition parties. Its author had tried to find the previous leaders of the party and to re-build his contacts in Nazi Germany. This was his assessment of popular attitudes to politics:

> The problem is that the average worker is primarily interested in work, and not in democracy. People who previously enthusiastically supported democracy now show no interest whatsoever in politics. I suppose one must be clear about the fact that in the first instance men are fathers of families and have jobs, and that for them politics take second place, and even then only when they expect to get something out of it.

It is clear that many of the people who bought into the Nazi Party were not like Hähnel, who was a passionate believer. They may have acted as if they passionately believed in it but actually they were just supporting the new regime because that was the way to get on. Further evidence for this comes from the work of Professor Robert Gellately who has conducted research into the relationship between the Gestapo and the general German population during the 1930s.[1] He came across an appraisal written about a man called Heinrich Müller who was the head of the Gestapo from about 1939. Though most people say he was killed at the end of the war, some on the fringe believe he escaped. The appraisal of Müller was written by the local Nazi headquarters in 1937 and had been ordered by Himmler and Heydrich. It is a personnel report to assess his suitability for high office. When the report's compilers investigated Müller's background they became rather worried with what they found. He had been a policeman before 1933 and this is what the report said:

> It must be acknowledged that he proceeded against these [left-wing] movements with great severity, in fact partially even ignoring the legal regulations and norms. It is not less clear, however, that Müller, had it been his task, would have proceeded just the same against the right. With his vast ambition and relentless drive he would have done everything to gain the appreciation of whomever might happen to be his boss, in a given system.[2]

What is fascinating is that despite the fact that the report raised concerns about his ideological equivocation, when Himmler read the report he had no problem with this aspect of Müller's character and promoted him, because the Nazis were nothing if not politically pragmatic. I wonder to what extent this appraisal of Muller is a true assessment of the majority of human beings; it is certainly a description that one could apply to the majority of people I met who were involved in these sorts of societies. Certainly they just wanted a quiet life, and if that involved being in a corrupt, evil society and just looking out for the best, that's OK. Before we think, therefore, that this is something peculiar to German, Russian or Japanese societies, there is some very interesting work that has been conducted about collaboration in the Channel Islands showing that it was a sought-after posting for a German Army soldier, as there was no strong resistance, a few of the local girls married German soldiers, and the climate was pleasant. We are lucky we do not know what would have happened if Britain had been occupied; remember that in France the ranks of the Resistance did not swell until it was clear which way the war was going.

As a result of our research for the programme, it became clear that we needed to find a member of the ordinary German population who had collaborated with the oppressive forces of the regime. Robert Gellately found from his research into a lovely town in the south of Germany called Würzburg that contrary to the popular image of the Gestapo as this large organisation which solely relied on oppressing and spying on the mass of the population, the reality was that the Gestapo seemed to rely to a large extent on denunciations being posted to them; they were not desperately proactive. Indeed they received so many of these denunciations, that Gellately came across an internal Gestapo memo, saying, 'We cannot possibly process all of the denunciations that are coming to us.'

Naturally, we wanted to examine how this could happen, and the mentality of the denouncers. We looked at the case of a lady called Ilse Sonja Totzke; there was a suspicion that she was Jewish, and also that she was a lesbian. One of the key denunciations was written by a lady called Resi Kraus (Maria Theresia Kraus) who was then about eighteen or nineteen, a voluntary denunciator as far as one can gather from the file. We decided to attempt to find this woman. When we eventually found her, Tilman Remme (the Associate Producer) and I went out to Würzburg and did an interview with her.

Even now, some years later, I still do not know what on earth was going on there. Tilman and I spent hours preparing for that interview, we knew we were very lucky to get it, but the one thing that we had not prepared for was that her position would be, 'That is my signature, that is my address, but it's nothing to do with me.' Perhaps Kraus simply did not like this woman, Ilse Totzke, who had a little house at the bottom of her garden; these denunciations were often used for settling a lot of private quarrels. Ilse Totzke was eventually deported to Ravensbrük and she died there, as far as can be established. Resi Kraus continued with her life; ironically it was Hitler who said, 'People only remember from their past what is convenient for them' – perhaps she has just removed from her memory an uncomfortable and inconvenient fact.

From the inception of the *Nazis* series, we had regarded it as absolutely vital that we interview a member of the *Einsatzgruppen*. To me this would be even more important than talking to the *Sonderkommando* or the camp guards at Auschwitz or Treblinka, because what went on behind the German Army in the east was the beginnings of the Holocaust. One particularly horrific aspect of this history relates to the *Einsatzgruppen* in the Baltic States, where very many people who took part in the killing were not Germans, but volunteers from those countries. And they lined up people at the edge of pits and shot them: men, women and children. In fact it was as a result of this killing that Himmler began to look – as he put it – for 'more humane methods of killing', and by that he meant not more humane for the people being killed but for the killers, as he was concerned about the psychological damage to those who were actually doing the killing.

We wanted to find someone who had been doing this and, crucially, someone who would be as honest as we felt they could be in such an interview. We were lucky that the fall of the Berlin Wall gave us access to Komitet Gosudarstvennoi Bezopasnosti (KGB, Committee of State Security) archives in Moscow, enabling us to go through the records of people who had been tried and convicted for war crimes by the Soviets. We came across two or three people who had not been executed by the Russians basically because they had informed on others; clearly some kind of deal had been done, and so these men had spent twenty years in a gulag instead. Tracing these people in Lithuania we went to talk to them, and one or two we did not quite think were being honest with us. We actually interviewed quite a few people that were not included in the final programme, because we just could not accept their account. But this man, Petras Zelionka, was included, and I still think he is being as accurate as he can be. This is a man who was a Lithuanian peasant who volunteered to be a member of a Nazi killing squad, in the summer and autumn of 1941.

The nearest I get to understanding him is in the answer he gives to the question about shooting the children, where he says 'it's a kind of curiosity'. One of the problems with interviewing old people is that actually they were not like that then, they did not look the same, they were young people; most of the men we interviewed were describing their actions between the age of eighteen and twenty-four. We recently did a series on prisons, and the producer came back to me after the research and asked, 'Do you know most crime is committed by people between the age of eighteen and twenty-four?' I said, 'Yes, I do actually.' These killers were young men, drunk a lot of the time, and they hated the Jews. Interestingly enough in that part of Lithuania there was no real problem with the Jewish population before the Germans arrived, but there were all sorts of rumours about: 'Oh, they'll cheat you in their dealings.' But what became clear was that many of the non-Jewish members of the population saw the opportunity to steal the Jews' property. I interviewed a number of 'bystanders' from one village who witnessed a particular pit killing. As the Jews were herded out of the village, the other villagers all walked out behind and followed them along to the pit. The Jews were lined up by the pit and when they were forced to strip they actually threw their clothes to people in the village that they liked; people also spoke about the fact that the whole area was covered in torn bank notes as the Jews did not want their killers to have the money.

Why did Zelionka agree to give us an interview? Well what was going on then in the Baltic States during filming really worried me, and may give us a clue. If I had a pound for every Lithuanian, Latvian and Ukranian who has said to me, 'Did you know Marx was a Jew?' I would be rich. Because quite independently of Nazism, many of the people of these countries appeared to have bought into the Nazi propaganda, that Judaism equals Communism. So when we were in Lithuania, the country had just been freed from, as many people saw it, the shackles of Communism. And someone like Petras Zelionka – I am guessing at his motivation here – is not unhappy to be interviewed because Communism has gone and in his mind that was also the creed of the Jews. He is not actually saying, 'I did my bit', that you know 'we were kind of embryonic fighters against Communism, in killing the Jews', but I think that is the line he is pursuing. When we filmed him in a Lithuanian army fort where some other killing had taken place, a young army officer in his early twenties was showing me round; he spoke very good English, and before the interview he said, 'Petras, men like that, they're heroes you know', and I replied, 'Well I don't think so', and he said, 'Oh they were persecuted afterwards, persecuted by the Communists.' And I said, 'Well look what they did.' He said, 'No, no, you're a journalist, and you're missing the story, the big story, the big story isn't what "we" did to the Jews, the big story is what the Jews did to us.' This is a young man in his early twenties who had no other reason to tell me this; we were just talking, I was not going to interview him.

So when people say, 'Oh all this is a kind of historical irrelevance, stop going on about it', I always think of that moment. Because it seems to me, in a broader sense, that what we are talking about here is something that is a profound part of the human condition – the search for scapegoats, the desire to have a quiet life, the desire for personal gain, the tendency to victimise particular groups and so on. I am not sure that there is any less potential for that kind of behaviour in the world now than there was then.

We called the series *The Nazis: A Warning from History*, precisely because of that thought which occurred to us all when we were making it. There was a German-born philosopher called Karl Jaspers who was persecuted by the Nazis[3] and after the war Jaspers wrote about the nature of history, talking specifically of the Holocaust:

> That which has happened is a warning. To forget it is guilt. It must be continually remembered. It was possible for this to happen, and it remains possible for it to happen again at any minute. Only in knowledge can it be prevented.[4]

Everything I have learnt in meeting and interviewing all these people confirms me in the view that Jaspers was right – which is not a very cheerful way of ending, but there you are.[5]

Notes

1   See R. Gellately (1991) *The Gestapo and German Society: Enforcing Racial Policy*. Oxford: Clarendon.

2   For this published version of Rees's paper, the exact wording of this quote was taken from Rees's book to accompany the original television series. See L. Rees (2002) *The Nazis: A Warning from History*. London: BBC Worldwide, 58.

3   Karl Theodor Jaspers (1883–1969) was born in Oldenburg and studied medicine, initially specialising in psychiatry and psychopathology. He was Professor of Psychology at Heidelberg University (1916–20) and then, from 1921, Professor of Philosophy until he was dismissed by the Nazis. His work was banned but he stayed in Germany and was awarded the Goethe Prize in 1947 for his uncompromising stand.

4   This quote is taken from the introduction to Rees's book to accompany the series – Rees 2002: 11. Rees had himself found the quote in a book by Ian Kershaw, but it originally appears in K. Jaspers (1953) *The Origin and Goal of History* (transl. Michael Bullock) London: Routledge & Kegan Paul, 149. Jaspers' whole discussion of the Nazi concentration camps, the meaning of them for mankind and how we might avoid a repetition of these horrors, is inspiring and worth reading in full, especially chapter 3 – 'The Future'.

5   In January and February 2005, to mark the sixtieth anniversary of the liberation of Auschwitz, Rees's new six-part documentary series, *Auschwitz: The Nazis and the 'Final Solution'*, was broadcast on BBC2.

15   *Kitty – Return To Auschwitz*

Peter Morley

In 1978 Yorkshire Television's (YTV) Managing Director, Paul Fox, invited me to produce and direct a quartet of one-hour documentaries, telling the stories of acts of extraordinary courage displayed by women in the Second World War. Each of these would focus on an individual's lone fight against Nazism and all it stood for.

When I met YTV's research team we established the criteria for the choice of people and their experiences for inclusion in the series. Very simply, these should be largely untold stories, and the chosen women had to be able to speak English and be willing to travel back to the locations to tell their stories. The research team was led by Kevin Sim who later joined me as YTV's co-producer.

While I was finishing a film I was making for EMI, they set off to find and compile a list of potential candidates. Once free, I would go and meet them, explore their stories, and we would then whittle down the list and make a final choice. Some weeks later, as I went around the various countries to meet these women, it became more and more difficult to choose between them. The courage and heroism they had displayed in pursuit of a common cause deserved the inclusion of each and every one of them. Sadly television schedules are not that accommodating.

One of the names the team had discovered was Kitty Hart. They were deeply impressed by the story of her survival at Auschwitz, and begged me to include her, urging me to go up to Birmingham to meet her. But I was reluctant to do that as I could not see how her story matched the criteria we had laid down. All the other candidates were mature women who had made conscious decisions to fight evil regimes, ready to take appalling risks, willing to sacrifice themselves and their families. Kitty, on the other hand, was an immature 12-year-old who was engulfed by events. She had been on the run with her mother for nearly four years, initially in her own country, Poland. Then Kitty's father procured false Aryan papers for them both and, bribing some officials, got them on to a transport taking slave labourers to work inside Germany. This, he hoped, might increase their chances of survival. They would never see him again. In 1943 they were betrayed; their false identities were discovered and they were arrested, tried and dispatched to Auschwitz, not because they were Jewish, but because they had entered Germany illegally. Kitty was now sixteen.

Hers is a complex story of courageous self-preservation and ultimate survival. If we were to go ahead and tell her story, it would have to be a one-off documentary and not part of the series I had been engaged to make. In any case, I had some reservations about taking a survivor back. In spite of this I was persuaded to go and meet Kitty, and on the train going up to Birmingham I rehearsed my reasons why I felt we could not go ahead and film her story.

On meeting her I soon realised that she was counting on being taken back to Auschwitz and that the researchers had previously hinted that this was likely to happen. My initial misgivings about this project were about to intensify. She took me over to the mantelpiece in her living room and handed me a small transparent Perspex presentation stand. Mounted inside it were two separate pieces of human skin, each one bearing a camp number – one was Kitty's, the other her mother's. They had them removed from their arms when they finally settled in England after the war and their display on the mantelpiece served as a visible and constant reminder of their time in Auschwitz. Kitty had prepared a light lunch and when we sat down she produced a small round loaf of bread she had baked, and ceremonially cut off one slice. As she held it up for me to see she said that this slice represented 'life or death – the daily Auschwitz bread ration' used by the inmates both for sustenance and for bribing and bartering. Every day, since settling in Birmingham after the war, she observed this ritual of cutting off just one slice, although now her loaf contained the most nutritious ingredients. After lunch we sat down in her living room and I got the full impact of her fight for survival delivered with an unstoppable eloquence that left me speechless and exhausted. In the early evening I made my excuses to return to London, with another visit planned for the following week.

On the journey back to London I tried to analyse the situation. Here was a survivor with an almost unbelievable story to tell, and a most persuasive way of telling it. She appeared to 'live' Auschwitz every day of her life, being surrounded by memorabilia to recall her experiences. She told me that right through the post-war years she had felt completely detached from that particular part of her life. She had refused to get involved emotionally in the past and said that she just pretended that it did not happen: 'I didn't allow my brain to take it in – I couldn't go on living if I did.' And yet, she had surrounded herself with Auschwitz artefacts to remind her, every day, of the very events she had refused 'to take in'. I was confused.

She had little time for what she called the trivialities of life, like getting wet when it rains. Was this how she was able to cope with memories? Was she burdened by a feeling of guilt? What effect would a return to Auschwitz have on her – could it be damaging? Was I prepared to accept the responsibility of taking that risk and possibly facing accusations of media manipulation? Would YTV concur? It was a troubled journey.

On my next visit I learned a great deal more about Kitty. We got on well and I was able to ask her many questions. I got the impression that she not only wanted, but also probably needed, to go back – maybe to find tangible and convincing proof that she had, in reality, lived through this hell, survived it, and now, 33 years later, was seeking confirmation.

I then discovered that Kitty's eldest son, David, a young doctor, was very keen to see Auschwitz and would gladly fly over from Canada to accompany his mother. He also said that he thought the time had come for his mother to make the return journey. Accompanied by her doctor son she would be in safe hands, and that finally persuaded me that this was a risk worth taking.

I could now go ahead and get ideas on how to translate all this into a film. The elements of the story were becoming clear, and now the film's style had to be established in the light of details about the location and all the logistical problems that were bound to arise. So the first step was to go and see Auschwitz for myself.

The emotions stirred by my arrival at Auschwitz-Birkenau are hard to describe. None of the films and programmes I had made touching on the Nazi period (the earliest was in 1959) prepared me for what I was experiencing now. From the top of the main building's watchtower, as far as the eye could see, loomed this vast camp. It had never occurred to me to think about its physical size; Auschwitz statistics are measured in a headcount of people, not in acres. Seeing it now from where I was standing, high up over the camp's entrance, it became painfully obvious that to have an intake of millions of people at one end, only to reduce them to ashes at the other, required facilities on a massive scale. The few films I had seen on the Holocaust had not made this clear to me, and now there was an opportunity to find a way of filming Kitty Hart and her son that would convey an impression of the obscene size of Auschwitz. This then would be a story of survival as seen through the eyes of one person, set against the infinite scale of this horrendous site.

Some of my YTV colleagues had suggested that a reporter should accompany Kitty and interview her. I felt that it would be an intrusion, and might stifle Kitty's natural style of delivery. In any case, the prospect of a mother telling her son what she and his grandmother had to endure would carry far greater conviction.

So the style for the film was taking shape. I had got to know her well enough to be pretty certain that once she entered Auschwitz-Birkenau, she would take control of the situation and pour out her recollections to David, peppered with anecdotes. This was going to be a very raw film, and its style, if one can call it that, was one of restraint – purely observational.

On my return I went up to York to put my plans to Paul Fox who was very supportive. I warned him that the main risk was Kitty's reaction on arriving at the camp, taking one look and deciding she could not go through with it. And I would be left stranded with the YTV crew, with no film and a blown budget. Typically, he backed the project. I then suggested that YTV should consider Kitty's story as a one-off television film. And that is what happened. The series that was finally called *Women of Courage* would consist of four programmes and the film now known as *Kitty – Return to Auschwitz* became a single 90-minute documentary.

November 1978, and shooting was about to start. Kraków is about fifty miles from Auschwitz and the closest city to it. We were all booked into the Holiday Inn – an inappropriate name if ever there was one. Kitty and David arrived the following day and over dinner I was able to brief them both. I explained to them that very early in the morning they would travel to Auschwitz in a taxi (our only mode of transport) and that the sound assistant would wave them down about a quarter of a mile out of sight of the camp's main gate. He would then wire them up with radio microphones, and send them on their way. The driver would be instructed to drop them at the main gate; I was keen to capture her reaction on seeing the outside of the camp for the first time. I explained that the crew and I would be inconspicuous. We would keep our distance and simply observe them with the camera, and follow her wherever she chose to take David. I would not offer any suggestions or instructions. There would be no prompting or cueing; in fact I would not be speaking to her at all. From the moment the taxi stopped and dropped them off, they would be on their own. Kitty then told me that she was worried because she was very uncertain about how she would react on seeing the camp again. I crossed my fingers.

It was only after the filming in Auschwitz-Birkenau had been completed that the director Peter Morley spoke to Kitty Hart. (Photo courtesy of Peter Morley)

I knew that we might have to walk huge distances and could be miles away from the camera truck and so to ensure uninterrupted filming, the cameraman, sound recordist and I weighed ourselves down with as many film magazines as we could carry. In order for the three of us to be able to hear every word spoken by Kitty and David, the cameraman and I also wore headphones, and I kept very close to him so that I could whisper instructions into his ear. We were a small, mobile and compact unit.

November 18 – a very cold morning – and we were ready. As the taxi approached we started filming and I held my breath as Kitty and David got out. She paused for a moment and then took her first tentative steps through the main gate of Auschwitz-Birkenau. I felt that we now stood a fair chance of bringing back a unique film.

We followed them into the camp keeping a distance of about twenty yards. I did not want to intrude. When she was inside the camp Kitty stopped, looked and sobbed. At that moment I had to fight back my tears. Later the cameraman warned me that these opening shots might be slightly out of focus as the eyepiece of his camera had filled with his tears.

When Kitty had composed herself she said to David: 'I have come to speak for all the people who have died here...' and from that moment on she took command of the situation and never drew breath. She explained that she was doing all this because some people were denying that it ever happened, and soon there would be no one left who survived Auschwitz, and she owed it to future generations to come here and explain what happened, before it was too late. And so for two long days, with the camera running, we just followed her, and time and time again she surprised David and us with the most dreadful revelations.

I noticed quite early on that a curious change was taking place between mother and son, as though their natural relationship had been temporarily suspended. On the few occasions when she did break down in the middle of some poignant recall, he found it awkward coming close to her, hesitant in putting his arm round her shoulder. His few questions to his mother were quickly put down; she found it hard to tolerate interruptions to her flow of recollections. She seemed to resent his presence, but was glad that there was someone who would listen to her. I sensed that she felt to be under great pressure to prove to herself that the millions of memories she had lived with all these years were really true. But now time was running out – she was in a great hurry.

There was just one rare occasion when she put a question to David, wanting to know from him whether she should feel any guilt about some of the actions she had been forced to take in order to survive? He reassured her about that.

On that first day we filmed continuously for six hours. We followed Kitty for miles never knowing where her explorations were leading to next. Bad light and total exhaustion brought that day's shooting to an end. I purposely did not contact Kitty after we had returned to the hotel that night, and the next morning we continued exactly where she had left off. By the end of that day the most important footage was in the can, and I had not spoken to her once.

Yet there was one particular event during the filming which troubled me for a little while. Kitty had looked for and found the block where thousands of women at a time were herded in for their almost waterless ablutions. It was black inside, there were no windows, and so we could not follow the two of them into the darkness. But we kept the camera running and heard David exclaim that he had found a shoe. 'Oh my God,' said Kitty, 'leather shoes … that meant life or death for somebody. To have a pair of leather shoes meant fifteen days bread ration – so either you ate or you had your pair of leather shoes.' As she walked out into daylight caressing this battered object I whispered to the cameraman that no one would believe this. I had seen a mountain of many thousands of similar shoes in the Auschwitz museum. What was a single one doing in this pitch-dark block? How did it get there? Had it languished there since 1945 when the Russians liberated the camp?[1]

I had to think twice whether to include this sequence in the final cut. If someone thought that I had planted that shoe in advance for the sake of 'good television' might it not undermine the honesty of the whole film? The same could also be thought when Kitty finds the pits where people were burned alive. With a stick she digs around in the ashes and finds a human bone. 'This represents a small proportion of the four million', she says to David, 'and perhaps your grandparents.' Had someone planted this small bone fragment? Should this sequence also end up on the cutting-room floor? I believe that if you do not have complete faith in the veracity of your own material, and embark on a course of dubious self-censorship, you should not be making this type of film.

Kitty and David soon returned to London and I spent another day filming at Auschwitz picking up linking and atmospheric footage. Then I travelled to Warsaw with the crew to shoot one of the *Women of Courage* documentaries. We were back in England a week later. I was very keen to telephone Kitty to find how she had reacted to the trip. And I got my biggest surprise yet. Tearfully she said to me that she felt terrible because she had let me down, let the crew down, let YTV down. I asked her what she meant, and she said: 'All the trouble you have taken, all that expense of flying everyone to

Auschwitz, and I never opened my mouth once.' And she had never stopped talking for two solid days.

When I had finished the cut, she came down to London and I screened it for her. She was dumbfounded. She could hardly believe that it was her saying all this. I ran the film again, and then, slowly, she began to realise the full extent of her reactions on setting foot again in Auschwitz.

The response to the initial ITV network transmission was very positive, with huge press coverage. Kitty was inundated with letters, even those optimistically addressed to 'Kitty, Birmingham'. I was intrigued by a few telephone calls from viewers who wondered where I had found that old black-and-white footage I used in the film. In fact, I deliberately did not use one frame of archive film. The word-pictures Kitty painted in people's minds were far more graphic than old newsreel film. Extraordinary.

The film was shown on television around the world and was well received. It collected a clutch of international awards. Two of these were particularly poignant. In 1981 in Berlin, of all places, *Kitty – Return to Auschwitz* won the prestigious Prix Futura. When the Burgormaster of Berlin presented me with the prize, the irony of it did not escape those who attended the ceremony. In 1985, Japan staged what they termed the first 'International Television Festival'. The organisers had combed the world for what they considered to be the best documentaries ever made. They selected a long list of international productions, and then invited the directors of each one to Tokyo. We had to address a huge festival jury made up of 150 television producers and directors, and then screen the film. After they voted, the NHK chairman presented me with the Tokyo prize. Two weeks later they showed *Kitty – Return to Auschwitz* on their network. The reaction to this foreign documentary was so overwhelming that they repeated it the following week. But what puts all these awards into the shade is the most valuable reward of all – the lasting effect the return to Auschwitz had on Kitty herself. The film we made produced results that totally changed her attitude to her incarceration and to her survival.

Over twenty-five years have now elapsed. We have kept in close touch, and I have witnessed, with admiration, the new life-style Kitty has chosen after her cathartic return trip. She now faced these unspeakable experiences in a new light. My early misgivings about the great risk of taking her back to the camp had faded into the background. When at first I got to know her in Birmingham, I felt that probably she needed to go back, but I had no inkling that her pilgrimage would result in such a profound change to her life. Gone is the mantelpiece display of her and her mother's preserved camp numbers, gone is the ritual of baking the Auschwitz loaf, gone is the memorabilia that cast such a negetive spell on her past. Instead, there emerged a new positive attitude to life in general, and to her experiences and survival in particular.

Ever since the film's transmission in November 1979, she has been in huge demand. She has lectured in dozens of schools on the Holocaust. She has visited her hometown, Bielsko, where the Jewish community, which included thirty members of her family, perished in the Holocaust. She has taken student trips to Auschwitz and has played an active role in countering those who have denied that any of this ever happened.

The raw style of this film, eschewing cold statistics, interviews and conventional filmmaking, has managed to establish a truth about this camp that is unchallengable – and thanks to her courage and her eloquence, Kitty gave the word, Auschwitz, a new meaning.

Note

1 The presence of the shoe has remained a mystery. At the time I queried it with the caretaker of Birkenau, and he too was totally baffled. The fact that it was pitch-black inside this ablution block may have caused the relic to escape detection since the camp's liberation in 1945.

16   Some reflections on Claude Lanzmann's approach to the examination of the Holocaust

Raye Farr

Shoah (1985) has been lauded as 'the film event of the century' (Paul Attanasio, *Washington Post*), and 'among the greatest films ever made' (Gene Siskel, *Chicago Tribune*). In the roughly twenty years since Claude Lanzmann's soul-shattering film appeared, much that has been written and said about it has focused on the prescriptions and proscriptions implicitly embodied in its form and content. We are now able to move beyond the boundaries of *Shoah*'s nine-and-a-half edited hours to look at the wider canvas of Lanzmann's work on the Holocaust and at the scope of what he captured in the estimated three hundred hours of footage he shot for the project between 1974 and 1985.[1]

Lanzmann has created two further films, each based on an interview that he chose not to use in *Shoah*: *Un vivant qui passe: Auschwitz 1943, Theresienstadt 1944 (A Visitor from the Living*, 1997) and *Sobibor, 14 octobre 1943, 16 heures* (2001). These films work powerfully on their own, and also give us a chance to broaden our perspective on what Lanzmann pursued with his camera team in the many years of filming the places and the people that could still evoke memories, traces, fragments of the different stages of the process of annihilation. *Shoah*, however, is the main subject of this chapter and our point of departure here.

The place and the word

Shoah shattered the calm edifice of traditional documentary approaches to history. The working title of the film was 'Le Lieu et la parole: The Place and the Word'; Lanzmann's camerawork and probing questions lead his viewers to places and words that few have encountered before, and that perhaps no one has encountered in such mass and juxtaposition. Layer upon layer of 'traces of traces'[2] carry us on rivers of time, forgetfulness and memory, on journeys that seem without end but end with ruthless finality, journeys along train tracks stretching out in diminishing perspective, carrying their freight to end points that immeasurably diminished our humanity and the legacy of the twentieth century.

For those unfamiliar with *Shoah* and his two subsequent, closely related films, it may be helpful briefly to outline Lanzmann's method. Starkly beautiful landscapes and human revelations of cruel facts comprise Lanzmann's film transport for the journey. On this journey he eschews the familiar tools and devices that have become staple ingredients of non-fiction films about the Holocaust. Not only does he reject archive film and photographs, he also discards voiceover narration. For Lanzmann, any attempt to impose a linear narrative on the event immediately entails reduction and falsification – in short, misrepresentation. Instead, the structure of the film is circular; images and words circle obsessively around the sites of destruction, moving ever closer to an elusive centre. Extra-diegetic music is replaced by silence and, on occasion, by songs sung by the witnesses. For Lanzmann, there can be no shying away from the ultimate goal: annihilation. *Sho'ah* in Hebrew.

Is Shoah a documentary?

Shoah has also been called 'the greatest documentary about contemporary history ever made, bar none, and by far the greatest film I've ever seen made about the Holocaust'.[3] Yet Lanzmann himself does not consider *Shoah* to be a documentary. There was considerable discussion during the symposium about the nature and definition of documentary film. Lanzmann would doubtless have been reluctant, in terms of his anticipated appearance at this event, to appear on a programme billed as dealing with documentaries in a slot immediately following the *World at War* panel. The first time I met Lanzmann, in a small elevator in the Holocaust Museum in Washington, I referred to his film as a documentary. His reaction was memorable; I won't make that mistake a second time.

Why this vigorous rejection of such a label? This is how Lanzmann himself defines the film, in the book *Au sujet de Shoah*: '*Shoah* is not strictly a documentary film in that scenes in it are staged and rehearsed. The role of *mise-en-scène* in the film is indeed crucial'.[4] When pressed for an alternative label, Lanzmann invariably refers to the film as 'a fiction of the real'.[5] How do we make sense of this provocative formulation? Lanzmann contends that it is ethical to fictionalise the reality of the Holocaust, rather than the reverse, for to attempt to authenticate a fiction, in the manner of Spielberg for example, is to breach the 'circle of flames' which surrounds the event.[6] In *Shoah*, by contrast, the production of fiction becomes the condition of possibility for authentic testimony.

Close attention to the images sheds light on this procedure. One of the most haunting sequences of the film occurs towards the end of the testimony of the survivor Abraham Bomba, a barber by training, whose job it was in the Treblinka *Sonderkommando* to cut the hair of the men, women and children about to enter the gas chamber. Lanzmann decides to interview Bomba in a barber's shop in Tel Aviv, placing a pair of scissors in his hands and a customer in front of him. The result, in the filmmaker's words, is 'a definitive cinematic scene … Perfect *mise-en-scène*'.[7] But Lanzmann's staging of this scene undermines its own fiction; Bomba, urged by his questioner to re-enact the physical actions he performed under duress in the camp, eventually finds himself unable to go on, and his hitherto coherent testimony breaks down under the pressure of re-surfacing memories. For Lanzmann, 'it is in this moment that the truth is embodied'.[8]

Despite Lanzmann's protestations to the contrary, there are of course good reasons why *Shoah* is often considered to be a documentary. To the film scholars who have spent the last twenty years debunking the conceit that documentary is a truthful endeavour, these elements of art, artifice and fiction would not disqualify *Shoah* as a documentary. After all, they are not unrelated to what an earlier generation of Grierson-inspired British documentarists called 'the creative treatment of actuality'.[9] Even without the traditional elements of archive film, photographs, 'talking head' experts and a chronological or linear narrative, the film is still recognisably one that would fit within the contemporary television category of the 'factual'. Moreover, the characteristics that define it as 'factual' were once, for British and European documentary makers, cardinal rules that defined documentary production: no script, no sets, a willingness to let your witnesses or 'real people' dictate the content and flow, and finally, real historical subject matter.

Definitions and categorisations aside, Lanzmann's singular approach to the atrocity sheds fresh light on ongoing debates about whether there is or can be a 'pure' form of approach to this subject. It seems evident that there are many different forms, rather than one pure form, and that trouble ensues when we attempt to define what the purest approach might be. Moreover, for all the ethical and aesthetic principles underpinning Lanzmann's approach, it is highly questionable whether a single normative formula could be maintained in the face of so complex and idiosyncratic a historical phenomenon as the Holocaust, not to mention its legacies: survivors and their memories, survivors' children and their own psychic scars, the guilt of survivorship, the immeasurable void left by those who perished.

Some survivors and scholars of the Holocaust believe that the Holocaust is such an immense, complex and profound subject that it is simply beyond representation. For Elie Wiesel, even Lanzmann's epic cannot adequately convey the event in its totality:

> There are really neither words nor means to capture the totality of the event ... In spite of the testimonies, memoirs and superhuman efforts of survivors, we will never know how Auschwitz and Treblinka were possible – for the killers as well as the victims.[10]

In my view, this position is not at odds with the position articulated by Lanzmann in *Shoah*. Indeed, this impossibility of representation is Lanzmann's point of departure, and the reason for his decision to make a film in the present, about the present.

Is the essence of the Holocaust 'unspeakable', as is so often claimed? If, as many suggest, the Holocaust created a unique void and disjuncture within human history that can never be truthfully conveyed, then the most that each honest attempt – in whichever medium – can aspire to do is to peel back another layer of the scar-tissue of memory, fact and documentation that has accumulated around the event, in order to bring us a little closer to its core.

Lanzmann gives this 'unspeakable' killing a name: Shoah. Isaiah 56: 5 ('I will give thee an everlasting Name') open's the film and is the heading of each chapter on the recent DVD version of *Shoah*. Lanzmann gives us the places and the words. He accumulates perspectives, both human and environmental. He circles the locations and gathers details. The multiple languages of witnesses and interlocutor, mediated on-screen by interpreters, reverberate with meanings that simultaneously bridge and break the human links in this history, raising further questions about what can and cannot be told. The layering of nationalities and countries of origin and the placement and displacement of witnesses across the globe weave a tapestry in dimensions that cannot be dissected: 'It is a film of geography, of topography.'[11]

More precisely, then, how does Lanzmann approach the Holocaust and create his extraordinary film? The special characteristics that distinguish *Shoah* from other films on the subject merit some elucidation.

The absence of archival images

Lanzmann's refusal to illustrate or validate the testimonies in *Shoah* by means of archive film and photographs is one of the most striking aspects of his approach, though it is not unique in films about the Holocaust. As contributions to this volume by Peter Morley and Orly Yadin show, a number of filmmakers have decided to reject the use of archive images, preferring – like Lanzmann – to place testimony at the heart of their work. Most had qualms about the way audiences might react to the unremitting violence and horror portrayed by so many archival images. But Lanzmann objects to such images on very different grounds. He points out that, strictly speaking, there is virtually nothing to show of the procedure at the core of the annihilation: mass murder in the gas chambers. Most of the images that have entered into collective memory are, in an important sense, peripheral to the event itself, such as those recorded by Allied cameramen at the liberation or by Nazi filmmakers in the Warsaw ghetto for propaganda purposes. Such images, in Lanzmann's account, have little to tell us about death in the gas chambers, hence his decision to abandon the archive and create images of his own. 'The point of departure for the film was', he explains, 'the disappearance of traces: nothing remains but a void, and it was necessary to make a film out of this void'.[12]

Camerawork, sound and space

Motion, silences and timeless images create a stream for our increased consciousness of the fragments that remain, of human beings who entered the Holocaust, looked into the black hole, stepped into the gas chambers, longed for death but were driven by the instinct to survive and the burden of bearing witness. In place of archival film, photographs or documents, the landscape of the Holocaust provides the visual and often the cognitive substance of *Shoah*. The camera takes the viewer on a journey back to the sites of the mass murders, allowing us time to stand, to look, to absorb and to try and fail to comprehend.

The camera technique is almost commonplace in its simplicity. The camera looks in our place, it points, walks, pans and tracks; the camera is the arm of the guide sweeping across the land. There is no trickery; it simply leads us and shows us the locations. It is the viewer who is invited to scour the landscapes for meaning, to contemplate the sites of the crimes in the serenity of the present while attempting to decipher its relationship to the traumatic past. Speaking about his film, Lanzmann refers to these mnemonic sites as 'non-lieux de mémoire' ('non-places of memory').[13] Like the images themselves, this formulation articulates the double negation of presence and of memory which was the ultimate aim of the Nazi project. What is arguably most striking in this film about genocide is the absence of any images of dead bodies. Instead, Lanzmann offers us images of absence: of unpeopled spaces, bodiless cemeteries, empty tombs, of traces under erasure.

Accompanying us on this journey to and through the 'non-lieux de mémoire' are the timeless sounds of local birds, of trains – always the trains – and of the slow rhythmic clopping of horses' hooves. Insistently linking past and present, the sounds of the trains and the horses produce a hypnotic and soothing sense of continuing forward motion that invites us to join others on their journey, to venture with them towards the unknown, the unspoken, the unimaginable – that which so many have tried to forget.

Testimony and Lanzmann's encounters with witnesses

Lanzmann's camerawork, the film's length, and the editor's art also invite us to search the faces of those he asks to bear witness, encouraging us to weigh their words and watch their eyes. The eyes that have seen what we think we want to know are not so clear about the matter of re-living the past. Lanzmann has described how he sought to re-animate, to reincarnate the processes of extermination through testimony. But the witnesses' relationships to Lanzmann's endeavour are continually shifting, as is reflected in their facial expressions, their words and their silences. Can one uncover what lies beneath the stones of Treblinka? Should we? Must we? Such are the implicit questions that inflect the various forms of resistance the witnesses mount against Lanzmann's enquiries.

In a seminal essay entitled 'In the Era of Testimony', Shoshana Felman offers an eloquent re-reading of *Shoah* as a reflection on the meanings and functions of testimony. Felman argues that Lanzmann's film explores and redefines the conflicted relationships between testimony, history and art. Crucially, she asserts that bearing witness to the Holocaust is at once necessary and impossible, a paradox which is central to *Shoah*: 'The necessity of testimony which [the film] affirms derives in reality, and in an absolutely singular way, from the impossibility of testimony which the film at the same time dramatises.'[14] According to Felman, every survivor testimony in *Shoah* simultaneously bears witness to this impossibility of testimony. If *Shoah* is a film about testimony, it is equally a film about silence, about the loss of voice, about that to which we can never bear adequate witness.

Void, amnesia, silence

I would like to focus on a sequence from *Un vivant qui passe*, a film about the International Committee of the Red Cross (ICRC) inspection of the camp at Theresienstadt, or Terezín, in June 1944. With the help of his accomplished editor, the late Sabine Mamou, Lanzmann created *Un vivant qui passe* from footage of an interview in 1979 with the head of the ICRC delegation, Dr Maurice Rossel. A Swiss citizen whose main task was to check on the conditions in the POW camps, Rossel visited Auschwitz in 1943 where he had a polite conversation with the camp commandant, whom he thought was quite a gentleman. Rossel then headed the ICRC delegation to Theresienstadt which, as is described elsewhere in this volume, had been tidied and elaborately 'beautified' in preparation for their long-scheduled visit.

The film's title is a reference to Rossel's perception of the inmates' view of him as he walked through the camp: 'a visitor from the living'. Indeed, the film is structured around a series of gazes; we, the viewers, watch Lanzmann watching Rossel in his armchair describing the prisoners watching him at the time of his visit: 'Only their eyes were still alive.' Lanzmann's suspicious, critical gaze is thus the lens through which we view Rossel as he exhales cigar smoke and attempts to justify his failure to take action at the time. To paraphrase: I would have done nothing differently. What could I report other than what I saw? Of course it was a sham. But why did none of the prisoners dare to say so in my presence? Or to slip me a note?

Many other remarkable and revealing interviews recorded by Lanzmann for *Shoah* were omitted from the final version because they did not fit into its architecture; that is, they remained in some respect peripheral to the mechanisms of genocide which are the film's central subject. Viewers of *Shoah* do not have the opportunity to see, for instance, some extraordinary interviews with female witnesses of different kinds, because it was principally men who were the active participants in – and extremely rare survivors of – the working system of mass killing.

Conclusion

I would like to conclude by describing an early scene in *Shoah* which, in my view, demonstrates the complexity and profundity of Lanzmann's approach to the Holocaust. Simon Srebnik, who survived his boyhood experience of Chelmno during the war, returns to the village with Lanzmann, where he re-enacts his wartime role of the singing prisoner and labourer who enchanted locals and Nazis alike, reconnecting to the place and to the words of the familiar German and Polish songs. In the extended scene that unfolds, Srebnik is at once child and adult, captive and free, simultaneously celebrated and implicitly reviled by the Polish villagers.

Like Srebnik's musical re-enactment of the past in the present elsewhere in the film, this scene positions the viewer precariously between the two historical moments. We watch Srebnik's face, at first shy and uncertain as the villagers praise the memory of his lovely voice, then increasingly uncomfortable as a crowd gathers in front of the church where Lanzmann is filming, eager to be where the camera is and to speak of their memories of the war. Their fond memories of the boy prompt them to 'remember' how they tried to help the Jews. And as a procession of priests and worshippers exits the church in the background, celebrating a Catholic feast in all its timeless ritual, Srebnik shrinks increasingly into himself, his expression visibly changing as more and more locals crowd around him. At this point they coalesce into a contained mob, agitated and energised, an antisemitic chorus, competing with each other to 'explain' why the Jews were targeted. Their explanations are oblique, their bias and prejudices both unselfconscious and unconscious. While the members of the crowd are unaware how much they are revealing, Srebnik knows, as do Lanzmann and the viewer. For me, this is one of the great moments of cinema and of historical insight captured on film. Intercut with shots of the villagers, the images of Srebnik's lonely eyes and haunted face, a face from which the fixed smile has by now faded, offer us a horrifying insight into the Holocaust and its legacies.

One does not smile after seeing *Shoah*, after glimpsing the nature of annihilation – not for a long time. In a certain way, Neal Ascherson wrote in 1986, Lanzmann had to make himself inhuman to achieve the immense humanity of this great film. I can only concur with his conclusion, 'Every human being should see this film.'[15]

Notes

1 The United States Holocaust Memorial Museum in Washington has acquired the outtakes of *Shoah*, in partnership with Yad Vashem in Jerusalem. I have been working since 1997 with my colleagues to reconstruct the 16mm film negatives into their original sequencing, as they were filmed and before the many, many years of editing produced the nine-and-a-half-hour release version. These outtakes comprise a

unique collection that I think many will find of great interest in using as a resource in the years to come. There will eventually be an opportunity to study the rushes, which include some fully intact interviews, as well as the unused portions of those interviews that constitute the basis of the 1985 film. There are approximately 250 hours of outtakes, including 67 interviews and 15 location shootings. Of those interviews, eight are very long, among which are Filip Müller and Richard Glazar from Lanzmann's film, but the longest interview of all was not touched for the nine-and-a-half-hour film. That is the interview with Benjamin Murmelstein, who was part of the Judenrat, or Jewish Council, at Theresienstadt; it comprises 74 camera rolls, ten minutes each. There are also 42 interviews that run between three and four hours, and 17 short interviews. So there is an extraordinary wealth of footage that will be available, with accompanying transcripts, and will gradually be accessible to view on video. In the meantime, in tandem with a local laboratory, we are putting the pieces of negative together like Humpty Dumpty, matching the edge numbers to the rushes that were used in the cutting room, synchronising them with the 16mm magnetic tracks, sometimes remade from the original audio recordings, preserving image and sound on new film copies that are then transferred to videotape – in order to reconstitute and preserve for posterity the remarkable encounters between Claude Lanzmann and some of the witnesses on both sides of the process of the attempted annihilation of Europe's Jews.

2   C. Lanzmann (1990) *Au sujet de Shoah, le film de Claude Lanzmann.* Paris: Ouvrage collectif, éditions Belin, 295.

3   M. Ophuls (1985) 'Closely Watched Trains', *American Film*, 11 November 1985, 18.

4   Lanzmann 1990: 1.

5   Ibid., 301.

6   See, for example, 'Holocauste, la représentation impossible', *Le Monde* (Supplément Arts–Spectacles), 3 March 1994, vii.

7   'Parler pour les morts', *Le Monde des débats*, May 2000, 15.

8   Lanzmann 1990: 298.

9   A definition of documentary film attributed to John Grierson by Forsyth Hardy in his introduction to the 1946 edited volume of writings by Grierson, *Grierson on Documentary*, Forsyth Hardy (ed.), London: Collins, 11.

10 E. Wiesel (1985) 'A Survivor Remembers Other Survivors of the Shoah', *New York Times*, 3 November.

11 Lanzmann 1990: 287.

12 Ibid., 295.

13 Ibid., 280–92.

14 S. Felman (1990) 'A l'âge du témoignage', in Lanzmann 1990: 77–9.

15 N. Ascherson (1990) 'La Controverse autour de *Shoah*', in Lanzmann 1990: 235.

17   But is it documentary?

Orly Yadin

My film *Silence* (1998) (co-produced and co-directed with Sylvie Bringas) is a short animated film. It contains no archival images of the Holocaust, no interviews with survivors, experts or eyewitnesses, no shots of the locations where these events took place, and yet it is a documentary and a true story. Just as the title of this volume suggests, all forms of documentary are merely *representations* of reality and in that sense, an animation film is no different from any other film style.

So many films and television programmes have been made over the past fifty years about Holocaust-related experiences that when my friend Tana Ross, a survivor, asked me in 1996 to make a film about her own story, I refused. Tana was born in 1940 in Berlin and was sent as a child to Theresienstadt. By some miraculous coincidence her grandmother had been sent separately to the same camp, found her and kept her hidden until liberation. In 1945, her grandmother and five-year-old Tana were sent to Sweden where they had relatives. Tana's mother had died in Auschwitz but Tana did not discover the details until much later. Basically, throughout her childhood and adolescence, she was taught to, and made to, keep silent and not to ask questions of her relatives. Only when she left Sweden as an adult, on her journey to start a new life in the US, did the Swedish uncle and aunt hand her a bunch of letters they had kept all these years: letters sent to them from Berlin by her mother, begging them to obtain visas for her and her baby daughter. To what extent they were responsible for not helping the family escape from Germany in time we shall never know, but obviously, they too had kept silent. Like many survivors, Tana became skilled at adapting to new surroundings and blending in.[1] Until quite recently she even kept her concentration camp experiences from her friends. There were so many silences relating to her story – self-imposed and inflicted on others – that we originally thought of calling our film *Silences*. Eventually we decided that one generic term, *Silence*, would stand for more than the plural of the word.

Whilst I was interested in Tana's story for personal reasons, I could not imagine, initially, how to produce a film that would shed new light on survivors' experiences and how to reach out to a new audience. The only visual documentation that Tana had of her childhood was a couple of photographs and three letters. Apart from the Nazi propaganda film made of Theresienstadt, there was no footage that I knew of that could help illuminate her story. I was not interested in filming yet another interview with a survivor talking about events she experienced at a much younger age. So, I kept on saying no to the idea of making a film. Tana, however, was persistent. She was determined to end her silence, but did not want to face an audience herself.

At the time I had a production company that specialised in animation films. Over ten years I had produced a variety of animation films – almost all based on true stories or 'issue' subjects. I am not sure, therefore, why it took so long for the penny to drop. One day, however, I had a flash of inspiration and realised that if we could animate her childhood experiences and enter the realm of imagination that way, then the film could work for us.

Before describing in more detail how we constructed *Silence*, here are a few more general thoughts about the compatibility of animation and documentary.

Animation can be the most honest form of documentary filmmaking

I write this partly to provoke, partly because I believe there is much truth in this statement. The power of the photographic image is so great that even the most sophisticated of viewers easily forgets that any documentary we see on the screen is not a transparent record of life but a filmmaker's interpretation of it. This could be merely in the choice of framing and lighting, in setting up situations, or in the way the shots are edited together to give new meaning. The honesty of animation lies in the fact that the filmmaker is completely upfront about his or her intervention with the subject and if we believe the film to be true it is because we believe the intention was true. In historical documentaries, where frequently there is no suitable footage to be found of a specific event or a specific person, filmmakers choose to re-enact, to film modern-day locations, to use graphics. They might even resort to using the 'wrong' footage in desperation! A documentary animation film claims from the start: what you are seeing is not a photographic record but it is nonetheless a true re-presentation of a reality.

Animation is less exploitative of its subjects

One of the advantages of using animation when making a documentary about a living person (even when it is about their past) is that there is no danger of being uncomfortably voyeuristic. So often we see a film that penetrates into the really personal domain, into sensitive subjects (and first-hand experiences of the Holocaust certainly fall into that realm) and I tend to ask myself to what extent is our interest one of real concern and to what extent a morbid and voyeuristic fascination with the subject. Opting to use animation is a gesture of respect by the filmmaker towards the subject. It also points to the limitations of traditional documentary methods in adequately revealing the survivors' (or other personal) experiences.

Animation can take the viewer to locations unreachable through conventional photography

Animation can show us an un-filmed past and can enter the depths of human emotions. A child's experience of being in a concentration camp as remembered fifty years later – how can this be conveyed? Through archival footage of children found by the Allies at the end of the war? Through the symbolic effects of dark and light? By filming an interview with a 60-year-old woman and trying to imagine her as little girl? Or … by creating a child's world through animated images. This, in a nutshell, was what convinced me to proceed with developing the film. As producers of animation films, our hope was that telling the story in this way would enable us to recreate the little girl's point of view and help the audience to identify with the central character. We did not want to use clichéd archival images and did not feel that an interview with Tana could achieve the same impact. As the development of the film progressed, and the more we talked with Tana, we realised also that there were other points of view we wanted to put across. We wanted to question the war-time role of her Swedish relatives through the range of Tana's emotions, but without attributing blame that was not proven. We wanted to show the inherent racism in Sweden – attitudes never expressed directly but which still had an effect on a little dark-haired girl amongst her blond classmates. We tried to construct the images in such a way as to imply all this without having to spell it out. Animation is very useful for saying a lot in very few frames, and saying it ambiguously enough for the audience to bring their own interpretation and experience to the screen.

Animated characters can seem more real than actors

Perversely, a strange thing happens with the so-called non-realistic medium of animation: once we, the audience, accept that we are entering an animated world, we tend to suspend disbelief and the animation acquires a verisimilitude that drama-documentaries hardly ever achieve. In drama-documentaries, however convincing the actors may be, the viewer never wholly forgets that they are actors standing in for someone else, someone who really existed but cannot be seen.

Tana leaves Sweden clutching her mother's letters. *Silence* (1998) (© Orly Yadin and Sylvie Bringas)

Tana in a classroom in Theresienstadt, in *Silence* (© Orly Yadin and Sylvie Bringas)

The background to *Silence* is the Holocaust. The story itself is about a damaged childhood and the strategies for survival that an orphaned child develops when prevented from speaking out about her memories and pain. It is also the story of lost identities and the search for new ones.

Tana came to me with a poem-like piece about her childhood, co-written to music by the composer Noa Ain and commissioned in 1995 by the municipality of Stockholm for an on-stage performance. This text needed to be adapted to the medium of film. It was beautiful in itself, but very long, wordy and too sentimental to be used as a sound-track. Animation can condense a remarkable amount of material with utmost fluidity and the film had to be precisely eleven minutes in duration (a Channel 4 commission). Gradually we deconstructed the poem and stripped it of sentiment and of words that could be better expressed through images. One option was to interview Tana and then edit the interview to length, but we decided that with such a short film and so much to say, the voiceover had to be scripted as tightly as the visuals were storyboarded.

We decided that the film would have two main sections with visual styles to echo the two locations of the film: Theresienstadt and Stockholm. We chose to work with two animators whose work we knew: Ruth Lingford with her black-and-white wood-cut-style images (reminiscent of Käthe Kollwitz) for the camp scenes, and Tim Webb for the colourful, crowded, Swedish part of the story. For the Swedish section, we were initially inspired by the drawings of Charlotte Salomon and showed them to Tim as a guideline for the kind of cinematic framing we were interested in.[2] We then worked on a storyboard and on re-writing the voiceover. From the storyboard and a rough voiceover guide we set about hiring our team – animators and painters to flesh out the film. We recorded Tana's reading of the script only after the picture was locked. Up until the last minute, as the film was taking shape, we kept fine-tuning the words. One of our main concerns was not to spell everything out and to leave space for the viewer to bring something of themselves to what they saw and heard. Throughout the whole process, we collaborated closely with Tana who commented on all our ideas. At times we walked a tightrope between respecting her sensitivities and trying to take the viewer into a more objective, universal sphere. I am pleased to say that my friendship with Tana survived the tensions of filmmaking.

Silence has been shown throughout the world – on television, in film festivals, in schools and in museums. In Sweden it is apparently now compulsory viewing for high-school kids. Reactions to the film have followed a similar pattern: initial scepticism at the combination of 'animation and Holocaust' or 'animation and documentary'; then very strong and emotional reactions to the film itself and an understanding of the medium we had chosen. A historical documentary, regardless of the media it uses – archival footage, dramatic reconstruction or animation – succeeds when it takes you to the heart of a historical moment and has a clear vision of what it is trying to say. I hope we did that.

Notes

1   Tana left Sweden for the US as a young woman of twenty and has been living in New York ever since. She has two daughters and two grandsons. She is a documentary filmmaker, a photographer, an interpreter and a tour guide.

2   Charlotte Salomon was a young Jewish German artist who kept a flamboyant visual diary of her middle-class Berlin life until she was forced to escape to France where she was eventually caught by the Gestapo and deported. Charlotte Salomon died at Auschwitz in 1943.

18   *Silence*: the role of the animators

Ruth Lingford & Tim Webb

RL: I was asked to work on *Silence* (1998) on the strength of a short film I had made called *Death and the Mother* (1998) which, though drawn digitally, has the appearance of woodcuts. It was in black-and-white, and had a strong gritty look. Tim Webb and I were involved in some of the thinking and planning for *Silence*, although directorial decisions were made by Orly Yadin and Sylvie Bringas. The starting point was a piece of writing by the protagonist, Tana Ross. We also looked at Tana's photographs, and at a variety of archive material. The colour sections of the film were based on the paintings of Charlotte Salomon, an artist who died in the Holocaust but who kept a diary of paintings about her life (published as *Charlotte Salomon, Life or Theatre?*).[1] These paintings had a particularly beautiful use of colour and also a distinctive narrative approach, where different phases of the story flowed into each other on the same page.

My brief was to animate the sequences set in Theresienstadt. The gritty, black-and-white look was very different, and it was a tough job for Tim and I to find common ground in terms of character design, and in the sequences where one world, in memory, changes into the other. For me, these moments are the strongest in the film, where a horrible and repressed memory exerts its grip on the safe and colourful present.

The film was very challenging to make. Orly and Sylvie had made a decision early on not to be too grim, not to use horrific images. So my job was to evoke the misery of Tana's situation without resorting to scenes of obvious horror.

Animation's access to the language of metaphor and transformation allowed, I think, a subtler and more concentrated portrayal of the situation than would have been possible using live-action drama. Images such as the one where the children transform into cockroaches and are swept away with a giant broom have, I think, an effect that are both visceral and thought-provoking. Using animation makes it clear that this is a subjective account. It is not trying, like drama-documentary, to blur the edges of objectivity. Animation can allow the production of strong harsh images without repelling and alienating the audience.

On a technical level, I animated the black-and-white sequences on an Amiga computer, drawing straight into the computer with a digitising tablet and pen and a simple programme called Deluxe Paint. In some sequences, I started from photographic reference. After I had finished the animation, the frames were transferred on to a Mac, which Sylvie then treated with a glow-effect. The decision to apply the glow-effect came late in production, and I was rather put out, as a lot of my detail was lost. But looking at the film from this distance, it seems like a good decision, and has worked well.

At the end of the animation process, it was rather daunting to finally meet Tana. I was really delighted that she liked what we had done.

Storyboard for *Silence* (1998) (© Orly Yadin and Sylvie Bringas)

TW: I was asked to be the animation director on a five-minute section of *Silence*. My section of the film covered Tana's life in Stockholm where she grew up after the war. To contrast this period with her time at Theresienstadt it was decided that we would use colour. As a guide to help me realise this section, Orly and Sylvie introduced me to the brilliant sequential paintings of the Jewish painter Charlotte Salomon. Salomon produced more than 700 (thinly disguised) autobiographical paintings during a two-year period of the war. Eventually she was captured and killed in a death camp. As the film was about Tana, a survivor from the same period, ethically I thought it was right to use Salomon's paintings as inspiration.

During the animation process I would meet with the directors, who would give me revised versions of the script to take away and storyboard in pencil. Initially the drawing did not go too well. So instead I decided to try storyboarding using small gouache paintings and, though the paintings took longer to produce, this proved to be a better method.

When the script and storyboard were finalised, we went into full production working in the same building as the directors. I redrew the paintings in pencil so that the animation could be done. After the animation was approved, the drawings were then each used as a guide for a small team of art workers to paint. The art workers used the original colour paintings from the storyboard as their guide. The painting style had to be tightened for animation, as the image would have 'boiled' if each frame was as loose as the storyboard or Salomon's painting. Each frame is an individual painting, unlike most conventional animated films where the characters are 'drawn' on to one level and the background 'painted' on another.

Note

1   C. Salomon (1981) *Charlotte Salomon, Life or Theatre?: An Autobiographical Play*. Translated from the German by Leila Vennewitz, with an introduction by Judith Herzberg. New York: Viking Press.

19 Oświęcim/Auschwitz: the shooting goes on...

Mira Hamermesh

In June 2003 members of my family from England, Israel and Mexico gathered in Poland to visit the places of my parents' martyrdom. First we travelled to Łódź, our native city, to conduct the ceremony of saying 'Kaddish', the prayer for the dead, at our mother's grave at the Łódź ghetto section of the cemetery. There, she had died of hunger in May 1943.

At Auschwitz, we paid respect to our father (grandfather to the younger generation), who was in the last transport from the Łódź ghetto to reach Auschwitz-Birkenau. The end of the war was only months away but even then the gas chambers were still working at full speed.

Before the war Oświęcim, renamed by the Germans 'Auschwitz', was an obscure small town close to Kraków. Its population was approximately 5,000 souls, of whom 40 per cent were Jews. Its only claim to distinction was a biscuit factory that was embossed with the town's name. Fate could not have prepared a more bitter irony for this peaceful town condemned by history to be forever associated with the vast Death Camp complex. Oświęcim did not deserve its later evil reputation. For Polish people, Oświęcim/Auschwitz is simply called *tam* ('there').

To inmates, crossing the gates with the inscription 'ARBEIT MACHT FREI', it was a place that seemed to have gathered into itself the hate and savagery of the whole world, carried by an unstoppable force.

It was an unusually hot June day when I was travelling from Auschwitz via Kraków back to Warsaw. The train was rushing through fields that were breathing dry heat. The treetops crowned with leaves, tossed by a breeze, were nodding to each other like friendly neighbours.

I sat opposite an old woman with a tattooed concentration camp number on her arm. Noticing that I was looking, her eyes followed mine and in a telling gesture she gently ran her fingers over it. Her action made me think of a creased page from an old book that one tries to smooth out, in order to make sense of the crumpled text. I knew from research that the six-figure number would have been done in a hurry and that the watered-down blue ink could have been jabbed into the arm with a blunted needle.

'I was *there*', she said, breaking the silence. Her advanced age had thinned her skin, now swollen with rivulets of protruding veins, but the number had stayed as blue as the passing sky. Even her death will not erase the Nazis' obsession for turning people into administrative files. Replacing a person's name with a number was the first step in the process of dehumanising the inmates.

I tried not to look at her number. I knew that the numbers inscribed on the skin of each survivor, in their permanency, contain stories that could fill volumes. Train journeys often turn into a kind of confessional on wheels.

Her name was Isolda Klein and she was born in Warsaw in 1918. New York has been her home since the end of the war. She had decided to come back to Poland for the commemoration of the sixtieth Anniversary of the Warsaw Ghetto Uprising, the month-long battle against the German military might by a handful of poorly-armed youngsters which took the Germans by surprise.

She told me: 'I was in a group that was led out through the sewers.' I had seen such scenes in Andrzej Wajda's 1956 film *Kanał*, in Holocaust museums and in photographs taken by the Germans of groups of ghetto fighters with raised hands, emerging from bunkers or sewers. The girls wore men's caps. 'Once out of the ghetto,' she continued, 'the first thing I did was to find a Polish hairdresser who would peroxide my black hair into straw blond. Through my university contacts, a friendly priest provided a false baptism certificate. Under an assumed name and religion I began a new life.'

In wartime Warsaw she had learnt to look at passing Germans soldiers with confidence. Young and attractive, in high heels and wearing an elegant hat she would parade her good looks … while her heart trembled with fear – 'Mind you, for a Jew on the run, appearance was a life saver.' Even now, Isolda Klein was just as well-groomed; her hair, tinted ash blond and elegantly set, was in sharp contrast to the rest of her lined face and sad-looking eyes. Her thin lips were painted crimson red, which I regarded as her declaration of the triumph of life.

None of the films or television documentaries about the German occupation of Europe could convey the fact that in Poland any attempt to shelter Jews on the run from the ghettos meant a death sentence. Some Poles risked their lives to help Jews but others, smelling fear in the hunted Jewish faces, made a profit by delivering the victims to the Gestapo and collecting the reward. Isolda described how she was followed and blackmailed by such an individual. Neither the Madonna medallion she was wearing around her neck nor the possession of a fake baptism certificate could save her. The dark roots of her hair betrayed her as a Jew. Sent to Auschwitz, she was healthy enough to pass the many selections.

Her American-born children were against their mother's visit to Poland. 'Why go to Poland now? At your age! Think of your high blood pressure and heart problems.' 'Ach, what do they know? They haven't been *there*!' A sad smile lifted the drooping corners of her thin lips. Her eyes were fixed on my wrist – free of a number. From her expression I could read her conclusion: 'You too have not been *there*.' This was neither the time nor the place to tell her that yes, I had been to Auschwitz more than once – but not as an inmate. In fact, the most recent visit was my fourth.

My first visit was prompted by a cinema outing back in 1960. I had settled in England after the war and had studied painting at the Slade School of Fine Arts. My marriage to an Englishman had helped distance myself from the emotional burdens that 'the Final Solution' imposes on those connected to it. For years I had managed to keep it at arms' length. Then, at one stroke, the protective shield was blown apart, of all places, at the Academy cinema in Oxford Street. In the dark auditorium, watching Andrzej Wajda's 1954 film *A Generation*, history and my heritage had come to claim me and I was drawn back into a world that should have consumed me together with my parents.

The experience left me with an irresistible urgency to find my mother's grave in the Łódź ghetto cemetery. Soon after, I went to Poland to seek out information about it and also to discover my father's fate in Auschwitz-Birkenau.

My pilgrimage to Poland, for such it turned out to be, was ill-timed. I had arrived in a country gripped by an extremely severe winter. The Łódź cemetery was covered under a thick layer of snow, not a time to look for an unmarked grave. It suited my pilgrim's mood to see the land of my birth covered in a white, frozen shroud.

The frustration due to my failure to locate my mother's grave was compensated by my encounter with students from the Łódź Film School. It led to the projection of the graduation film of their colleague, Roman Polański. The impact of his film, *Dwaj Ludzie z Szafa* (*Two Men with a Wardrobe*, 1958) created a desire to be able to combine my painterly imagination with my need to tell stories. Perhaps I too could become a student there, I mused idly. But I lived in London, was married, had a child, and the film school was in Poland! The thought about the film school was left behind as I proceeded to my next objective: via Kraków to Auschwitz.

In Kraków, a helpful hotel receptionist arranged a lift for me to the concentration/death camp in the car of a visiting VIP from France, a guest of the Ministry of Culture. He was a professor of contemporary military history researching the fate of French prisoners of war. The road from Kraków was hilly and the unsoiled whiteness of the snow cloaked the landscape. How different it would have appeared to the Jews squashed inside the cattle trains, peering through the gaps of the boarded-up windows. While riding in the comfort of a car my thoughts turned to my father's ride in the cattle train to Auschwitz.

Passing the infamous gate with the deceptive inscription, I anticipated that the black letters cast in iron would crush me with powerful emotions. Nothing of the sort happened; a numbness of feelings prevented my heart from stirring. The crisp frosty air felt light, the winter sky was crystal clear and the sun was shining. Ironically, the snow rendered the place obscenely beautiful. I was deaf to the murmur of agony left by those who had passed through these gates.

I had come in the hope of getting closer to my father whose shadow was trapped in this space and of picking up a handful of ashes. The ruins of the chimneys of crematoria do not evoke the taste of ashes or the smell of singed flesh that used to fill the air in all seasons. The inmates, who were made to stand in the endless punishing roll calls, knew the source of the belching smoke.

Documentary films about concentration and death camps create an illusion of seeing with one's own eyes. The unblinking eye of the camera faithfully records the skeletal men and women wearing bizarre striped 'pyjamas', moving like zombies amongst heaps of dead bodies, but it cannot capture the thoughts, dreams and prayers of the victims.

The snow crunched under my fur-lined boots and I thought about the inmates who wore thin cotton garments and wooden clogs, freezing in the severe Polish winters. It was, of course, a vain attempt on my part to imagine that I could perceive this place through my father's eyes.

As a guide, I had used the book *This Way for the Gas, Ladies and Gentlemen* by Tadeusz Borowski, a former inmate who, in his ferocious detailed description, gives an idea of what greeted the stunned and starved Jews after the doors of the cattle trains opened. Dazed, they tumbled down the ramps, greeted by blows and shouts: 'Schnell! Schnell!'

I made my way to the only surviving gas chamber and discovered I was not alone. The French professor was staring at the ceiling with the fake shower fixtures from which instead of water the Zyklon B gas used to be released. To my surprise, he pulled a folded skullcap from his pocket and covered his head. In an almost inaudible voice he began the recitation of the 'Kaddish'. I moved close to him, a wounding grief united us – two Jewish mourners. The Professor cried for his family, and I for mine. This improvised service filled me with the tranquil piety necessary to bring me closer to my father's last choking breath. It also held at bay the demon-driven scream for revenge.

The second time I went to Auschwitz-Birkenau was in 1962. The 'unreasonable' desire to become a filmmaker led eventually to being accepted as a scholarship student at the Polish Film School in Łódź in 1961. I was one of the few Westerners to be admitted during a more relaxed period of the Cold War. Little did I know that the four years of training to become a film director would also become my apprenticeship to life behind the Iron Curtain, as well as exposing me to the effects of the 'Oświęcim Factor'.

This time I came to Auschwitz-Birkenau as a budding film director to shoot my first school exercise, a short feature. The script for my film *Take a Deep Breath* (1962) was an adaptation of a story by Ryszard Palczynski, who had based his novella on a real event that took place in Auschwitz-Birkenau. It is a tale of a Kapo who fell in love with a Jewish girl. The reason why I chose this story was to gain a better understanding of what is so perplexing and inexplicable about the Holocaust. Franz represented to perfection the character of the Kapo who was a villain in one part of the camp, and a love-stricken hero in another.

Franz was a Pole from Silesia who, in the function of a Kapo, had earned the nickname of 'Franz the Killer'; people even feared his shadow. Measured by Auschwitz's standards of brutality, his savagery was never short of new tricks. One of his favoured punishments was to place a plank of wood over the victim's throat and get two other prisoners to balance at each end.

Franz's downfall coincided with the arrival of a transport from Theresienstadt, the 'model' ghetto/camp in Czechoslovakia. A special area was set aside for the newly-arrived Jews within Auschwitz, but located at a distance from the major death camp. Before their arrival, the Commandant in charge had handpicked a team of Kapos who were briefed to be extra polite when receiving the new batch of prisoners. As a perverse kind of a joke, 'Franz the Killer,' was included.

The well-orchestrated charades had a dual purpose. Firstly, to reassure the new arrivals about the tolerable conditions at Auschwitz where families were kept together and the chance of work was promising. Secondly, to get the new arrivals to write postcards to the people left behind in Theresienstadt. To this end even their journey to Auschwitz took place in passenger and not in cattle trains. The Germans did everything to keep the Theresienstadt inmates ignorant about what Auschwitz stood for, and that beyond the wooded ground and the barbed wire, the smoking chimneys were not those of factories but of the crematorium.

The new transport of a few thousand Jews were indeed received in a civilised manner and led in an orderly fashion to their allotted barracks. Franz was approached by a mother with two teenage daughters about help with their heavy suitcases and he, with a smile, obliged. Later Vera, the youngest, requested an aspirin for her 'Maminka's' headache and he immediately ran to get it. By degrees, they had begun to regard the 'nice

Kapo' as their protector and renamed him affectionately 'Franta Our Angel'. He did not disappoint them; he did everything to make their life more comfortable.

At first, Franz's watchful superiors, knowing his sadistic disposition, were greatly amused by the perfection of 'Franz the Killer's' charade. They did not know that he had fallen in love with Vera, the younger of 'Maminka's' two daughters. Eros in Auschwitz proved to be a cruel god of love. Lovesick Franz, knowing the secret of the family's ultimate fate and the date of the impending gassing, became frantic to save Vera, at any cost. He used every means at his disposal: bribery, his illegally stashed gold and diamonds, disregarding the risk to his own safety.

The night before the fatal 'action' was due to take place, he informed Vera about what awaited them and that he had arranged for her safety. At first she disbelieved him but when persuaded about the truth she would accept his help only if 'Maminka' and her sister would be included. This was an impossible request. Heart broken, in their parting scene he instructed her how to die: '*Take a deep breath, death comes quicker this way...*'

My film, *Take a Deep Breath*, ended with this dramatic scene. With more footage and experience, it should have ended in keeping with the author's account of what happened to Franz afterwards. He was punished by the authorities for his lapse into humanity by being singled out to personally supervise the removal of Vera's family from the barracks. Determined to die rather than to carry out his duty, he threw himself on the electrified barbed wires. He was pulled off and, half-alive, was forced to watch how 'Maminka' and her daughters were driven into the gas chamber. He was tortured as an example to others, while making sure that he stayed alive to take more punishment. After the war, Franz was tried by the Poles and sentenced to life imprisonment for the murder of many inmates.

During the five days of filming, the cast and the crew, including myself, were lodged in the concentration camp, living at the Auschwitz Museum guestrooms. When waking up, I watched from the bedroom window how the daybreak mist lifted slowly, like a gigantic curtain, to reveal in its stillness, ghosts waiting to re-enact the drama of death. The spirit of Auschwitz seemed to live on in the presence of the barbed-wire enclosure, the watchtowers and the overgrown railway trucks. The sound of barking of the neighbourhood dogs carried echoes of the past.

Even many years later a powerful stench lingered on in the derelict wooden barracks, a mixture of rotting damp soil and urine that refused to evaporate. No amount of wind blowing through the cracks of the wooden boarding succeeded in wiping out the vestiges of these odours of death. The empty wooden bunks, standing like scaffolding, were filled with inscriptions scratched with hairpins or knives, forks or various blunt instruments. The death camp 'graffiti' cries out in many languages: names, dates, SOS appeals, lines of poetry, messages of the despair and hope left by forgotten people.

All of us were receptive to the messages from the past – of the eight crew-members, five of us (and I was the only Jew) had relatives who had passed through here. One day, we ventured to the archive offices to search through the records for family names. As for my father, there was no trace of the last Łódź transport. By that time the bureaucratic niceties were abandoned, he and his companions were led straight to the gas chambers. My Polish colleagues were more successful.

Loving the Dead (1991) (© Mira Hamermesh)

In the evening, instead of going to sleep, we would huddle together in one of the rooms and with the help of generous helpings of vodka managed to spark laughter by telling obscene jokes. It was a kind of 'hangman's humour'. Did we hope that our laughter would appease the restless spirits?

After the filming, we left flowers on the empty bunks as if they were coffins. I swore never again to set foot in Auschwitz. Years later, I was asked what it felt like to film in a place where the carnivorous earth was nourished with the bones and flesh of one's relatives...

In my attempt to get away from the subject of the Holocaust, my future filmmaking for television made me span the globe: *Two Women* (1975) was shot in England and Hungary; *Maids and Madams* (1986) in South Africa; *Talking to the Enemy* (1988) in the Middle East; *Caste at Birth* (1990) in India. Most of the films dealt with conflicts, oppression and processes of dehumanisation of people. These films have been widely distributed and some have won international awards.

Despite my oath never to return, I returned to Auschwitz-Birkenau in 1991 to shoot the film *Loving the Dead*. This was due to a challenge from a BBC commissioning editor. When I presented a new project with locations in China, she commented: 'Mira, why not consider a film closer to home?' It was a timely reminder that I have been running away from anything to do with Poland and the Holocaust.

So once more, I passed the gate with the sickeningly ironic inscription, this time with a professional crew. By now, due to the political changes in Poland, Auschwitz was no longer a place controlled by the heavy hand of communist propaganda that had perverted much of historical truth. Gone were the ubiquitous descriptions of 'fascist criminals', and the Jews and the Gypsies were finally acknowledged as the chief victims of the Holocaust.

In *Loving the Dead* I ventured to explore who in Poland remembers their missing Jewish neighbours and how do the Poles cope with the task of sharing their land with the legions of Jewish ghosts. Above all, I hoped that the personal motive could make the reality of the Holocaust more concrete and banish the abstraction of 'six million' that had become a cliché. The driving motive was to give substance to the people who once had lived there and left so many traces of their existence on the Polish landscape, to transform absence into presence and lend a voice to those who were silenced. I sensed that by using in the film the story of my parents, victims of the Holocaust, it could serve as a thread from which to weave a much larger fabric, delineating details of the Polish-Jewish cultural heritage, saddled with a record of a troubled co-existence at times. But most importantly, I managed to locate my mother's grave hidden for years by lush vegetation that had rendered the ghetto section of the Łódź cemetery inaccessible. The process of filming symbolised for me an act of peacemaking with the dead.

20 Seeing and hearing for ourselves: the spectacle of reality in the Holocaust documentary

Elizabeth Cowie

As an audio-visual record, the documentary film or video is a memory-machine. It can make present events available for re-viewing, at which time they become a remembered past. Yet archival footage, like any recording of actuality, does not offer us simple facts, just the spectacle of the past. The contingent circumstances of recording may not only produce audio-visual information which is incomplete or indistinct, but the situations and places, as well as the kinds of people and their actions, may not be known to us and we may wonder who these people are, whether they are related as family or perhaps are friends or neighbours? Why do they appear sad? Where are they going? We will seek answers, but there is no 'ideal chronicler' who can inform us without also interpreting the images and sounds. Instead it is through the accounts and comments of participants, witnesses and historians that we come to understand the meaning of what we see and hear, and who thereby remember for us.

Remembering, however, is not only the recall of past events; it may also be the re-encountering of emotions in relation to those past events. It is a process we characterise as mourning if the past we remember is characterised by loss. In remembering the Holocaust, should we remember not only the events and their facts and figures, but also the experience, that is, the loss? The Holocaust documentary can inform, but it can also – in bringing us to feel as and to feel for those we learn from and learn about in the documentary – enable us to form our own memories. Such remembering, for most of us, will not be in relation to our personal experience of the events in the past, but our present experience of the representation of past events. For, as James Young has commented, we cannot now know of the Holocaust, or indeed any era, 'outside the ways it is transmitted to us in its representations'.[1] The ways in which we may come to know and to feel through the Holocaust documentary is the focus of the present chapter.

Our knowledge of the Holocaust, however – as recorded on film and in photographs, and in the documentaries made about it – is caught in the paradox that seeing does not translate into a simple and proper knowing. While the photographic and cinematographic apparatuses that emerged in the nineteenth century gave rise to the idea of an unlimited access to reality in unmediated recordings of reality, as if through the camera we might create a record of everything that an all-seeing God might have surveyed,[2] our access to the sounds and images of recorded reality is always partial, for the camera and its microphone necessarily frames and hence cuts out from the wider ongoing contingency of the world just this scene, this event, these actions, that person, her speech. Documentary, then, looks for us and, in its selections and ordering, constitutes a particular form of narration of the factual and the objective through which it becomes knowable, thus producing a documentary epistemology in which we are enabled not only to see but are also brought to know.

In recognising this we may feel a sense of loss for what we can imagine but never know, namely the reality before its fall into mediation and hence interpretation through narration. Technical developments from the late 1950s made possible highly mobile sync-sound and image recording which liberated the observing eyes and ears of documentary, and enabled ordinary people to give their testimony and tell their stories to camera.[3] A more directly observational cinema arose,[4] in relation to which spectators, by adopting the looks and sounds of documentary as their own, might feel that they are not only overlooking and overhearing events and actions but able to get in close and move around as if themselves a participant. The out-of-focus shot, or the action heard but not seen, that might interrupt such an illusion becomes read instead as an indicator of the documentary truth of the moment of recording as one of 'uncontrolled reality' in which there is no possibility of getting a better shot in a second take.[5] The new 'direct-documentaries' enable a sense of an immediate and full access to the recorded historical reality whereby seeing for ourselves affords us the satisfying knowledge of the evidence of our own eyes, even though we know that our eyes are easily deceived and that, 'while photographs may not lie, liars may photograph'.[6]

The direct filming of observational documentary, however, can become a more improper knowing, and perhaps voyeuristic, when used to entertain in 'reality TV' programmes such as *Big Brother*, which satisfy our curiosity through hidden cameras. Yet audiences, while objectifying the real people who take part, also identify with them. That the recorded 'seen and heard' is not simply knowable or evidential, but requires interpretation that can become misinterpretation, presents a particularly acute dilemma for the documentary representation of the Holocaust. As the concentration camps were liberated, still and ciné photographers documented the shocking evidence they found of Nazi brutality and inhumanity that had produced the scenes of 'starvation, cruelty and bestiality', described by General Eisenhower.[7] The visual records of the army cameramen and the broadcast and printed reports of the war correspondents testify to what they saw and heard not only from Allied soldiers but, most tellingly, through the testimony of those liberated from the camps. The accounts sought to witness for contemporary audiences at home, as well as for future generations, the horror, brutality and suffering of those held in the camps through their twin regimes of slave labour and extermination. Their success is attested by Susan Sontag who later recalled her reaction as a 12-year-old: 'Nothing I have seen ... ever cut me as sharply, deeply, instantaneously ... When I looked at those photographs something broke ... I felt irrevocably grieved, wounded, but a part of my feelings started to tighten; something went dead; something is still crying.'[8] The images began to seem too shocking, too traumatic, for citizens who had already suffered directly or indirectly. Moreover it subsequently became clear that the shocking images led to other unintended and unwanted responses, whereby the survivors and the dead became dehumanised through being objectified as victims, and thus recreating old stereotypes.[9] Seeing with one's own eyes is clearly, then, not a matter of simple objectivity but also of affect, of an emotional response and with it, perhaps, a defensive reaction of denial, or even anger at the victims for the anguished horror they have aroused.

The Allied records provided visible evidence of atrocities but not necessarily of the organised and systematic murder of proscribed groups and races, most especially of Jews, in 'the Final Solution' agreed at Wannsee in January 1942, much of the documentation for which the retreating SS had destroyed. The painfully haunting scenes from Bergen-Belsen of emaciated corpses being bulldozed into a mass grave which can be seen in many Holocaust documentaries (including the 'Genocide' episode in the series *The World at War*) evoke both the mass nature of the deaths the Nazis brought about and its mechanised inhumanity, yet this understanding arises metaphorically in relation to an image of burial by an Allied soldier, and of victims not of the gas chambers, but of the ravages of illness and deliberate starvation the Nazis had perpetrated.

It is of course almost exclusively only Nazi material that is contemporaneous with the genocide they carried out. While certainly authentic, such archived material is not straightforwardly visual evidence; its partiality and incompleteness is the result not only of the accident of survival, but also the process of selectivity in its recording. We see the transport wagons and the many people – the young, the old, the sick, families and friends – with anxious faces being herded aboard, but there are no images of the horror experienced by these unwilling travellers or the terror they endured in the gas chambers. The objectivity of these images as found reality seems profoundly compromised in being recorded as evidence of the Nazi's successful achievement of their desired Final Solution. The camera's look as objective observer with which the viewer so naturally aligns themselves is here the optical viewpoint of a Nazi cameraman, suggesting as well his subjective point of view in his mental apprehension of the scene, and with which we will want nothing to do. Yet these images also record living people doomed, each recognisable; amongst those faces boarding the trains, behind the camp wires or in the ghettos, might be found friends, neighbours and, most hauntingly of all, relatives, who could be recognised – or imagined – not only as parents or brothers and sisters, but as the grandparents or great-grandparents of children born long after.

A different kind of evidence of the acts of genocide is found in the traces and remains recorded by the Allied photographers on the liberation of the death camps, but whose role as evidence must be explained to audiences. The Soviet archive footage of the storerooms at Auschwitz-Birkenau full of the suitcases the transportees carried there, or the piles of spectacles or, what is even more disturbing to see, the mountains of hair, all bear silent witness to a story of murder which is thus indirectly told. In Alain Resnais' film, *Nuit et Brouillard* (*Night and Fog*, 1955), the shots of what appear to be shower rooms, filmed in the now-empty and abandoned camp at Auschwitz, reveal strange marks scratched in the ceiling which, the voiceover chillingly informs us, were made by those imprisoned there as they struggled against the poison they breathed. Here the scene – the physical place of gassing – fails as visible evidence until the testimony lying within the scene as an index of the suffering experienced is recognised and explained.

Night and Fog is a documentary in the tradition of the 'creative treatment of actuality', impassioned and personal. Made ten years after the liberation of the camps, it is the first historical account, seeking to present not just visual evidence but also to show why the Holocaust happened, and to engage its audiences both politically and emotionally through its aesthetic form. Alternating colour footage of the Auschwitz camp's remains in Poland – which fail to reveal their bloody history – with black-and-white archive footage, much of it shot by Nazis, the film is profoundly shocking. A voiceover narration explains what we see in awful detail, as well as with compelling irony – cataloguing the architectural styles of the different camps, for example – which makes all too obvious what Hannah Arendt described as the banality of evil. Irony arises as well in the unspoken narration of the image-track in the many contrasts it presents, notably between the contemporary colour footage of the camp remains, in some shots almost overgrown by nature's verdant invasion, and the archive footage of the rise of Hitler. The present-day actuality is rendered in long shots and travelling camera movements, or carefully framed frontal views creating a rhythm and tone to these images which is matched with panning camera shots in the archive footage. The past appears as a trace in the remnants of cinematic memory and its relation to the present is as loss and concealment, namely, of a historic reality the knowledge of which – both physical and in terms of our historical understanding – has become hidden, overlooked, denied even. The music, composed by the German exile Hans Eisler, unites the work as a sensory as well as intellectual experience.

Night and Fog was highly controversial on its release in France in 1955 and subsequently; as a result the film is itself a document on the history of the representation of the Holocaust, and of the writing of the history of the war and post-war period in France itself and Europe more generally (though the term Holocaust would not yet have been used). Despite being censored and its exposure curtailed in 1956 (as detailed by Christian Delage in this volume) the film prompted intense public debate about the camps as well as French involvement in the deportation and subsequent genocide of Jews, and collaboration in general during the period of the Vichy government and Nazi occupation of France.

Night and Fog's controversy concerned not only its account of the past but the way it related that history to contemporary France and the extreme measures the French Government was then pursuing against the popular uprising in Algeria. The commentary included a timely warning which is no less relevant today:

> And there are we, who look at these ruins with sincerity, as if the old concentration camp monster lay dead and buried beneath them. We, who feign a renewal of hope faced with this receding image, as though there was a cure for the plague of the camps, we who feign to believe that all this happened only at one point in time in one country and who did not think to look at what surrounds us, and who do not hear the unending cry.[10]

The film focuses on the barbaric acts of deportation, slave-labour, medical experiments and mass-murder conducted by the Nazis involving ordinary French, political deportees as well as those racially targeted. But in not identifying Jews as the overwhelming majority of victims it has been seen subsequently as participating in a certain denial of the antisemitism which was at the heart of a Nazi racial policy that nevertheless also included the Slavic peoples as well as Gypsies as racially contaminating in the new Third Reich. *Night and Fog* and its controversies makes clear the complexity of what must be remembered in the Holocaust documentary.

It was the landmark Thames Television series, *The World at War* (1974, made in co-operation with the Imperial War Museum), in its episode 'Genocide', that brought the Holocaust to mass television audiences in Britain for the first time. Its aim was to produce a television history that drew on the visual and in which the authenticity of its images and commentary was supported by the stories of those who had experienced the events. These interviews offered not just oral testimony, however, but were also a powerful and emotional focus for empathy and identification, as well as at times antipathy. In seeing the face as well as hearing the words of the camp survivor, or the prison guard who describes his horror and outrage on seeing the process of gassing, we become engaged directly. Moreover the testimonies are themselves documents not merely in terms of their information but also their jokes and anecdotes as well as idiosyncratic styles of speech and address to camera which bear witness to the particularity of each individual and to the moment in time and the context or place of their speech. It is an embodied discourse.

Testimony constitutes the whole of Claude Lanzmann's extraordinary and compelling *Shoah* (1985). The Holocaust is made present through the words of surviving witnesses, of Jews who lived through the horror of imprisonment in the camps, of officials and administrators, and of the Germans and Poles who lived alongside the camps. We are moved by their stories and by their own often very emotional responses to their accounts which remain partial, intermittent and incomplete. Lanzmann rejected the use of archive footage, or any representation of the past; instead he is concerned to produce an encounter with the past in the present through forms of re-enactments and re-encounters in the historical place of their experiencing, or in a place both similar and different – an Israeli forest, for example – which invokes the absent and past space of horror. At the film's opening, Polish villagers hear again Simon Srebnik, Chelmno survivor, and remember how he sang for his German captors. We see these witnesses encounter their Holocaust past, performed for Lanzmann and his camera; the responses of anguish and pain in remembering on the part of surviving victims is profoundly moving while the complex mixture of relief and distress in acknowledging that past and their role in it which most – both Jews and non-Jews – had sought to forget, as well as the denials and self-justification of the perpetrators, is disturbing and thought-provoking. The embodied speech of a survivor penetrates the images of a landscape in which we can see no atrocities, while the voice describes how, as he disinterred the victims some months earlier of the shooting squads for the burning which would remove any evidence of the genocide, he uncovered his wife, and the film returns us to his anguished face in the present of his remembering. The problem of embodied memory which is not properly remembered as a 'story' is explored in Orly Yadin's powerful 1998 documentary animation *Silence* which is based on a survivor's recollection of her fragmented understanding as a small child of why she has been sent abroad without her mother.

These films document the memory of the living. How should the Holocaust documentary remember those now dead? James Young has argued eloquently for the commemoration of the victims of the Holocaust through remembering their living reality as family members, as part of their communities, and as participants in the culture and identity of their homelands.[11] It is this which *Maelstrom: A Family Chronicle* (1997) by Péter Forgács achieves so well. The film intercuts archive footage with home movies from two families. We follow Max Peereboom's camera as he records the marriages, births, family celebrations and holidays of himself and his Dutch Jewish family between 1933 and 1942, juxtaposed with amateur footage of scenes of Crown Princess Juliana's wedding and, ominously, a National Socialist Youth Storm Camp, and a Dutch Nazi

Training Camp in Terborg. A different kind of remembering is introduced through the home movies of the second family: here we see another successful man, proud father and doting grandfather, namely Arthur Seyss-Inquart, the Austrian Nazi Party minister appointed Reich Commissioner for Occupied Dutch Territories. The juxtaposition of images produces a connection and similarity between the families which our knowledge forcefully undermines, effecting instead a powerful and poignant contrast between the Peerebooms, whose lives we have come to know and care about through Max's camera, and this other father and filmmaker who will ensure their annihilation.[12]

The Peerebooms live again for us through Max's camera and its record of events that took place over sixty years ago. In re-presenting these images the film commemorates this family and the living community it was a part of, while also narrating their loss, for we already know the ending of the story Max himself will be unable to go on to tell. Here, Forgács says, is the film's structure of spiralling maelstrom and he asks 'At which sequence, which episode do you realise the swirl, when do you start to become anxious and feel their end?'[13]

The final scene in the film is of the Peereboom family packing the night before their deportation to Auschwitz. Michael Renov writes:

> As we watch, a female voice recites the list of personal articles to be allowed each deportee: a mug, a spoon, a work suit, a pair of work boots, two shirts, a pullover, two pairs of underwear, two pairs of socks, two blankets, a napkin, a towel and toilet articles. We are here face-to-face with the banality of evil.[14]

For as spectators we are painfully suspended between two times: 1943, when we watch the Peerebooms and enter into their hopes and fears for a future thay can still imagine, and the present time of viewing with our knowledge of their fate. Through this suspense[15] the film's re-presenting of these fragments of family home movie enacts a 'remembering' that engages the viewer in coming to know of loss as an emotional experience summed up by the words 'if only'. It is a personal memory of loss, even though we ourselves never knew the Peerebooms, which draws us into a work of mourning that is also a commemoration.

Notes

1   J. E. Young (1990) *Writing and Rewriting the Holocaust*. Bloomington: Indiana University Press, 149.

2   The early panoramic photographs are precursors of Cinerama and with computer-controlled cameras it is perhaps now possible to produce a total record in all four dimensions of an event, though it would only be comprehensible by an individual person through a process of selection and montage, or by serialising the images in time and hence losing the simultaneity of the images of the event, limited as we are to eyes fixed in one plane only.

3   The development of lightweight 16mm cameras which could be hand-held, together with the new zoom and telephoto lenses, enabled the camera to penetrate scenes and capture the sounds directly in sync with the new lightweight magnetic tape recorders.

4   This has been the aim of many of the filmmakers associated with American 'direct cinema', notably Richard Leacock, the Maysles brothers and D. A. Pennebaker, who all worked on *Primary* (1960) and for later

directors such as Frederick Wiseman.

5 It is an index or trace of the failure of the camera to accurately record the scene, and thereby becomes a sign, a convention, whereby such fuzziness, or out of focus, or shaking camera/image, signifies 'documentary reality', used by fiction and non-fiction filmmakers alike.

6 L. Hine, 'Social Photography, How the Camera May Help in the Social Uplift', *Proceedings, National Conference of Charities and Corrections*, June 1909. Reprinted in A. Trachtenberg (1980) *Classic Essays on Photography*. New Haven: Leete's Island Books, 111.

7 P. Novick (2001) *The Holocaust and Collective Memory*. London: Bloomsbury, 64.

8 S. Sontag (1977) *On Photography*. New York: Farrar, Straus and Giroux, 19–20.

9 Novick 2001: 64. Paul Salmons, Holocaust Education Co-ordinator, Imperial War Museum, London, in his notes to teachers comments: 'Some history departments still use explicit photographs of Nazi atrocities in an attempt to communicate the full horror of the Holocaust. But should our objective be to shock and horrify? What do young people actually learn from such an approach? Too often Jews become defined by the Holocaust, dehumanised and objectified.'

10 The original French text is: 'Et il y a nous qui regardons sincèrement ces ruines comme si le vieux monstre concentrationnaire était mort sous les décombres, qui feignons de reprendre espoir devant cette image qui s'éloigne, comme si on guérissait de la peste concentrationnaire, nous qui feignons de croire que tout cela est d'une seul temps et d'un seul pays, et qui ne pensons pas à regarder autour de nous, et qui n'entendons pas qu'on crie sans fin.' This original text is from R. Raskin (ed.) (1987) *Nuit et Brouillard by Alain Resnais: On the Making, Reception and Functions of a Major Documentary Film: Including a New Interview with Alain Resnais and the Original Shooting Script*. Åarhus: Åarhus University Press, 65–130. A translation of the entire script can be found at: http://simplyscripts.com/b.html

11 J. E. Young (1993) *Holocaust Memorials and Meaning: The Texture of Memory*. New Haven: Yale University Press, 132.

12 We may remember as well that Seyss-Inquart himself will be condemned to death following his convistion for war crimes at the Nuremberg Tribunal. He was executed in 1946. This knowledge – while perhaps offering the dubious comfort of revenge – thus also re-asserts the rule of human rights and justice against Nazi inhumanity.

13 Péter Forgács, in an interview with Bill Nichols, '*The Memory of Loss*: Saga of Family Life and Social Hell', in *Film Quarterly*, 56 (2003), 4, 6.

14 M. Renov, 'Historical Discourses of the Unimaginable: Péter Forgács' *The Maelstrom*', conference paper at 'Visible Evidence', 2000.

15 Forgács has said 'It is like the suspense of a Hitchcock film. We know ahead of time that the innocent victim will fall into the hands of the killer. We want to warn her/him: watch out! And our palms are sweating. We can't help, and here – in my films – it anticipates real blood, real suffering' (Ibid., 9). But, in contrast to a Hitchcock film, it is not play-acting.

SECTION IV

THE HOLOCAUST IN FEATURE FILMS

During the symposium and in this book we deliberately focused on European cinematic treatments of the Holocaust. We felt that American or Hollywood films treating the subject were already well-known and due to the power of American film distribution had tended to drown out many other perspectives. Indeed one of the complaints during the various symposium discussion periods, especially on day four (devoted to feature films), was how difficult it was to see prints or obtain video copies of numerous important continental films about the Holocaust. Moreover, we felt that as the conference had been conceived to explore further the film aspects of the Museum's Holocaust Exhibition, it was right to examine films emanating from those nations which had been at the heart of this experience. Even with a superficial knowledge of the films related to the subject, and after discussions with the International Federation of Film Archives (FIAF) and colleagues in various European archives, it was clear to the symposium organisers that there were many important films on the Holocaust that had so far only been seen by a handful of film scholars and critics based in the UK. The European Holocaust cinema was also older and more established than its Hollywood counterpart; in fact, as Trudy Gold's chapter demonstrates, Hollywood did not produce any films on the subject until the late 1950s. With greater and easier cultural exchanges with the countries of Eastern Europe now possible, the symposium provided an opportunity to bring these films to a wider audience. However, given the important role that Hollywood films have played in raising awareness of the Holocaust, even creating a 'cultural memory' of the event in nations such as the UK and the US, we felt that we should start this section with Gold's chapter, which offers an overview of Hollywood's treatment of the subject.

An important theme introduced in this opening chapter, and one subsequently tackled by Ewa Mazierska and Giacomo Lichtner, is the representation of the Jew within the cinematic representation of the Holocaust. The common link between Hollywood's treatment of the Holocaust and that of Polish, Italian and French cinema is the fact that these are often de-Judaised accounts. The ethics of how a filmmaker should represent the Holocaust, indeed whether a filmmaker should tackle the subject at all (as agonised over by Jack Gold), is just as important in this section as in the 'documentary' chapters. Trudy Gold explores this in a number of ways; for example, questioning whether humour or farce can and should be used to represent the Holocaust. This theme is taken up again in the survivors' 'right to reply' session where it is the impact of Hollywood feature films about the Holocaust that dominates the debate. As with the documentary section, one can discern two broad methods of treatment, with *Escape From Sobibor*

(1987), *Schindler's List* (1993) and a number of American films adopting the classical narrative realist model, and European filmmakers, particularly those based in Eastern Europe, exploring a range of non-realist and reflexive approaches, often, as in the case of *Pasażerka* (*Passenger*, 1961/63) and *Daleká Cesta* (*The Long Journey/Distant Journey*, 1949) a mixture of many methods. This is not to say that filmmakers working in the classical narrative field stuck rigidly to the conventional approach; for example, both Jack Gold and Steven Spielberg introduced elements associated with documentary and European 'art house' cinema for ethical and stylistic reasons.

This section also looks at the place of Holocaust film in society, with two of the chapters (those by Ian Wall and Anna Reading) and the 'right to reply' session attempting to assess how feature films have influenced and could promote greater understanding of this subject.

In her overview of Hollywood's treatment of the Holocaust, Trudy Gold begins by explaining an anomaly: how it was that the Jewish heads of the main Hollywood studios could ignore Nazi policy towards the Jews. In fact, as Gold explains, it was not until the Eichmann trial in 1961 that Hollywood began to tackle the subject seriously. She then charts the development of the representation of the subject, picking out and evaluating various repeated themes (Zionism, the survivors' tale, the Holocaust and comedy or farce), and examines in more detail key films such as *Judgment at Nuremberg* (1961) and *Schindler's List*. Gold's essay also cites a number of less well-known Hollywood and partly American-funded European films, that merit more attention.

Jack Gold's chapter is an account of the making of *Escape From Sobibor*, a film for television that he directed in 1987. The author provides an almost confessional exposé of the anxieties and difficulties he had in realising the remarkable true-life story of the attempted escape of six hundred Jews from the Sobibor death camp. During the symposium, Gold's presentation, and in particular the remark that he would have preferred to film in black-and-white, stimulated an extended debate about aesthetics and truth. Black-and-white, although technically 'less real' than colour film, was commonly perceived to be the historical medium of the past. According to Ian Wall, one group of young people so closely associated monochrome images with the period of the Holocaust and the Second World War that they refused to accept the authenticity of colour film of the liberation of a concentration camp (shot by George Stevens).

Gold then gave his thoughts on the ethics of dramatising scenes of atrocity. For example, he would not have considered reconstructing a scene within the gas chambers at Sobibor (as Spielberg later did for scenes at Auschwitz in *Schindler's List*), and had also rejected a scene he had filmed in which a baby that had been shot by a member of the SS was then kicked. Pushed by a member of the audience to explain whether this was out of consideration for a fictional dead child, or for dramatic reasons (that is, following the law of diminishing returns) Gold recalled that he had been motivated by a fear of alienating his audience as well as repugnance. Jack Gold and Anna Reading doubted whether any artistic representation could be as effective or horrific as that suggested in the mind of the viewer. Moreover, Gold could not recall an artistic representation of the Holocaust that could match the horror of actuality footage of Holocaust atrocities.

We leave it to the reader and the viewer to decide how successful Gold was in finding a compromise between the needs of entertainment and authenticity. Without seeking to influence this assessment, a number of conference delegates were impressed that

Gold's film had explained, at least partly, why resistance had been so difficult for camp inmates. Clearly, as the experience of Sobibor shows, it was generally only with the assistance of soldiers (in this case Soviet POWs) that untrained, peaceful civilians, had been able to overcome their natural revulsion to kill, and could be organised so as to vanquish their armed guards.

In turning to the educational imperatives of Holocaust representation through feature films, Ian Wall offers a model for an integrated approach to teaching the Holocaust through film, based on the work of Film Education, a film industry-funded charity that promotes the study of cinema in schools. Wall describes the education materials and teaching module that was prepared for schools to accompany the video of *Schindler's List*, a copy of which was distributed for free to every school in the UK. He then suggests a number of topics that should be raised with students who are examining the Holocaust through film and how the teacher and student might tackle less familiar film categories particularly relevant to the Holocaust, namely, documentary, newsreels and amateur film.

Anna Reading's chapter then describes her research project to assess how young people's 'cultural memory' of the Holocaust, in three different countries (the US, Britain and Poland), was influenced and shaped by film and television. Anna's pioneering study, which used a variety of surveying techniques, reveals that this influence is not straightforward as an individual's reception of a film or video is shaped by the subtle interplay between various forces: a viewer's culture and ethnicity; gender; and the 'interpretative framework' in which the film or video was viewed.

Jiří Cieslar's chapter is an examination of the long-forgotten Czech Holocaust film *The Long Journey*. Made by the celebrated Czech dramatist and filmmaker Alfréd Radok, this is a remarkably inventive and accomplished film which has had a great influence on Czech cinema. For example, one can see echoes of the stylistic approach adopted by Radok in Jan Němec's *Démanty noci* (*Diamonds of the Night*, 1964). Cieslar places the film in historical and political context, covering the period when Czechoslovakia was occupied by the Germans and the post-war Stalinist regime, during which Radok's career was hampered by State repression, ultimately forcing him into exile. Further, the very characteristics of expressionism and experimentation which make *The Long Journey* unique and won it many plaudits at the time of its release, put it at odds with the prevailing artistic climate of socialist realism. Cieslar then goes on to examine the complex narrative structure Radok used to tell the story of the Holocaust as it affected a middle-class Jewish family. Finally, he offers an assessment of Radok's masterpiece in comparison with other artistic representations of the Holocaust.

Ewa Mazierska then contributes an overview of Polish cinema and the Holocaust, focusing on three key films of the genre: *Ostatni etap* (*The Last Stage/The Last Stop*, 1948), *Passenger* and *The Pianist* (2002). Her chapter is fully grounded in the cultural and political developments that has shaped that society since the war and looks especially at the place Jews have held in Poland's memory of the war.

Italian Holocaust films, as Giacomo Lichtner explains, have been only superficially about the Holocaust, with the filmmakers being more deeply concerned with Italian society, its complexities and contradictions. Lichtner examines this anomaly by reference to the history of Italy's Jewish community, through the Italian experience of the Second World War and by a considered analysis of a number of important films. The study focuses on internationally acclaimed films such as *Il Giardino dei Finzi-Contini* (*The Garden of the Finzi-Continis*, 1970) and *The Night Porter* (1974) as well as less known classics such as *Kapò* (1960) and *L'Oro di Roma* (*The Gold of Rome*, 1961). Lichtner also spends some time evaluating the contribution of *La vita è bella* (*Life is Beautiful*, 1998). Usefully placing it within the context of Italian cinematic traditions, he offers a less jaundiced view of Roberto Benigni's efforts than is the norm.

In turning to the 'Survivors' Right to Reply' chapter, the transcript of this session has only been lightly edited, with the original voice of the participants retained as much as possible. As well as wanting to recreate the atmosphere of this session, ethically we felt that it would be wrong not to give a verbatim account of the discussion which was led by a panel of three survivors and chaired by Trudy Gold. As well as Holocaust survivors and their family members, the audience included filmmakers, academics and educators. One of the highlights of the symposium, the debate in this session ranged over many issues, but inevitably there was much discussion about the rights and wrongs of two of the most popular and controversial Holocaust films, *Schindler's List* and *Life is Beautiful*. Esther Brunstein's remarks, during a discussion the previous day, perfectly encapsulated the prevailing sense of ambivalence that many survivors had with *Schindler's List*. She explained that while the film had provoked her grandchildren to show real interest in her experiences of the Holocaust, she had been upset by numerous historical inaccuracies in the film. For example, at the end of the film, 'Schindler's survivors' had sung 'Jerusalem the Golden', a song penned in the 1960s; she felt a far better choice would have been the partisan song 'Don't Ever Say this is the Final Road'. Despite such reservations, many of the younger members of the audience were impressed with the open-minded manner in which the survivors discussed film and other artistic representations of the Holocaust. Perhaps this arose from the fact that many members of this group of survivors were involved in Holocaust education, and thus aware of the wider value of more 'popular' but less historically rigorous accounts of the Holocaust. One of the characteristics of this session was the humour that underpinned the contributions as well as the determination of the survivors present to pass on their stories to future generations. All agreed that feature films had opened a door for them to tell their stories to a younger generation in schools. Having seen *Life is Beautiful*, or *Schindler's List*, school children wanted to hear the 'real life' stories that they began to relate to their own lives and families. The discussion returned again and again to the survivors' belief in the value of showing feature films in an educational context. Yet we began this book with Trude Levi's doubts about the wisdom of showing *Life is Beautiful* once there are no longer survivors around to tell their own stories. This tension between the need to find ways of communicating to younger generations while preserving historical truth is of greater relevance as each year passes.

21 An overview of Hollywood cinema's treatment of the Holocaust

Trudy Gold

The story of the Holocaust can never be realistically told. Six million men, women and children were murdered, six million untold stories. Consequently all the feature film-maker can ever do is to recreate a small part of the tragedy.

Even the word 'Holocaust' is problematic because it means sacrifice, completely subsumed by fire. Many people prefer the term *churban*, meaning ruin, destruction or desolation. Others prefer *sho'ah*, meaning great catastrophe. Periodisation is also an issue: the murders mainly occured between 1941 and 1945, but between 1933 and 1939 the Nazis socially, legally and economically isolated the Jews and between 1939 and 1941 they were herded into ghettos.

Writers and poets have stated that language itself is inadequate to describe what is considered to be the nadir of Western civilisation. Paradoxically there is a commandment, *shahor*, to remember, and cinema at its best can be memory inscribed on celluloid. Yet the history of the portrayal of the Holocaust in English-language cinema, particularly in films emanating from the US, is a curious phenomenon. Many of the émigré filmmakers working in Hollywood in the 1930s and 1940s were German and Austrian Jews. They may have worn their Judaism lightly, but it was due to Hitler that they lived and worked in America, and they had a clear awareness of Nazism and its leader (although this was still, of course, before 'the Final Solution'). But despite the Jewish ancestry of the majority of studio heads and many industry practitioners very few films made in the period 1933 to 1939 even allude to antisemitism. Goebbels called the cinema the most powerful propaganda weapon of the twentieth century, so why did these men, who had the knowledge and the means, not make use of it?

One does not have to look very far to see the reason for this. The film moguls took part in the creation of the American dream, and their Jewish identity was at odds with the dream, which existed to express a homogeneous American identity. And, even after Hitler came to power, American films were still very popular in Germany. The studios had agents in Europe, and they wanted their films to sell there. Warner Bros. did want to start making films about what was happening in Germany (not least because their agent in Germany was murdered by the Nazis) but American isolationism and anti-semitism dulled the home market for such films. After the British entered the war in 1939 Joseph Kennedy visited Hollywood and warned them of the dangers of producing anti-Nazi propaganda films. It was, he said, 'Europe's war'. But, after Pearl Harbour the studios did begin to make anti-Nazi films – their arsenal included such films as Ernst

Lubitsch's brilliant *To Be or Not To Be* (1942), *The Seventh Cross* (Fred Zinnemann, 1944) and *The Hitler Gang* (John Farrow, 1944).

A few pre-war films had explored the issue of antisemitism. One was *The House of Rothschild*, made in 1934; another was *The Life of Emile Zola* (William Dieterle, 1937), which centred on the Dreyfus affair, but in many ways the affair is de-Judaised. It was not until 1947 that two films were made on the subject of antisemitism: *Gentleman's Agreement* and *Crossfire*. Both were made by non-Jewish directors, Elia Kazan and Edward Dmytryk respectively.

So at what point do attempts begin to depict on screen what the Holocaust was and what it meant? This was a challenge not only for filmmakers, but for other media as well. When was the enormity of the Holocaust realised? When was the fact that killing Jews was as important to Hitler as winning the war really put on the agenda? How many people wanted to read or hear survivors' testimonies? In the 1960s and 1970s, with the publication of Raul Hilberg's *The Destruction of the European Jews* and Lucy Dawidowicz's *The War against the Jews*, historians began to examine the crimes.[1] The writings of Elie Wiesel and Primo Levi were not published in English until the 1960s and there was an obscuring of the issues, even in history books.[2] When I studied history in the 1960s, the Holocaust was a footnote; it was treated with dignity, but there was no attempt at exploration or detailed study. It is therefore not really surprising that there was very little ventured on film.

The first film to portray a concentration camp was *The Young Lions* (Edward Dmytryk, 1958) starring a young, blond Marlon Brando as a good German soldier who, making his way back to rejoin his regiment across a disintegrating Germany at the end of the war, comes across a concentration camp. Although the representation is muddled and inaccurate, it did attempt to represent what a concentration camp was like. *The Diary of Anne Frank*, directed by George Stevens and released the following year, produced a very de-Judaised, universalised account. Then came the trial of Adolf Eichmann.

There is no doubt that the long-running Eichmann trial in Israel in 1961 had a profound impact on the world. By bringing to justice the bureaucrat seen as most responsible for the implementation of the Final Solution, the Israelis were able to create a show trial which revealed to the world the full horrors of the Holocaust. It was headline news everywhere, the Russians opened up their archives, and evidence became public. For Hollywood, the Eichmann trial paved the way for an extraordinary film, *Judgment at Nuremberg* (Stanley Kramer, 1961). Like Kramer's *Ship of Fools* (1965) a few years later, *Judgment at Nuremberg* is a message film, but also a Hollywood blockbuster, with Spencer Tracy, Burt Lancaster, Judy Garland, Maximilian Schell and a host of other stars of the era. It focuses on the lives of four judges who joined the Nazi Party. Although it was not obligatory to join the Party in Hitler's Germany, to remain a judge after 1935, you had to wear the swastika on your robe. These four Nazi judges find themselves having to enact immoral laws, since under Nazism morality and legality have no connection.

The film's story centres on the Feldenstein case. Feldenstein is an elderly Jew who has a 16-year-old gentile friend; he is her landlord, and he looks after her. Then he is accused of having sex with the girl. In 1935, under the Nuremberg Laws sexual relations between Jews and Aryans were a crime, and Feldenstein is executed. Burt Lancaster plays a man who, before the war, was a great international lawyer. He is appointed judge for the Feldenstein case and in one very powerful scene he tries to justify, in tiny, human terms, why Hitler has come to power.

Judgment at Nuremberg does show footage of the camps being shown in the courtroom, but we, the cinema audience, are not exposed fully to the scenes that they have to watch.

The next important film was Sidney Lumet's *The Pawnbroker* (1965), the story of a professor, played by Rod Steiger, who loses everyone he loves in the camps, but survives, goes to New York (where he has a distant relative) and becomes a pawnbroker. He has become a man without feelings. His shop assistant, a young Puerto Rican, acts as the catalyst that unlocks his feelings once more: in one memorable scene he asks the pawnbroker the secret of the Jews' success in commerce. Gradually, through their relationship, you see the professor-turned-pawnbroker coming to life again. Through the flashbacks, this is the first Hollywood film that actually exposes camp experiences, bringing to the screen a sense of the horror the man has been through.

Zionism also came to the big screen. Leon Uris wrote *Exodus* in 1958, and in 1960 it was made into a film starring Paul Newman as Ari Ben Canaan, and directed by Otto Preminger. Because of the impact of *Exodus*, Uris was awarded the tourism medal from the State of Israel.

Exodus was not the only film of the 1960s to extol the birth of Israel. *Judith* (Daniel Mann, 1965), starring Sophia Loren as a Holocaust survivor, stretched beyond the bounds of imagination, but *Cast a Giant Shadow* (Melville Shavelson, 1966) was a huge box-office hit bursting with macho men, including John Wayne and Kirk Douglas. It tells the story of Colonel Micky Marcus, who was the highest ranking American soldier to go to Palestine after the Second World War, to volunteer to fight for the survival of the Jewish state. All these films, in their different ways, link Israel's birth with the Holocaust, as if the Holocaust were a justification for the state of Israel.

After the Six Day War, when Israel was again perceived to be threatened with extinction, a great many books about the Holocaust appeared, and more documentaries were made. *The Man in the Glass Booth* (Arthur Hiller, 1975) is a strange film based on a stage play about a death-camp survivor who pretends to be a Nazi, so that he should be arrested and put on trial in Israel.

As we move into the 1980s more personal stories of survivors of the camps were portrayed on screen. The controversial *Sophie's Choice* (Alan J. Pakula, 1982) takes its audience into the camps, while *Max and Helen* (Philip Savile, 1990) was based on a Simon Wiesenthal story. *Triumph of the Spirit* (Robert M. Young, 1989), the story of a boxer, is actually set in the camps. *Music Box* (Costa-Gavras, 1989) is set in contemporary America and tells the story of a Hungarian who is put on trial for his role in the Final Solution, following the release of secret documents from Soviet archives.

Television blockbusters in the 1980s included screen treatments of Herman Wouk's *The Winds of War* (1983) and *War and Remembrance* (1988), both directed by Dan Curtis, *Inside the Third Reich* (Marvin J. Chomsky, 1982), which interspersed documentary with drama in the increasingly popular 'faction' genre, the mammoth six-hour *The Nightmare Years* (Anthony Page, 1989) based on the writings of William Shirer, and the screening on BBC2 of a German series, *Die Geschwister Oppermann* (*The Oppermann Family*, Egon Monk, 1983), which detailed the life of German Jews up until about 1937, again using a mixture of documentary film, newsreel and drama. Jack

Gold's *Escape From Sobibor* (1987) was a feature film that told of a real escape from a death camp.

Any attempt to recreate reality in fiction raises the questions of why fictionalise an event rather than present the work as a documentary. But the dramatisation achieved for *Escape From Sobibor*, and later for Steven Spielberg's *Schindler's List* (1993), was to attract a much larger audience. *Schindler's List* was seen by a quarter of the population of Britain, nearly a third of the population of Germany, and had a profound effect on global consciousness of what the Holocaust was. Roman Polański's film *The Pianist* (2002), the story of the pianist Władysław Szpilman and the Warsaw Ghetto, was a mainstream, award-winning success, despite Polański saying that the Holocaust could never be filmed.

The strength of Spielberg's film derived from his subtlety and skill as a filmmaker, but its success was also partly due to timing. *Schindler's List* was released in Britain at the approach of the fiftieth anniversary of the end of the Second World War. It also coincided with Holocaust Studies being added to the core curriculum in England and Wales. We could now say that there are so many films, documentaries and dramatisations about this subject that we are in danger of saturation.

A final category of films about the Holocaust to consider – and it seems at first almost obscene to write the two words in the same sentence – is those that combine humour and the Holocaust. Can humour be used in an attempt to convey the enormity of this catastrophe? Should it be used? There are two types of film in this genre. The first are the films that ridicule Nazism, and these began with Charlie Chaplin's *The Great Dictator* (1940). Chaplin was not a Jew, but had a Jewish girlfriend, the actress Paulette Goddard (who is also in the film), and he said: 'I was determined to go ahead, for Hitler must be laughed at. Had I known of the actual horrors of the German concentration camps, I could not have made *The Great Dictator*, I could not have made fun of the homicidal insanity of the Nazis. However, I was determined to ridicule their mystic bilge about a pure-blooded race. As though such a thing ever existed outside of Australian Aborigines!'[3] The film aroused a great deal of controversy when it was first shown, and it is important to recall the political climate at the time: this was 1940, the United States was not yet in the war, the appeasement lobby was strong and vocal and Joseph Kennedy was telling Hollywood moguls to keep clear of such sensitive subjects.

In 1942 one of the great directors of the Weimar era, Ernst Lubitsch, who came to Hollywood in 1926, made *To Be or Not To Be* (remade by Mel Brooks in 1983, less successfully). It tells the story of a troop of actors in Poland just as Hitler invades, and holds Nazism up to ridicule. At this period the real evidence of what the Nazis were doing was only just beginning to filter through, but Lubitsch said that if he had known about the camps he would not have made his film.[4]

Mel Brooks' *The Producers* (1968) is the story of a Broadway producer, brilliantly played by Zero Mostel (who came straight from the Yiddish Theatre). The producer is a professional failure who is reduced to seducing rich old ladies. Then an accountant, played by Gene Wilder, comes to visit. As he looks through the desperate producer's accounts, he comes up with an interesting proposition: 'Do you realise you could make more money out of a flop than out of a hit, providing you have enough investors and the play closes on the first night?' So the schemers set out to find the worst play ever written – and find a musical based on the life of Adolf Hitler with, of course, its show-stopping torch song, 'Springtime for Hitler'. *The Producers* has become an iconoclastic cult classic and Mel Brooks reprised his success 35 years later when he brought *The Producers* to the New York and thence to the London stage.

The other aspect of this genre is to introduce humour into the camps. An excellent television film was the black comedy *Genghis Cohn* (Elijah Moshinsky, 1993) written by Stanley Price. It is about a man who before the war was a comedian in Germany, a cabaret compère in the mould of the M.C. of Bob Fosse's *Cabaret* (1972). He returns after the war to haunt his murderers.

Another controversial film to have appeared is *La Vita è Bella* (*Life is Beautiful*, 1998), made by the Italian director Roberto Benigni, which won an Academy Award for Best Foreign Language film, and describes itself as a fable. (The film and its reception is discussed in greater detail by Giacomo Lichtner later in this volume.) It received criticism as well as plaudits, but could well be opening another flood gate – it was soon followed by a French-Romanian production *Train de Vie* (*Trenul Vietii/Train of Life*, Radu Mihaileanu, 1999) which is total farce set against the backdrop of the Holocaust.

It is of course impossible to transcribe a tragedy such as the Holocaust, with all its crimes, wounds and stories, in completeness and perfection, to the screen. Since *Schindler's List* movies about the Holocaust abound; some are excellent, some indifferent, some risible. Many survivors have stated that when they are no longer here no one will be left who has an inkling of the real truth. And then the fear is that we will only be left with Hollywood.

Notes

1   R. Hilberg (1961) *The Destruction of the European Jews*. London: W. H. Allen; L. Dawidowicz (1975) *The War Against the Jews*. London: Weidenfeld and Nicolson.

2   E. Wiesel (1960) *Night*. Translated by Stella Rodway. London: Macgibbon and Kee; P. Levi (1960) *If This is a Man*. Translated by Stuart Woolf. London: Orion; P. Levi (1965) *The Truce: A Survivor's Journey Home from Auschwitz*. Translated by Stuart Woolf. London: Bodley Head.

3   C. Chaplin (1978) *Charles Chaplin: My Autobiography*. Harmondsworth: Penguin, 388.

4   It was not until late 1942 that the American public received official confirmation of the Nazi campaign to annihilate the Jews. On 24 November Rabbi Stephen Wise, President of the World Jewish Congress in New York, held a press conference to announce that the US State Department had investigated and confirmed reports about the Nazi extermination campaign against European Jews. And on 17 December the governments of the USA, Britain and ten Allied countries released a formal declaration confirming and condemning Hitler's extermination policy towards the Jews. See www.ushmm.org/research/library/faq/right.htm

22 *Escape From Sobibor*: a film made for television depicting the mass escape from Sobibor extermination camp

Jack Gold

As part of the preparations for the execution of 'the Final Solution', three death camps were built in eastern Poland: Belzec, Sobibor and Treblinka. It is estimated that at Sobibor, which became 'operational' in April 1942, 250,000 Jews were murdered during the camp's existence. Six hundred Jews were kept alive to maintain the camp. In October 1943 they attempted a mass escape and three hundred survived. A few days later Himmler ordered that the camp be destroyed.

When I was first approached to direct this film I resisted the idea. This was an instant almost intuitive reaction to the idea of 'yet another Holocaust film'. The actual story of this film, the escape, was subsumed by the feeling that the Holocaust was being exploited by commercial television. Also, I considered the impossibility of the true portrayal of its horror in a film suitable for a mass audience. I had obviously read about and seen many terrifying images on the process of the Holocaust. I am no poet so metaphor on this level was beyond my reach. I also felt that there was only one true way to show such obscenity … unadulterated realism. Such reconstruction is impossible under any civilised circumstances, and the script I received, though based on survivor's accounts, was a mediation by dramatic reconstruction. My instinctive antipathy was encapsulated by my subsequent reading, years later, the following quotations on the inherent dangers in tackling the subject. Firstly, from Elie Wiesel on the NBC *Holocaust* Series:

> It was untrue, offensive, cheap … an insult to those who perished, and those who survived … it transforms an ontological event into soap opera … We see long, endless processions of Jews marching towards Babi Yar … we see naked bodies covered in blood … and it's all make believe … People will tell me that similar techniques are being used for war movies and historical recreations. But the Holocaust is unique, not just another event … This series treats the Holocaust as if it were just another event. Auschwitz cannot be explained, nor can it be visualised. The Holocaust transcends history … the dead are in possession of a secret that we the living are neither worthy of, nor capable of recovering … The Holocaust (is) the ultimate event, the ultimate mystery, never to be comprehended or transmitted. Only those who were there know what it was, the others will never know.[1]

The second quotation comes from the critic Molly Haskell:

How can actors, how *dare* actors presume to imagine and tell us what it felt like! The attempt becomes a desecration against, amongst others, the Hebraic injunction banning graven images.'[2]

I was deeply affected by the essence, the rationale of these quotations. However, (there is always a 'however') I was eventually swayed to commit to the film by two factors. The first was the perennial cry exclaimed by the survivors of Sobibor: 'Bear Witness!' – an appeal echoed by Primo Levi and George Steiner. Levi, the Auschwitz survivor, said that one of the recurring nightmares he had while he was an inmate of the camp was trying, after the war was over, to describe what he had seen and experienced there to an indifferent or unbelieving audience. The agony of not being able to communicate to others the nature of so transcendentally an important experience compounded the agony of the experience itself.[3] For George Steiner, the act of bearing witness was partly a way of defying the whole logic of Nazi genocide: 'My whole life has been about death, remembering and the Holocaust ... Namelessness was Hitler's taunt ... "Who remembers the Armenians?" I have had to be a "remembrancer".'[4]

In addition, I was influenced by the major effect of 'bearing witness' inspired by the transmission of the *Holocaust* series. When it was shown in Germany in 1979 a German journalist wrote: '...only since, and as a result of *Holocaust* does a majority of the nation know what lay behind the horrible and vacuous formula "The Final Solution" of the Jewish question. They know it because a US filmmaker had the courage to break with the paralysing dogma ... that mass murder must not be represented in art.' The television showing was also 'widely credited with a decisive role in the Bundestag's decision, later that year, to abolish the statute of limitations on war crimes'.[5]

The second factor (in addition to 'bearing witness') that swayed me was the existential nature of the escape itself. Not just the mechanics of the event, but the demonstration of the Jew taking control over his own destiny, even in the most elemental situation where death was seemingly inevitable. The belief that the Jews went like sheep to slaughter was pervasive. The reasons behind this apparent behaviour were complex, detailed and overpowering. Here was the opportunity to reveal the terrifying bravery of ordinary people, not trained militarily (except for the Russian prisoners), but civilians, craftsmen, workers, women, children.[6]

These factors finally compelled me to direct the film, and then a different set of problems arose. How to reveal a historic event? How to communicate something that actually occurred? Any filmmaker has three basic choices, not mutually exclusive: (i) Direct evidence, using actuality film, newsreel, home movies, still photographs, sound recordings of the events as they happened. This method could not apply to Sobibor; there was no such evidence, or certainly none that was discovered; (ii) Witness accounts. These will be made by participants or spectators, remembering and recording their experiences on film, sound or the page, subsequent to the event. This was a major possibility. There were living survivors. There were some historical records, though very few directly relating to Sobibor. In fact Claude Lanzmann made such a film using one survivor only, in the manner of *Shoah* (1985). Richard Rashke's book *Escape From Sobibor* is based on accounts by the survivors. His detailed research involved interviews with eighteen of the thirty living survivors (as of 1982) around the world.[7] He checked and cross-checked searching for authentication; it was this book that formed the basis of the film; (iii) Reconstruction. This method might involve the participants or their representatives i.e. actors. (There are of course other approaches possible, for example the metaphoric or the comic; but neither was considered in relation to this project.)

The decision to use this method to tell the story invites the severe criticisms quoted earlier, nevertheless reconstruction was the style chosen. The reasons are twofold. First-ly, the intention was to engage as large an audience as possible, not only to inform and educate them, but also to enable the income from a mass audience to justify the great cost of reconstruction. It is not really a chicken and egg situation so much as a 'double helix', an entwining of motives. Secondly, the term 'documentary', however honest, au-thentic and emotional the content, does not attract large audiences. More attractive is desire, the recounting of a story, identifying with various characters. Of course this can be effected in documentary, but communicating the feeling and experience of events, the shaping and compression and extension of time, the heightening of emotion and stimulating the imagination is most accessible through drama. 'Documentary' has a tendency to keep people at arm's length. Remember the audiences for NBC's fictional *Holocaust* series, a drama that followed ten years in the lives of two fictional fami-lies through the genesis and history of the Holocaust: one hundred million Americans watched nine-and-a-half hours over four nights. As was 'often observed at the time, more information about the Holocaust was imparted to more Americans over those four nights than over all the previous thirty years'.[8]

The first step in the making of the film was to write a script. The producers, Martin Starger, Dennis Doty and Howard Alston commissioned Reginald Rose (*Twelve Angry Men,* 1957) to adapt Richard Rashke's book for the screen. The characters and events are faithfully presented and masterfully shaped into a dramatic form. I do not use the word 'story' because that sometimes has the implication of 'fiction'. My appearance in the process was after earlier drafts of the script were completed.

My observation was that we should try to draw out the horrors of the camp and to further articulate questions and responses relating to the behaviour of the inmates. Our intention was to be as authentic as possible by emulating the documentary form. This approach permeated every aspect of the production: casting, design, camera and sound.

The basis of success in such a film, after the all-important script is agreed, lies in the casting. The main characters to be portrayed were a disparate collection of Jews, mainly from Eastern Europe but also from Holland and Russia. There were also Ger-man soldiers and Ukranian guards. In addition to these main parts were the hundreds of other prisoners. The language of the film was English (for basic commercial reasons). The importance and care in the casting, in addition to the talent of the actors, was that they would look not only Jewish but also 'ordinary', not bringing the baggage of famili-arity but enhancing the documentary feeling. One factor in attracting large audiences is the presence of 'stars', and we were fortunate in only having two 'known' faces in the film. Rutger Hauer, a big, blond, blue-eyed Dutchman played the Russian soldier leader Pechersky, and Alan Arkin played Feldhendler. I was uncomfortable with this as a mat-ter of principle, but full of admiration for the superb quality of their performances. The majority of the other principal actors were English, Dutch and Yugoslav. The German parts were played by Germans. The mass of the prisoners were played by Yugoslavs who at least were and looked East European. It must be evident by now that the film was made near Belgrade for reasons of topography, logistics and economics.

The design of the film was vitally important. The actual camp had been destroyed after the escape, but with Alan Starski, a Polish designer, the reconstruction was as authentic as possible. Survivors contributed their memories and the fact that Sobibor was similar in design to Majdanek made the task less difficult.

It is opportune at this moment to draw attention to the invaluable help the survivors gave. They were involved in the original book, the development of the film, the appearance of the camp and their clothes, the behaviour of the guards and the prisoners. Some of them were with us throughout the filming. In fact at a pre-filming gathering some of the survivors mixed with the actors portraying them, and they picked them out, they 'recognised' themselves. These survivors were our touchstone for credibility.[9]

Credibility was important. The problem was to accommodate the preconceptions and expectations of the audience. They had seen newsreels and documentaries of the camps – the malnutrition, emaciation, the rags, the pyjama-like uniforms, the filth, the physical disabilities. Sobibor apparently was not like that. When the Jews got off the trains those destined for extermination went directly to the designated part of the camp. The people we were concerned with were in the working part of the camp. Six hundred of them. These had the pick of the discarded clothing. To avoid disease this part of the camp was kept relatively clean and the diet was apparently sufficient to sustain the work-force. Another hurdle was that it was not possible in the 1980s to get malnourished actors. This was compounded by the fact that we were filming during a heat-wave and despite all efforts – embrocations, sun-hats, umbrellas – the actors had healthy looking tans. The result was that the audience do not get the images they expect, an inhibition to credibility. Another inhibition may seem inconsequential that we were filming in colour. Our recollections of images of the camps are in black-and-white. Colour softens, it militates against the documentary effect especially with this subject.

The film crew was international. The cinematographer, Ernie Vincze, is an Hungarian ex-patriate, his crew was English, the assistant directors were Yugoslav and the rest were English and Yugoslav. All the ingredients were in place. We had rehearsals of the scenes. I made the actors drill under an army sergeant to get used to strictly obeying humiliating orders, to be screamed and shouted at. I showed films of the camps to the cast and gave them copies of *The Informed Heart* by Bruno Bettelheim (a survivor of Dachau and Buchenwald) to read. For the German actors I showed documentaries of the training of SS soldiers and antisemitic propaganda. All these efforts were to try and give a basis for an authentic, informed realisation of their parts.

We tried to recreate for the audience what it was like to be in Sobibor at that time. Maybe a measure of our success is revealed in the following incident. Thomas Blatt, one of the survivors who was with us throughout the filming, was then about sixty years old; in the film he was portrayed by a young teenager. Thomas was with us when we filmed the climax of the film, the escape. We filmed over five days, hundreds of people running to the forest through exploding minefields, machine-guns firing, a cacophony of screaming excitement. Filming finished and a few hours later, on the last day, Thomas – clothes torn, glasses broken – was brought to us by some locals who had found him wandering, lost, bewildered, in the forest … to which he had escaped! It transpired that the re-creation was so authentic to him that he changed from spectator to participant. Over forty years vanished; he was again a teenager rushing to freedom. The reconstruction had become reality. I felt that all our work had been climactically vindicated.

Notes

1   E. Wiesel (1978) 'Trivializing the Holocaust', *New York Times*, 16 April 1978, 2.

2   M. Haskell (1978) 'A Failure to Connect', *New York*, 15 May, 79.

3   P. Levi (1995) *If This is a Man* and *The Truce*. Translated by Stuart Woolf. London: Abacus, 66. See also P. Levi (1988) *The Drowned and the Saved*. London: Michael Joseph, 1–2.

4   G. Steiner (1985 [1965]) 'A Kind of Survivor', in *Language and Silence: Essays 1958–1966*. London: Faber & Faber, 119.

5   P. Novick (1999) *The Holocaust and Collective Memory: The American Experience*. London: Bloomsbury, 213. In 1979 after the showing of the series, the Bundestag abolished the Statute of Limitations relating to war crimes. I would like to here acknowledge the enormous help I received from Peter Novick's book throughout this time.

6   See Novick 2000: 137–42.

7   R. Rashke (1983) *Escape From Sobibor*. London: Michael Joseph.

8   Novick 1999: 209.

9   The following survivors were with us on the set at various times during filming, giving invaluable advice and support: Thomas Blatt, Stanisław Smzajzner, Itzhak and Eda Lichtman, Chaim and Selma Engel, and Esther Terner.

23   The Holocaust, film and education

Ian Wall

'The premier demand upon all education is that Auschwitz not happen again. Its priority before any other requirement is such that I believe I need not and should not justify it.'
– Theodor Adorno[1]

Learning about the Holocaust

In this chapter I shall look at ways in which films have been used, and could be used, in teaching about the Holocaust. Anyone intending to teach school students this subject must tackle a number of key issues. Firstly, there is the need to consider how the Holocaust came about and, secondly, to consider the significance of the Holocaust and its lessons for us as members of a democratic society, attempting to live with one another in an atmosphere of understanding and co-operation. Both of these must be underpinned by a comprehension of what happened during the years 1933–45 as well as the roots of the Holocaust in a far deeper vein of antisemitism, which goes back centuries (an approach adopted by the Jewish Museum in Berlin). In England and Wales, the Holocaust is taught within what is called Key Stage 3 of the National History Curriculum. Usually, this teaching will only occupy a short period of time (six hours or slightly more) when students are aged between 11 and 13. However, teaching about the Holocaust can also take place within other subjects – English (through studying works of non-fiction such as *The Diary of Anne Frank* for example), Citizenship and Religious Studies. Each of these will have their own learning outcomes, specified by the subject requirements. To examine Holocaust teaching in each of these disciplines would only highlight the fragmented approach to Holocaust studies within the current school curriculum. In addition we must also look at the place of film within the National Curriculum. References to the study of the moving image appear within the requirements for English, and film is also mentioned as a possible 'source' for examination in History lessons. Film and Media Studies, whilst both being growth subjects within the school curriculum, are not compulsory for all students, appearing as they do in option choices at GCSE and A Level. However, despite these passing references, one must wonder exactly what approaches teachers, who might wish to use film within the History curriculum, would take when teaching the Holocaust.

From my own experiences as a teacher at a comprehensive school in central London, I found that within History, there was a tendency to use film as illustrative material, to allow students to see 'what it was like'. This approach, to both documentary footage and feature films, fails to answer basic questions about the construction and values of each type of film. The History teacher might point out factual errors in a feature film, but accept the surface 'reality' of the film.

In forming the organisation Film Education in 1985, I sought to avoid this approach to film within the curriculum, and instead looked at ways in which the 'reading' and the critique of a film could be reflected and refracted, through the application of the key critical approaches of the subject itself.

Thus, within film studies, the key themes of study include language, narrative, representations, audiences, institutions and values/ideology. How do these reflect those key areas already included in the school approach to, for example, the study of English? With the exception of 'institutions' all of these key concepts were studied, but with a slightly different emphasis. Our philosophy was not to put the differences between texts into conflict; one text is not better than another – they are different. We wish to explore the positive benefits which could be gained from comparison – how one text reflects another and the ways in which it uses its own specific signifying practices to convey meaning.

The majority of our work at Film Education is based around feature films currently in distribution; I shall be discussing a key project that we undertook for *Schindler's List* (1993). Before doing so, it is important to consider our approach to the teaching of history through feature films and its specific relevance to the teaching of the Holocaust.

We firstly ask what type of history we are shown in feature films. Do they do no more than show us what the period depicted in the film would have looked like? Do they tell us more about the values of the culture that produces them as opposed to the culture that they seek to represent? Key influences on our thinking have been the work of Pierre Sorlin and Robert Rosenstone.[2] In *Visions of the Past* (1995) Rosenstone makes these points about mainstream films that deal with historical subjects; these have been our guiding principles when creating study materials:

a) The mainstream film tells history as a story, a tale with a beginning, middle and end. A tale that leaves you with a moral message and (usually) a feeling of uplift.

b) Film insists on history as the story of individuals, either men or women (but usually men) who are already renowned, or men or women who are made to seem important because they have been singled out by the camera.

c) Films offer us history as the story of a closed, completed and simple past.

d) Film emotionalises, personalises and dramatises history … it gives us history as triumph, anguish, joy, despair, adventure, suffering and heroism.

e) Film so obviously gives us the 'look' of the past – of buildings, landscapes and artefacts – that we may not see what this does to our sense of history.

f) Film shows history in process. The world of the film brings together things that, for analytic or structural purposes, written history often has to split apart. Economics, race, class and gender all come together in the lives and moments of individuals, groups and nations.[3]

Looking at Rosenstone's six points, we have to question whether feature films can help answer our key questions on the Holocaust. Are we being given the 'what' without the 'how' and the 'why'? A film allows no time for reflection, debate or verification. We are carried along by its narrative flow. We are involved with individual characters as opposed to broader issues.

The key issue to be raised, beyond a simple aesthetics of film, is the morality of the reconstruction and the representation of the Holocaust itself. We need to ask students to think about how and why feature films strive to look 'authentic' and how this 'authenticity' might differ from concepts of historical truth. By authenticity, I mean the ways in which the film refers back to historical images and footage from the period in which the film is set and thus tries to create images which 'look right', so that the historical drama with which we are presented appears in some way as a historical 'document'.

The Schindler's List project

In 1995, every school in the United Kingdom received a free video copy of the film *Schindler's List* accompanied by a study guide and a 20-minute video documentary telling the story of the Holocaust. This coincided with the video release of the film. Thus whilst the package was of benefit to schools it was also of use to the marketing strategy for the video. News coverage, both in the press and on radio was generated (even going as far as my one and only appearance on *Today* on Radio 4).

Why *Schindler's List*, a mainstream Hollywood film and not a different film, say an art-house film such as *Obchod na korze* (*The Shop on Main Street*, 1965) or *Au revoir, les enfants* (1987)? The most basic answer to this question is money. The project was partly funded by CIC Video (the video distributors of *Schindler's List*), repeating what had happened in the US where schools were also given copies of the film. Film Education believed that the film had to be put in context and so additional funding was raised to produce the guide and the video documentary. Our major concern was that the film would be screened and that students would then see this as *the* Holocaust. To counteract this tendency, we placed *Schindler's List* in its context as a 'film' and then as a representation of one small part of the Holocaust.

Returning to the question, 'why not an art film', finance aside, to have done so would have meant attempting two major tasks. Firstly, the one which we would be dealing with anyway – the representation of the Holocaust on film and, secondly, to attempt to give young students (and probably a large number of teachers!) an understanding of how independent art-house film operates as a communication medium, compared to a mainstream, Hollywood, narrative film.

© Film Education

Schindler's List contained more than enough for the students to consider, without presenting them with the additional task of grappling with the nuances of an art-house film. They would also have to have some understanding of the history of the Holocaust. Altogether, we thought this would have been too much for students ranging between 13 and 15 years old. The very accessibility of *Schindler's List* to students was one of its attractions, as it allowed us to raise a variety of wider questions about the representation of the Holocaust.

However, first we had a practical problem – how to show a 15 certificate film in a classroom, when the majority of students would be under 15? We had already encountered this problem with the theatrical release of the film, when we organised 25 screenings of the film for students in cinemas around the country. In the end the problem was resolved as these were classed as private screenings, and so certification did not apply. Schools were asked to gain parental permission so that students under 15 could attend. The same approach was used to enable distribution of the *Schindler's List* video to schools – private screenings and parental permission.

In creating the study materials and accompanying documentary, we were presented with a number of challenges. The first of these was to position our work within the general trend of Holocaust studies and to identify those questions that had to be addressed; most of these seem to be encapsulated in the following statement by Yehuda Bauer:

Why is the Holocaust a central experience of our civilisation? Is it because what happened once, can happen again? Is it because modern technology has helped to uncover hidden and frightening recesses of man's potential for evil? Is it because we have seen how people become enmeshed in a bureaucratic hell which leads them into the negation of first themselves and then of others? Is it because we see in the Holocaust the heights of the human spirit as well as its abysses? Is it because some of us ask where was God, and others ask where was Man?

It is these and similar questions that cause more and more people to devote their attention to the Holocaust, the mass murder of the Jewish people during the Nazi period.[4]

When considering sources that can be used in teaching, and particularly film, we need to question the ways in which source material can help answer these questions.

Before asking students to question the film itself, we wanted them to think about the nature of film and the different types that they might encounter – newsreel, documentary and the feature film. When looking at the Holocaust, I would add amateur film, a category better known as 'home movies'. By this I mean the footage, often employed in Holocaust documentaries, which although usually shot anonymously, we know from the image quality and point of view to have been taken by members of the German military, who were either involved or present at deportations and massacres.

Students were asked to think about the function and intention behind the shooting or production of each type of film, and then what 'truths' and problems each category would present to a historian studying the Holocaust.

When looking at newsreels, students should be encouraged to examine the purpose of the newsreels and their potential audience. They need to consider why the newsreels represented Jews, and the events leading up to the Holocaust, in the ways that they did. Students also need to think about how audiences in Germany might be willing to accept such images. One must also ask what is not shown in newsreels of this period, what was hidden from German (and international) audiences?

Even more than for newsreels, although documentaries purport to show the 'truth' about a particular subject, they are, in fact, total constructions. Within the canon of Holocaust documentaries, Claude Lanzmann's *Shoah* (1985) has been immensely important as it has questioned two of the key filmic strategies commonly adopted by documentarists: the use of archive footage (that was originally shot for other purposes such as newsreels) and the use of dramatic reconstruction. Lanzmann's approach calls into question all those documentaries where images of extermination, persecution and execution have been employed as background material; in a manner that may, unintentionally, realise the antisemitic propaganda aims of the original cameraman. Lanzmann's problematising of archive film should be raised with students who are looking at documentaries – how is historical footage used and where might it have come from. (See the chapter by Raye Farr on Lanzmann's films in this volume, where these issues are discussed in greater depth.)

Finally, we turn to amateur footage. The most basic question we must ask is, why did the perpetrators film scenes of transportation and execution? To help them navigate their way through this difficult area, we asked students to consider the purpose of their own 'home videos', what sort of events they recall and why they made them. In translating these ideas across to the Nazi/German photographers who created their own images of Jews *in extremis*, we can raise issues about Nazi attitudes to Jews and why these images might have been created. In thinking of memory and recall, we must ask what sort of 'memories' were created here and why.

Having considered these four categories, we then proceeded to examine *Schindler's List* itself. Because of the success of the theatrical release of the film, we assumed that students and teachers would be aware of the film and also have an awareness of the 'Holocaust' which had been created by the film. It is tempting to say that for many people, the Holocaust is now viewed through *Schindler's List*. However, the film shows us only one aspect of the Holocaust, and Spielberg could be seen as having chosen one particular Holocaust story that had a 'happy ending'.

This led to a discussion of the scriptwriting process. Students must consider the demands placed on a Hollywood writer, who must take a dark subject (one that could have been a depressing, downbeat movie), and turn it into a life affirming work, fulfilling the expectations of audiences for a Hollywood film told within the classical narrative format.

One key aesthetic point about *Schindler's List* is that for the most part it is filmed in black-and-white. Students were asked to reflect on the effect this had on them as members of an audience and their interpretation of the events. It is a fact that most people believe all film covering the events of the first half of the twentieth century was shot on black-and-white stock. This common misconception led Spielberg to film in this way, but the choice of black-and-white film stock might also be seen as part of Spielberg's strategy to change the way people perceived his film: it gave *Schindler's List* a 'documentary' feel, and black-and-white film is a look closely associated with European art-house cinema. Thus, Spielberg deliberately distanced himself from a typical Hollywood moviemaker's approach to the subject. Other tactics adopted for the same purpose were: the absence of stars; emotional restraint (until the overblown ending);

Oskar Schindler (Liam Neeson) in a scene from *Schindler's List* (1993). (© Universal City Studios, Inc. and Amblin Entertainment, Inc.)

avoiding the use of non-diegetic music; and the occasional use of a hand-held camera to give the film a 'verité' style.

This discussion then led on to other 'aesthetic' questions about what the audience is seeing. We ensured that students understood the constructed nature of film and examined the ways in which messages are transmitted in film, by looking at production factors such as editing, *mise-en-scène*, lighting, and narrative construction. Exercises on image and scene analysis ensured that the student could come to an understanding of how this process occurred.

Whilst looking at these key filmic issues, we did not want to lose sight of the historical context in which the events took place. Thus the guide included, and referred to, historical sources which students could use to interrogate both the narrative of the film and also raise questions about what was not shown.

How successful was the project overall? A quotation from *Teaching the Holocaust* gives some sense of the impact:

> Spielberg's *Schindler's List* is the most frequently found Holocaust video in English schools, not least because of Spielberg's generosity [sic] in donating a specially edited version to every school in the UK.[5]

Although the film was not 'specially edited', it is interesting that no reference is made to Film Education or the supporting materials that were provided. Could this mean that teachers simply slipped the film into what they were already teaching and paid no attention to the approach offered within the study guide?

Our own feedback suggests that this was not the case. Significant number of teachers contacted Film Education for additional copies of the guide and still ask for copies of the guide and the documentary. Research that we carried out at the time suggested that this was the most popular set of materials that we had circulated to schools.

Its effect on the film industry, particularly regarding the documentary video, was dynamic. Following on from the project, we subsequently produced 49 television programmes for the BBC 'Learning Zone' on a variety of filmic subjects, all accompanied by guides on individual films, all funded by the industry and most still requested by schools.

This project also had a significant effect on the ways in which we have approached subsequent projects about historical feature films.

Producing history

In conjunction with my co-director and producer at Film Education, Jane Dickson, we have now produced two programmes dealing with the Holocaust.[6] The video that accompanied *Schindler's List* is, we feel, the least satisfying of the three. When producing it we fell into the trap of using newsreel and amateur film as wallpaper to accompany a brief history of the Holocaust. It also incorporates footage from the film itself in an unproblematic way in order to illustrate historical events and issues. A popular alternative approach would be to use dramatised reconstructions of events.

Our next foray into this area was to examine the Holocaust film genre as a whole, a task that we tackled over two programmes. The first discussed many of the issues outlined above regarding different film types and the kinds of 'truths' each could offer.

Jews going to work in Oskar Schindler's factory, in *Schindler's List*. (© Universal City Studios, Inc. and Amblin Entertainment, Inc.)

Covering a variety of films and documentaries, the programme posed questions for students which demanded that they looked at films as a way of coming to terms with historical events and the ways in which they are portrayed on film.

In the final and most successful programme, we asked Holocaust survivors to talk about their experiences and to tell us what they felt about those films which have depicted the Holocaust. We felt the survivors' contributions were the most important, not only for their comments on historical accuracy but more importantly their thoughts on how faithful the films had been to their experiences, and how well they had dealt with the deeper philosophical and human issues that surround the Holocaust – the immorality, the inhumanity.

The deaths of six million Jews may forever be beyond the understanding of mankind. All we can do, through the study of the Holocaust, is to hope that what we teach and the way that we teach it will ensure that we remember for the future.

Notes

1   T. Adorno (1998 [1967]) 'Education after Auschwitz', in *Critical Models, interventions and catchwords*. Trans. Henry W. Pickford. New York: Columbia University Press, 190.

2   P. Sorlin (1980) *Film in History: Restaging the Past*. Oxford: Blackwell; R. Rosenstone (1995) *Visions of the Past: The Challenge of Film to our Idea of History*. London: Harvard University Press.

3   Rosenstone 1995: 55–61.

4   Y. Bauer (1978) *The Holocaust in Historical Perspective*. London: Sheldon Press, 3.

5   S. Hector (2000) 'Teaching the Holocaust in England', in I. Davies (ed.) *Teaching the Holocaust: Educational Dimensions, Principles and Practice*. New York: Continuum, 108.

6   The programmes (*The Holocaust on Film* – Parts 1 and 2) were broadcast in April and May 1998 on BBC1.

24 Young people's viewing of Holocaust films in different cultural contexts

Anna Reading

How do viewers respond to representations of the Holocaust in films and on television? What role does film actually play in the construction of people's 'socially inherited memories' of the events?[1] This chapter examines critics' responses to various Holocaust films and then discusses the results of a recent study of young people in different cultural contexts, in which encounters with Holocaust films emerged as a significant element in the construction of their socially inherited memories of the events.

Scholar Miriam Bratu Hansen argues that responses to Holocaust films can be divided into three kinds: official publicity surrounding a film's release; discussions by critical intellectuals; and reports on the public's reception of a film.[2] With the first two, the main concern is with the relationships between the history of the events themselves and the ethics and problems of representing this in film. These tend to be either positive endorsements of the manner of representation and the role film can play in educating people about the events, or they are highly critical of the film as a popular mass medium to represent the Holocaust.

Of those critics and academics that are critical of the possibilities of film, most arguments centre around the feature film. Hollywood versions of the Holocaust are said to sanitise the events into a simple story of triumph over tragedy. The terrible moral dilemmas that people faced are ignored and replaced with simplistic choices and a safe cheerfulness. The Jewish dimension of the Holocaust is superseded by the telling of the story in a way that emphasises that this could have happened to any ordinary American family. In US filmed versions of the Holocaust, it is argued, the tendencies have been towards the universalisation, trivialisation, vulgarisation and popularisation of events.[3]

The feature film that generated the largest amount of critical media coverage and raised debates about how best the Holocaust could be represented was Steven Spielberg's feature film *Schindler's List* (1993). Reviews, academic critiques and commentaries considered many different aspects of the film. Some of these explored the reception of the film by audiences in Germany. Others discussed the ethics and choices that went into the filmic representation in which Spielberg had chosen to use black-and-white throughout most of the movie. Critics centred on the film as a Hollywood product, arguing that its commercial imperatives trivialised the events; some did not like its use of classical narrative or the focus of the film given to the perpetrators as opposed to the history and lives of the 1,100 rescued Jews. There were those that maintained that the film was as at fault for trying to represent the unimaginable. Some journalists, believing that film should have a specific social and political function, reflected on the 'educational efficacy' of the film following its reception by black high school students in Oakland, California. The students were asked to leave the cinema after laughing at the portrayal of Nazi violence towards Jews.

With *Schindler's List*, however, as well as other feature films and documentaries about the Holocaust, critics have emphasised the positive role of the film in the cultivation and creation of knowledge and understanding of the events. Prior to the Holocaust being on the national curriculum in the UK, for example, film was a major medium in which the events entered collective memory. *Schindler's List* was praised for its educational value and its achievement in reaching such a broad public in so many countries with the difficult subject of the Shoah. Similarly, in the 1970s the American television serial *Holocaust* was endorsed by some for bringing into the home the events on a human scale. Jeffrey Shandler has argued that television programmes about the Holocaust mean that people are able to learn about the events in ways that bring its meaning into people's everyday lives, rather than placing it in another realm that they could more easily forget.[4]

In contrast to the mixed responses often given to feature films, documentaries and video-taped testimonies about the Holocaust have been generally positively received. The advantage of the face-to-camera interview is that it can hand down to us non-verbal memories, the facial expression, the ellipses and silences, 'the point at which memory will not enter speech'.[5] Video testimonies can be said to restore the humanity of Jewish people: we see them in colour in their family and home environments, which is very different from the reduction by Nazi-shot black-and-white photographs of Jewish people to hollow-eyed victims.

Underlying all these responses, though, is an assumption that Holocaust films in some simple and direct way affect our understanding and memory of the events. What is lacking with this is sufficient empirical material that explores the actual reception of Holocaust films as part of people's everyday lives. Where this is explored it is either through anecdotal reports by journalists of viewers' responses in cinemas,[6] or social science-based studies that somewhat mechanistically seek to gauge public awareness of the Holocaust following an event or film.[7] Further, these studies are based on responses by specific national publics.[8] What interested me, however, was a more complex and culturally situated understanding of the different ways in which young people's reception of Holocaust films are part of a cultural legacy that is forming their socially inherited memories of the events.

Hence, this study was based on cross-cultural qualitative research with young people under the age of 35. The choice of countries – Poland, the UK and the US – arises firstly from my academic background, as someone who has lived and worked in these countries and who hence has some understanding of young people, their languages and cultures. Secondly, because of the differing cultural mediations and experiences of these countries during and after the events themselves, they provide important comparative material for reflection and analysis. Poland, for example, under Nazi occupation, was the site of the key death camps. After the war, in Poland social memories of the Holocaust were constructed in relation to the Communist State, while in the UK and the US they were constructed within the Western capitalist order. At the same time, it should also be noted that the Jewish and Polish diaspora during and after the Holocaust links these three countries very strongly.

The research consisted of life-history work with 54 men and women aged between 16 and 34 from varied cultural and religious backgrounds in the cities of London, Gdansk, Kraków, Łódź, New York and Washington DC. Predominantly high school and college students were asked to write and talk about the 'socially inherited memories' of the Holocaust that they had developed and inherited through various social and cultural channels, including films.

The results of the study suggested that young people's memories and historical knowledge of the Second World War and the Holocaust came through a wide range of mass media and cultural forms, including television programmes, film, museums, history books and literature, comic books, games acted out as children, watching football games, memorial sites as well as the local environment and geography, encounters with survivors, teachers and peers. For Americans and British respondents the internet was also significant. By far the most significant means of learning about the events were personal encounters with survivors, teachers or family members.

This, in turn, is reflected in the fact that the most influential factor in terms of young people's viewing and reception of Holocaust films is the 'interpretative community' in which people were raised. In short, this is the way in which people internalise inherited stories and memory practices socially agreed by their family and community as necessary to their making sense of themselves in relation to the wider world. Thus, for young Jews and Poles or second and third generation Poles in the US and Britain, the Second World War and the Holocaust was something that was always present in their lives whether overtly spoken about or not. This was especially the case for young Jews; they asserted that they were immersed in Holocaust memory for as long as they could remember – there was no 'first' memory. In contrast, for non-Jews in Britain and the US, television programmes were often their first memory of the Second World War and the Holocaust, often initially in the form of comedy programmes in which the subject arose.

Secondly, within these differing interpretative communities, socially and culturally inherited memories of the Holocaust were handed down neither predominantly through film nor through any other mass medium, but through family members, especially grandmothers. For example, grandmothers were described as having the cultural authority to indicate to grandchildren which version should be accepted as representing the truth, when there were differences between the public version of history taught in schools and the version taught through the family in the private sphere. Hence one Jewish American respondent described how her grandmother helped her negotiate the differences between her school textbook in which the Holocaust constituted 'just a coupla lines' and the more detailed version of the Holocaust inspired by her Jewish family's memories (Rebecca, aged 24, Depth Interview, Washington DC, 1999).

It was fathers, however, who played a key role in giving anchorage and interpretation during the viewing of films and television programmes about the Holocaust. In all three countries, films and programmes on television were recollected within the context of watching them with their father present:

> My father watched a lot of military movies so I kind of connect it with that ... I think my
> first introduction was in high school ... but the actual memories of connecting it to the

actual tragedy of the Holocaust was during those movies, watching those movies with my father. (Michael, aged 29, Focus Group, Washington DC, April 1999)

However, it was not only the interpretative community and within this the structure of the family that was brought to the viewing of Holocaust films and their interpretation. The gendered identities of individuals within these contexts was significant in terms of the importance that film had in relation to other media used to represent the events. Thus, young women in all three countries gave greater emphasis, overall, to the importance of reading books in the development of their understanding and integration of the history of the Holocaust, but men gave greater emphasis to viewing moving images. One Polish woman, for example, described visiting Auschwitz with her parents who carefully explained the history and the context of what happened there. In the same year, she encountered the history of the Holocaust while watching a documentary about it on television. She said the two encounters remained separate in her mind until she was in her twenties when they became linked through her own reading of Holocaust related books. Likewise, a British woman, also 32, said that for her the images of the Holocaust after seeing a short and very shocking documentary at school at the age of 12 remained with her for a long time in a separate part of her mind. She said it was as if the events took place in another Europe – one different from the one in which she travelled and then lived in for six months when she left school … It was only later, through reading both Holocaust history and literature that the reality of the Holocaust became more fully integrated into her broader knowledge, understanding and feelings – her socially inherited memories – of our century.

Young men, in contrast, gave more emphasis to the moving image in a number of ways. Generally they began their written life history accounts with an early memory recollected from watching television documentaries and feature films on the Second World War (rather than specifically the Holocaust) at home. From this, events for young men were often described as being integrated through games at school that were based on imaginative re-enactments of films they had seen. Men described how as children they were able to identify with characters in the films and act out roles in the games that they played in the playground. Although girls were not excluded from these games, as one Polish man pointed out, it was more difficult for them to be involved since there were not many female characters from the films that they could play (Tomasz, aged 20, Catholic, Pole, Łódź, Depth Interview, April 1998). Young women rarely described playing games inspired by films at school as providing key moments in the development of their socially inherited memory of the Holocaust.

The gendered identities of young men and women are, undoubtedly, constructed differently in Poland, the US and the UK and within the different ethnic groups within these. Yet despite this, the actual content recalled and remembered from Holocaust films and still images was clearly differentiated along the lines of gender. For example, women respondents in all three countries more often remembered and described images of child victims, or women being forced to abandon established roles as mothers by leaving their children. Men more often recalled and described an image of direct violence as significant to the development of their memory:

A SS officer like just shot 'em right in the head and the bullet and the blood was coming out man, you know ... they just left 'em there to die, so it was really touching. (Todd, 16 years old, Focus Group, New York, April 1999)

In the same film – *Schindler's List* – whereas women tended to remember 'the girl in the red coat' wandering the street in Kraków after the ghetto and its people were destroyed and forcibly moved, men remembered scenes of shooting or violence. Men described images as meaning more emotionally than words: 'the visual images to me were more than a lot of words – bring home the depth of the hurt' (Peter, aged 29, Focus Group, Washington DC, April 1999).

Young people experienced the meaning and place of Holocaust films as changing over time and in relation to representations of the events in other media. An African American man, for example, who had been posted to Germany with the American armed forces in the early 1990s, described how his most important socially inherited Holocaust memory concerned a visit to Dachau concentration camp in Germany with his mother when she was over from the US to see him:

> My first emotional connection with the Holocaust was watching her cry as we walked through it ... now when I watch movies and documentaries I have a different perspective. (Peter, aged 29, focus group, University of Maryland, Washington DC, April 1999)

The meaning of historical events articulated within films is thus not fixed or discretely and permanently made by one film or visual moment. Rather, the 'effect' in terms of meaning is intertextual: the same film may be understood and integrated into young people's memories in different ways over time and in different ways following the experience or consumption of other media in which the memory of the events of the Holocaust is represented. A Holocaust film is not a closed system existing in isolation with a particular set of effects. Rather, individuals make meaning from a film about the Holocaust in relation to other films, in relation to books, conversations, museums, memorials and other mediations of events.

Conclusion

Young people's reception of moving images related to the Holocaust are in some ways no different from responses to film and television programmes generally: a multiplicity of meanings are generated by viewers who watch them from within the context of their particular communities. These interpretative communities, each with their particular belief systems and histories, provide context and anchor the meanings and impact of the Holocaust films. In this way, the viewing of Holocaust films and television programmes should not be seen simplistically in terms of discrete, fixed texts for the conveyance of information or effecting awareness. Rather they should be understood as part of a complex processes of identification and non-identification with the historical past for young people in different cultural contexts. Holocaust films are viewed from within a structure of thought and feeling imbued through a particular epoch, as well as people's gendered structures and identities. Holocaust films are also viewed in relation to other encounters over time with the history of the events through other films, as well as a broad variety of other media from museums to books.

There are, though, some differences that are distinguishable between films and television programmes about the Holocaust and the reception of other moving images. Films about the Holocaust are more important to those brought up within interpretative communities and environments in which the social inheritance of the Holocaust is not overtly part of the memories handed down within everyday life. Amongst Jewish respondents, part of their historical endowment is the inculcation and internalisation of an understanding of the Holocaust so that it appears 'natural' rather than socially acquired as for other respondents. For them, films are viewed from within this fabric of 'naturally' acquired understanding. Nevertheless, what is also important to note is that the non-Jewish young people in this study articulated a responsibility to understand the Holocaust. Thus 'the structure of feeling' for contemporary young people in relation to the Holocaust is that they feel they should know about the events and should speak about them. This is unlike, for example, the blanket of denial and silence for the generation in the United States immediately after the war.[9] Consequently, an understanding of the reception of films about the Holocaust needs to be understood within this structure of feeling and within the changing temporal context this implies. The experience, memory and meaning of the Holocaust for one generation will be different from another; thus a film like *Schindler's List* does not have 'one effect' on an audience, but, rather its meaning will change over time and in relation to other texts. Finally, in contrast to the more distant or abstracted knowledge of the Holocaust, acquired through, for example, lessons at school, young people's responses show that the history and personal stories of the Holocaust encountered through film seemed to develop in them an acknowledgment, an empathy for the facts in terms of their human meaning in people's everyday lives.

Notes

1   For a discussion outlining the definition of memory and socially inherited memory in relation to the Holocaust see A. Reading (2002) *The Social Inheritance of the Holocaust: Gender, Culture and Memory*. Basingstoke: Palgrave Macmillan, 15–16.

2   M. B. Hansen (2001) '*Schindler's List* is Not *Shoah*: Second Commandment, Popular Modernism and Public Memory', in B. Zelizer (ed.) *Visual Culture and the Holocaust*. New Brunswick, NJ: Rutgers University Press, 147–51.

3   See, for example, A. Insdorf (1989) *Indelible Shadows: Film and the Holocaust*. Cambridge: Cambridge University Press.

4   J. Shandler (1999) *While America Watches: Televising the Holocaust*. New York: Oxford University Press.

5   J. Young (1988) *Writing and Rewriting the Holocaust: Narrative and the Consequences of Interpretation*. Bloomington: Indiana University Press.

6   See for example, F. Rich (1994) 'Schindler's Dissed', *New York Times*, 143, section 4, 6 February.

7   For publication of these, see for example C. Y. Glock, G. J. Selznick and J. L. Spaeth (1966) *The Apathetic Majority: A Study Based on Public Responses to the Eichmann Trial*. New York: Harper and Row, and *International Journal of Political Education*, 4, 1–2 (May 1981), a special issue on the impact the television series *Holocaust* had on the American public.

8   See also, for example, G. Eley and A. Grossman (1997) 'Watching *Schindler's List*', *New German Criticism*, 71, 41–62.

9   P. Novick (1999) *The Holocaust and Collective Memory: The American Experience*. London: Bloomsbury.

25 Living with the long journey: Alfréd Radok's *Daleká cesta*

Jiří Cieslar

Alfréd Radok's *Daleká cesta* (*The Long Journey* aka *The Distant Journey*, 1949) is something of a legend in the Czech Republic; even during the forty-year period when it was banned in Czechoslovakia, it remained in the collective consciousness as one of the country's film masterpieces. For example, the celebrated Czech literary figure and former Czech president Václav Havel, who was in his youth Radok's stage assistant and a close friend, wrote important analytical essays on Radok's work and also penned a very admiring obituary when the director died in 1976.[1]

Internationally, *The Long Journey* was well received when it was released, being awarded, in 1951, the New York Critics prize for the 'Best Foreign Film'. It is to this day the definitive Czech film about the Holocaust, even when compared with such celebrated and internationally recognised films of the 1960s as *Démanty noci* (*Diamonds of the Night*, 1964), directed by Jan Němec; *Obchod na korze* (*The Shop on Main Street*, 1965), directed by Ján Kádar and Elmar Klos, *Transport z ráje* (*Transport from Paradise*, 1962) and *...a pátý jezdec je strach* (*...and the fifth horseman is fear*, 1964), both directed by Zbyněk Brynych, and *Dita Saxová* (1967) directed by Antonín Moskalyk. Long since forgotten abroad, it is hoped that, with the release of a new English sub-titled print and its screenings at the Imperial War Museum in 2001, there will be renewed interest and appreciation of Radok's masterpiece.

The plot of this cinematic work of art is very personal to Alfréd Radok (1917–76), who was half-Jewish and lost a large part of his family in the Holocaust. His father and grandfather died in a transit camp – the ghetto town of Terezín (Theresienstadt) where much of *The Long Journey* is set. For the last months of the war, Radok was himself imprisoned in the detention camp of Klettendorf near Wrocław (Poland), from which he managed to escape. *The Long Journey* was Radok's first film and was made only three years after the tragic events that engulfed his family. He shot the film partly in Prague's Barrandov film studios and partly on location in Terezín; an experience which was particularly difficult and painful.

The Long Journey was filmed in the autumn and winter of 1948–49, a very difficult and dark period in Czechoslovakia, just following the Communist regime's assumption of power in February 1948. As it was to turn out, Radok's film was to be one of the last expressions of cultural freedom in the country for a very long time. At that time, however, this freedom was already being curtailed by new censorship, a fact that influenced the final shape of the film and also the amount of exposure it enjoyed. The expressionistic style in which the film was made aroused the suspicions of the new regime and, after its first run in March 1949, *The Long Journey* had only a limited release and was then banned completely; ironically at exactly the same moment that it was receiving awards in New York. It was typical of that era of Czechoslovak history that words such as expressionism, formalism and structuralism were more like accusations than technical or aesthetic terms. The Czech people were not able to see *The Long Journey* again until after the Velvet Revolution, when in 1991 it received its television premiere.

The whole of Radok's life seems determined by an atavistic fate. After *The Long Journey*, he was only allowed to make two more films: in 1953 he shot a mediocre musical called *Divotvorný klobouk* (*The Magic Hat*) and in 1956 he made a comedy in the 'art nouveau style' called *Dědeček automobil* (*The Grandfather – Automobile*). In 1960 he was one of the founders of Laterna Magika, an internationally recognised multi-media venue (theatre, film, dance and music). After a short period he was forced to leave, a pattern which was to be repeated as Radok tried to develop a career in the theatre; driven from one theatre to another (he was twice forced to leave the National Theatre), he was unable to realise his dream of forming a permanent troupe of actors. Three days after the occupation of Czechoslovakia in August 1968, Radok escaped to Göteborg in Sweden and his name became taboo in Czechoslovakia. He worked in the Swedish theatre with little success as he had problems both with the actors and in tackling a foreign language. In 1976, during a short stay in Vienna, Radok died of a heart attack.

Narrative structure

The Long Journey has a strange and complex narrative structure, operating on three levels. On the first, it is a melodrama about a mixed marriage between two young doctors from the same hospital, a Jewish woman Hana (Blanka Waleska) and her Aryan colleague Toník (Otomar Krejča). Their wedding has to take place in virtual secrecy and is set against the dark backdrop of the recently introduced antisemitic laws and the issue of the first call-up papers for 'the long journey', transports to the concentration camps. The second part of the film is set in Terezín. The film's third narrative element is provided by archival sequences of newsreel and propaganda footage; these comprise the film's 'documentary' prologue and excerpts linking certain sections of the plot.

The first part of the story takes place in Prague, in 'the ghetto without walls', in an environment tainted with fear and anxiety about the future. The story begins when the leading character, Dr Hana Kaufmann, is dismissed from her position. It is a sad fact that the first order of the Czech government in the 'Protectorate of Bohemia and Moravia', and made only two days after the Nazi occupation of the country, was to exclude 'non-Aryan' doctors from their practices.[2] The action then continues chronologically, showing the impact on the lives of the main characters of successive measures taken against the Jews, starting with the scene when Hana and Toník are forced to cancel a trip to the theatre as a consequence of the order forbidding Jews to visit theatres and other cultural events; the film's plot mirroring an edict enforced in the Protectorate on 1 September 1941.

The second narrative level takes place in Terezín where first Hana's family and later Hana herself is transported. Ironically, it was not until the Nazi occupation that the garrison town, with its high, red-brown, surrounding wall, served the purpose to which it had been built. However, this time the fortress was designed to imprison people rather than protect them from hostile Prussians.[3]

Hana scrubbing the paving stones in Terezín. (© Národní Filmový Archiv)

The majority of the ghetto's inmates came from the Protectorate of Bohemia and Moravia (about 60,000), but deportees were also sent from countries in the West, such as France, Holland, Belgium and so on (see the chapters in this volume by Becker and Fantlova-Ehrlich). Within the ghetto there was also a Gestapo prison, the so-called Little Fortress, where the severest conditions existed. Here Radok's father, Viktor, was tortured and murdered. Understandably, Radok was not able to go into the prison during the filming of *The Long Journey*.

To create the illusion of freedom, the Nazis granted the Jews a highly dependent form of self-government within the ghetto. After a while, the prisoners were even given limited freedom for cultural expression. So in Terezín a very specific, semi-legal cultural environment existed. Many concerts, cabarets and operas were performed (for example Verdi's *Tosca* and Smetana's *The Bartered Bride*) at night in Terezín's houses. The premiere of the children's opera *Brundibár* by Hans Krása was performed in Terezín, an event recalled in a scene in *The Long Journey* when a group of children sing a song from the opera. Drawings, scores, poems and secretly-written diaries, for example by Alisah Shek or Erich Kassler, survive to record Terezín's cultural life.

The Germans created the pretence that Terezín was a 'model ghetto', recording the life of the town in a 'documentary' film (see Lutz Becker's chapter in section two) and even allowing a delegation of the Red Cross to visit. To prepare for this inspection, the Jews were compelled to make the town look presentable for the international visitors, an episode recreated in Radok's film in the absurd scene in which the women wash the pavement of one of Terezín's streets.

Hana among a crowd of prisoners at Terezín who have panicked, hearing of the arrival of a 'transport' from the East. (© Národní Filmový Archiv)

Terezín's reality was, therefore, strange, complex, absurd and full of contradictions. From time to time, this closed world was also hallucinatory and incredible. As an expressionist stage director, Radok drew upon these characteristics and moods. He saw Terezín in a subjective and imaginative way, as a nightmare, as an inner and very personal experience. In contrast with the documentary style of the Polish feature about Auschwitz, *Ostatni etap* (*The Last Stage/The Last Stop*, 1948) made by Wanda Jakubowska, Radok created a vision of Terezín as a large, crazy, grotesque, railway station, a vestibule to the extermination camps, as a place of chaos. It is a place without floors and ceilings and with many obstacles: steps, bars, oblique walls and with mysterious sounds off-screen.

Five years ago I screened *The Long Journey* to one of Terezín's former prisoners, who was very disappointed with it. As he said to me, 'There was order in Terezín, not this kind of chaos'. He could not accept the artistic licence with which Radok approached the subject nor the style he adopted to represent Terezín.

Radok not only drew on elements from his imagination, but also from the dreadful reality of Terezín. For example, we see the night-train travelling along the narrow streets of the town centre. Although this scene is like a dream, it was based on the reality of Terezín, an occurrence that was for Radok a powerful metaphor for the madness of the prison ghetto.

These metaphorical scenes can be viewed as ceremonies or rites at the heart of the melodrama. The protagonists in these scenes take on symbolic features when the meaning or significance of the moment and situation increases. Naturally enough, there are more of these symbolic scenes in the second part of the film, which is set in the ghetto. Two striking examples concern the transports to and from the East. The first is set at night in one of the streets of Terezín, as a Jewish band, standing on a hearse, play as the Jews trudge slowly past in the rain to take their 'transport to the East'. The second occurs at the end of the film, as Hana waits by the tracks for a train from the East bringing typhoid patients. Her face is not seen, only the silhouette of her body as a black statue.

One of the first examples of this highly stylised and symbolic treatment of the action occurs when the family is still in Prague. This is the scene showing Professor Reiter's suicide following Hana and Toník's wedding. The scene is characterised by unusual camera angles and an impressive soundtrack, which is dominated by the sound of a pianist practising scales in a room above, the scales getting louder and faster as the drama develops. The room also contains a variety of symbolic objects: a rucksack, marked with the number 402, a sinister reference to the family's future status as prisoners; a globe standing on the table, symbolising the world to which the Professor refused to escape; and a clock that has stopped. The audience does not see the moment when the Professor jumps from the open window to the pavement below; instead, the action is conveyed via sounds from the street, then the camera pulls dramatically away from a close-up of the Professor's cigar to show, in mid-shot, the open window. This scene does more than relate Reiter's fate: it gives us a general perspective on the Jewish situation; it is symbolic of the Holocaust; and it is also a tribute to the exceptional courage of those who chose suicide to escape the suffering of the 'transports' and the concentration camps.

An artistic report

Archive film sequences comprise *The Long Journey*'s third narrative layer. To retain a link with the fictional narrative, Radok used an innovative technique in which a frame, frozen from the previous dramatised scene, shrinks into the bottom right-hand corner of the screen and is then held within the wider frame throughout the archive sequence. One of these archive sequences follows the suicide scene as an expressive counterpoint, and comprises German newsreel footage of Prague castle with the Deputy Reichsprotektor Reinhard Heydrich, SS head Heinrich Himmler and the Sudeten German leader, Karl Hermann Frank.[4] For the archive film sequences, Radok used footage from the German propaganda newsreel series *Die Deutsche Wochenschau* (June 1940–March 1945) and also Leni Riefenstahl's famous propaganda film *Triumph of the Will* (1935). These sequences referred to a larger external history, which, although remote from the story of Radok's characters, ultimately has a fatal impact on their lives. The archival sequences also place Radok's characters within the wider history of the war as it unfolds. Finally, during the 'documentary' prologue, Radok compares Nazi propaganda slogans with the real situation of the war. For example, a statement at the Nuremberg rally by Fritz Reinhardt is translated in the ironic, weary voice of the commentator, 'Wherever we look new order is being built', the film cutting from the rally to a sequence of archive film, in which the camera pans across an enormous manufacturing site and finishes on an aerial view of the prison huts of Auschwitz. The tone of the narrator's voice adds greatly to the power of Radok's commentary and provides an intimate and warm aspect to the film.

As it turns out, Alfréd Radok shot some of the 'documentary' footage himself, thus *The Long Journey* can be seen as a mixture of genuine archive film and intentional mystification. A method that relates to Radok's concept of the ideal film as an 'artistic report', a multi-dimensional structure in which different points of view can be compared. *The Long Journey* contains an array of these different film elements (archivally sourced propaganda and newsreel footage; a pastiche of factual film; a feature film; and an expressionist camera, sound and lighting style) and was undoubtedly influenced by Orson Welles' *Citizen Kane* (1941). In an interview in the Czech daily newspaper *Mladá fronta* (December 1947), Alfréd Radok cited *Citizen Kane* as his greatest artistic experience of that year.

Without claiming that *The Long Journey* is as celebrated or as great a film as *Citizen Kane*, the two films are stylistically similar and share an expressionist viewpoint. There are also many interesting similarities between Welles and Radok. Both directors came to the cinema from the theatre, but far from being hindered by their lack of experience of film production, Welles and Radok found this liberating and endeavoured, in an almost exhibitionist manner, to demonstrate how creative they could be with the medium. They also relied on the skills of very experienced film technicians, above all cameramen; Orson Welles used Gregg Toland and Radok used Josef Střecha.

Representing evil

The Long Journey only represents a fragment of Radok's original intentions for the film, which was based on a synopsis written by Erik Kolár who had been imprisoned in Terezín. Radok and Kolár wanted to represent evil 'in the others' (the Nazis), but also as it was manifested 'in us', i.e. Czech antisemitism whether hidden or openly expressed. In the end this subject occupied far less of the film than they had intended, and was only represented in minor characters such as the caretaker who shamelessly steals Jewish possessions and Toník's father, a man whose 'everyday', non-aggressive antisemitism prevents him from attending his son's wedding. Radok and Kolár's original screenplay contained a far more prominent demonstration of antisemitism: paralleling a scene in which German students watch the execution of Jewish professors in Berlin with a scene showing Czech nationalist students fighting people sympathetic to the Jews. It is very likely that the Communist censors were not happy with these particular insights into domestic antisemitism.

Radok's inexperience did not always have a positive impact on the film, for example he drew rather old-fashioned performances from his actors. In spite of this, *The Long Journey* is a very important film because it shows the evils of war at a number of symbolic levels: as a Holocaust tragedy; as the universal tragedy of man; and lastly as a metaphor for an inner prison which potentially threatens each of us.

During the Imperial War Museum symposium, one of the delegates explained that the Holocaust was for him 'a thing of the present, a present state of mind'. Of course, but the Holocaust is also, at least for me – a person who did not live during the Second World War – a phenomenon of profound 'archetypes', to use the term coined by Carl Gustav Jung. The Holocaust draws on the archetypes of violence, fear, anxiety, and perhaps even the creativity that the prisoners of Terezín expressed to protect themselves. Interestingly, over the course of the symposium, various sequences of archive footage were repeated in a number of different films. I was particularly struck by the sequence showing the female camp guards being escorted away from the barracks at Bergen-Belsen. I see the mysterious impact of this repeated scene not only, of course, as an echo of archetypal imagery, but also as one of the repeated scenes, figures and atmospheres from our dreams.

Radok's picture of Terezín is a vision of the inner experience from which no one can escape. The last scene of the film is set in Terezín's cemetery, sometime after the end of the war. As the camera surveys the bleak field of crosses, the commentator's weary voice remarks that 'man was victorious'. He follows this glib comment by naming a long list of concentration camps and ending with the following statement: 'Seven million died in the concentration camps. Over 140,000 from all over Europe went to Theresienstadt. Only a few survived.'

It is as if Radok, through the devise of *mise-en-scène,* is trying to relate to the viewer that here is a specific experience that cannot be overcome. This experience remains and what do we with it? This question does not only concern the survivors of the Holocaust, but all of us.

Some decades after the end of the war, writers and filmmakers began to produce work that probed more deeply into the Holocaust and the issues the phenomenon posed for humanity. But long before the books of Primo Levi, Jean Améry, Rudolf Glazar and Claude Lanzmann's film *Shoah* (1985) demanded our attention, Alfréd Radok's *The Long Journey* brought audiences a startling and profound interior view of the Holocaust.[5]

Notes

1. Havel assisted Radok on two theatrical productions, *The Swedish Match* and *The Woman Thief of London.* His essays on Radok's work have not been published in English; however, there is a detailed survey of Radok's career, including a number of quotes from Havel, in J. M. Burian (2002) *Leading Creators of Twentieth-Century Czech Theatre.* London: Routledge. Here is an excerpt from Havel's obituary of Radok: 'His life was interlaced with tragic paradoxes. On the one hand, Czech theatre owed few others as much as it did him for so many truly new and inspirational impulses, from which whole generations of younger directors drew and which helped so many actors to an artistic rebirth. On the other hand, this same Czech theatre gave few others as little opportunity to enjoy the results of his work, to develop them in peace, and to live to have them justly appreciated. In Radok's fate was something of the fate of an outlaw, an Ahasvera; almost always he was driven away from his work precisely at the time when it began to bear fruit.' Václav Havel, 'Alfred Radok: an obituary', in Burian 2002: 59. Other writings about Radok by Havel include: 'Radok dnes' ['Radok Today'], in '*Do různých stran*' [*In Various Directions*], Prague: Lidové noviny, 1989, 318f, originally written in 1986; *O divadle,* Prague: Lidové noviny, 1990, 394; 'Několik poznámek z *Švéské zápalky*' ['Several notes from *The Swedish Match*'], in *O divadle,* Prague: Lidové noviny, 1990, 376f.

2. The Germans occupied Czechoslovakia on 15 March 1939. The German occupiers imposed a new name on Czechoslovakia, the 'Protectorate of Bohemia and Moravia', which did not include most of Slovakia, now independent due to pressure from the Germans. Consistent with its status as an autonomous part of the Reich, the Head of State remained the Czech President Hácha and the Government of the Protectorate was still led by the pre-invasion Czech cabinet headed by Prime Minister Rudolph Beran. However, the Czech leaders' authority was contingent on the Germans, as they were ultimately answerable to the German representative in the Protectorate, the Protector of Bohemia and Moravia, Konstantin von Neurath.

3. The ghetto of Terezín was established in November 1941. On 3 May 1945 the Germans handed Terezín over to the Red Cross and on 8 May it was liberated by the Red Army.

4. Karl Hermann Frank (1898–1946) was the deputy leader of the SDP, the Sudeten German Party. After the

German takeover of Czechoslovakia in 1939, he was made Neurath's deputy with the post of State Secretary for the Protectorate of Bohemia and Moravia. He was sentenced to death by a post-war Czech court and publicly hanged near Prague on 22 May 1946.

5   Editors' note: Cieslar's slightly contradictory statement here probably refers to the date at which books such as Levi's *If This is a Man* were published in Czechoslovakia. Primo Levi: *Se questo è un uomo* (*If This is a Man*) (1947); *La Tregua* (*The Truce*) (1963), translated into English as *The Truce: A Survivor's Journey Home from Auschwitz*, translated by Stuart Woolf. London: Bodley Head, 1965; Jean Améry (1912–78): *Jenseits von Schuld und Sühne* (*Beyond Guilt and Atonement*) (1966). This book was translated into English in 1980 as *At the Mind's Limits: Contemplations by a Survivor on Auschwitz and its Realities*. Bloomington: Indiana University Press; Richard Glazar (1920–): *Treblinka, slovo jak z dětské říkanky*, Prague: Ústav pro soudobé dějiny AV ČR, 1994.

26 Double memory: the Holocaust in Polish film

Ewa Mazierska

The Second World War is regarded as the single most important event in Polish history of the twentieth century. Yet prior to the mid-1980s the term 'Holocaust' was hardly used in official discourses. As a person who grew up in Communist Poland in the 1970s and early 1980s I remember that in history lessons we were repeatedly told that in the war Poland suffered a greater human loss than any other country, reaching six million people, but no teacher mentioned the ethnic and religious background of those who died or the way they lost their lives. As a result, we assumed that the vast majority of them were 'ordinary' Poles who died on the battlefield.[1] When the concentration camps were mentioned, it was again suggested that these were places where the Nazis extermi- nated predominantly Poles, as opposed to Polish Jews and Jews from other European countries.[2]

Why have the Jews been excluded from the Polish memory of the war? Some his- torians, including Piotr Wróbel, explain the phenomenon with reference to Polish an- tisemitism and the social and cultural separation of Polish Christians and Jews: 'The Holocaust did not change the Polish stereotype of the Jew. After centuries of separation, most Poles had no corporate feelings of a common suffering with the Jewish people'.[3] Several intellectuals writing on Polish-Jewish relations sought justification for this phe- nomenon in concepts of trauma, repression and the return of the repressed, an explana- tion even advanced to explain the post-war silence of Holocaust survivors and the recent evolution of Holocaust consciousness in Israel, Europe and the United States.[4] Accord- ing to the trauma theory, Polish feelings of guilt for their treatment of Jews during the Nazi occupation, intertwined with the shock of witnessing their extermination, was so intense and distressing that it had to be repressed.[5]

The situation began to change in the mid-1980s, largely because of the easing of censorship which allowed new evidence of the extent of Jewish suffering and the nega- tive role Poles played in the Holocaust to be placed in the public domain. Two events are of particular importance in this perspective: firstly, the Polish premiere of Claude Lanzmann's *Shoah* (1985), a film which focused on Polish indifference and widespread collaboration with the Nazis in the acts of ethnic cleansing of Jews; and secondly, the discovery, thanks to the book *Neighbours* (2001), written by Jan Tomasz Gross, of the Polish massacre of 1600 Jews in the village of Jedwabne, an event which took place in July 1941.[6] These events deeply upset and offended Poles, but also forced them to look at the Holocaust afresh, facing up to the idea that they were not the 'Christ among nations' as they liked to perceive themselves.[7]

I will suggest that until the collapse of communism, Polish cinema, like Polish history in general, played down the significance of the Jews' extermination during the war. I will refrain from claiming that simple antisemitism was the main reason for that, although it was clearly a factor in the way the Holocaust was portrayed by some filmmakers. Other factors include: a desire on the part of filmmakers to represent the war as a conflict between fascism and communism, rather than as an ethnic or colonial war; to produce 'patriotic' films by extolling Polish suffering at the expense of others nations, especially Jews, which was particularly the case of Andrzej Wajda's films;[8] and to erase any doubts that during the war Poles did not help their Jewish 'neighbours' as much as they could.

Films about the concentration camps were made in every period of Poland's post-war cinematic history and by filmmakers who had different thematic and stylistic interests, and political allegiances, as well as different experiences of the war. Some directors were imprisoned in the concentration camps, others learnt about them from historical sources and artistic renderings. It is not possible to analyse all of them in this chapter; therefore I will focus on the three films which achieved the greatest national and international recognition and best reflect the attitudes in Poland to this subject at different times of Polish post-war history, as well as serving an excellent prism through which to look at other aspects of Polish past.

The first film which fulfils these criteria is *Ostatni etap* (*The Last Stage/The Last Stop*, 1948) by Wanda Jakubowska which received numerous awards in Poland and abroad, including the Award of the World Peace Council in 1951. Jakubowska was an ardent believer in communism and conveyed her views both on- and off-screen, being the main representative of socialist realism in Polish cinema and one of the highest profile filmmakers to join the Polish United Workers Party (Polska Zjednoczona Partia Robotnicza) after the Second World War. Accordingly, *The Last Stage* can be regarded as a 'Holocaust film', documenting the experiences of people incarcerated in concentration camps, and a socialist realist film, proclaiming Stalinist ideology through a particular rhetoric and style.[9]

During the Second World War Jakubowska was engaged in the resistance movement, which led to her arrest in 1942. She spent six months in the Pawiak prison in Warsaw and was later transported first to the Ravensbrück concentration camp and then to Oświęcim (Auschwitz), from which she was freed on 18 January 1945. The years in the camps constituted her most important experiences, both in terms of her personal life and artistic development.[10] Indeed, four of her films are set during the Second World War and three of them deal specifically with the issue of the concentration camps. The project of *The Last Stage* was actually conceived during Jakubowska's incarceration. She shared her ideas with many fellow prisoners and they passed her their stories to be included in the project. The co-author of the script was fellow prisoner, Gerda Schneider, a German, who, like Jakubowska, dreamt of making a film about life in Auschwitz.

Jakubowska's film portrays life in the women's part of Auschwitz-Birkenau until it was liberated by the Red Army and focuses on the resistance movement in the camp. It has no single main character, but at least three women can be regarded as leading heroines: Marta, a Polish Jew who works as a translator; Anna, a German nurse and communist, and the Russian doctor, Eugenia. In spite of their different nationalities, there are many similarities in their views, behaviour and position in the camp. All have senior posts thanks to their skills and influence and the respect held for them by their

Scene from *The Last Stage* (1948). BFI 3231 (© Studio Filmowe "Oko")

fellow prisoners. Eugenia will go to any length to procure medicines for her patients, Anna helps her and Marta organises the smuggling of essential commodities into the camp and tries to uncover the Germans' plans. Their attitude is strongly contrasted with another hierarchy, imposed on the prisoners by the Nazis: the system of block leaders. Apart from being individuals, Marta, Anna and Eugenia serve as symbols of the main enemies of fascism: Jewry, communism and the East, with communism serving as a 'common denominator' of these three women. It was thanks to the cooperation of these three forces that the Nazis were eventually defeated, both on the small scale of the concentration camp and in the war as a whole. Again, this idea of international solidarity is in tune with the communist principle of privileging internationalism at the expense of the welfare of one's nation. Characteristically, if Jakubowska shows any group of women in a less favourable light than the others, it is the Poles. The block leaders are mainly Poles and the greedy, haughty and utterly incompetent wife of a pharmacist, who becomes the new doctor in the female camp, is also Polish. Her character can be regarded as a criticism of the Polish pre-war bourgeoisie, the class who the owners of chemist shops epitomised.

Reaction to the film, at the time of its premiere in 1948, was very positive both in Poland and abroad. The reasons for this phenomenal success are complex and it is impossible to establish all of them. However, some factors reappear in the opinions of critics and film historians. First, as Tadeusz Lubelski notes, is simply the subject of the film. At the time the film was made, Poles were keen to see films about the war. When in 1947 the popular Polish film magazine, *Film* conducted a survey amongst its readers, asking them what themes they favoured in cinema, the most common answer was the Second World War.[11] At the end of the 1940s there was also a desire in many other countries (such as Russia and Yugoslavia) to see the war on screen. Secondly, the strong pacifist message of *The Last Stage* captured the popular mood in both the East and the West, when everyone worldwide needed to console themselves with the assurance 'never again' which ends the film.[12] Over the next few decades the mood both in Poland and abroad changed; pacifism was no longer taken for granted, and the Soviet Army was associated with an oppressive force, rather than with those who liberated Auschwitz. This affected the reception of Jakubowska's later films, devoted to the issue of the camps, which was cooler than that of *The Last Stage* despite *Koniec naszego świata* (*The End of Our World*, 1964) being in many ways her most accomplished film. Third and perhaps the most important reason for the immense popularity and appreciation of *The Last Stage* is Jakubowska's use of what Tadeusz Lubelski describes as the 'witness strategy', which means representing a particular reality from the point of view of a person who either has first-hand experience of it or uses the insight of other witnesses.[13] However, Lubelski persuasively argues that the witness strategy was intertwined in *The Last Stage* with the strategy of propaganda, typical of socialist realism. It was further compromised by Jakubowska's conformity to certain Hollywood conventions, which prevented her, for example, from showing the emaciated bodies of the prisoners, or their infestation with vermin. Nevertheless, its pioneering status in the 'Holocaust genre' and the effect it had on its viewers can not be overestimated.

While *The Last Stage* belongs to the socialist realistic paradigm in Polish cinema, *Pasażerka* (*Passenger*, 1961–63) was directed by one of two principal creators of the Polish School: Andrzej Munk (the second is Andrzej Wajda). This distinction had major implications for the ideology and style of the film. Hence, while Jakubowska foregrounds in her film the resistance movement of the prisoners, Munk, in line with the Polish School ethos, avoids loud proselytising and concentrates on documenting typical days and nights in the camp, what can be described as the camp's 'normality'. The struggle of the prisoners against their oppressors, although not ignored, is pushed to the

Liza, the overseer in *Passenger* (1961–63). BFI 161527 (© Contemporary Films)

background and typically revealed through its effects. For example, in one episode we see that the vicious dog belonging to the Nazi guard has been killed. It is suggested that the prisoners killed the dog, but their action is not shown. Similarly, we learn that a Jewish child was saved by Polish female prisoners, but we never see the child or the care it received from its rescuers.

In documenting ordinary life in Auschwitz, Munk's film reflects an important literary trend in Polish literature about the camps, as represented by works such as *Medaliony* (*Medallions*, 1945) by Zofia Nałkowska and the short stories of Tadeusz Borowski, although the direct literary source for *Passenger* was a radio drama, written by Zofia Posmysz-Piasecka. These authors tried to document with minute precision how the 'Nazi machine' worked and what effect it had on its victims and perpetrators, without making any explicit moral judgement. However, their passionless narration hides an outrage and bewilderment as to how it all could happen. Moreover, Borowski is renowned for regarding the Holocaust not as a catastrophe imposed on 'good people' from without and an aberration in the history of European civilisation, but as its end. In his outlook on the camp there was no fundamental distinction between the oppressor and the oppressed: both were eventually corrupted by the system and were prepared to betray even their closest ally to save their lives or even to receive small privileges.[14] As Ewelina Nurczyńska-Fidelska observes, while Munk utilised Borowski's dispassionate style, took on board many of Borowski's ideas and was aware of the corrupting influence of the camp's mechanisms on the prisoners, he did not share the writer's utter pessimism.[15]

In line with Borowski's idea that in the concentration camp the lives of oppressors and victims were closely linked in a moral sense by belonging to the same cruel microcosm, *Passenger* has two main characters. One is Liza, a German who during the war belonged to the SS and worked in Auschwitz as overseer of a division which sorted the confiscated belongings of the people who were sent to the crematoria, the other is Marta,

Marta, the prisoner in *Passenger*. BFI 342882 (© Contemporary Films)

a Polish prisoner, who was sent to the camp as punishment for an anti-Nazi conspiracy. The film takes the form of an extended flashback, triggered by Liza's unexpected meeting with Marta on a cruise liner travelling to South America more than a decade after the war. Worried that her husband, who accompanies her on the journey, will be approached by Marta who might accuse her of involvement in the Nazi operations and in need of self-exoneration, she tells him how miserable her own position was during the war and how she tried to 'save' Marta. Later, however, tormented by her conscience, she provides us with the second and more truthful version of events. We learn that she did not really want to save Marta, but to change her into an accomplice in her crimes and her grateful and obedient slave, using a method of 'carrot and stick'. For example, she allowed her to meet her fiancé who was incarcerated in a different part of the camp, but later sent her to the death block as punishment for her defiance. This version shows Liza not as a humble soldier, forced to take part in the war and a person who tried to be as noble as possible in adverse circumstances, but as an active follower of the Nazi formula who was even more devious than many – apparently – more cruel members of fascist organisations.

While Liza has a chance to present her version of events in Auschwitz, we learn about Marta only through Liza's unsympathetic and jealous gaze at her Polish 'slave' and her self-pitying memory. In most scenes Marta is mute and her actions are interpreted as being ungrateful and malicious to Liza. This, however, is enough to learn that (not unlike Jakubowska's heroines) she remained strong and altruistic. Ultimately, as Nurczyńska-Fidelska observes, Marta was also freer than Liza, because she managed to retain control over her thoughts and deeds, while Liza submitted to the fascist system and her sense of duty.[16]

From this thumbnail synopsis we can infer that, not unlike Jakubowska, Munk played down the issue of the prisoners' nationality. Marta is a Pole, as is her fiancé, but the reason for that appears to me not to be the author's desire to concentrate on Polish suffering at the expense of Jewish, but Munk's outlook on the Second World War as a product of a particular ideology and system. It was born in Germany and affected predominantly Jews and Poles, but as Borowski argued, could happen anywhere in Europe and affect everybody, irrespective of their nationality, age, education or social class.

The history of the making of *Passenger* deserves a separate study for which there is insufficient space here. However, one fact cannot be ignored: Munk did not manage to finish his film, as he died in a car accident during its shooting in 1961. The final version was completed in 1963 by Munk's collaborators, including the fellow Polish School author, Witold Lesiewicz. Rather than shoot the scenes which remained in the script they decided to edit the film from the existing material. The result is that the contemporary part of the film is reduced to a series of photographs. Consequently, *Passenger* is much more a film about life in Auschwitz than in the original project. Another result is the fragmented style of the film, with photographs and off-screen commentary replacing parts of the narrative. I suggest that while at the time of the film's premiere this could have been regarded as a weakness, in light of later films about the Holocaust, and the discussions of how this subject should be depicted, this fragmented style now feels like its strength. In particular, the lack of a 'smooth', Hollywood-style plot and the numerous gaps in the narrative, which bears a resemblance to a documentary, supports the idea that those who embark on making films about the Holocaust should recognise art's ultimate inability to tell the whole truth about this tragedy. Despite being unfinished, *Pas-*

Adrien Brody, in *The Pianist* (2002) (© UIP)

senger is regarded as Munk's masterpiece and became his most awarded film, including the FIPRESCI Award in Cannes.[17]

The last film I shall examine is *The Pianist* (2002) by Roman Polański, a film awarded a Palme d'Or at the Cannes Film Festival and Academy Awards for best director and best leading actor. Although it is a co-production of four countries: France, Poland, Germany and the United Kingdom, I feel justified in considering it in this chapter on the grounds of the director's nationality, its literary source, the choice of the main character, as well as the fact that it was shot in Poland, only a few miles from the site of the Warsaw ghetto. At the same time it cannot be denied that Polański's film was made largely for an international audience, to which can be attributed the language in which it is shot: English, as well as the largely British and American cast, including Adrien Brody in the leading role, with Polish actors playing only minor parts. Consequently, we need to contextualise the film differently from the two discussed previously, situating it not only against the background of Polish but also foreign films about the Holocaust and the discussions they triggered amongst historians and film critics. Two films in particular should be taken into account: the previously mentioned *Shoah* by Claude Lanzmann and *Schindler's List* (1993) by Steven Spielberg. Thanks to a painstaking reconstruction of the German 'machinery of destruction', which precludes any sensationalism, using place to invoke what is absent (instead of replicating the past) and concentrating on the stories of those who perished, *Shoah* became the paradigm of an 'honest' or 'true' film about the Holocaust, almost the ultimate Holocaust film.[18] For the same reasons it was the antithesis of a commercial movie, defined by an individual hero, a classical narrative and a happy ending. Moreover, as previously mentioned, *Shoah* deeply offended Poles.

By contrast, *Schindler's List* was a commercially successful film that was greeted with sympathy in Poland. Not only were Poles grateful to Spielberg for using a largely Polish crew, including the cinematographer Janusz Kamiński and production designers Allan

Starski and Ewa Braun who received Academy Awards for their work, but also for re-fraining from accusing the Poles for Jewish suffering. At the same time, the film was criticised for such vices as focusing on those who survived the camps because 'stories of the saved distort [history] because they exclude stories of the drowned',[19] inflating 'the rescuer's role'[20] at the expense of the victims, and producing a 'simulacra' of the Holo-caust, rather than looking for and interrogating its traces in the present.[21] Spielberg was also accused of 'Hollywoodisation' of the Holocaust by making it fashionable, a part of popular culture which, in the opinion of many historians and Holocaust survivors, is an unsuitable fate for a subject as serious as the most horrific act of ethnic cleansing in hu-man history.[22] Some Jewish critics even questioned Spielberg's right to make a film about the Holocaust. For example, Sever Plotzker described *Schindler's List* as a 'film made by a rich and spoiled Jewish director, master of fictional hits, who tries with his fabricated document to express his pained Diaspora Jewishness'.[23]

Hence, the question which Polański (who previously rejected an offer to direct *Schin-dler's List*) had to ask himself prior to embarking on this subject was how to avoid similar criticisms, but at the same time make a film which would be commercially successful and not offend his Polish friends, such as Andrzej Wajda, for whom *Shoah* was anath-ema. It seems that he managed to find the perfect formula to avoid these dangers. Part of the recipe was, so to speak, Polański himself. For example, David Thompson writes that '*The Pianist* is ... as near-perfect a marriage of subject and artist as could be imagined'.[24] Being a Holocaust survivor gave Polański a credibility to embark on this subject which no Polish director had enjoyed since Wanda Jakubowska. This 'authentic' aspect of the film was seized upon by the Polish press. Authors of reports from the set mentioned, for example, that Polański asked the costume designers to change some details in the costumes of German policemen on the ground that they did not conform to his memory of the war. Moreover, as a Jew he could not be accused lightly of making a film which undermines Jewish suffering. The second part of Polański's recipe for a successful Holo-caust film was its literary source: the memoirs of a Holocaust survivor, the pianist and composer, Władysław Szpilman. Accordingly, the Jew, rather than a 'good German' as in *Schindler's List* or a 'good Pole' and a 'good communist', as in many Polish films about the camps, is the main protagonist of the story. At the same time Szpilman can be regarded as a model of a Jew assimilated into the culture in which he was brought up, not unlike another character in the Polish Holocaust film: Korczak in Wajda's film of 1990, whom I have elsewhere described, borrowing the term from Isaac Deutscher, as the 'non-Jewish Jew'.[25] Szpilman's own son, Christopher Szpilman describes his father as somebody who could not live anywhere except Poland.[26] Needless to say, this category of Jews is accept-able to the majority of Poles, even those with antisemitic views.

Szpilman's memoirs consists of two main parts: his life in the ghetto and his lonely struggle to stay alive after the ghetto's annihilation and the Warsaw Uprising. Szpilman's account of life in the ghetto strikes as sympathetic to Poles. If he is critical of anybody, it is largely of some of his fellow Jews who collaborated with the Nazis and took advantage of their less fortunate compatriots. Yet even this criticism is free of any hatred or bitter-ness. Although he never acted against the welfare of other Jews, on the contrary, he was involved in the resistance movement, in common with Borowski, Szpilman reveals a perfect understanding that in extreme situations the most natural human reaction is to fight for our own survival even at the expense of the welfare of those close to us. This understanding, according to many Polish historians and war survivors, is lacking in many Jewish accounts of the Holocaust.

Szpilman's survival is a combination of several factors. One of them is his own will to live, as well as to tell his story and be able to play the piano (in this respect he is similar to Jakubowska who also dreamt about continuing her filmmaking career when the war was over). Others include the help that he received from Polish friends and a German officer, who did not kill him, but helped him to stay alive by bringing food to him in his hiding place. Szpilman survives the war, but the image of his emaciated body and the awareness that all his family perished in the gas chambers makes the closure of Polański's film rather different from a Hollywood-style 'happy ending'.

On the whole, Polański's adaptation is regarded as very faithful to its literary original in terms of its construction of characters, narrative and ideology.[27] The only major difference concerns its structure: the second part is extended in comparison with Szpilman's memoirs. As a result, in his lonely time of 'clinging to life' Szpilman comes across as a more active and ultimately, more noble and heroic figure than in his own biography, thus preventing the criticism that in Holocaust films Jews are represented as weak and passive. At the same time the familiar figure of the 'good German' does not lose its greatness (which in Szpilman's book was closely linked to his Catholicism, while in Polański's film to his love of music), and there is still space for some Poles to show their willingness to help the Jews. The true villains are the Nazis and the Stalinists – the latter are responsible for the destruction of the 'good German', who after the war dies in a Russian camp. Hence, Polański's film is a voice against oppressive and tyrannical ideology, rather than against a particular nation or ethnic group which fought in the war.

Paradoxically, by showing no hatred towards any ethnic group, only to ideas planted in people's heads or enforced by the 'sword', Polański's film is close to Jakubowska's rendition of the Holocaust. Moreover, it contains the same type of difficult optimism as *The Last Stage*, which is lacking in Borowski's and Munk's accounts of life in the concentration camp, as well as in Lanzmann's *Shoah*. Both directors admit that the Holocaust was an extreme atrocity, but it was not the end of humanity or civilisation. For those who survived life goes on and can even bring happiness and joy. The important thing is to remember and ensure it never happens again.

Notes

1   Different historians provide different estimates of the Polish and Jewish losses during the war. However, what is agreed is that even if the loss was equal (about three million Christian Poles and three million Jews), the meaning of those losses was different to both the Poles and the Jews. Polish Jewry ceased to exist whilst the Polish nation survived. Moreover, the Jews depended on Polish help while Poles profited materially from the Jewish catastrophe. See Wolentarska 2004.

2   For the treatment of the Holocaust in Polish history textbooks see A. Radziwiłł (1989) 'The Teaching of the History of the Jews in Secondary Schools in the Polish People's Republic 1949–88', *POLIN: A Journal of Polish-Jewish Studies*, 4, 402–24, and E. Traba and R. Traba (eds) (1999) *Tematy Żydowskie*. Olsztyn: Wspólnota Kulturowa Borussia.

3   P. Wróbel (1997) 'Double Memory: Poles and Jews After the Holocaust', *East European Politics and Societies*, 11, 3, 569.

4   See E. Ochman (2004) *Remembering the Polish-Jewish Past a Decade after the Collapse of Communism*, PhD thesis, European Studies Research Institute, University of Salford. Ochman refers to such sources as S. Friedländer (1993) *Memory, History, and the Extermination of the Jews of Europe*. Bloomington, and Indianapolis: Indiana University Press; D. LaCapra (1994) *Representing the Holocaust: History, Theory, Trauma*. Ithaca, London: Cornell University Press; and D. LaCapra (1998) *History and Memory After Auschwitz*. Ithaca, London: Cornell University Press. A similar theory was used to explain why the world did not know about Oskar Schindler's case for so long.

5   See E. Ochman (2003) 'Jedwabne and the Power Struggle in Poland: Remembering the Polish-Jewish Past a Decade after the Collapse of Communism', *Perspectives on European Politics and Society*, 4, 2, 171–89, and Ochman 2004.

6   J. T. Gross (2001) *Neighbours: The Destruction of the Jewish Community in Jedwabne*. Princeton, Oxford: Princeton University Press; see also Ochman 2003 and 2004.

7   See Adam Krzemiński, quoted in Ochman 2004.

8   See E. Mazierska (2000) 'Non-Jewish Jews, good Poles and historical truth in films of Andrzej Wajda', *Historical Journal of Film, Radio and Television*, 20, 2, 213–26.

9   See E. Mazierska (2001) 'Wanda Jakubowska's cinema of commitment', *European Journal of Women Studies*, 8, 2, 221–38.

10 See B. Mruklik (1985) 'Wierność sobie: Rozmowa z Wandą Jakubowską', *Kino*, 6, 5–9; 20–1.

11 See T. Lubelski (1992) *Strategie autorskie w polskim filmie fabularnym lat 1945–1961* (Kraków: Wydawnictwo Uniwersytetu Jagiellońskiego), 76.

12 This was definitely the case in Russia and Yugoslavia. Apparently, the film also got a good reception in the US due to its pacifist message. There is no contradiction between the desire to see war on screen and the pacifist message of the film. On the contrary, Jakubowska wanted to show war on the screen to demonstrate how cruel and unnecessary it is, in short – to prevent it in future. Films about the war often contain a pacifist message.

13 Lubelski 1992: 75–83.

14 See T. Borowski (1992) *This Way for the Gas, Ladies and Gentlemen*, trans. Michael Kandel. London: Penguin.

15 E. Nurczyńska-Fidelska (1982) *Andrzej Munk*. Kraków: Wydawnictwo Literackie, 164.

16 Ibid., 163.

17 FIPRESCI is an international organisation of film critics.

18 See M. Rawlinson (1999) 'Adapting the Holocaust: *Schindler's List*, intellectuals and public knowledge', in D. Cartmell and I. Whelehan (eds) *Adaptations: From Text to Screen, Screen to Text*. London: Routledge, 113–27.

19 Omer Bartov, quoted in Rawlinson 1999: 117–18.

20 Raul Hilberg, quoted in Rawlinson 1999: 119.

21 See Miriam Bratu Hansen in Rawlinson 1999: 120–21.

22 Ibid., 121.

23 Sever Plotzker, quoted in Y. Loshitzky (ed.) (1997) *Spielberg's Holocaust: Critical Perspectives on Schindler's List*. Bloomington: Indiana University Press, 206.

24 D. Thompson (2003) 'The Pianist', *Sight and Sound*, 13, 2, 58.

25 Mazierska 2000: 214–18.

26 I. Kalinowska (2002) 'Być synem Szpilmana', *Kino*, 9, 14.

27 See J. Płażewski (2002) 'Zeznanie przed trybunałem historii', *Kino*, 9, 15–16.

27 For the few, not the many: delusion and denial in Italian Holocaust films

Giacomo Lichtner

Italian society is one of many contradictions and Italian Holocaust films have not escaped this characteristic. Many of the most famous Italian filmmakers have attempted to come to grips with this subject, and all but a few have ended up speaking of something else. In other words, the films discussed in this chapter are only superficially about the Holocaust, and are far more concerned with Italy, Italian class relations, even Italian regional characteristics. This is the most notable peculiarity of a film genre that was slow to start – 1960 saw the first films concerned with this subject, but they remained solitary examples for at least a decade – and then developed according more to the guidelines of contemporary Italian cinema, history and culture than to those of the historiography of the Holocaust. An initial explanation for this lies in the particular nature of the Italian Jewish community, whose degree of assimilation was much higher than in other European countries. Moreover, in contrast to other states with highly integrated Jews, such as France or even Germany, Italy was home to a relatively small community and in modern times had not experienced the mass immigration of Hasidic Jews from the East.

This does not mean, however, that one cannot identify a category of Italian Holocaust films but that the boundaries of this category are somewhat loose, including films such as Roberto Rossellini's *Il Generale della Rovere* (*General della Rovere*, 1959) or Lina Wertmuller's *Pasqualino Settebellezze* (*Seven Beauties*, 1975), which are not strictly about the attempted genocide of European Jewry. The former is the story of a cynical and apolitical Italian conman, turned martyr by a new awareness of the collective struggle against the Germans. It only includes a fleeting, though significant, glimpse of anti-Jewish persecution, while focusing on indifference and conformism as survival mechanisms. The latter is a black comedy about a Neapolitan petty gangster who somehow ends up in a German concentration camp. *Seven Beauties* is a film about the moral price of survival, and although there are no Jews in it, its representation of the concentration camp has persuaded most scholars to consider it a Holocaust film. Both these films use the wartime context to comment on the indifference and moral indolence of Italians, during as well as after the war.

Undoubtedly the best-known film in this genre is Roberto Benigni's award-winning Holocaust fable *La vita è bella* (*Life is Beautiful*, 1998). Visually beautiful and full of contradictions, this work suits a tradition of successful Italian comedies, usually released at Christmas: the only time of the year when one or two well-distributed domestically produced films manage to compete with and often overcome American imports. The

Life is Beautiful (1998): Benigni's physical comedy enters unfamiliar territory. (© Buena Vista International)

traditional ingredients for such hits are a comedian, an array of regional dialects, a beautiful leading lady, and a number of comic set pieces. It is perhaps not worth pausing too long over the all-too-familiar plot of *Life is Beautiful*, except to say that this film is not really about the Holocaust as much as it is about a father-child relationship and the faith in innocence as a shield against life's 'ugliness'. Because in spite of its title and its artificial ending, in spite of its own simplistic message, what one can discern from Benigni's film is in fact that life is not always beautiful.[1] Indeed, immediately after the characters' arrival in the concentration camp, Benigni seems to begin to deconstruct his film's own fairytale structure and reject its axiom. The climax of this rejection is reached with the father's (Guido's) death, but suddenly denied by the child's (Giosuè's) triumphant exit aboard a US tank,[2] to re-establish the dominant ethics of the film. The final voiceover reinforces the film's contradiction and furthers its problematic falseness. Where in the initial voiceover a supposed omniscient narrator had stated 'This is a fairytale, as in fairytales there is sadness, and as in a fairytale there are marvels and happiness', the final one reveals this narrator to be Giosuè's adult self, who can confidently declare 'This is my story, this is the sacrifice my father made for me'.[3] Ceasing to be a fairytale, the film's narrative structure assumes the form of a survivor's memoir. Moreover, this ending fails to come to terms with the inevitable implication of the liberation of the camps: death. Only life interests Benigni and inevitably that renders his film joyous yet quite inappropriate to its setting.

Among the main problems in *Life is Beautiful* is that the pain it conveys is an individual rather than a collective one. The grief the spectator feels is at all times centred on an individual – the suffering father, the son who has lost him, the mother separated from her family – not the enormity of the crime or the communities wiped out. A sense of the Holocaust as a collective tragedy is absent from the film. It is in fact a common trait of Italian Holocaust filmography to represent pain from an insistently individualistic point of view. Of course this particular trend does not necessarily entail an inability to grasp suffering, and stories of individual bravery or survival are bound to fascinate filmmakers and entertain audiences. Nonetheless, approaching the Holocaust from an individual perspective carries the danger of considering the Holocaust an experience that ends with the conclusion of the story of the character(s) involved. This chapter aims to trace this and other tendencies in the history of Italian Holocaust cinema and examine them so as to move the discussion beyond *Life is Beautiful*.

Kapò (Gillo Pontecorvo, 1960), *The Night Porter* (Liliana Cavani, 1973) and Wertmuller's *Seven Beauties* all focus, each in its own way, on the individual man or woman and how they deal with the struggle between survival and morality. *Kapò*, the French-sounding pronunciation of which knowingly hides the Italian origin of the word, tells the story of a young French Jewess (Edith) who tries to survive in a concentration camp first by assuming the identity of a non-Jewish inmate, and later by becoming a kapo, prostituting herself for the Germans and administering her share of violence to her fellow prisoners. *Seven Beauties* is not entirely dissimilar inasmuch as its main character also sleeps with the threatening camp chief, becomes a kapo and is forced to choose inmates to send to death and later to shoot one himself. *The Night Porter*, an Italian-directed European co-production starring Dirk Bogarde and Charlotte Rampling, is instead a refined psychological thriller. Set in Vienna in 1957, the film tells the story of a survivor of the camps, Lucia, who recognises in the night porter of her hotel the SS doctor, Max, who had taken her as his protégé in the camp. Liliana Cavani employs a series of alternate flashbacks to reveal to the audience that Lucia survived by accepting Max's 'attentions'; indeed, that the two had engaged in a sadomasochistic sexual relationship. The relationship is restored as the two characters attempt to recreate camp conditions. However, this time they are both victims, as Max's secret association of former SS murder the re-united 'lovers' in order to silence potential witnesses. All three films have interesting things to say: the first about what Primo Levi would later call 'the grey area', where the struggle for survival clashes with one's ethical beliefs;[4] the second about national and regional character, and the indifference and lack of a sense of civil duty on which Fascism thrived; the third about the fragility and ambiguity of the ego.

Both *Kapò* and *The Night Porter* ultimately fail: the former by giving in to a redeeming ending where Edith chooses a cathartic death, which negates all the director had said so far about the grey area;[5] the latter by letting itself be drawn in by the morbid fascination of suggesting that we are all both victims and persecutors, and that the relation between these is in fact one between two sides of the self. Moreover, in their effort to find a line neatly separating human and de-humanised, all three films share an unfortunate choice: they all use the physical prostitution of their characters as the symbol of their loss of humanity. But as survivors have made clear, there was no 'line' to cross, but a long process of unrelenting humiliation, initiated by not being considered citizens and being denied one's rights and duties. It is interesting that Francesco Rosi, in his 1996 adaptation of Primo Levi's *La Tregua* (*The Truce*), should introduce an entirely fictional sexual encounter between Levi and another former inmate to signify his crossing back into the human congress. Levi does not need to signpost his reintroduction to 'feeling

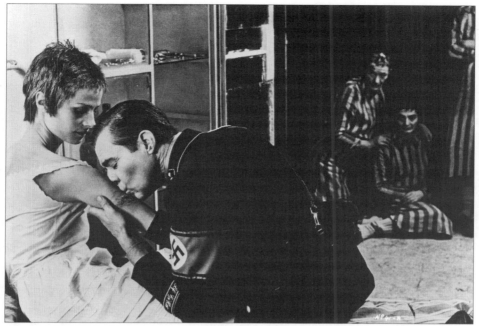

Crossing the line: as Lucia accepts Max's approaches while other inmates watch, sex confirms its preferred status as a symbol of dehumanisation in *The Night Porter* (1973) BFI (© Lotar Films)

human' because his whole memoir is about such return. Rosi on the other hand reduces the Italian author's account of his post-liberation journey to a biopic that fails to manage that leap from the particular to the universal that differentiates Levi's work from that of other survivors.

The Truce has another major fault of willingly playing down Levi's Jewish identity to represent him first and foremost as an Italian, a left-wing activist and an intellectual. But if Levi was indeed the first two of these things, and was – almost to his irritation – considered to be the third as well, his being a Jew was undoubtedly central to both his life and work. Rosi's revisionist effort starts when he edits to create a link between Levi's red-and-yellow Star of David and the Red Star of the liberating Soviet forces, so as to identify him above all as a political deportee. Rosi fabricates scenes not only in an attempt to make the film more attractive but also to adapt Levi's message to his own. Thus a critical part in the book in which Levi meets two Russian Jewesses who doubt his being Jewish is ignored, while his meeting with an Austrian lady who doubts his being Italian plays a central role, giving the character-Levi (played by John Turturro) a chance to claim his Italianness. In the same way, the final scene of Rosi's film contains an edited version of Levi's poem *Shemá* – the epigraph to *Se questo é un uomo* (*If This is a Man*, 1946) – significantly without its final biblical curse. It is a fitting ending to a film that insists throughout on representing Primo Levi as manifesting a distinct hint of Christian forgiveness.

Rosi is in good company in his inability to relate to his character's Jewishness. The representation of Jewish identity has indeed been a complex issue for Italian filmmakers grappling with the Holocaust. The Jewishness of Benigni's main character is entirely superfluous, its only function being that it allows the director to set his film during the Holocaust. Luchino Visconti's two films, *Vaghe Stelle dell'Orsa* (*Sandra*, 1965) and *La Caduta degli Dei* (*The Damned*, 1969), are much more concerned with Oedipal undertones and class relations, and with the pursuit of power within the state and family structure, than with the Holocaust or Jewish identity. Even Vittorio De Sica's *Il Giardino dei Finzi-Contini* (*The Garden of the Finzi-Continis*, 1970), despite representing beautifully the dynamics of the Jewish community of pre-war Ferrara, has its real interest in class identity and relations. So much so that only at the end of the film, when the Jews are deported and class barriers are removed, can a feeling of communal identity be developed among them.

Carlo Lizzani's late neo-realist effort *L'Oro di Roma* (*The Gold of Rome*, 1961) is perhaps better inasmuch as its main character is indeed the Roman Jewish community, which it tries with care to portray. He does this by examining its position as an integral part of Rome since ancient times, while remaining distinctly Jewish in its rites and customs. Lizzani is aware of the powerful forces at play here: the organisation of the community and the difficulty in fleeing experienced by Jews whose ancestors had stopped being 'wanderers' long before. He succeeds in portraying the Jews' certainty, held by many to the very last, that the Pope would not allow the mass deportation of the Jews from his holy city. A belief fed by the still vivid memory of centuries of humiliating and painful, but usually not fatal, Papal persecutions. Despite all this Lizzani's film can

Death of a city: Roman Jews are transported from the centre of the Italian capital, less than a mile from the Holy See, in *The Gold of Rome* (1961). While Lizzani empathises with the community as a whole, he clearly identifies its passive acceptance of German measures as a fatal failing. BFI (© Movietime)

sometimes adopt a didactic and melodramatic tone. Moreover Lizzani ends up associating religion with extinction by showing a rabbi preaching calm and prayer instead of a struggle for survival, a young man (David) having to accept the need to commit violence in order to live, and a young woman (Giulia), married to a Catholic man, leaving her husband to join her father in his fate. Giulia, just like Edith in *Kapò*, chooses to assert her Jewish identity but pays the ultimate price. The director seems to favour David's heroism over Giulia's martyrdom.

The Gold of Rome is the product of a pedagogic concept of art and a clear political belonging. Lizzani's David, the brave, committed and lonely working-class hero, is entirely idealistic; yet if the film is critical of religion it is also at all times aware and respectful of Jewish identity and the Holocaust's place in it. The same cannot be said of all Italian Holocaust films. *The Garden of the Finzi-Continis*, already briefly mentioned, is excellent in its representation of the middle-class Ferrara Jews, the difficulty in accepting the loss of their place in society, and the disbelief at the racial laws initiated by a country they felt their own. De Sica's film leaves no ambiguity as to who issued and executed the persecutory laws: quite uniquely, no Germans appear in his film. The first half of *Life is Beautiful* is similarly clear about Fascism's responsibility, as well as wryly sarcastic about its mannerisms, bureaucracy and pomposity. Otherwise, since neo-realism, Fascism has been ridiculed in order to avert blame from, rather than apportion it to, Italy. Neo-realism helped the political construction of a historiographical orthodoxy establishing the Resistance as a glorious movement (which it may have been) involving the overwhelming majority of Italians (which it certainly did not). The neo-realist Fascist is either an idiotic figure of comical nature, often even physically an object of derision, or a pusillanimous, impotent slave of the Germans. The latter, on the other hand, become the embodiment of all evil, viciousness and vice.

The mythologisation of Italy's anti-Fascism contributed to its self-administered absolution from the accusation of racism that the 1938 laws directed to it. Long after the demise of neo-realism, Italian Holocaust films continued to prefer setting their action abroad: *Kapò* in France; *The Night Porter* in Austria; *Jona Che Visse nella Balena* (*Jonah Who Lived in the Whale*, Roberto Faenza, 1990) in the Netherlands. A debate on Italy's racial laws took place on their fiftieth anniversary, in 1998, but the lack of a serious analysis of Italy's responsibilities, before Susan Zuccotti's 1987 book *The Italians and the Holocaust*, has certainly affected the way Italian cinema has represented the Holocaust. It is a fact that the racial laws contained clauses that allowed several exemptions, that they were executed with Italian, rather than German, efficiency, and that the population proved mostly uncooperative. It is also true that Fascist Italy – unlike Vichy France or other pro-German European governments – never sent Jews, whether foreign or Italian nationals, to the slaughter; that Italian generals did not allow the deportation of foreign Jews from Italian occupation zones in Greece, Yugoslavia and southern France; that 85 per cent of Italy's Jewry survived the Holocaust. Crucially however, 6,800 Italian Jews did not return from the camps.[6] Instead of congratulating themselves on the high number of survivors, Italians need to question why so many died.

In the 1930s and 1940s some antisemitism existed in Italy like everywhere else, and its origins were many and varied. The degree of racial antisemitism was minimal, but there was a religious bias based on the accusation of deicide, traditionally made by a Catholic Church whose only solution to the 'Jewish Question' had always been their conversion. There was then a circumstantial, political anti-Judaism, which was developed by Mussolini for a number of reasons – among which the attempt to awake in the Italians a sense of racial belonging – and carried a following not of fanatics but of conformists and opportunists. There was finally a casual antisemitism based on distrust and ignorance of the Jews' different customs. All in all though, Italy's main problem was not antisemitism but indifference: a national tendency that affected Italian politics as a whole, not exclusively in its wartime racial relations (and still does). That is probably why some of the best examples of Italian films related to the Holocaust make their most insightful points on complacency rather than persecution, on Italy rather than on the Holocaust.

Italy has so far lacked both the myth-shattering counter-orthodoxy of a film like Marcel Ophuls' *Le Chagrin et la Pitié* (*The Sorrow and the Pity*, 1969) and the messianic thoroughness of Claude Lanzmann's *Shoah* (1985). Yet Rossellini, De Sica, Pontecorvo, Lizzani, Wertmuller and others have attempted to represent the Holocaust and what made it possible, mirroring some Italian myths, evading taboos and addressing fears. Their work helps us more in our effort to understand Italian culture and history than the Holocaust or how it is possible to represent it. Benigni's *Life is Beautiful* comprises many of the traditional faults of Italian Holocaust filmography, but also a new approach. This is not so much in its comic style but more in its fairytale structure: a partially successful attempt to find a new language in which to talk about this tragedy. It has been particularly helpful insofar as it has kick-started once again the debate over memory and history. The emergence in the last few years of excellent films such as the Frazzi brothers' *Il cielo cade* (*The Sky is Falling*, 2000) and Ettore Scola's *Concorrenza sleale* (*Unfair Competition*, 2001), is a case in point. For its influence to prove long-lasting, however, it is essential that we allow this debate to go beyond the film itself, to outlive controversy and gossip and become a serious re-evaluation of past trends. To do this, we must avoid both censorial excesses and a worrying tendency to use films not as the artistic representation of an historical event, but as the means to sell to the wider public a particular version of history.

Notes

1   The origin of the film's title is to be found in a part of Trotsky's diaries written from his Mexican bunker a short while before being murdered. About the film's title, the French director Jean-Luc Godard suggested it should have been 'Life is beautiful at Auschwitz'.

2   The choice of an American tank has gained Benigni further criticism as most commentators interpreted the concentration camp as being that of Auschwitz, which was liberated by the Soviet army. However, although the vast majority of Italian Jews were indeed sent to Auschwitz, the film never states the location of the camp. Both the unspecified location and the US army tank belong to *Life is Beautiful*'s fairytale nature.

3   The initial voiceover was added on the advice of Miramax's Harvey Weinstein.

4   See P. Levi (1988) *The Drowned and the Saved*. London: Michael Joseph.

5   Lino Miccichè reports that the film's producers intervened to change the original ending, which did not contain Edith's sacrifice; L. Miccichè (1985) *Cinema Italiano: gli anni '60 e oltre*. Venice: Marsilio, 114.

6   These figures are from S. Zuccotti (1987) *The Italians and the Holocaust*. New York: Basic Books, 24–5, citing Milan's Centre for Contemporary Jewish Documentation (CDEC).

28　The survivors' right to reply

Trudy Gold, Rudy Kennedy, Trude Levi, Frank Reiss

The 'right to reply' session, during the symposium held at the Imperial War Museum, 26 April 2001.

Trudy Gold: Good afternoon, everyone. We felt very strongly that as we were going to put on a symposium on the representation of the Shoah in film, it would be absolutely wrong not to invite survivors to have an opportunity to give their views on how they feel about this. I am delighted to introduce Trude Levi and Rudy Kennedy, who survived Auschwitz and who, for quite a long time, have been going into schools to tell their stories to young people. I know that in the audience are many others who have been working in education for many years, so welcome, and I hope you will all participate in the discussion. We are also very privileged to have here Frank Reiss. Frank was one of the few Czech children to have actually survived the war in Czechoslovakia – he was hidden and finally deported to Theresienstadt, which thankfully he survived.

　I'd like to start with a question: is it possible to recreate the events of that devastating period, particularly in a feature film? We heard earlier from Jack Gold, who is an incredibly sensitive filmmaker, talking about the kind of problems he faced when he tried to represent what is probably the unrepresentable, in *Escape From Sobibor*. Trude, how do you actually feel about the plethora of films that are coming out, particularly in the past fifteen years, now that there are attempts to portray scenes in the camps themselves?

Trude Levi: Well it's a very difficult question, because I think the only approach is to do what Jack Gold did, to underplay not to overplay, to leave something to the imagination. As soon as it is overdone then it becomes kitsch. It lowers the whole quality, certainly of the film, but also the quality of what has to be conveyed. *Schindler's List*, for instance, opened the doors for us into schools, into universities. From the moment that *Schindler's List* was released, we had a much better opportunity to speak out and to get in contact with young people. Therefore I think it was a very valuable film, even though it has got its weaknesses.

Then there are other films, like Roberto Benigni's much talked about *Life is Beautiful*. This is not a Holocaust story, it's a love story, which uses the Holocaust as the ultimate sacrifice, but it's not a Holocaust film, and I don't think it should be used in twenty years' time, in ten years' time – when we are not around any more – to tell what is true and what is not true. It certainly should never be shown to young people as a way to educate them.

TG: I want to bring Rudy in on that, because I know he has some very strong views on *Life is Beautiful*. But first of all, Rudy, how do you feel about representations of the Shoah, particularly in feature films?

Rudy Kennedy: I think it's an immensely difficult thing to do, because in every one of these films I see something missing, from my point of view. Of course, I'm very biased: I was there, I'm a survivor, so some of my feelings, and my judgement, are terribly biased. But some films are better than others. I would agree with what Trude says: although *Schindler's List* had many shortcomings, it is a film we could hang something on, something useful educationally.

The other film, the Benigni film – it's soft pornography, in my opinion. It shows the love of a father for a son, which is natural, and then, in order to make it stronger, it uses Birkenau as a backdrop. That annoys me. I feel that Benigni chose to use the background of a concentration camp in order to attract attention. I can't agree with that. Another thing very wrong about that film is that it has the father making jokes of the Germans. We see it all the time, when he took the child, when he gave him food to eat, and it's just crazy. The Germans were laughing at us. It's so untruthful, I can't imagine it, or any of the sequences Benigni shows. From my point of view, they are impossible, quite impossible. Lastly, it doesn't matter with an audience like you, or with Jewish people who have generally seen or heard about the Holocaust, but for non-Jews hearing and seeing about it for the first time, I can hear them saying: 'Look, it wasn't that bad. They were able to steal food, they could do all these little tricks, the Germans look really silly. They didn't have such a bad time.' This bothers me a lot.

TG: Frank, would you like to comment now?

Frank Reiss: Yes, thank you. Humour in films, you know, just boils down to who can take what. Somebody can joke with me about Theresienstadt, and many jokes have been made. I will give you an example. When I was growing up after the war, people would ask me 'Where were you in the war?' So I would name the three concentration camps in Slovakia, and then Theresienstadt. They would say, 'Theresienstadt, don't even talk about it, that was a sanatorium!' That was the label. So I can listen to jokes about Theresienstadt, I can even make a few. But if somebody makes a joke about Majdenak, where the ashes of my father are, I would not tolerate that.

On the Benigni film, I totally disagree. I found it wonderful, to have portrayed the love for that child, and for the father, marching to his death, still able to maintain the illusion for his child, I liked that. Of course it was not a concentration camp, of course it was not reality… So anybody takes from it what they can.

What I dislike in films is the selectivity: when we get outraged, and when we don't get outraged. *Schindler's List* is a fraud. It is a fraud for one simple reason. Every movement has a need to create saints, and the Holocaust movement has a need to create saints too, be it Elie Wiesel or others. And it doesn't suit me. Schindler was a man, deeply involved in the Nazi movement, not only in the Nazi movement, but in the Secret Services, involved in preparing that staged invasion of a German radio station. He was on the blacklist of Czechoslovakia after the war. I do not know the details, I'm not a historian and I never tried to get access to the documentation, but so much is true. He was a Nazi, and if you read what his wife says about Schindler, you will have rather a different impression from the one Spielberg gives.

I want to end with one thought. Whether we, as survivors, like something or not, whether our contemporaries like something or not, history will be made long after we are gone. If a gladiator appeared today, he would say: 'What kind of an idiot is this, describing gladiators this way?' If Napoleon, or Moses, appeared they would think the same – that's now how it was, that's not me.

TG: I think one of the issues, sixty years on, when what happened in the Shoah is taught more and more, is that it's not just for the story of what happened, but also a warning to humanity. I hear this so often now from teachers, that what they're trying to extract from the Shoah are the ethical lessons, looking at the whole scenario – the victims, the perpetrators, the bystanders, those who rescued, and those who resisted. There are now available the books, the eye-witness testimonies, most of which have now been put on videotape, there are films of the liberation, and also Nazi footage; these are what we are leaving behind for future generations.

But this symposium is about film, and today is particularly about feature film, and I think it does raise an awful lot of questions about what we are trying to transmit to future generations, because I don't believe you can make an accurate film about the Shoah. For the six million who died, there are six million stories that can never be told. We get glimpses and, as Jack [Gold] said, sometimes art itself is a medium of transmitting a message, but what are your thoughts on that, Trude? Looking at, say, all the films made so far, do you feel that, collectively, they give an accurate representation, or an attempt at a representation?

TL: It is an attempt, but it's not an accurate representation. Accurate representation can only be done with documentation. The moment it becomes a feature film, it can't be accurate representation. So the question always is: How sensitively has it been done? How sensitive is its approach and what is included? I agree with Frank, for instance, that the Benigni film is a wonderful film, I think it's an absolutely wonderful film – but I don't think it's a Holocaust film, and it definitely should not be used in education. It's all together wrong to view it as representing the Holocaust, even though, I know, even in Auschwitz there were some children hidden. Italians were always wonderful with children, and I could even imagine that a child could have been hidden, it would have been possible. But of course quite a lot of situations portrayed in the film weren't possible. This certainly isn't a film which should be used for teaching about the Holocaust. But films are very valuable, because unfortunately quite a lot of young people, and indeed older people, will switch off a documentary, but won't switch off a feature film, so if it's done sensibly and intelligently, then they get something out of the feature film.

I have gone into many schools, and spoken to lots of groups, and to hear survivors speaking of their experiences is the only true representation. In every letter that I receive, people say: we have seen lots of films, we have read books, but the only time we really understood what had happened was when we heard a survivor speak. So the survivors' testimonies are, I think, the most important things, and these are what have to be preserved and have to be shown. They bring it really close, and they bring it down from the six million to the one person, to the individual, and that means something.

FR: One of the most fascinating things in life is that you don't just have black and white; there are the shades. In the late 1970s, I was stationed in Rome working on an American refugee programme. Our director there was a Hungarian Jew, named Eva Elias [sic] – if she is alive, she would be almost ninety now. During the war Eva had the good fortune to get to Italy and to be interned in an Italian concentration camp. And she told me – and this is where I recall Benigni – that in the morning she would take five prison guards and go to the ocean, and teach them how to swim, then they would return in the evening. Now if you showed that in a film, most people would probably say: now this film is really demeaning the Holocaust and making a joke of it. Yet this was the experience of a survivor.

RK: Well, I think it all depends what use you make of the film. As an entertainment film, the Benigni has some good points. But the fact is that the setting is clearly meant to be a concentration camp. There should be a sign, bigger than the one on the film saying it's a fable, that says in very large letters: This is not the truth, it's just showing the love of a father for his son. That would be different. Otherwise people will not understand it, and will think, why are these damn Jews saying that life in a concentration camp was so terrible? This is the problem. I know that other people think differently, that's life, but I don't think I would change my view on this. I don't make a big deal out of it, and I don't want you to think that I'm now going to tell you my story, but I just want to add that my own father stayed alive in Auschwitz until he found I was safe. Every father would do this and save their child; that is normal. But to make jokes out of it … My father died three days later.

[At this point the debate opened to questions from the floor]

Esther Brunstein: I fully agree with Rudy on this. I found it very difficult to digest that when a child is hidden during the day, and when the father comes home, and he says I want my money, and I am hungry, how you can say the whole thing is not happening. You know it's pretence, and how he can say, 'It's all up, it's all up, they are making buttons out of us.' It's not a line for humour. The only sentence which I found meaningful was when the father says 'People don't do things like that.' But people did do things like that.

Joan Salter: I'm also a survivor. I think when we take into account films as education, we have to remember that all history is filtered, and that even with a documentary, the minute you start editing it, you are putting a slant on it. It's a known psychological fact that two people can be standing next to each other, and what they see will be two different things, and we should not forget that. There is one aspect of films as education that is beginning to worry me. It was alluded to briefly in *Schindler's List*, when they sang 'Jerusalem is Golden'. Film, whether for television or for the big screen, is a very expensive medium. There has to be finance, and finance involves satisfying the market's expectations, attitudes, polemics etc. I am becoming a little concerned, not just about film but a lot of other aspects of the Holocaust, that a lot of the material that's coming out is presented as black and white: every German was horrendous, every Jew was marvellous. I think this is as dangerous as some of the other things that we're talking about, because it's not true and it's not human nature, and if we try to trivialise it by treating it as such, then you're not going to achieve anything.

Dina Iordanova: Listening to you it seems that the context of the discussion is education, and film in general used in education. But I have only heard two films mentioned so far: *Schindler's List* and *Life is Beautiful*. Are these the only two films that have been made? Are these the only two films that need to be discussed here? What I would like to hear you say is what films you believe are the films that educationalists should be using. There are a number of takes on the Holocaust, it's not necessary that we talk only about films that were made recently. There are films like Wertmuller's *Seven Beauties*. There is *The Night Porter*. There is *The Shop on Main Street*. There are a number of Polish films. There are plenty of Holocaust films. And you, as survivors, are saying that you may not be about in ten years' time, so probably something that you should consider are which films you would like to see screened in the classroom. I would really appreciate hearing something on that.

FR: By the way I'd like to say I don't subscribe to the premise that I won't be around ten years from now!

TL: I haven't seen all the films you mentioned, but *The Shop on Main Street* is certainly a wonderful film, a very valuable film, and one that should be shown, because it is pretty much correct. I'd also like to mention a much more recent film that was shown very little, and that was *Sunshine* [1999]. It was basically not a Holocaust film, it was a very beautiful film, and if the sex scenes had not been in it, which didn't add anything and made it much too long, it would have been a great film. It was the first film, the only film, that showed historically correctly what happened in Hungary, how the army behaved, how the Hungarians behaved, Hungarian antisemitism. It was historically absolutely spot on, and therefore it is a very valuable film. But unfortunately it was spoilt by the superfluous sex scenes, most probably included for financial reasons, though

Szabó [the director and co-writer István Szabó] disputed that, and said he wanted to show that in different generations sex was approached in a different way – though he didn't show it very well.

TG: Rudy, are there any films that you would consider putting forward as an attempt at an accurate depiction?

RK: I can't really put my finger on it, it's very difficult, you're talking about education?

TG: No, not just education, I think we have to widen the discussion.

RK: Well there are many films, even the old BBC films, which are fantastic in my opinion for showing what went on. I think why we home in on *Schindler's List* is, as Trude quite rightly said, that before it there was very little talk about the Holocaust. It was suppressed. In my case, for fifty years I didn't touch on it, for a number of reasons. One was, I was never asked. I didn't want to talk about it, because I didn't think people would believe me. So it was the Schindler film that broke the silence. You could then go to schools to talk to the children about it, and we found we didn't have to start at the beginning: do you know the Holocaust? Do you know what it means?

Obviously every year it's a different class, but the children have seen much more, know much more. We can come into a classroom, and can start by saying: 'This is my experience, don't get too depressed by what I'm going to show you – look, I'm alive, Hitler didn't succeed all the way, and at the end of it I'll give you a few bits and pieces of paper to remember things.' Very often I'm speaking to non-Jewish children, but when I go to see Jewish people, because they know more, I quote them Pastor Niemöller's words, and that goes down very well. I say, 'We give you these talks, not because we want to unburden ourselves, because we want you to realise how, in a country which was believed to be highly cultural, highly technological, people were highly trained or highly educated, things changed overnight. Hitler came in 1933. In 1933 I was still playing in my home town with children on the same street. When Hitler came to power I was a lone child, the only Jew. The antisemitism was immediate, we didn't have to wait long for Hitler to get it across; there was obviously an underlying antisemitism, we mustn't forget that.'

Another point I want to underline is that, as Trude said, when we go to schools we are believed. Historians will tell us that what we remember is highly marginal, we learnt it probably from the books we read, from them, they were already constructed. This worries me more than what films will be shown after we're gone, quite frankly. Because we can't stop the so-called historians, and if they can't find some document, they suddenly become, not historians, but people who only believe in something if it's in a document. They are making a terrible mistake when they don't believe us, when they say 'We can't trust you'. And I could tell you several occasions where this has been very powerful.

I think, if anything, there's been too much about the Holocaust. Some people say, and I agree, that it has become a business.

TG: So what you're saying is that the representation can be distorted in many other ways than in film.

RK: Yes.

TG: Does anyone else want to come in on this one?

Fred Knoller: I'm a Holocaust survivor. There are two types of films that we are talking about, and we are all thinking about the future, about education when we are no longer around, what future generations will see and will read about what happened during this period. Just as there are two types of books, biography and fiction, there are two types of film: documentaries and entertainment. I must say I am in full agreement with Rudy, that lousy film of *Schindler's List* is a tremendous help. I lecture in schools all the time, and wherever *Schindler's List* has been shown in advance, there is the most incredible attendance. And not only the attendance, but the reaction of the children was quite fantastic, the questions they ask are the best ever. So I think we should think about what we select for the future, which films are going to be shown, and somehow or other, if educationalists would consult with us Holocaust survivors, we could help them to choose the right films.

FR: After our generation has gone, in fifty years' time something else will happen, truth will be written, which today you still cannot approach, about man's behaviour towards man, regardless of whether they had the sign of the SS, KAPO, or Star of David on their arm. Remember that marvellous statement by Niemöller: 'First they came for the Communists, but I was not a Communist – so I said nothing … And then they came for the Jews, but I was not a Jew – so I did little.'[1] But there will be also a paragraph about his antisemitic writings; and that when we talk about Janusz Korczak, there will be the wonderful writing about his antisemitic writings. So we will have a chance to be intellectually much more honest, because it's not going to cut into living beings. And we should maybe pay some thought to this development.

TG: That's an extraordinary idea, what you're saying is that only with a gap of time can we really have intellectual objectivity.

FR: Intellectual honesty.

Harry Fox: I'm a survivor. First of all, I don't like this business about being reminded how long I'm going to be in this world. I have a young family, and I wouldn't dare tell them how old I am, never mind how long I have to go! It's all about today.

We've been speaking to schools for a number of years, long before *Schindler's List*. But no matter how much hard work we did, it didn't mean very much. *Schindler's List* put us on the map. Whether we like the film or we don't like it is not important at all, the fact is that it depicts what happened. Whether there is some fellow who is a Nazi, whatever Schindler was, it's unimportant – it shows the camps. I know some of these camps, and it gets absolutely right what happened there. Therefore when we go into schools now there is more credence to our memories. We're told all that rubbish about how the memory fades, but we all know that as time goes on the long-term memory gets stronger, you only forget where you live, or what happened yesterday, but you do not forget those things. So, that takes care of *Schindler's List*.

Now, the other film, *Life is Beautiful*, I liked the film, whether it is a Holocaust film or not. I think Benigni made a nice film. I had a father in the camps with me, right through 1945. I'm a survivor because I had a father. If I hadn't had my father with me I wouldn't be here talking to you. When they were looking for youngsters, my father hid me. You know we had those straw mattresses? Some nights I was in there, because he figured it was better not to be about while they were looking for young children. His brothers didn't do it for their children, and none of them survived. So I know what he did for me, and I know what a father would do for a son. Whether he does it with jokes, or he does it another way, is not really important, because he gives his life, no problem at all. He just stopped a bullet for his son. I think the truth will come out anyway, rest assured, it isn't what you say, and whether somebody says 'It couldn't have happened', because it did happen. I think that is put to bed now. When I am asked, 'What about those who deny the Holocaust happened?', I say, 'Choose another question, because we don't bother with that one any more, we all know, we don't bother.' The fact is that the truth comes out in the end. We're finding out things now that we didn't know about, because they are open-ing the files. So I wouldn't worry about the truth. Somebody says. 'It wasn't six million, it was five million, it was only three hundred thousand...' all this nonsense, but the truth comes out. I don't think we need to worry on that account. As far as films are concerned, of course it is a business, films are a business, and whether you like it or not, films like *Life is Beautiful* are going to be made because we don't have the power to stop them.

TG: Thank you, Harry. I think a very important question was raised [by Dina Iordanova] when she said, 'What other films would you consider?' The point about *Schindler's List*, in this country anyway, is that because a quarter of the population saw it, it did raise levels of interest and understanding to an incredible degree.

The majority of teachers will tell you they don't have much time to show film, so it's usually documentaries that are actually seen in the classrooms, rather than modern fea-ture films. *The World at War*, especially episode 20, is probably the most widely shown documentary at the moment. *Lessons of the Holocaust*, which Rex Bloomstein and Rob-ert Wistrich made, is also very widely shown in the classroom. But I think one of the problems is that teachers haven't had much access to foreign-language films and so are missing out on the many excellent films that have been made in Poland, in the Czech Republic and in France. As a teacher myself, I would use extracts from *The Pawnbroker* and from *Judgment at Nuremberg*, because I had the luxury of time.

We seem to be focusing on what films we would use in education, but films aren't just about that, are they? They are made for entertainment on one level, or perhaps they're made to get home some sort of truth. I think that's another thing we have to distinguish. Nobody here has actually said 'We are opposed to our experience being shown at all in feature film.' Does anyone feel that strongly about it, or have we become very pragmatic?

Daniel Faulkner: I'm a survivor. It has been mentioned before that no single film can describe the Holocaust and what it meant for those who lived through it. I want to come back to *Schindler's List*. When I went to see it, when it was shown for the first time in London, people came up to me and said, 'Tell me, was it really like what they showed on the film?' I said, 'Yes, in some respects, yes. But one thing they could not show was this terrible mortal fear, every minute of every day, that we had to go through.' And this is what could not be put on celluloid, the most important aspect, this fear, fear every minute of the day, that a whim of somebody else could finish your life.

As for Benigni's film, this was a fable, a fable well described. In fact, when Korczak was led to the Umschlagplatz [collection point, in Warsaw from where Jews were transported by train to Treblinka], I happened to see it from a cellar in the street, and he told the children that they are going on an excursion, and they have to put on their Sunday best; this was a fable because he didn't want to frighten the children, and the love of the father for his son was so great, that he made a comedy out of it.

TG: Do you all know about Janusz Korczak? He was a great educator in Poland and he set up an orphanage in the Warsaw ghetto, where he taught, kept the children's minds alive. As Frank has said, there are some certain shadows to Korczak, but he is becoming a sort of symbol.

Christian Delage: I am an historian. I just wanted to say two or three things. Maybe we can make a distinction about which films we could show in a classroom, rather than simply see on the screen. I don't know if you know the pictures I am going to mention. *None Shall Escape* was made by André de Toth in 1943 in the USA and describes a deportation, and a revolt by Jewish people. Wanda Jakubowska's *The Last Stage* has been screened here and is very important because it was made so soon after 1945 by somebody who was in this camp, and it's incredible that she went back with some of the people she was with, to make this film. Whatever you think of the content of these films, or the way they are made, I think it very important to consider their historical context, when they were made, and for students to be conscious of this.

The third film I would like to bring up is much more recent, made in 1998. It is a French one, maybe you don't know it, but it a very good picture. It was made by Emmanuel Finkiel [the film is called *Voyages*], a Jewish filmmaker. When they arrive at Auschwitz we can say that the film stops, because for the filmmaker, it is very difficult for him to go back again to this camp, knowing all what has been done, between 1945 and now. So it's a kind of interrogation of how can we still have a memory of what's happened once the last survivor will no longer be around.

Finally, I would like to ask the survivors what they think of the co-existence of film and testimony. I mean in the classroom, obviously it's not the same for the students or the pupils to see a picture, and to hear about what a survivor is saying. Isn't there a problem in the confrontation of the two of them? In an exhibition, for example, you can have both the object, some film and so on, and here in the Imperial War Museum you have testimonies on video screen, and you have archival footage. Both times I visited the Exhibition, the people were mostly in front of the archival footage, instead of in front of the testimony screen. I mean I think it's a problem that we must talk about.[2]

RK: Whenever I go to a school, I take with me transparencies, which shows my home – I was lucky to find some pictures – I show our local synagogue, then I show it burnt down. In other words, they get the feeling of what was going on. I also show them where I was liberated in Belsen. I show them some of the people lying on the floor there. I think we have to do that in order to make an impact. After all, the Holocaust is something very important, we can't just make it a good story, a fairy story. So this is what I do, and I agree with you that unless you have something like that, it's very difficult to really get across what went on.

Luke Holland: Everybody is mediated through film. I'm a documentary filmmaker and, I suppose I ought to add, an actor as well. So I've got a foot in both camps. I recently spent five weeks in Israel playing the part of Doctor Kalkovsky in the new Amos Gitai movie.

This was a most extraordinary experience for me, coming from a background in documentary film. I've always been under the illusion – one I still sort of treasure – that documentary films are really where it's at, and feature films are the sort of over-indulged and bloated younger relative. After the experience of trying to get into the part of Kalkovsky, the Jewish refugee from Heidelberg who ends up in Israel during the last years of the British mandate, I found myself thinking that, in this heavily mediated, rather Orwellian world characterised by spin and dissimulation, perhaps feature films get closer than documentaries to the kind of universal tools to which we all aspire. As a result of this experience, I have acquired a new respect for the feature medium. The film, incidentally, is based on a short story by Arthur Miller, and Miller also features in the film, so look out for it, it's called *Eden* [2001].

But I wanted to make one or two other points, if I can go on for a second. Trude's comment about *Life is Beautiful* had me thinking. It's not just filmmakers who are selective, in a sense audiences are also selective when they come to the film experience. To suggest, as you did, that this is not a film about the Holocaust, but a film just about a relationship, and in a sense one can somehow expunge the Holocaust element, is a bit like saying that the chap who killed Kennedy was a jolly good shot, let's compliment him on his shooting, but ignore the consequence of his action. I think things are connected in a very real sense.

The other point I wanted to make was that when the large Holocaust Exhibition was opened here last year, Mr Crawford, the Director of the Museum, was asked, I think by somebody from the BBC, why it had taken so long for the Imperial War Museum to address this issue. He made a number of points in response, among them, 'Well, the Jewish community has had some difficulties in deciding how best to commemorate this event.' I felt the answer could be presented much more concisely. I think it's about the Cold War. The issues that we are dealing with here have in some sense been put on hold for fifty and more years, before *Schindler's List* was released in 1993 or thereabouts, then in 1994 the Museum in Washington opened, followed, in 1996, by the Jewish Museum in Berlin, the Museum here not until 2000.

These are contemporary phenomena which are only made possible by the change in political circumstances globally. The de-Nazification process effectively stopped in Germany soon after the war. The Germans may have been bad guys, but they were our bad guys, as it were, and keeping the Communists at bay had suddenly become the important issue. And all the filmmaking until quite recently, in my view, has been squeezed through this template of the Cold War, but now we are revisiting, archives are opening, we're able to ask questions that we weren't able to ask before.

As many of you know, I know Rudy Kennedy very well because we made a film together for the BBC called *I was a Slave Labourer* about the issue of compensation of Jewish slave labour. We've been on an international tour, and I was recently in China with the film. Mr Kennedy is frequently asked, why has it taken you so long to ask for compensation for slave labour?, to which he responds that you don't answer questions unless they are asked. No one was asking Mr Kennedy and his colleagues about the issue of compensation for slave labour. It was put on hold until very recently. It also is a post-Communist-collapse phenomenon, if you like.

RK: I think I ought to say something here, in case you get the wrong impression. The film was actually made, so I agreed to do this. I had two stalkers: one was him [Luke Holland], the other was the bunch of journalists, who followed me round as well. But the point here is, we did the film because we wanted to get the truth, and we wanted to record the memories. When I talked to lawyers, they said 'Oh, you can't go to court, they are not going to do this. The only thing you can do is ask for money, then we can come in and do something, and we can sue....' As you've seen it's not until we actually become serious and got these class-action lawyers going that suddenly Germany turned round, or turned the tables on us and started a foundation. And that gives me another way to tell you, that I have a great fear, because the sum of money which was agreed – and it's a derisory sum, and it's not going to go very far, and we haven't got it yet, and may be somebody will ask me why not – it is important to realise that a large sum of money has been taken out of the total, which is ten billion Deutschmarks, to set up a Future Fund, which will be run by German industry. The historian, again I bring up the historians, who was acting with [Chancellor Gerhard] Schröder for the German government, is called [Lutz] Niethammer and in an interview or article in *Der Zeit*, a German paper, he said: 'The survivors have to thank the people who employed them, because otherwise they would have gone straight to the gas chambers.' Can you imagine what that did to me? I've been following this guy ever since, and he may well be the one who will be running this [the Future Fund]! So my fear is this foundation, which is going to be an exchange of people, teachers, professors will come there, and exchange things, I think the Holocaust will disappear. We are going to become politically correct, it's already happened, and this will be genocide. It will be said, 'Well, yes, the Holocaust ... the Jews had a very hard time, and maybe five, to six, or three to eight millions were killed, but then there were twenty-five million in Stalingrad and so on, and look what happened in Africa...' And we will disappear. And the German industry is very, very ... they are looking for selling things, they will make sure of this, and we have no way of stopping this.

FR: I want to thank Mr Kennedy, who brought up Future Fund, because this demonstrates that you cannot escape humorous thoughts, I thought to myself: a future fund for slave labour?!

Annie Fox: I'm not a survivor, but I'm married to one. Now I do think films are important, and films of the survivors' testimonies are also very important, because there is a danger that so many people now talk about the Holocaust that the actual enormity of it is sort of washed over in a sentence, like 'The Holocaust, oh yes, there was six million.' When it comes down to one person, each of those six million was one person, and each of the survivors are one person, and they lost all the people that they loved and they've been through a trauma. In *Schindler's List* there is a scene where the one bit of colour on screen is a child's coat, that blush of pink – you see that little child walking along, and then you see the coat lying on the ground. That brought it down to the individual. Somehow we need to convey the feeling that it actually happened to real people, it wasn't just history, in the sense of something that happened a long, long time ago, which we're not involved in, but to actually give some inkling that it was a real thing for every single person.

In educational terms, it can then be linked to one's behaviour to the person next door. There's a village in Poland where they turned on their neighbours, so it can be that close to hand. And that can come out in films, even in *Life is Beautiful*. You can see some people watching that film, trying to see their experience of the Holocaust in it and not finding it, but if you view it in another way, as the relationship of a father to a child broken because of the Holocaust, that's a way of looking at the impact of the film. Words can be in danger of being over-used, numbers are so huge that they become meaningless and miss the actual tragedy of communities. My husband today was more upset, in a way, by seeing the photographs of life before the Holocaust, the sight of all that's been lost, the life, the laughter, the culture, and everything. People forget, even now they forget the individual in the hugeness of the tragedy. But I think that juxtaposition of individual testimony with a film that can bring out the nearness, that we're only, all of us, flesh and blood, and that's what people did to each other.

TG: Thank you, I think that is a splendid note to finish on.

Notes

1   According to Peter Novick, there is no contemporary record of Pastor Martin Niemöller's first (oral) delivery of this recital, which amounts to a 'confession of his moral failure during the 1930s'. However, the version reprinted here is, according to Novick, the one authorized by Niemöller's widow: 'First they came for the Communists, but I was not a Communist – so I did nothing. Then they came for the Social Democrats, but I was not a Social Democrat – so I did nothing. Then they came for the trade unionists, but I was not a trade unionist. And then they came for the Jews, but I was not a Jew – so I did little. Then when they came for me, there was no one left who could stand up for me.' See P. Novick (1999) *The Holocaust and Collective Memory: The American Experience.* London: Bloomsbury, 221 and 237. Novick believes this was said by Niemöller in the late 1940s or early 1950s, but a version also appeared in the *National Jewish Monthly* of May 1941 and is reprinted in *Teaching the Holocaust (A Teachers' Pack).* London: The Spiro Institute, 1994.

2   In subsequent correspondence, Delage further qualified his comments: 'Actually I wanted to say that the IWM's exhibition, as in the permanent exhibition at the US Holocaust Museum in Washington DC, the visitors are first offered a historical discourse, in which the footage about the camps is an important part. It looks like, at the end, the two museums are focusing on the video testimonies, as if they were the ultimate source of knowledge about the Holocaust. My opinion is that if they may be emotionally moved by the words of the survivors, the visitors are more deeply questioned by the contemporary images, i.e. the photographs of the period and the films made in 1944–45. I mean too that the so-called 'duty of memory' which would claim that it is better to go and see the camps in order to understand the Final Solution than to read a book or gain access to documentary historical evidence is not so legitimate. By the way, it was a big issue for the American team in charge of the preparation of the Nuremberg trials: Robert H. Jackson wanted a documentary trial and and not a trial with a lot of witnesses.'

SECTION V

LEGACY AND OTHER GENOCIDES

'But what intrigues me, is the image that makes someone want to do something ... What would it have been about *Behind Closed Eyes* that might have said to you "My life is no longer the same, I've got to try and do something, my awareness has been created"?'

– Rex Bloomstein

For filmmakers Rex Bloomstein, Daniela Zanzotto and Annie Dodds, documentaries about the Holocaust led naturally onto, or were part of, an examination of contemporary instances of the abuse of human rights, oppression and genocide. While each filmmaker is concerned with effecting social change, each has come to their subject from very different perspectives. In this final section, we explore the actuality and investigative reporting shown in David Harrison's film *Journey Into Darkness* (1994), the social campaigning of Rex Bloomstein's series for television, the social history of documentary filmmaker Daniela Zanzotto and the unique project of creating a 'Crimes Against Humanity' exhibition for the Imperial War Museum.

In David Harrison's film about Rwanda, one can see parallels in the way the programme was shot with those films that reported the discovery of German atrocities towards the end of the Second World War. In June 1994, Harrison and Fergal Keane, of the BBC's *Panorama*, went into Rwanda. The film they shot of the genocide that was taking place was one of the first reports to come out of the country, and certainly the first one shown on British television. Rather like the experiences of the military cameramen who entered Bergen-Belsen, Harrison and his colleagues were unprepared for the scenes that greeted them, nor where they able to grasp the full significance of what was happening – that this was an organised attempt at genocide. Harrison's contribution to this volume is gripping reportage, a vivid eye-witness account of what a BBC film crew was able to see and record in the midst of the genocide being perpetrated. But it is also a history of how the film itself has become involved as a witness to the genocide. Ten years later, while Harrison and his team were filming in Rwanda to commemorate the tenth anniversary of the genocide, their original film was being used as evidence against the perpetrator of a massacre in Nyarubuye. While Harrison's programme won awards, and received positive feedback from the audience, he writes of the frustration that the team felt when greeted with a deafening silence from political circles, from those lawmakers who could make a difference. As we know, the international community did little to intervene militarily in Rwanda despite this and many other journalistic programmes and reports.

One of the major concerns for the filmmaker Rex Bloomstein in making his series *Human Rights, Human Wrongs* was that it should have an effect on the viewing public.

Bloomstein has examined the denial of human rights in a number of films about the Holocaust and the Third Reich, including *Traitors to Hitler* (1979), *Auschwitz and the Allies* (1982) and *The Longest Hatred* (1989). Aspects of this subject were also explored in his films about the British prison system, notably *Lifers* (1984). But Bloomstein's historical examination of the Holocaust and state oppression under the Third Reich led naturally to a concern with contemporary examples of the abuse of human rights, and a series of ground-breaking, campaigning televisions series broadcast on the BBC in the 1980s and 1990s.

In some cases, public reaction to the programmes did make a difference. Bloomstein estimated that following the *Prisoners of Conscience* series, six out of the forty individuals who were featured were released as a direct consequence of the programme being broadcast. However, a more important point was that the films were part of a much broader campaign not just to help individuals who had been imprisoned without trial, or tortured, but to raise the conscience of viewers as to the continuing problem of human rights abuse.

Struck by the parallels between the French government's treatment of the Jews during the war, and contemporary French attitudes to race and immigration, filmmaker Daniela Zanzotto saw little point in examining the Holocaust if the lessons it told for the present were not made explicit. In 1997 Zanzotto began a documentary film project in La Cité de la Muette, a council housing estate at Drancy in the suburbs of Paris. During the war the estate became an internment or transit camp for Jews on their way to the labour and concentration camps in the East. With a tone and conviction remarkably similar to that of Alain Resnais and his colleagues who made *Nuit et Brouillard* (*Night and Fog*, 1955), Zanzotto explains her determination that her film *Les Voix de le Muette* (*If the Walls Could Speak*, 1998) should not be a historical documentary that would be hermetically sealed in the past; but one that would be stylistically and politically relevant to young people. Less of a campaigning documentary, Zanzotto's film is a meditative piece linking what happened in the past to the present preoccupations of those living in the housing project at Drancy. She makes an explicit connection between the memory of what happened in that place, and how those living there see it today, and in a larger picture, how the circumstances of the housing project in Drancy reflect on the French attitude towards immigrants. In effect, the film asks whether this is a landscape in which the deportations to death camps could happen again.

Each filmmaker in this section has been concerned with audience reaction, and at the symposium it also became clear that for campaigning filmmakers, access to the networks is a pressing issue. Hence the last contribution from Suzanne Bardgett and Annie Dodds has a unique value for filmmakers, the opportunity to make a film about recent abuses to be shown in an educational context and in a museum setting. The 'Crimes Against Humanity' exhibition showcases a video describing recent acts of ethnic violence and other crimes against humanity. The video has pointed to the parallels between the Holocaust and instances of post-war genocide. Suzanne Bardgett explains the background to the creation of the genocide exhibition, the brief for the video and the design of the viewing space while Annie Dodds explains how she and her colleague James Barker realised their brief and overcame the various conceptual and practical problems in producing a 30-minute documentary, which covered a century of killing from the Armenian genocide of 1915 through to the Rwandan genocide of 1994. Both Dodds and Bardgett emphasise the importance of the design of the viewing room. Placing the viewer in front of a large screen in a blanked-out setting, the documentary shares the concern of all the filmmakers in this section, exhorting the viewer to witness, to reflect, to act.

The publication of this book coincides with the launch and distribution of a number of new feature films and documentaries released to mark the tenth anniversary of the genocide in Rwanda. As David Harrison discusses in his chapter, Fergal Keane and the *Panorama* team returned to Rwanda to make *Killers* (2004) for broadcast on BBC. Other recent documentaries of note, and which were screened in 2004 at the Imperial War Museum, include Greg Barker's 120-minute *Ghosts of Rwanda* (2004) for Frontline/ WGBH Boston. Barker's film is a powerful and comprehensive retelling of the story, but with a particular focus on the admirable efforts of the small multinational community who stayed behind in Rwanda to minimise the slaughter. Interestingly Barker's film celebrates the heroism of Captain Mbaye Diagne, a Senegalese member of the UN force who, through charisma and powerful negotiating skills, managed to save the lives of many Tutsis, partly by secreting them in a hotel in Kigali, a haven which is now a central feature of two of the recent feature films on the subject, *Hotel Rwanda* (2004) and *Sunday by the Pool in Kigali* (2005). Sadly, unlike Paul Rusesabagina, the manager of the hotel and central figure in *Hotel Rwanda* (played by Don Cheadle), Captain Diagne was killed by mortar fire while supervising efforts to protect more Rwandans from the genocide. Also screened in the Museum's season were, from France, Anne Aghion's *Gacaca, Revivre ensemble au Rwanda?/Gacaca, Living Together Again in Rwanda?* (2002), about the government's attempts to achieve some reconciliation in the country through the Gacaca courts, a system that traces its origins to pre-colonial times, and Belgian filmmaker Sarah Vanagt's *After Years of Walking* (2003), which explores the role that the teaching of history played in the genocide. A forthcoming German-British documentary on the subject is *Shooting Dogs*, directed by Michael Caton-Jones and produced by David Belton, who decided to make the film after failing to erase his memories of covering the genocide for *Newsnight*. One of the first dramatised films to be produced on the subject is *100 Days* (2001), directed by Nick Hughes and produced by the Rwandan Eric Kabera. Made in Rwanda and using a cast largely comprising amateur actors, the film tells the story of a local Hutu official who is persuaded to implement the government's policy of genocide toward the Tutsis.

We are still too close to the events of 1994, and indeed these films, to make sense of the genre; however, one does notice that a few familiar themes are beginning to emerge. Commentators have remarked on the unrivalled power of film to convey the emotions surrounding genocide and, as some claim, that without grasping the fear, horror and raw emotion that gripped Rwanda in those four months, one fails to understand what is currently happening in central Africa today. Many express the hope that the timely release of films on the Rwandan genocide may motivate audiences to exert pressure on politicians to stop the savagery now taking place in Darfur.

There is also a strong interest in the landscape in which the genocide took place, with filmmakers and journalists returning to the sites of these atrocities to conjure up the ghosts of these horrific events, and even to re-enact them (for example in *100 Days*). But in addition to the sites of grief and trauma, there has been an interest in those locations, notably the Sabena-owned Hotel Mille Collines in Kigali, which became havens of sanctuary from the horrors in the streets outside.

Perhaps inevitably, and harking back to the kind of criticisms levelled at feature-film treatments of the Holocaust, some critics have accused *Hotel Rwanda* of trivialising the Rwandan genocide, of glossing over crucial historical details and of reducing key figures to cinematic archetypes (in one review, the actress Sophie Okonedo, is accused of performing the role of Rusesabagina's wife like a 'damsel in distress'[1]). We also notice the tendency of documentarists and feature filmmakers to look for tangible heroes – Rwandan versions of Oskar Schindler – around and through which the story of the genocide can be told. One welcome improvement on Holocaust cinema, however, is that filmmakers working on Rwanda have been sensitive to make Africans the hero figures; we do not notice a de-Africanisation of the story or the characters. But there is one strand in this evolving debate about the cinematic representation of the Rwandan genocide that has no parallel with Holocaust cinema, and that is the position taken on the issue of the representation of perpetrators. As the reader will recall, the documentarists Michael Darlow and Laurence Rees presented convincing arguments in favour of interviewing the perpetrators of the Holocaust. However, this was an argument borne out of the need for historical understanding; at no stage did these filmmakers discuss any obligation on their part to empathise with the perpetrators, in fact both filmmakers were anxious that the viewers did not think they sympathised with these killers and adopted strategies to distance themselves from the SS guards, *Einsatzgruppen* killers, informers and other interviewees. By contrast commentators and filmmakers on the Rwandan genocide have begun to argue that some of the killers were also victims and brutalised people, perpetrators who may also deserve our sympathy and understanding. Clearly when many of the killers were children themselves, there is an obligation on filmmakers to be far more even-handed in the portrayal of this genocide than would have been possible or justifiable in the case of the Holocaust. As Micheala Wrong explained in *The Guardian*, in a survey of the recent crop of new films on Rwanda:

> These moviemakers face a double challenge. While they want us to see through the eyes of the victims, any director who fails to probe the minds of the perpetrators – those Hutu villagers who were terrified and bullied by their mayors and local officials into taking up machete and hoe and slaughtering their friends and relatives – will be providing only a partial account. A film about Rwanda's genocide that doesn't grapple with the impenetrable riddle of how ordinary, decent folk were persuaded to do such extraordinary, indecent things has fallen at the first fence. I didn't understand it in 1994; I don't understand it now.[2]

Notes

1   Xan Brooks (2005) *The Guardian*, 25 February.
2   Micheala Wrong (2005) *The Guardian*, 18 February. Wrong is the author of *I Didn't Do it For You: How the World Betrayed a Small African Nation*. London: Fourth Estate, 2005.

29 Human rights: does anyone care?

Rex Bloomstein

The denial of human rights has been an underlying theme of much of my work in documentary and this has been particularly true in the number of films I have produced and directed on the Holocaust. The planned extermination of the Jews and the revelations of the death camps at the end of the Second World War led to a determination that these barbarities should never happen again and directly to the modern machinery of human rights.

Antisemitism's fanatical grip on Adolf Hitler and those who commanded and serviced the machinery of destruction, and the acquiescence of sections of the German population, had devastating consequences in instigating the project of genocide. It has to be said even members of the Allied bureaucracies were not free of racist attitudes towards the Jewish people. The fear of antisemitism for instance was a crucial factor in the remarkable lack of action and reaction amongst the millions of American Jews as news filtered out about what was happening to their fellow Jews trapped in the Reich. So the poison of hatred toward Judaism and Jews nurtured through millennia had its apotheosis in the twentieth century, and its manifestations are there to be seen.

I examined and explored these issues in *Auschwitz and the Allies* (1982) in an attempt to provide insight into the Allied response to the greatest site of mass murder in history. In *The Gathering* (1982), an accompanying film, harrowing personal testimonies were interspersed with a record of the meeting of several thousand Holocaust survivors. Their search for lost relatives, their guilt and joy at survival and their continuing traumas were a haunting experience for anyone present in that hall in Jerusalem.

Other documentaries followed: *The Longest Hatred* (1989), a trilogy that charted the unique history of antisemitism and its manifestation in modern society; *Liberation* (1995) featured the stories of Allied soldiers who were the first to enter the Nazi concentration camps; *Understanding the Holocaust* (1997), a specially designed video for an educational pack entitled 'Lessons of the Holocaust', an aid in the teaching of the Holocaust in the history and religious studies syllabuses of the UK National Curriculum; and *The Roots of Evil* (1997), a three-part series in which I explored why acts of terror and destruction seem endemic in the human condition.

But as our title suggests there is a potential problem in trying to make human rights both interesting and compelling to an audience, particularly a television one. The subject can be arcane, legalistic and stuffed full of the language of diplomacy – which often is intended to obfuscate and mire debates in UN-speak. Attend a session of the UN Commission of Human Rights, as I have done, and you will know what I mean. There are exceptions such as the Universal Declaration of Human Rights, which is a magnificent document and its articles form the basis of many subsequent Covenants, Conventions and Treaties.

Here are some of the articles of the Declaration:

Article 3:   Everyone has the right to life, liberty and security of person.
Article 4:   No one shall be held in slavery or servitude; slavery and the slave trade shall be prohibited in all their forms.
Article 19: Everyone has the right to freedom of opinion and expression.

It has been said that human rights have become the idea of our time. But every day we see and hear evidence that suggests these dense but valiant attempts to bind nations to codes of conduct in the treatment of their citizens, and the citizens of other countries, in peace and war, are blatantly ignored. The effect on most of the world's citizens is despair and cynicism at the gulf between intention and reality. A gulf that can become an abyss, when a minority or a majority turns upon its fellow countrymen in a series of steps which are often taken under the world's gaze leading to gross violations of human rights. The first step is denigration and vilification – a process that leads to de-humanisation – 'they are no longer human like you or I' – then comes economic and social isolation – then hopefully, capitalising on the rest of the world's ignorance and more significantly indifference – the final step. Extermination. Genocide. So violations of human rights, wherever they may be, whatever they may be, are ignored at our peril.

The rule of law is crucial in any debate or analysis, historical or contemporary, of any situation regarding human rights. A devastating example of the law being suborned to the interests of the State and one that has been captured on film is the People's Court trials of the men who plotted to overthrow the Führer on 20 July 1944. These show trials were presided over by the infamous Dr Freisler. Hitler is reported to have said that 'the traitors should not be allowed to make long speeches, Freisler, our Vyshinsky, will see to that'. Vyshinsky was Stalin's notorious chief prosecutor during the Russian treason trials of the 1930s.

Dr Goebbels, the Reich Minister for Propaganda, ordered that a film be made of the trials to be distributed amongst the armed forces as a warning against those who would consider treason. The stark images of Freisler haranguing members of the officer corps went down so badly at showings to army units that the film was quickly withdrawn. It is believed that Hitler himself ordered that the executions of the leading plotters, which included Field Marshal von Witzleben, should be filmed and the footage be sent to him to view. These films have never surfaced into the public domain though they are thought to exist. However, several hours of the specially-shot film of the trials surfaced in the 1970s having been obtained covertly by a West German film production company from an archive in East Germany. These fragments and sequences, which showed brave and often broken men under interrogation by Freisler revealing the part they played in the attempt on the Fuhrer's life, formed the basis of the film I made telling the story of the Plot called *Traitors to Hitler* (1979).

What better figure to avenge this attempt on the life of the Führer than the cruel, eloquent and cynical Roland Freisler. Thwarted in his ambition to become Minister of Justice, from 1937 to 1944 he condemned over 5,000 people to death as the red-robed

Roland Freisler during the 'Bomb Plot' trials (IWM)

president of the People's Court.[1] He subordinated all human feeling to the dogma of National Socialism and vehemently followed the line that individuals must not only be punished for treasonable acts but also for treasonable thoughts. He became known as the 'Robespierre of the Nazi revolution'. He presided over a court which openly subverted every notion of justice, a court in which the lawyers for the defence vied with each other to present their clients' guilt. An officer who was forced to attend as an observer was the former Chancellor of Germany, Helmut Schmidt. The point of the trials was not to establish guilt, as most had pleaded guilty; Freisler's task was to ridicule, humiliate and destroy the conspirators psychologically in order to satisfy Hitler's thirst for vengeance. All the conspirators had been manacled, deprived of sleep and tortured in order to reveal the extent of the plot. Most of the conspirators were hanged on the same day.

Article 5 of the Universal Declaration says 'No one shall be subjected to torture or to cruel, inhuman or degrading treatment or punishment'. So where do the torturers come from – is the torturer a recognisably human being – if so, how is he able to do what he does to the defenceless man or woman before him? The awful truth is that one does not have to be a sadist or a psychopath or a paranoid psychotic to become a torturer. Usually such men are weeded out as too unpredictable. Torture occurs mainly in non-democratic countries but it can certainly occur in democratic ones.

It was in 1987 that I noted a column in the *Times* newspaper called 'Prisoners of Conscience', written by Caroline Moorehead and based on campaigns developed by Amnesty International. It struck me that I could replicate her column highlighting cases of innocent men, women and even children falsely imprisoned, but this time do it for television. I co-opted Caroline Moorehead and we first went to Channel 4 who in fact turned us down. We then persuaded the BBC to commission us to produce ten 5-minute programmes over two weeks – Monday to Friday in December when Human Rights Day falls.

Among the things we wanted to do was obviously to get the audience to watch such a series, and then to get them involved in trying to secure the release of an innocent person; to do what human rights organisations all over the world were doing, in bringing attention to the often appalling conditions and treatment that prisoners endured. A further point decided was to get well-known and distinguished people to present the programmes and thereby raise the profile of the series. The first programme in our *Prisoner of Conscience* series was presented by Sting.

What then were our main difficulties? We first did all we could to check the authenticity of the case. Secondly, as it was practically impossible in most of the cases to do our own filming, it was vital to acquire as many photographs of the prisoner we were featuring as well as family members, the prison in which he or she was being held and any other visual references that we could find. This included film footage either given to us by human rights groups or bought from news organisations, or most commonly from the BBC's own news and current affairs departments. We also established a network amongst the NGOs led of course by Amnesty International and its UK branch. So what effect did we have? An average of 10,000 people either wrote or rang the BBC for an information pack that gave details of how and where to write protesting at the featured

The first programme in the *Prisoner of Conscience* series was presented by Sting, who appealed on behalf of Soh Sung, a South Korean who was arrested in the spring of 1971 following his involvement in student demonstrations. At the time of the programme, Soh Sung had been in prison for 19 years; during his imprisonment he was tortured into making a confession and attempted suicide to avoid further questioning. He was since been released and is now teaching human rights law in Japan. (© BBC Worldwide/Sting/Soh Sung)

person's imprisonment. Of the 64 prisoners of conscience shown over those five years over forty are now free. An average audience was around one million. It is actually impossible to ascertain precisely what influence these programmes might have had in directly obtaining the release of the innocent people whose cases we revealed or how many of the audience were inspired to become involved and actively support human rights organisations such as Amnesty International. But undoubtedly we had some effect.

After five years of these programmes, it became obvious that the numbers of prisoners of conscience was in decline, as regimes around the world found other ways to intimidate those they deemed their opponents, using the terrifying weapon, for instance, of disappearance. It was time to change. So we devised a new format based on a 10-minute slot again with a presenter and again retaining a personal story, but this time taking as our focus a different subject or issue such as genocide, censorship and slavery. We reduced the programmes to five, and as before spread over the second week of December. Again the public were asked to phone for an information pack. The new series was called *Human Rights, Human Wrongs*.

A 14-year-old boy based in Eindhoven sent me this poem after watching an episode on Japanese prisons.

Jail in Japan.
Eyes forward, no left, no right,
no daylight to be seen.
No people, no life to tell you why,
Every night it's all the same, change is not an option.
Pressure brings blood to your wrists that beg for freedom;
The windows with no glass aren't on your side.
No one to see, no one to disagree with,
no one to tell it to.
No left, no right,
all is wrong that should make it right.

I had been much impressed by Amnesty's Urgent Action campaigns on behalf of individuals or groups under threat. So in 1998 as part of a Human Rights Season commemorating the fiftieth anniversary of the Universal Declaration of Human Rights, we decided to make ten five-minute films, which we called *Urgent Action*. These concentrated on particular cases with explanatory commentary and no presenters. We created a web site and automated answering system, giving names and numbers of ambassadors and embassies. They were shown as usual in the second week of December. Viewers were given a number and urged to protest about the situation facing our subject. We were able to commission our own filming using BBC correspondents, stringers and human rights groups and even in one case a charity. A total of 17,000 people rang the BBC – some 25,000 contacted the BBC's website and several ambassadors got very unhappy indeed. The programme that got the most response was *Women under the Taliban* (1998).

Fashions change, new programme controllers come in and so it was in 1999 that our last series of *Human Rights, Human Wrongs* were made. In all we did five years of these programmes. Our record number of calls was for an episode presented by Whoopi Goldberg on 'violence against women' – nearly two thousand. Audiences again averaged

Women in Afghanistan (© Amnesty International)

a million. One postscript should be mentioned. At the end of virtually all our human rights programmes Caroline Moorehead, my co-producer, and I would always use these words to our audience 'if you would like to protest about…' and then give details of the address or telephone number for people to contact about the case. The BBC's compliance and editorial policy unit decided in their wisdom after ten years of these programmes that the use of the word 'protest' was going too far for the BBC. They insisted it be changed. Rather than not do the programmes we elected to say, 'If you would like further information…'. That edict rather summed up why it was all over.

It was the hope of the world that it would learn from the horrors of the Second World War, that nations would draw closer together, and correspondingly be less violent towards fellow states as well as their own citizens in the light of these past experiences. We might suppose that, for instance, the communications revolution would be the engine of tolerance. But knowing more does not necessarily bring understanding and acceptance of others. It is true that the Cold War is over and that worldwide technologies such as the internet have indeed advanced at an extraordinary rate yet, paradoxically regimes and governments continue to inflict brutalities on their citizens. What lessons then are still meaningful so long after the Second World War and the experience of other genocides that have since taken place? It is my contention that the greatest lesson to be learnt is the need for a continuing moral and practical response to abuses of human rights.

Note

1   Roland Freisler was President of the People's Court from September 1942 until his death in February 1945.

30   *Journey Into Darkness*

David G. Harrison

Panorama's Journey Into Darkness was probably the first documentary-length film on any network on the killings in Rwanda. It was shown on BBC 1 on Monday 27 June 1994. The brief was simple – try to find out what was going on in Rwanda and who was behind the killings.

I had been filming in Africa for over twenty years for the BBC, particularly in Southern Africa during the Apartheid years, in Rhodesia during the war of independence and next door in Mozambique during the last days of Portuguese rule. I had also produced an eight-part BBC series, *The Africans: A Triple Heritage*, with the distinguished Kenyan academic, Ali Mazrui, filming in sixteen African countries over three years.[1]

But nothing had prepared us for what we discovered in Rwanda. It was all the more shocking because of the optimism that prevailed in Africa at this time. Nelson Mandela had been released; the elections in South Africa had taken place in April 1994. We were busy broadcasting the good news from Pretoria. The pictures of a beaming Mandela, shaking hands with outgoing President de Klerk, went round the world. Yet some 1,500 miles to the north these savage events were unfolding, in a small place called Rwanda that none of us knew much about.

For me it was even sadder because I had come to appreciate that in Africa memories of hard times are often short. When it comes to remembering the excesses of previous colonial masters or enemies, Africans show an extraordinary readiness to forgive. After 27 years in jail that was the message that Nelson Mandela personified.

Before Mandela's release I had written a book about Afrikaner Nationalism and the way the 'The White Tribe' had imposed its will on South Africa.[2] I ended expressing the fear that the country would end in conflagration. How wrong that proved. There was trouble in the early years when Mandela was trying to organise elections, but in the end the mainly Zulu Inkatha party did agree to sit down with the ANC. The Afrikaners chose the ballot box, not the gun.

But now, these easy theories were being turned on their head in Rwanda. Reporter Fergal Keane and I set off in early June to join up with cameraman Glenn Middleton and soundman Tony Wende both from Johannesburg. We met in Nairobi then went on to Uganda. We hired two Land Rovers plus drivers. The war was at its height. We had to be self-sufficient – with food, water, petrol cans, sleeping bags, mosquito nets, generator. Tony Wende, our quartermaster, made sure of every last detail. We headed south into Rwanda behind the lines of the Rwandan Patriotic Front (RPF), who had invaded Rwanda from their base in Uganda. Their aim was to drive out the Hutu government who had initiated the slaughter of Tutsis and of any moderate Hutus who stood in their way.

Within hours of crossing the border we were filming at an orphanage, hearing the stories of children whose parents had been cut down in the early days. We met politicians stunned by what was happening to their country. One had lost his wife and all his children. Our guide was an officer in the RPF's invading army, Captain Frank Ndore. He took us to a church in the parish of Nyarubuye in the southeastern province of Kibungo. It was nearly dusk as we approached. There were scattered bodies in front of the church and – as we walked into grounds of what had once been a school – dozens then hundreds more. The smell was overpowering. We simply filmed as we went, discovering ever more gruesome sights: severed limbs, crushed skulls, piles of bodies, men, women and children. Glenn Middleton, our cameraman, remembers above all 'the stench of rotting corpses'. But he went on: 'The light was fading. We knew what we had to do. We sort of went on autopilot. We barely spoke.' In the church itself there were single bodies, under the wooden benches, one curled up below one of the Stations of the Cross. Frank said they were all local Tutsis who had fled to the church for sanctuary once the orders to kill had been passed down to the local authorities from the hard line government in Kigali.

Frank was keen to move on. The armed Hutu gangs, the *Interahamwe*, which he said had done the killing, were still in the district. They came and went as they wished across the nearby Tanzanian border. It was dark by now. We took a last shot of the front of the church in the car headlights then drove nervously down the dirt track. The nearest village, Rusumo, was about ten miles away. We were mighty relieved to get there and find an abandoned office where we camped for the night.

Down the corridor we found two badly wounded youngsters being treated by survivors. One, a girl named Valentina, had a bad wound on the back of her head and the fingers of her right hand severed. The carers told us they had been cut off when she tried to ward off a machete blow. The hand looked green and gangrenous. The helpers had no drugs and only improvised bandages. We handed over our feeble supplies of Paracetamol and some sweets. We thought Valentina had no chance of living.

Next day we met and filmed more survivors. They all insisted that the man who organised the murders, distributing weapons and machetes, was the *bourgmestre* of Rusumo, Sylvestre Gacumbitsi, a former secondary school teacher. A man named Silas showed us Gacumbitsi's house where we stole his photograph from the wall. Silas said Gacumbitsi had fled to Tanzania. And that's where we tracked him down in a vast refugee camp named Benaco. He was in charge of distributing Red Cross rations to the hundreds of Hutus who had run away before the advancing RPF army. He was not pleased to see us. Nor were his pals. We simply walked up to him with camera turning and put the accusation that he had organised the killing at Nyarubuye. He denied it all, insisting he had never been near the place. 'But the local Tutsis insist they saw you there', said Fergal. 'Ah, those Tutsis, they are liars', was the answer. Back in Rusumo we showed the interview to our friends the survivors. 'That's the man', said Silas. They were in no doubt. It was a telling moment in the film.

Next day we drove to the capital Kigali where the battle to control the city was coming to a climax. The RPF were using light artillery and mortars to drive out the vastly superior numbers of the government army, the Forces Armées Rwandaises (FAR). In the Red Cross hospital we saw the terrible toll being taken on the civilian population both by the war and the *Interahamwe*. We saw and filmed the crashed plane of President Juvénal Habyarimana. It had landed in the garden of his presidential palace. The assassination was the signal for the start of the killing. At that stage no one knew who had shot down the plane. The hardliners within the government were suspected, angered at Habyarimana's readiness to try to negotiate peace with the RPF. The hardliners, for their part, insisted that the RPF had murdered their President and called on all loyal Hutus to avenge his death. The mystery of the plane crash has still not been solved.

From Kigali we made a wide detour and drove south into Burundi to meet Rizu Hamid, a fellow *Panorama* producer who had been setting up filming on the government side. She took us back into Rwanda to the provincial capital Butare. At every settlement we ran the gauntlet of *Interahamwe* thugs at road blocks. They smelled of beer; they flaunted grenades, guns and machetes. They wanted cigarettes. 'We are looking for *inyenzi*, for spies', they told us – literally 'cockroaches', the scornful term for the RPF. There was no doubt what happened to any they identified. In an equally chilling encounter Rizu took us to meet the Vice Rector of Butare University, Dr Jean-Berchmans Nshimyumuremyi. He said all the Tutsis in Butare had 'left'. He had seen nothing of massacres. 'Did so many Tutsis deserve to die?' asked Fergal. There was a long pause. 'When you have a war situation', said the Vice Rector, 'can you avoid the killing of people?'

The *Prefet* of Butare, Sylvain Nsabimana, took us to meet a crowd of Tutsi refugees who had sought protection in front of his office. He insisted they were safe. Next day he organised a convoy of orphans and escorted them himself to the Burundi border stopping to ensure their safe passage at every *Interahamwe* road block. Of course we filmed. On the way back we learned from the radio that the *Prefet* had been sacked, his job taken by a senior military man. That night, when we tried to go back to see the Tutsis camped at the *Prefet*'s office, the army would not let us through. The RPF invaders were reported to be within twenty miles of Butare. It was time to leave.

With this assortment of experiences Fergal and I headed for London (upgrading ourselves to club class). We arrived bleary-eyed but buoyant with the certainty that we had a powerful story. The same day the French announced 'Operation Turquoise', their plan for military intervention to stop the fighting. At our BBC base at White City there was no discussion. We had to get the film ready before it was overtaken by events. We had two cutting rooms, two picture editors, six days and six nights before our slot on the next *Panorama*.

There was no time to agonise over what we should and shouldn't show, nor indeed to discuss whether this was or wasn't genocide. The atrocities at Nyarubuye, the survivors' stories, our hunt for Gacumbitsi and his denials stood on their own. The viewers would make up their own minds. Nsabimana's story was more difficult. We knew that government officials had not just condoned the killing of Tutsis but had organised it. But here was a *Prefet*, deep in government territory who insisted that he was protecting the Tutsis camped in front of his office. Then we had filmed him leading a convoy of orphans to safety in Burundi, stopping at every *Interahamwe* roadblock to warn off the thugs. Had he organised it all for our benefit? We had no means of knowing. And what became of the Tutsis he was protecting? We never found out. We ended the film with this dichotomy. The 'good guy' had lost his job, apparently for behaving like a human being and saving Tutsis, while the 'bad guy' was still handing out aid, courtesy of the Red Cross, in a refugee camp in Tanzania.

The film was shown on BBC1 at 9.30 pm on Monday 27 June after the main news. We completed it minutes before transmission. Every time I watch it I am aware that the sound balance at the beginning is not right (we re-mixed the international version). Some haunting music we came across in Rwanda is just not brought through enough. It was my fault. I wasn't there for the final mix. I had gone back to the cutting room to check the sub-titles. The audience was 2.1 million, less than the *Panorama* average. The *Sunday Independent* called it a 'devastating report'.[3] Thomas Sutcliffe, in the daily *Independent*, said, 'it didn't add much to what we already know about that sorry country'.[4] Victoria Brittain, in *The Guardian*, praised some 'subtle and powerful images'.[5] Fergal received a few letters from people who said they had been moved and one from a man who said he was sick and tired of watching blacks killing each other. There was no political reaction at all. Our bit of sleuthing, tracing the perpetrator of one of the worst massacres to a UN refugee camp in Tanzania, met with a deafening silence. For good measure I then came down with malaria, courtesy of Rwanda, but at least I felt I was paying my African dues. Still, we had a morale booster at the end of the year when *Journey Into Darkness* won the Royal Television Society's 1994 award for the Best Foreign Film and another award from Amnesty International.

A year later when we went back to Rwanda to make another *Panorama* about French involvement in the whole tragedy I met a 'Mountie' from the Royal Canadian Mounted Police seconded to the International Criminal Court.[6] His job, with the full might of the UN behind him, was chasing *genocidaires*. Gacumbitsi was on his list but all he knew was that he was 'somewhere in Tanzania'.[7]

By July 1994 the war was over. The RPF government of national unity under Paul Kagame was installed in Kigali. Soon after, former *Prefet* Sylvain Nsabimana was arrested and charged at the International Criminal Tribunal for Rwanda in Arusha as one of the so-called 'Butare Six'. His defence counsel lost no time in requesting our film as part of his case. Far from participating in the genocide, the defence pleaded, he had done his best to save lives. The case, involving the whole hierarchy of Butare province, has dragged on ever since, complicated by accusations of interference with witnesses.

It was not until June 2001 that the former *bourgmestre* of Rusomo, Sylvestre Gacumbitsi, was finally arrested in Tanzania. He was taken to Arusha and charged with Genocide, Complicity in Genocide and with three Crimes Against Humanity – extermination, murder and rape. This time it was the Counsel for the Prosecution who asked for our film. Fergal Keane was invited to give evidence and early in 2003 underwent some bizarre cross-questioning from Gacumbitsi's defence lawyer. He maintained that his client had not been at Nyarubuye. The defence also said they had a report from forensic experts who had proved that 'the footage taken by Fergal Keane was taken at three different times and that the bodies that were filmed and photographed were skeletons of many years back.' We had heard the accusation many times that, if there were atrocities at Nyarubuye, they had been committed by the RPF as they invaded the country. But to be accused of faking the whole lot was new. What about the smell, we thought. Had we faked that too?

While Fergal was in court in Arusha we were already beginning our own investigation into the events at Nyarubuye for a film to mark the tenth anniversary of the genocide in April 2004.[8] We met a widow who recalled a meeting near Rusomo where Gacumbitsi had urged Hutus to attack Tutsis: 'Don't let them get away, burn their houses.' The next day she said she was caught and raped by a man who told her, 'We can do what we want because we have Gacumbitsi's permission.'

Another survivor, who had been called to testify as an anonymous witness at Arusha, told us that Gacumbitsi gave orders to separate Hutus from Tutsis among those seeking refuge at the church. Then, a further order: 'Take your tools and get to work. You hit snakes on the head.' We also met Gacumbitsi's former police bodyguard, an ex-soldier who had been with the *Bourgmestre* in the days leading up to the Nyarubuye massacre. He described how he brought two people, who looked like Tutsis, to Gacumbitsi. 'He said: "Why are you bringing them to me? Don't you know what you are supposed to do?" I told them to turn and face the other direction. Then I shot them dead.' He was cautious about appearing in the new film but eventually agreed. He was afraid that Gacumbitsi's friends still at large might use witchcraft to kill him.

A moving moment was to meet up again with Valentina, the girl whom we had first filmed in 1994 on the point of death. She had recovered, was back at school and hoping to go on to study to become a chemist. She had lost all her immediate family at Nyarubuye and was now living with an aunt in Kibungo. She said she couldn't bear to go back to her home village and see killers she knew out on provisional release.[9]

Some ten miles from Nyarubuye in a school classroom at Gitwe eighteen men from the village of Rukira were on trial for their involvement in the church killings. Astonishingly they were lodged at night in two offices across the road from the school, guarded only by two lightly armed warders from Kibungo prison. Dressed in pink Rwandan prison garb they sat around the building, cooked for themselves and received regular visits and food from their wives and children. Why didn't they run away, since all were facing long prison terms if they were found guilty? 'There's nowhere to go', one of the prosecutors told us. 'If they cross into Tanzania they would soon be picked up. They are better off here getting regular food and seeing their families.'

We took two of the prisoners – their leader, 38-year-old Gitera Rwamuhizi, and Evariste Batare, also 38 – back to Nyarubuye. By tradition in Rwanda in rural areas farmers give up one day's work a week for the community. They call it *Umuganda*. Gitera remembered the day in April 1994 when they were told that 'Today's work is to go to Nyarubuye to kill Tutsis.' They took clubs, machetes, spears, bows. It was a two-hour march. When they got there they encircled the church where the Tutsis from the area had taken refuge. The gendarmes threw in grenades. 'Then they sent us in to kill survivors. They said that if you leave one Tutsi alive you too will die ... They were being killed anyway so why not do it?'

Evariste said he wanted to take money off the dead but didn't get the chance: 'I had to carry out a fridge for one of the gendarmes.' But why had they killed people they knew? Gitera shook his head: 'These were people we lived with, neighbours, friends. When you went away you could leave your child with them and when you returned the child would be in good hands. We shared fire and water.' Evariste insisted that they had been told again and again that Tutsis were 'enemies of the state ... They invaded Rwanda, they shot down the President's plane. Tutsis within the state were hiding them, so they were accomplices. So we had to kill the accomplices.'

A Hutu farmer, out on provisional release after serving a nine-year sentence, gave another reason. He insisted that he had not been near the church but later had come across a 7-year-old boy, wounded by shrapnel from the grenades. He killed him with an *impiri* (a short knob-headed stick, used by Southern African tribes as a weapon): 'Once he was of that tribe he was supposed to be dead, everyone knew that.'

Those who refused to go along were killed. The *Prefet* of Kibungo, technically Gac-umbitsi's senior officer, was removed on orders from Kigali and later murdered as he tried to escape with his wife and children. I met the policeman sentenced to twenty years for his death. On my first two visits to Nsinda jail where he was serving his sentence, he would hardly speak. He said he received no visitors. His family lived far away. On my third visit he said he had been present when the *Prefet* was killed at a road block. He was found guilty, he insisted, only because he hadn't intervened: 'I was in charge of security, I had a gun and didn't stop them. So I am being punished.' Do you deserve it? 'Would it make any difference?'

On 17 June 2004 Sylvestre Gacumbitsi was found guilty on three of five counts – gen-ocide, extermination and rape. He had not only directed the attack at Nyarubuye church but had taken part himself, killing a man 'thus signalling the beginning of the massacres'. He had 'publicly incited the rape of Tutsi girls, by specifying that sticks should be stuck in their genitals in the event they resisted'. To the last he insisted that he had not been there. The defence still maintained that our film of the Nyarubuye episode was total fic-tion. Gacumbitsi was sentenced to thirty years imprisonment. The defence is appealing. So too is the prosecution, who want the sentence increased to 'the remainder of his life'. It is not expected that the case will be heard before Spring 2005.[10]

Notes

1   *The Africans: A Triple Heritage*, 9 x 55 mins, BBC 1, 1986, a co-production with PBS.
2   D. Harrison (1981) *The White Tribe of Africa*. London: BBC Publications. US edition published by Univer-sity of California Press, South African edition by Macmillan.
3   *The Sunday Independent*, 3 July 1994.
4   *The Independent*, 29 June 1994.
5   *The Guardian*, 28 June 1994.
6   *The Bloody Tricolour*, BBC1, 20 August 1995. Reporter Steve Bradshaw, Producer David Harrison.
7   The delay in the international response to the Rwandan genocide was the subject of another award-win-ning *Panorama*, *When Good Men do Nothing*, BBC1, 7 December 1998, Reporter Steve Bradshaw, Pro-ducer Mike Robinson.
8   *Killers*, BBC1, 4 April 2004. Reporter Fergal Keane, Producer Darren Kemp.
9   *Panorama* chronicled her remarkable recovery in *Valentina's Story*, BBC1, 10 February 1997. Reporter Fergal Keane, Producer Mike Robinson.
10   According to the International Criminal Tribunal for Rwanda (ICTR), a decision on Gacumbitsi's appeal against the sentence of thirty years imprisonment handed down in June 2004 was still pending (as of 31 May 2005). Those wishing to follow the case should refer to the ICTR website at www.ictr.org. In April 2005 the Appeals Chamber for the ICTR classed Gacumbitsi's case as 'seized for appeal'.

31 *If the Walls Could Speak (Les Voix de la Muette)*

Daniela Zanzotto

Bonjour la Muette: still from *If the Walls Could Speak* (1998) (© Disruptive Element Films)

A ten-minute ride on the RER (commuter train) from Notre Dame brings you to the *banlieue; banlieue* being the French word for the suburbs. But the outskirts of Paris is an area more akin to the inner cities of the UK and US, rather than the leafy suburbs, with many purpose-built estates housing a largely working-class community, a high percentage of which is of North African origin. The one thing that makes the generic *banlieue* town of Drancy stand out from the rest is La cité de la Muette.[1]

Designed by Eugene Beaudoin and Marcel Lods in 1934, La cité de la Muette was a modernist social housing project, based on the ideals of Le Corbusier. Beaudoin and

Lods planned five high-rise apartment blocks and a four-storey horseshoe-shaped block, forming a natural and protective enclosure around which community life could thrive; shops and a school were to be sited on the ground floor. At the time, La Muette was the largest and most ambitious government housing scheme in France. But before construction of the estate had been finished, the high-rise blocks became home to the police and their families, whilst the horseshoe block was turned into France's main internment camp for Jews (both French and foreign) who were to be deported.[2] La cité de la Muette (known as Camp de Drancy during the war) was the last stop in France before the long train journey to the labour and death camps of Germany and Eastern Europe. Between 1942 and 1944, 62,900 of the 76,000 Jews deported from France stayed in the Drancy camp for an average of two weeks; approximately two thousand of those passing through Drancy survived the camps.[3] The French government of the French State (L'État Français, 12 July 1940–20 August 1944)[4] took the decision to use La cité as a camp and it was run entirely by the French and their gendarmes between 1941 and 1943. During the period of French control, close to 38,000 Jews were deported, mostly to Auschwitz. When the Germans took control of the camp on 2 July 1943, the gendarmes stayed to help them, providing the guards to patrol outside the camp perimeter. A few years after the war, La cité was returned to its original purpose of providing homes for those on a low income; the new residents began moving in to their flats in 1947.

My grandfather was deported from the camp at Drancy in 1944. He did not return home. I had first visited La cité with my mother and grandmother. It felt strange to be in the place of so much sadness and pain, whilst the residents of the buildings went about their normal everyday business. I wondered what these people thought, if anything, about the past life of their home.

I also had an intellectual interest in the history of La cité and was curious to explore what this might represent in terms of wider concepts of the French nation. So, a year into a PhD programme on Comparative Literature, and after writing an MA thesis on eighteenth century French history and literature, I decided to embark on a short documentary film project about the history of La cité de la Muette. Part of my academic research had been to examine an ideological contradiction, built into the very fabric of the modern French nation at its inception: at a time when the eighteenth-century Enlightenment ideals of liberty, equality and fraternity were taking shape, ideals that would ultimately become the ideological backbone of the French Revolution and the ensuing French Republic, France's economic driving force was the sugar trade. This trade was dependent on colonialism and slavery, activities which, in my view, contradicted everything that the Enlightenment espoused. Liberty, equality and fraternity could not be for all. This contradiction resurfaced in a blatant fashion during the Second World War: with the very active involvement of the French in the deportation and murder of thousands of Jews. The fact that at the time and for a long period after the war, France overlooked or denied its active participation in the treatment of Jews, turning the blame instead on the Vichy government and the Germans, seemed to me very much in keeping with the hypocrisy of the French national ideology, as it had been founded in the eighteenth century.

I was also interested in the issue of national identity in French history. The treatment of Jews during the war had shown that the right to French nationality could be revoked at any time. I wondered if there were any parallels with the current relationship between the State and France's immigrant population? But I was also interested in popular concepts of national identity. I suspected that in the eyes of the 'French' most immigrants had a very tenuous hold on their new national identity: 'once an immigrant, always an immigrant'.

I enjoyed academic research, but was attracted by the idea of examining the history of La cité through film, as it offered a multi-faceted approach that could never have been achieved in a dissertation. Although I had not undergone any formal training in filmmaking, I had a keen visual eye, and was inspired by the example of an acquaintance who had made his first documentary with a Hi8 camcorder and a few microphones. Once I had embarked on the project, I found that the skills of research and analysis gained during my academic studies proved to be perhaps more valuable than any film school training.

So I set off to Paris with a Mini DV camcorder, unsure if I would be able to master the camera and record sound, let alone conduct interviews. But I was determined and threw myself wholeheartedly into the project. As the work progressed, I realised that I could not do justice to this complex and important subject in a short film shot over a few months. It warranted extensive research and many hours of interviewing and filming. The process eventually took a year-and-a-half and the result was a 52-minute documentary.

My intention was to make a historical documentary that would appeal to younger audiences, not usually willing to listen to a history lesson. I was convinced that a Holocaust documentary should try to make the horrors of the past relevant to a contemporary audience, but I often found the experience of watching documentaries about the Holocaust frustrating and alienating. As I was someone who had been directly affected by the Holocaust, I became concerned about how others of my generation, those with no personal connection to the subject, were responding to these documentaries.[5] At times it was the style of the conventional historical documentaries, with their didactic narrative voiceover, that alienated me. Other films were missing the larger social context that would allow the viewer a deeper understanding of the subject. Surely, we must try to learn something from such a painful episode in human history? What is the point of the 'past' if we cannot use it to mend our ways? Keeping the 'past in the past' is safer, less challenging, but also dangerous.

La cité de la Muette was the ideal vehicle to encourage this dialogue between past and present. Buildings with such a dramatic history are often turned into museums, and so they stay in the past. The appearance of this building had changed little since the war, but this was not because it had been preserved like a museum piece or memorial; on the contrary, the post-war use of La cité de la Muette had given the building a new lease of life. By bringing the two lives of La cité closer together we could begin to address the issues that concerned me.

As I was researching and filming *Les Voix de la Muette* (*If the Walls Could Speak*, 1998), it became apparent that people believed that the Camp de Drancy of the war and La cité de la Muette of today were two completely different places. This confusion perpetuated the popular post-war myth of the separateness of the French Republic and the wartime Vichy government. Even in a documentary about Drancy, made by Stephen Trombley in 1995 (*Drancy: A Concentration Camp in Paris, 1941–1944*), there

Holocaust survivor Henri acts as a guide, in *If the Walls Could Speak* (© Disruptive Element Films)

seemed to be very little connection between the internment camp and La cité today, as if the estate no longer existed or was not a real place, and certainly not the lively, bustling community that I knew. For me, making a film that moved between the past and present of La cité meant that this split could no longer be sustained and the lines between the ideologies of Vichy and the ideals of the French Republic could begin to be blurred, in terms that were literally concrete! Visually I reinforced this blurring by juxtaposing photographs of the estate when it functioned as an internment camp with scenes of La cité de la Muette today. I made this even more explicit by superimposing archive stills with images of La cité shot with my video camera. Recollections of episodes in the survivors' time in the camp were brought to life with sequences shot as the video camera moved around the estate grounds, the basements and stairwells. I also used this technique to present the larger history of the French treatment of the Jews. For example, contemporary video footage of buses run by RATP (Paris's main public transport operator) was used to illustrate the survivors' memories of being bussed to Camp de Drancy in vehicles owned by the same organisation.[6]

I decided that I should include interviews with Holocaust survivors who had been interned in Drancy, as well as with people who lived in La cité today, but beyond that I had no specific criteria for the interviewees. The idea was that the survivors' stories would provide the historical backbone to the film. I also wanted to explore the parallels between the survivors' experiences of possessing a dual identity (Jewish and French), with those of the contemporary immigrant community – this would provide a link between the past and present. However, my approach to documentary-making is organic:

although you have to have some basic ideas of what you want, mostly you find things along the way, and that includes the people.

Two of the survivors I found through my mother and the other two came from an organisation of Auschwitz survivors that, amongst other things, arranges for members to talk about their experiences in schools and other places. I made a conscious decision to interview survivors who were used to talking about their experiences (with one exception), as I was not equipped to give psychological support to someone who was sharing this subject for the first time.

The other interviewees I 'found' by spending time on the estate. For example, I met the Housing Officer while I was conducting research at a library, and he offered himself for interview. The post woman was a friendly and open character, and she was glad that someone was not making a film that was 'stuck in the past', so she readily agreed to be a part of the film. Interestingly, I filmed her at the end of the ten months of researching and filming – I had somehow managed to miss her – and the decision to make her the structural thread in the film was not made until we were editing. Many of the younger people who appear in the film were happy to talk because, as well as the usual questions about the camp, I asked them about their personal experiences of living in La cité and other issues in their lives.

There is a certain amount of mythology about the process of 'gaining people's trust' in documentary-making: there is no formula or 'easy way'. In my experience it is often just a case of talking to people, explaining what you're doing, and if they feel comfortable enough, they'll talk to you. If they refuse then there's always room for gentle persuasion and persistence, as was the case with 'Henriette', the older woman interviewed in the film, who was one of the first to move into La cité after the war. She had initially agreed to an interview, but then refused, I think out of fear and uncertainty about what I would ask her. When I explained what I wanted to do in more detail and expressed how important her contribution would be she changed her mind and agreed to the interview. Some people were annoyed when approached with questions about the history of La cité (one striking example is included in the film), but most reacted positively to the project and were at least willing to talk to me; it probably helped that they were used to people from the radio and television coming and asking questions.

I was struck by the amount of misinformation held about the history of La cité; in particular it was clear that the role of the French in the deportation of the Jews was a surprise to most people. When talking to a group of young men of Tunisian, Caribbean and Portuguese origin about life on the estate and its history, they told me that the Germans had run and guarded the camp. So I showed them a photograph of a French gendarme, distinguishable by his képi, at the entrance to the camp looking onto a group of prisoners. It took a few moments for them to realise what this picture showed, and they were genuinely surprised at the presence of a French gendarme. They spent some time looking at the photograph, discussing it and identifying parts of the building. It was almost as though they were trying to work through a revelation of betrayal. Here were young adults who had been to school and lived in this historic place, yet they knew nothing about the role of the French. It is perhaps one of the most significant scenes in the documentary.

As I had no formal camera training, in the first instance I defined my style in relation and in opposition to the Holocaust documentaries that I had seen. I wanted

A moment of realisation for some young men from La Cité, in *If the Walls Could Speak* (© Disruptive Element Films)

to make a documentary that reflected contemporary culture and was thus better able to communicate with young people. But my camera style developed organically, as I filmed; in some ways I was liberated by not having received any formal training, as I was not aware of any cinematic rules or conventions that I should adhere to.

I adopted a dynamic hand-held style for the archive materials, moving the camera across the still photographs to focus on individuals or details such as the star pinned to the coat of a Jewish child. Occasionally the movement of the camera is rapid, blurring the details of the photograph. I chose this treatment, rather than a more conventional static presentation of the historical images, as I wanted to bring the images to life. As there is no archive film of Drancy's internment camp, this method also lent the photographs the illusion of moving images.

Much of the film's style was achieved during the editing process. I knew that I wanted a generally fast and dynamic pace, and I worked with a talented editor who was able to translate my camera work, which was occasionally messy, into a coherent style. At times he would select footage that to me seemed unusable, but in the context of the style of the film worked well.

Consistent with my strategy of making a film in a contemporary style, I deliberately chose music for the soundtrack that would be familiar to young people and reflected the urban lifestyle of the young interviewees who now live in La cité. Except for one piece by the Hungarian folk band Muszikàs, that might be associated with a Holocaust documentary, all the music in the film was by dance, ambient and techno bands (Autechre, Morcheeba, Seafeel); a style that would be unexpected in a historical documentary.

As for the archival research, there were few documents covering the period from the end of the war to 1948, when La cité reverted back to being a housing estate. Apparently most of the housing documents had been destroyed by damp when they were stored in a basement, the rest were lost when the housing office moved headquarters. I did, however, find an extraordinary series of documents from the war years, held in the Paris Archives (which I included in the film). These were letters from the housing office requesting rent from the town of Drancy, for the use of La cité as an internment camp. In other words, because the Regional Department of Housing was unable to rent out the flats since the building was being used as a camp, the Department was asking Drancy's council to reimburse it for loss of earnings. Here was evidence of the petty bureaucracy of everyday life, the machinery of a governmental organisation of the French State (little changed at this level since the Republic) carrying on as if nothing had changed. Personally, I found this a compelling piece of evidence of the complicity of the French civil administration in the Holocaust.[7]

As well as a historical account of La cité, the documentary was to be an examination of the contemporary phenomenon of racism and antisemitism. One day, while setting up my camera and tripod, I was approached by a man, white and haggard looking, who proudly announced that he was the one who had vandalised the train carriage, sited at the entrance to La cité as a memorial to the Holocaust. It was clear that he was unstable, poor and incredibly angry with the government for not looking after him, blaming his lot on the immigrants, even though, as he assured me, he did have black friends. I in-

The 'memorial' carriage to La Cité's other history.

Poster for *If the Walls Could Speak*
(© Disruptive Element Films)

cluded the interview in the documentary as this man, although not an ideologically committed neo-Nazi (that is he was probably not a member of Le Pen's National Front), was the kind of person likely to be drawn to the arguments of the neo-Nazis, and thus was representative of one sector of the National Front's voting constituency. It was important to give a face to racism and antisemitism to help the viewer understand how such beliefs can flourish. Finally, in the context of a film that dealt with the Holocaust, the arguments against racism could be all the more powerful.

Towards the end of filming, as the country was gearing up for the local elections, I was told of a National Front Rally to be held in the centre of Paris and I decided, mainly out of curiosity rather than for the purposes of the documentary, to go and film the event. I went expecting to see the usual stereotypical neo-Nazi types. To my surprise, and this is why I included the rally in the documentary, the majority of people did not match the media image of right-wing racists, they were just ordinary French men and women, young and old, smiling, eating and enjoying themselves, like the French who had watched the Jews in the camp from their windows, or seen busloads of Jews being driven by, doing nothing and secretly glad that finally these people would be chased from their precious France. In the May 1997 elections, the National Front took second place in Drancy.

If the Walls Could Speak had muted success in France. It was shown on Planète (a cable channel and subsidiary of Canal+), but none of the main terrestrial broadcasters were interested, as apparently they had already dealt with the subject on several occasions. Well yes, they had, in the safest way possible, by keeping the past in the past, and avoiding anything that was too critical of the French.

However, the film was also shown at a fairly big festival in Créteil, the Festival International de Films de Femmes. I was nervous as this was my first Paris screening, and I was unsure about how people would react. So I was surprised when, after the screening, many members of the audience came up to thank me for making the film and making them aware of an aspect of French history of which they were completely ignorant! And these were Parisians.

The film won the award for the best documentary by a first-time director at the 'Out of that Darkness' film season at the ICA, London in 2000. It was also awarded a prize at the Festival Internazionale Cinema delle Donne (Women's Film Festival) in Turin, and it has been extensively screened at festivals around the world.

My ultimate wish is that the film will be included in history lessons in French schools.

Finally, for those who do not speak French, I would like to point out the irony in the name of La cité de la Muette. La Muette, literally translated, means 'mute woman'.

Notes

1   *Cité* is the French word for a housing estate.

2   The tower blocks were finished, but when the horseshoe block was turned into a camp, only the building's exterior was close to completion; the interior of the building had not been divided into flats, so there were just large, bare concrete spaces. The French opened the camp in 1939 to hold communists. It was then used by the Germans to hold French, British, Yugoslav and Greek POWs. In August 1941 the French government took the camp over to imprison Jews.

3   See S. Klarsfeld (1994) *Memorial to the Jews Deported from France, 1942–1944*. Paris: Fils et Filles des Déportées Juif de France (FFDJF).

4   The Third Republic was dissolved by the National Assembly by a vote held during a meeting in the Grand Casino in Vichy on 10 July 1940. L'État Français, the name given to the body set up to replace the Republic, was inaugurated by Marshal Petain's Vichy group on 12 July 1940.

5   As well as my grandfather, my grandmother's four brothers and four sisters were deported from France. Only the sisters survived.

6   RATP stands for Régie Autonome des Transports Parisiennes. Strictly speaking, the buses used to transport the Jews in wartime Paris, were run by the Société des Transports en Commune de la Région Parisienne (STCRP), the publicly-owned forerunner of the RATP. RATP was created on 21 March 1948, by combining the assets of the Compagnie du Chemin de Fer Métropolitan de Paris (CMP), which ran the Metro with STCRP, which ran the buses.

7   The Vichy government's policy towards the Jews is well covered in R. O. Paxton (2001) *Vichy France: Old Guard and New Order, 1940–44*. New York: Columbia University Press, 168–85. See also H. Rousso (1991) *The Vichy Syndrome: History and Memory in France Since 1944*. Cambridge, MA and London: Harvard University Press.

32 Exploring the common threads of genocide: the Crimes Against Humanity Exhibition at the Imperial War Museum

Suzanne Bardgett & Annie Dodds

SB: In December 2002 the Imperial War Museum opened an exhibition on the subject of genocide and ethnic violence. It is housed in the space above the Holocaust Exhibition, where the Museum's curved roof – removed from the busier galleries below – provides a striking vaulted tubular space, criss-crossed with a mesh of giant white steel ribs.

Visitors who arrive in this sparely-designed gallery find an exhibition made of just two elements: a 30-minute film which runs continuously on a wide floor-to-ceiling screen, and a table of interactive videos. An introductory text explains the exhibition's purpose – to allow visitors to explore why it is that ethnic violence and genocide have been so recurrent in the last one hundred years.

IWM 2005-1-1 (© IWM)

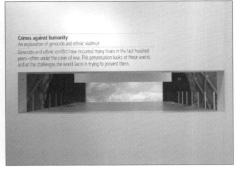
IWM 2005-1-11 (© IWM)

Visitors sit on simple, cubic concrete seating to watch the film, whose six self-contained sections mean that it can be joined at any point. It does not have a single-person narrative, but instead offers a series of thoughts from eight commentators – an academic, journalists, human rights workers, a lawyer, a soldier – who turn over the principal issues surrounding genocide and our response to it.

The film contains extremely distressing scenes – the aftermath of the 1994 Market Square mortar attack in Sarajevo, bloodied corpses left on the roadside after a killing spree by Hutu extremists in Rwanda, a body burned beyond recognition being lifted into a coffin in Kosovo, a Nazi official taunting an old Jewish woman. The witness testimony is likewise chilling – you hear the unending anger of a Cambodian woman whose entire family was murdered by the Khmer Rouge. It is thirty minutes of appalling education in one of the world's most perplexing subjects and its impact can be seen on visitors' faces.

Many comment that they find the Exhibition a surprising but valuable addition to the Museum's displays:

> 'Fascinating, enlightening, informative and thought-provoking. Death doesn't just happen in Europe and in the past. These concerns are immediate. We have to do something and the IWM is going some way to ensuring historical memory.'

When, in the mid-1990s, plans were first drawn up for the permanent exhibitions which would fill the planned major extension to our building, the concept favoured by the then Chairman, Field Marshal Lord Bramall, was for a large exhibition which would examine the notion of 'Man's Inhumanity to Man', including in it a full historical explanation of the Holocaust as well as other terrible events of the twentieth century.

We took Lord Bramall's vision and divided it into two – deciding that a detailed account of the Holocaust should form the larger part of the space (reflecting a clear demand for a narrative exhibition on this subject) and the upper floor devoted to an examination of genocide as a general theme: why it happens; what common features unite events in places as diverse as Cambodia, former Yugoslavia and Rwanda; and what the role of the international community has been and could be in trying to prevent genocide. A kind of post-script to the Holocaust Exhibition, in other words, which would offer visitors a space in which to contemplate the wider story.

Why this approach? Firstly, we recognised that the 1990s had seen a change in the nature of conflict. Of 120 wars in the 1990s, only ten were purely inter-state wars. Following the end of the Cold War, a new era had arrived in which the chief threat to international security was the collapse of states. Instances of ethnic violence within such 'failed states' accounted for nearly all the wars of recent years. Surely this phenomenon deserved investigation?

An exhibition on genocide, while ambitious, would be highly topical. The aftermath of genocide was constantly in the news: Slobodan Milosevic had been handed over for trial at the Hague, efforts were being made in Cambodia to bring to justice former Khmer Rouge officials, a UN mission was finally preserving peace and democracy in East Timor and the International Criminal Court was about to come into being.

Finally, it seemed meaningful and relevant to create a display which would stimulate our visitors to think about their own reactions to media reports of outbreaks of communal violence. The dilemma of whether or not to intervene in order to prevent ethnic bloodshed is one which looks set to recur again and again. The exhibition would – we felt sure – have the power to engage visitors on some of the most important international issues of the day.

Inspiration came in particular from Michael Ignatieff's trilogy on the face of modern conflict, *Blood and Belonging*, *The Warrior's Honor* and *Virtual War* while Leo Kuper's 1981 book *Genocide* and the work of the small but dedicated group of genocide scholars gave us a series of markers as to what events the exhibition should cover.[1]

To those – and there were some – who asked whether this was not taking the Museum outside its traditional subject areas, we were firm that this was a valid approach and one which would bring the Museum credit for tackling a difficult and 'off-putting' topic. By focusing on genocide, the Exhibition would amplify the lessons learned in the Holocaust Exhibition (opened in 2000) and complement it, and would answer the many comments we had from visitors to that exhibition wanting more information on instances of organised mass murder *since* the Second World War.

We realised that a conventional artefact, showcase and panels exhibition would not work. A film was surely the most effective way to engage the public on this topic – 'sit them down and make them think'. Not a dry distillation of the various theories of human destructiveness, but a finely-wrought production which would engage, move and educate.

We advertised our search for a suitable filmmaker in *Broadcast* magazine and got a strong response. A shortlist was drawn up and we asked those companies to explain how they would render the subject.

Our brief asked for a production which would combine both 'emotional power and historical integrity', and listed a number of key ideas we wanted conveyed. For example that genocides most often occur in states where there is rapid transition, or where the government promotes an extreme ideology; that Western governments will often turn their backs on genocides until it is too late; that turning the spotlight on violations of humanitarian law can affect the outcome; and that if the will is there to try and convict those who incite and commit mass murder, it can arguably act as a deterrent to others.

The competition produced some imaginative treatments. Two of the four short-listed companies wanted a degree of 'play-acting' within the gallery. One asked the visitor to imagine that an extremist regime had come to power in the UK, and invited them to examine their likely responses to such a scenario. Another involved a 'laboratory of human behaviour' mixing experiments which reveal how easily human beings commit 'crimes of obedience', intercut with testimony of real people who had lived through or witnessed the aftermath of genocide. Although well-intentioned, these approaches seemed fraught with problems. Perhaps such things could be staged in a 'single-message' museum like the Museum of Tolerance in Los Angeles, but in ours it felt uncomfortable.

Our eventual choice was for October Films, represented by Annie Dodds and James Barker, with whom my colleagues and I had worked for two intense, rewarding years in 1998 and 1999 making the 36 audio-visuals in the Holocaust Exhibition. Their treatment was closest to what we had ourselves envisaged and, crucially, we knew we could trust them to deliver a production which would sit happily in the Imperial War Museum – an institution with which they were both very familiar.

Once the film was finished we showed it to the front of house staff here. At first no-one spoke – it had been truly overwhelming. One person felt that it showed the *true* face of conflict – the reality of what it is to be killed by a massive shell explosion or burned or murdered with machetes – and that this needed to be seen in the war museum. Some thought that two particularly shocking sequences in the film should be taken out – they were simply too upsetting to be suddenly confronted without warning 'on a Sunday afternoon outing'. (Our response was to exclude those under sixteen, and put up prominent warnings of the upsetting nature of the material.) Another said she knew instantly that it would broaden the appeal of the Museum and that we should be proud of it.

A brief word about the design of the space. The main challenge was to make a virtue of the top floor's unusual – some might say intractable – architecture. We wanted a 'deliberately clinical/futuristic space giving a sense of scientific investigation' and an atmosphere which was 'apocalyptic, futuristic, meditative.' 'The design needs to be above all sensitive to the enormous loss of culture, livelihoods and lives which this small space and relatively simple concept will seek to embrace.'[2]

Casson Mann, our designers, proposed a single white structure as the central element – a space offering a symbolic choice to step in and engage full-on with what is being screened, or to stand at the edge of the space and look on from the sidelines. The large white 'table' hints at the roles bureaucracy and diplomacy play in both perpetrating and preventing genocide.

Embedded in this table are six interactive computer screens at which visitors can examine for themselves the historical background to particular genocides, or probe issues

IWM 2005-1-10 (© IWM)

IWM 2005-1-9 (© IWM)

like international justice or the aftermath of ethnic conflict. The style of these is deliberately factual and subdued, with black-and-white graphics and simple, informative maps. Victoria Cook, the research assistant in our Office, spent a year-and-a-half scripting and illustrating these interactives, with additional input from genocides expert Mark Levene of Warwick University, and Laurence Freedman of Kings College, London. Judging by visitors' comments, these seemed to have worked well. For example:

> 'A thought provoking climax to a great museum – brings all under this roof into focus, and lends everything resonance.'

The Exhibition has certainly broadened the Museum's remit and drawn in new audiences. Our programme of public events now carries films and talks on a much wider canvas of topics than before: 18 November 2003 saw a lecture by human rights lawyer Geoffrey Robertson QC on the hopes for the International Criminal Court, and in 2004 a high-profile one-day seminar to remember the Rwandan genocide – with commentators from Africa, Europe and the US coming together to address the failings of the international community in 1994. The Exhibition has attracted interest from the lawyers at the Hague, and from the Foreign Office, who now include a visit to it and the Holocaust Exhibition in a training programme for all new recruits.

The Crimes Against Humanity Exhibition has above all shown that the Museum is capable of addressing difficult contemporary issues and that the public will readily engage with this deeply distressing and demanding subject.

AD: The Imperial War Museum's brief to come up with a concept for a short film on genocide in recent times was one of the most challenging projects we have attempted as documentary filmmakers. As we thought through the implications of producing a short film encompassing a subject of such enormity and complexity, that would run as a continuous loop and be instantly comprehensible to the general public at any point, and be timeless enough to be shown for several years, we realised that a conventional documentary approach simply would not work.

The answer was to develop a simple but robust structure, which would release us from the traditional demands of historical chronology, story-telling and lengthy explanations. We began to think of the film in terms of a poem, consisting of short verses or sections, where words and imagery are condensed, but imbued with meaning, and can convey weighty ideas. Within this format we could explore thematically some of the fundamental processes common to many genocides and mass killings, even though the time, place and circumstances of events might be worlds apart – from episodes like the Armenian massacres of 1915, to Pol Pot's Killing Fields in Cambodia or the 1994 Rwandan genocide. By taking this approach, we hoped to shed light on some of the key points in the Museum's brief.

Our film set out to examine how the first steps to genocide can arise when, under conditions of conflict or extreme unrest, existing differences between people, be they national, racial, religious or political, are turned into something subversive and dangerous. How powerful elites leading the persecution of minorities use fear, repression and virulent propaganda to separate and dehumanise their victims, holding them responsible for all the nation's woes. How it then becomes increasingly acceptable for ordinary people to condone or carry out previously inconceivable persecutions, even against those close to them, culminating in mass murder. Although these acts, at a lower level, are frequently carried out by people fired up by crazy bloodlust, the project of extermination is devised calmly by those in power, who believe it to be a rational solution to a host of otherwise insoluble problems that threaten their national community.

We would show how the international community has always found it notoriously difficult to gauge the right response to state-sponsored mass killing; every argument for action being matched by a counter-argument for non-involvement. As people flee persecution, there is the inevitable divide as to whether we open our doors to them or try to stem the flow. Economic sanctions often hurt the victims more than the rogue regime and military intervention carries massive risks. How far do our moral, legal and ethical responsibilities extend for what happens elsewhere? Should we be prepared to intervene at a much earlier stage, not just wait until we have to respond to a major humanitarian disaster? And to what extent do our own actions, both economically and politically, contribute to conditions which could make genocide more likely?

If we do intervene, either unilaterally or through the United Nations, there is the question of how we deal with punishing the perpetrators. Since the Nuremberg trials, the idea of genocide as a crime against humanity was established and incorporated into the UN Declaration of Genocide in 1948. Recently, rape perpetrated as an act of war has also been included. Global ground rules have been established for the trial and punishment of those who commit genocide, from the heads of states to the ordinary individual, and steps have been taken to establish an International Criminal Court. But laws do not protect against the conditions for genocide and nation-states can go their own way.

We felt it important, in this film, to focus on the perpetrators, to hear how they rationalise their behaviour or deny responsibility: men like Adolf Eichmann, in charge of a vast, elaborate state-sponsored bureaucracy of death or Slobodan Milosevic, former president of Serbia on trial in The Hague, under whose rule thousands of Bosnian Muslims were slaughtered. How do ordinary Hutu men and women, machetes and clubs in hand, justify murdering their closest friends and neighbours? In similar circumstances, might we all be capable of the same conduct?

The film would also show the aftermath of genocide; not just how survivors are left deeply damaged by the experience for the rest of their lives, but how the effects can continue for generations. Even after the killing stops, whole societies can become fractured and dysfunctional if they are unable to confront their darkest history or even, as in former Yugoslavia and Rwanda, be condemned to repeat it.

Though the film runs on a continuous loop as these ideas are followed through, there is a beginning and an end marked by a short, silent, chilling montage of superimposed black-and-white photos which powerfully conveys the personal agony and loss caused by these human calamities. Each section, however, makes sense within itself and has a title to indicate its theme, helping visitors to grasp quickly what is going on. This approach was made possible by the fact that the accompanying bank of interactive programmes would do what the film could not do: deliver the specific historical stories, the facts, figures and points of information about all the main genocides in the time-span, from 1914 onwards. Though they were designed to be completely different in style, it was vital that the interactives and the film supported and complemented each other to offer a comprehensive provision of content in the presentation of the exhibition.

As the film was to be driven by ideas rather than stories, we had to find a way to construct a coherent central narrative. It became clear that, unlike the Holocaust exhibition films where the narrative is driven forward by the survivor testimony, which needs time for the stories to unfold and where you have to see the people on screen, something very different was required here. We especially wanted to avoid the constrictions inherent in seeming to have a single point of view, a film rooted in one authoritative voice, in the sense of using a written script and a spoken commentary.

Our solution was to suggest a narrative montage of different voices from sound-only interviews. By not showing the faces of our interviewees on-screen, we would allow the maximum flexibility to weave together a mix of historical, factual, philosophical and moral observations from a wide range of voices and the ability to make non-narrative visual references to the many genocides and mass killings of the last century. Above all, we could use that valuable screen time to focus on illustrating their words with the most arresting and haunting images, retaining an unbroken visual momentum in the film.

Having decided not to film survivors or interviewees, we felt nothing was to be gained by any additional filming. After all, nothing could be more telling or have more impact than footage or photographs shot at the time of events, and we knew there was a wealth of such material in archives and collections. Having given ourselves the liberty to use imagery in a non-narrative way, it required a massive research programme to acquire and view hours of footage from many parts of the world to select the most powerful images from which to assemble the film in the cutting room.

This was a tough undertaking, given the grim nature of the subject and the often harrowing images, some of which we were unfamiliar with. Acts of genocidal cruelty and inhumanity were to be found in all corners of the globe amongst all kinds of societies. The list was depressingly long and we could only refer to a small number. It made us keenly aware of how careful we would have to be to create a film that, while it did not in any way diminish or sensationalise the monstrous events it presented, allowed people to watch and become involved without being overwhelmed by the horror of the subject matter. We were helped in this by the format that made it possible for us to cut together an unusually wide variety of visual material within a short space of time.

At certain points in the film, for instance, we run attractive images of daily life in London, people relaxing in sunny Regent's Park, having a pint at a pub on the Thames, close-up faces of people going about their everyday routine. But these impressions of a prosperous, multicultural city are there to remind people that, in some measure, our affluence and stability is connected to poverty and insecurity elsewhere, that our own political and economic policies have far-reaching affects – be it the supply of arms to repressive regimes or trade practices which cause the collapse of poorer economies – that can help make conditions for genocide more likely. Though these scenes address vital, discomforting issues, the viewer is nevertheless afforded some visual breathing space to ponder on our common humanity.

The editing process was one of experimentation, trying out different juxtapositions of words and pictures and honing down a mass of material into a basic thematic structure. Only when a loose but coherent thread of ideas had emerged, which could be supported or led by the imagery, did we feel in a position to carry out the interviews to provide the principal narration.

We had already carried out a good deal of research, talking to people, reading books and articles, listening to broadcasts and films, to choose our eight interviewees; each uniquely qualified to discuss the subject of genocide, either as experts in the field or through their personal involvement in reporting events, particularly in former Yugoslavia and Rwanda.

Carrying out these sound interviews was very different to filming the survivor testimony interviews for the Holocaust Exhibition. Here, we had to plan our questions carefully and systematically to try to elicit short, clear answers which would specifically cover the ideas we wanted to include. By this time, for example, we knew that within the main themes, we wanted to include the significance of rape as a genocidal crime and the killing and dispossession of tribal peoples for their land and resources. We could not predict what our interviewees would come up with, but we were hopeful of obtaining some unexpected and powerful insights. In the end, they gave us more than we could have wished for. From their voices, interwoven with others from archive film, news and radio broadcasts, we were able to assemble a disturbing and memorable meditation on the subject of genocide.

Specially composed music was an additional element which helped give the film cohesion. Our music composer, Dan Jones, who saw versions of the film at different stages, discussed with us how music or sound could help unify certain sections, create links or, most importantly, provide space for reflection. Nowhere is this more evident than in the silent black-and-white stills montage where the spare, swelling musical motif, seems

IWM 2005-1-12 (© IWM)

to intensify one's gaze. With such extreme subject matter, we had to be very careful to avoid music which felt in any way manipulative of mood or emotion. The design of the exhibition space, incorporating a surround-sound system, made a considerable difference as to how subtly and creatively we could use the music. It enabled us to broadcast the entire soundtrack, especially the music and sound effects, to fill the space in a fuller, more enclosing way.

The film also gains enormous impact by being projected on a large screen in the austere, white setting – a very different experience to watching a television monitor or cinema film. Though people are free to sit, stand, move around or use the interactives, there is an atmosphere of intense concentration. The simple, elegant design, the dominating screen with its potent images, the spatial sound and the powerful narration, have combined to create a special space where people can contemplate the nature of genocide.

Notes

1   M. Ignatieff (1994) *Blood and Belonging: Journeys into the New Nationalism*. London: Vintage; M. Ignatieff (1999) *The Warrior's Honor: Ethnic War and the Modern Conscience*. London: Vintage; M. Ignatieff (2000) *Virtual War: Kosovo and Beyond*. London: Chatto and Windus; L. Kuper (1981) *Genocide*. Harmondsworth: Penguin.

2   Quotes from the design brief for the 'Crimes Against Humanity Exhibition', Holocaust Exhibition Project Office, 2001.

FILMOGRAPHY

The filmography below gives the basic details of relevant films and television series mentioned within the various chapters of this book. For more detailed information about Holocaust films, including many not discussed in the present text, the Cinematography of the Holocaust online database is recommended. Curated by the Fritz Bauer Institut, and available in English and German, it offers a comprehensive listing of relevant material searchable by various lists (Film Titles, Subject, Personal Names, and so on) and also has a free text search. See www.fritz-bauer-institut.de/cine/cine_e.htm for details.

100 Days (GB/Rwanda, 2001, colour, 100 minutes) Directed by Nick Hughes; produced by Nick Hughes and Eric Kabera; written by Nick Hughes. Main cast includes Eric Bridges Twahirwa, Cleophas Kabasita, Davis Kagenza, Mazimpaka Kennedy.

Achter Gesloten Ogen (Behind Closed Eyes) (Netherlands, 2000, colour, 100 minutes) KvO Films. Directed by Duco Tellegen; produced by Karel von Ossenbrüggen; originally four 25-minute television documentaries.

After Years of Walking (GB, 2003, colour, 37 minutes) National Film and Television School. Directed and produced by Sarah Vanagt; cinematography by Annemarie Lean-Vercoe; film editor Sarah Metcalfe.

Atrocities at Scafati, Near Pompeii, Italy; Advance of US Troops on Pratella and Prata Sanita, Italy; British Troops Enter Belgium Near Brussels; German Concentration Camp at Vught, the Netherlands; Capture of Celle, North East of Hanover, Germany; Starving Internees at Belsen Concentration Camp, Germany (allocated title) (GB/USA, 9/1943; 1/11/1943; 1945, b&w, c. 2 minutes) Part of a series of compilations of Concentration Camp material for use in Allied film productions. Held in the IWM Film and Video Archive as A70 514-72.

Au Revoir, Les Enfants (France/West Germany, 1987, colour, 104 minutes) Nouvelles Éditions de Films/MK2/ Stella Films. Directed, produced and written by Louis Malle; main cast includes Gaspard Manesse, Raphael Fejtö, Francine Racette, Stanislas Carré de Malberg.

Auschwitz and the Allies (GB, 1982, colour, 110 minutes) BBC. Produced by Rex Bloomstein; written by Piers Brendon and Rex Bloomstein.

Auschwitz: the Nazis and the 'Final Solution' (GB, 2005, colour, 300 minutes total) BBC. Directed by Detlef Siebert, Dominic Sutherland and Martina Balazova; written and produced by Laurence Rees.

Battle of the Books (GB, 1941, b&w, 7 minutes) Paul Rotha Productions (Sponsored by the Ministry of Information) Directed by Jack Chambers; produced by Paul Rotha; music by Charles Brill; commentary by Henry Ainley. Held in the IWM Film and Video Archive as UKY 380.

Belsen Concentration Camp, Germany: Interviews With Inmates (Reels 1 and 2) (allocated title) (GB, 23/4/1945 and 24/4/1945, b&w, 20 minutes) British Movietone News (Sponsored by the Ministry of Information). Photography by Paul Wyand; sound by Martin Gray. Part of a series of compilations of Concentration Camp material for use in Allied film productions. Held in the IWM Film and Video Archive as A70 514-97 and A70 514-98.

British Movietone News Issue Number 830a (GB, 3/5/1945, b&w, 10 minutes) British Movietone News. Commentary by Lionel Gamlin and Leslie Mitchell. Held in the IWM Film and Video Archive as NMV 830A.

Cabaret (USA, 1972, colour, 124 minutes) ABC Circle Films. Directed by Bob Fosse; produced by Cy Feuer; script by Jay Presson Allen (based on Joe Masteroff's stage musical and John Van Druten's play *I Am a Camera*, both derived from Christopher Isherwood's book *Berlin Stories*); main cast includes Liza Minnelli, Michael York, Joel Grey, Marisa Berenson and Helmut Griem.

La Caduta Degli Dei (The Damned) (Italy/West Germany/Switzerland, 1969, colour, 164 minutes) Praesidens/Pegaso/Italnoleggio/Eichberg. Directed by Luchino Visconti; written by Nicola Badalucco, Enrico Medioli and Luchino Visconti; main cast includes Dirk Bogarde, Ingrid Thulin, Helmut Berger, Renaud Verley.

Calling Mr Smith (GB/Poland [Polish Government in exile], 1943, b&w, 9 minutes) Concanen (Sponsored by the Polish Film Unit). Directed by Stefan Themerson and Franciszka Themerson; produced by Eugene

Cekalski; cinematography by Stefan Themerson and Franciszka Themerson; edited by Stefan Themerson and Franciszka Themerson; dialogue by Bruce Graeme. Held in the IWM Film and Video Archive as SIK 35.

Carl de Brouwer Amateur Film (two reels, with the allocated titles ***Cycling Tour of Rhineland, Germany 1936*** and ***Country Life in a Belgian Family During the German Occupation, 1942–1944***) (Belgium, 1936–44, b&w [part colour], 105 minutes total) Shot by Carl de Brouwer. Held in the IWM Film and Video Archive as MGH 4438 and MGH 4439.

Cast a Giant Shadow (USA, 1966, colour, 141 minutes) United Artists/The Mirisch Company/Llenroc/Batjac. Directed by Melville Shavelson; produced by Melville Shavelson and Michael Wayne; written by Melville Shavelson (from Ted Berkman's book); main cast includes Kirk Douglas, Senta Berger, James Donald, Angie Dickinson, Topol.

Le Chagrin et la Pitié (The Sorrow and the Pity) (France/Switzerland/Germany, 1969, b&w, 270 minutes) ORTF/Productions Télévision Rencontre SA. Directed and written by Marcel Ophuls; produced by André Harris and Alain de Séduy.

Il Cielo Cade (The Sky is Falling) (Italy, 2000, colour, 102 minutes) Parus Film/Viva Cinematografica/Istituto Luce/RAI. Directed by Andrea Frazzi and Antonio Frazzi; produced by Carlo M. Cucchi and Vittorio Noia; written by Suso Cecchi d'Amico (from the novel by Lorenza Mazzetti); main cast includes Isabella Rossellini, Jeroen Krabbé, Barbara Enrichi, Gianna Giachetti, Luciano Virgilio.

Concorrenza Sleale (Unfair Competition) (Italy/France, 2001, colour, 110 minutes) Medusa Produzione/Massfilm/MBAC. Directed by Ettore Scola; produced by Franco Committeri; written by Furio Scarpelli; main cast includes Diego Abatantuono, Sergio Castellitto, Gérard Depardieu, Jean-Claude Brialy.

Crossfire (USA, 1947, b&w, 86 minutes) RKO Radio Pictures. Directed by Edward Dmytryk; produced by Adrian Scott; written by John Paxton (from Richard Brooks' novel *The Brick Foxhole*); main cast includes Robert Young, Robert Mitchum, Robert Ryan, Gloria Grahame, Paul Kelly.

Czech Jewish Family Life in Pre-war Europe: Amateur Film by the Hartmann Family (allocated title) (Czechoslovakia, 1932–36, b&w, c. 30 minutes) Shot by Karel Hartmann and Jan Hartman. Held in the IWM Film and Video Archive as MGH 6432 reels 1–3.

Daleká Cesta (The Long Journey/The Distant Journey) (Czechoslovakia, 1949, b&w, 108 minutes) Filmové Studio Barrandov. Directed by Alfréd Radok; written by Alfréd Radok, Mojmir Drvota and Erik Kolar; cinematography by Josef Střecha; main cast includes Blanka Waleská, Otomar Krejča, Viktor Ocásek, Zdenka Baldová, Jirí Spirit, Eduard Kohout, Rudolf Deyl.

Démanty Noci (Diamonds of the Night) (Czechoslovakia, 1964, b&w, 63 minutes) Ceskoslovensky Filmexport. Directed by Jan Němec; written by Jan Němec (from the novel *Darkness Has No Shadows* by Arnost Lustig; main cast includes Ladislav Jánsky, Antonín Kumbera, Irma Bischofova.

The Diary of Anne Frank (USA, 1959, b&w, 170 minutes) Twentieth Century-Fox/George Stevens. Directed and produced by George Stevens; written by Frances Goodrich and Albert Hackett (based on their play); main cast includes Millie Perkins, Joseph Schildkraut, Shelley Winters, Ed Wynn, Richard Beymer.

Dita Saxová (Czechoslovakia, 1967, b&w, 103 minutes [original version]) Filmové Studio Barrandov. Directed by Antonín Moskalyk; written by Arnost Lustig and Antonín Moskalyk (from Lustig's novel); main cast includes Kristina Mikolajewska, Noemi Sixtova, Bohus Záhorský, Karel Höger, Martin Ruzek.

Drancy: A Concentration Camp in Paris (GB, 1994, colour, 55 minutes) Worldview Pictures. Directed by Stephen Trombley; produced by B;ruce Eadie.

Eden (Israel/Italy/France, 2001, colour, 91 minutes) R&C Produzioni/Agav Film/Les Films Balenciaga/Tf1 International. Directed by Amos Gitai; written by Amos Gitai, Marie-Jose Sanselme and Nick Villiers (from Arthur Miller's book *Homely Girl: A Life*); main cast includes Samantha Morton, Thomas Jane, Luke Holland, Danny Huston, Arthur Miller.

Élise ou La vraie vie (Elise, or Real Life) (France/Algeria, 1970, colour, 100 minutes) ONCIC/Port Royal Films. Directed by Michel Drach; written by Claude Lanzmann (based on the novel by Claire Etcherelli); main cast includes Catherine Allégret, Jean-Pierre Bisson, Martine Chevalier, Mohammed Chouikh, Bernardette Lafont, Marie-José Nat, Alice Reichen.

Escape From Sobibor (USA, 1987, colour, 143 minutes) Zenith Productions. Directed by Jack Gold; written by Richard Rashke and Reginald Rose; cinematography by Ernest Vincze; edited by Keith Palmer; main cast includes Alan Arkin, Joanna Pakula, Rutger Hauer, Hartmunt Becker, Jack Shepherd.

Der ewige Jude – ein Filmbeitrag zum Problem des Weltjudentums aka ***Der ewige Jude (The Eternal Jew; Le Péril Juif)*** (Germany, 1940, b&w, 67 minutes) Deutsche Filmherstellungs und Verwertungs GmbH (DFG). Directed by Fritz Hippler; written by Eberhard Taubert; music by Franz R Friedl. Held in the IWM Film and Video Archive as GWY 522.

Exodus (USA, 1960, colour, 220 minutes) United Artists/Carlyle Productions/Alpha. Directed and produced by Otto Preminger; written by Dalton Trumbo (from Leon Uris' novel); main cast includes Paul Newman,

Eva Marie Saint, Ralph Richardson, Peter Lawford, Lee J. Cobb.

The Final Solution – Auschwitz (GB, 1979, colour, 60 minutes) Thames Television. Directed and produced by Michael Darlow; executive producer Jeremy Isaacs; narrated by Eric Porter.

The First Theresienstadt Film aka *Theresienstadt 1942* (allocated titles) (Germany, 1942, b&w, 8 minutes). Directed by Irena Dodalová; written by Irena Dodalová and Peter Kien; produced under the supervision of Obersturmführer Otto; featuring Hans Hofer, Otto Neumann, Kamilla Rosenbaumova, Karel Švenk and Jakob Edelstein. Held in the IWM Film and Video Archive as MGH 3628.

Der Führer Schenkt Den Juden Eine Stadt (*Hitler Presents a Town to the Jews*) aka *Theresienstadt – Ein Dokumentarfilm aus dem Jüdischen Siedlungsgebiet* (*Theresienstadt – A Documentary from the Jewish Settlement Area*) (Germany, 1944, b&w, 10 minutes) Ufa. Directed by Kurt Gerron; written by Manfred Greifenhagen. Held in the IWM Film and Video Archive as MGH 5104.

Gacaca, Revivre ensemble au Rwanda? (*Gacaca, Living Together Again in Rwanda?*) (France, 2002, colour, 55 minutes) Dominant 7 Productions/Planéte Cable. Directed by Anne Aghion; produced by Philip Brooks, Laurent Bocahut and Anne Aghion.

The Gathering (GB, 1982, colour, 60 minutes) BBC. Produced by Rex Bloomstein.

Gaumont British News Issue No 1181 (GB, 30/4/1945, b&w, 10 minutes) Gaumont-British News. Held in the IWM Film and Video Archive as RMY 144.

Il Generale Della Rovere (*General della Rovere*) (Italy, 1959, b&w, 130 minutes) Gaumont/Zebra Film. Directed by Roberto Rossellini; produced by Moris Ergas; written by Sergio Amidei, Diego Fabbri, Indro Montanelli and Roberto Rossellini; main cast includes Vittorio De Sica, Hannes Messemer, Sandra Milo, Giovanna Ralli.

Genghis Cohn (GB, 1993, colour, 79 minutes) BBC. Directed by Elijah Moshinsky; produced by Ruth Caleb and Mark Shivas; written by Stanley Price (from Romain Gary's novel *The Dance of Genghis Cohn*); main cast includes Anthony Sher, Robert Lindsay, Matthew Marsh, Diana Rigg, Paul Brooke.

Gentleman's Agreement (USA, 1947, b&w, 118 minutes) Twentieth Century-Fox. Directed by Elia Kazan; produced by Darryl F Zanuck; written by Moss Hart (from Laura Z Hobson's novel); main cast includes Gregory Peck, Dorothy McGuire, John Garfield, Anne Revere, Celeste Holm.

German Civilians and One Wehrmacht Officer are Ordered by Colonel Sears of US 4th Army to See Results of Regime at Liberated Ohrdruf Concentration Camp, Germany, 7 April 1945; Liberated Ohrdruf Concentration Sub-camp, Germany, 6 April 1945; Liberated Concentration Camp, Holzen, Eschershausen, Germany, 8 April 1945 (allocated title) (USA, 6–8/4/1945, b&w, 11 minutes) US Army Signal Corps (Sponsored by US Army Pictorial Service). Cameramen listed as Cummings, Connell and Technician/4 Andrew F. Kier. Part of a series of compilations of Concentration Camp material for use in Allied film productions. Held in the IWM Film and Video Archive as A70 514-14.

Die Geschwister Oppermann (*The Oppermann Family*) (West Germany/GB/Austria, 1983, colour, 220 minutes) BBC/ZDF/ORF. Directed and written by Egon Monk (from Lion Feuchtwanger's novel); main cast includes Wolfgang Kieling, Rosel Zech, Till Topf, Michael Degen, Ilona Grübel.

Ghosts of Rwanda (USA, 2004, colour, 120 minutes) FRONTLINE (WGBH Boston)/BBC/Silverbridge Productions. Directed, produced and written by Greg Barker.

Il Giardino Dei Finzi-Contini (*The Garden of the Finzi-Continis*) (Italy/West Germany, 1970, colour, 95 minutes) Documentarfilm/CCC Filmkunst. Directed by Vittorio De Sica; produced by Gianni Hecht Lucari and Arthur Cohn; written by Tullio Pinelli, Valerio Zurlini, Ugo Pirro, Vittorio Bonicelli and Alain Katz (from Giorgio Bassani's novel); main cast includes Dominique Sanda, Lino Capolicchio, Helmut Berger, Fabio Testi, Romolo Valli.

Goebbels: Master of Propaganda (GB, 1992, colour, 50 minutes) BBC. Directed and written by Laurence Rees.

The Great Dictator (USA, 1940, b&w, 129 minutes) United Artists. Directed, produced and written by Charlie Chaplin; main cast includes Charlie Chaplin, Paulette Goddard, Jack Oakie, Reginald Gardiner, Henry Daniell.

Hijoji Nippon (*Japan in Time of Emergency*) (Japan, 1933, b&w, 100 minutes) Osaka Daily Newspaper Film Department/Ministry for the Army. Directed by Iyokichi Kondo. Narrated by General Araki Sadao.

The Hitler Gang (USA, 1944, b&w, 101 minutes) Directed by John Farrow; produced by Buddy G. De Sylva; written by Frances Goodrich and Albert Hackett; main cast includes Bobby Watson, Roman Bohnen, Victor Varconi, Martin Kosleck, Luis Van Rooten, Alex Pope, Ivan Trieseult.

Holocaust (aka *Holocaust: The Story Of The Family Weiss*) (USA, 4/1978, colour, c. 570 minutes) NBC. Directed by Marvin J Chomsky; produced by Robert Berger and Herbert Brodkin; written by Gerard Green; main cast includes Tom Bell, Joseph Bottoms, Tovah Feldshuh, Rosemary Harris, Ian Holm, Meryl Streep, Fritz Weaver. James Woods.

The Holocaust on Film (*Parts 1 And 2*) (GB, 1998/1999, colour, 30 minutes each) Film Education (for BBC

Education). Directed, produced and written by Jane Dickson and Ian Wall.

Hotel Berlin (USA, 1945, b&w, 98 minutes) Warner Bros. Directed by Peter Godfrey; produced by Louis Edelman; written by Alvah Bessie and Joe Pagano (from a novel by Vicki Baum); main cast includes Faye Emerson, Helmut Dantine, Raymond Massey, Peter Lorre, Alan Hale, Andrea King.

Hotel Rwanda (GB/Italy/South Africa, 2004, colour, 121 minutes) Kigali Releasing/Lion's Gate/United Artists. Directed by Terry George; produced by A. Kitman Ho; written by Terry George and Keir Pearson; cinematography by Robert Fraisse; main cast includes Don Cheadle, Sophie Okonedo, Nick Nolte, Joaquin Phoenix.

The House of Rothschild (USA, 1934, b&w [with colour sequence], 87 minutes) Twentieth Century Film Corporation. Directed by Alfred Werker; produced by Daniel F. Zanuck, William Goetz and Raymond Griffith; written by Nunnally Johnson (from the play by George Hembert Westley); main cast includes George Arliss, Loretta Young, Boris Karloff, Robert Young, C. Aubrey Smith.

Human Rights, Human Wrongs (GB, 1993–2000, colour, season of short television documentaries; 10 minutes each) BBC. Produced by Rex Bloomstein.

I Was a Slave Labourer (GB, 1999, colour, 70 minutes) BBC. Directed by Luke Holland; main cast includes Rudy Kennedy (as himself).

Ich Klage An (*I Accuse*) (Germany, 1941, b&w, 124 minutes) Tobis-Film. Directed by Wolfgang Liebeneiner; written by Eberhard Frowein and Harald Bratt (from Helmuth Unger's novel *Sendung und Gewissen*); main cast includes Heidemarie Hatheyer, Paul Hartmann, Mathias Wieman.

Inside the Third Reich (USA, 1982, colour, c. 200 minutes) ABC Circle Films. Directed by Marvin J. Chomsky; produced by E. Jack Neuman; written by E. Jack Neuman (from Albert Speer's book); main cast includes Rutger Hauer, John Gielgud, Maria Schell, Blythe Danner, Derek Jacobi, Trevor Howard.

Jew Süss (GB, 1934, b&w, 109 minutes) Gaumont British. Directed by Lothar Mendes; produced by Michael Balcon; written by Dorothy Farnum and A. R. Rawlinson (from Lion Feuchtwanger's novel); main cast includes Conrad Veidt, Benita Hume, Frank Vosper, Cedric Hardwicke, Gerald Du Maurier.

Jona Che Visse Nella Balena (*Jonah Who Lived in the Whale*) (Italy, 1990, colour, 100 minutes) Focus Film/ Jean Vigo International/French Productions. Directed by Roberto Faenza; produced by Elda Ferri; written by Roberto Faenza, Hugh Fleetwood and Filippo Ottoni (from Jona Oberski's book *Kinderjaren*); main cast includes Jean-Hugues Anglade, Juliet Aubrey, Jenner Del Vecchio.

The Journey of Butterfly (USA, 1996, colour, 62 minutes) Bolthead Communications Group. Directed by Robert E. Frye; produced by Robert E. Frye, Marcy Lefkowitz, Daniel Bergmann, Peter Chafer.

Jud Süss (Germany, 1940, b&w, 85 minutes) Terra. Directed by Veit Harlan; written by Ludwig Metzger, Veit Harlan and Eberhard Wolfgang Möller; main cast includes Ferdinand Marian, Werner Krauss, Heinrich George, Kristina Söderbaum. Held in the IWM Film and Video Archive as MGH 3605 (viewing copy only, kindly provided by the Goethe Institute).

Judgment at Nuremberg (USA, 1961, b&w, 178 minutes) United Artists/Roxlom. Directed by Stanley Kramer; produced by Stanley Kramer; written by Abby Mann (from his television play); cinematography by Ernest Laszlo; main cast includes Spencer Tracy, Marlene Dietrich, Montgomery Clift, Burt Lancaster, Richard Widmark, Maximilian Schell, Judy Garland, William Shatner.

Judith (USA, 1965, colour, 109 minutes) Paramount Pictures/Cumulus Productions/Command Productions. Directed by Daniel Mann; produced by Kurt Unger; written by John Michael Hayes (from a story by Lawrence Durrell); main cast includes Sophia Loren, Peter Finch, Jack Hawkins.

Kapò (France/Italy, 1960, b&w, 118 minutes) Vides/Zebra/Francinex. Directed by Gillo Pontecorvo; produced by Moris Ergas; written by Gillo Pontecorvo and Franco Solinas; main cast includes Susan Strasberg; Laurent Terzieff; Emmanuelle Riva; Didi Perego; Gianni Garko.

Kinodokumentary O Zverstrakh Nemetsko-fashiskh Zakhvatchikov (*Cinema Documents of the Atrocities of the German Fascist Invaders*) (USSR, 1945, b&w, 60 minutes) Central Studio for the Documentary Film. Directed by M. V. Bolshintsov. Compilation prepared for use as evidence during the Nuremberg Tribunal by the Chief Prosecutor for the USSR.

Kino-khronika No 9 (USSR, 2/1943, b&w, 11 minutes) Central Newsreel Studio, Moscow. Produced by I. Setkina, assisted by Z. Dembovskaya; cameramen include A. Regachovsky and F. Chukhlebov. Held in the IWM Film and Video Archive as RNC 9.

Kitty – Return To Auschwitz (GB, 1979, colour, 65 minutes) Yorkshire Television. Directed by Peter Morley; produced by Kevin Sim; with Kitty Hart.

Kolberg (Germany, 1945, colour, c. 140 minutes) Ufa. Directed by Veit Harlan; produced by Wilhelm Sperber; written by Alfred Braun and Veit Harlan (with uncredited input by Josef Goebbels); main cast includes Heinrich George, Kristina Söderbaum, Paul Wegener. Held in the IWM Film and Video Archive as MGH 3602 (viewing copy only, kindly provided by the Goethe Institute).

Koniec Naszego Świata (*The End of Our World*) (Poland, 1964, b&w, 154 minutes) Film Polski. Directed by

Wanda Jakubowska; produced by Stanislaw Adler (based on a book by Tadeusz Holuj); main cast includes Lech Skolimowski, Teresa Wicinska, Wladyslaw Glabik, Tadeusz Holuj.

Liberation (GB, 1995, colour, 60 minutes) Channel 4. Produced and directed by Rex Bloomstein.

Lift Your Head, Comrade (GB, 1942, b&w, 15 minutes) Spectator (Sponsored by the Ministry of Information). Directed by Michael Hankinson; produced by Basil Wright; cinematography by A. H. Luff; sound by William S. Bland; edited by Ralph Kemplen; music by William Alwyn; written by Arthur Koestler. Held in the IWM Film and Video Archive as CVN 211.

The Life of Emile Zola (USA, 1937, b&w, 116 minutes) Directed by William Dieterle; produced by Henry Blanke; written by Norman Reilly Raine; main cast includes Paul Muni, Joseph Schildkraut, Gloria Holden, Donald Crisp.

The Longest Hatred (GB, 1989, colour, 150 minutes total) Thames Television/WGBH Boston. Produced and directed by Rex Bloomstein; written by Rex Bloomstein and Robert Wistrich.

Loving The Dead (GB, 1991, colour, 56 minutes) Sered Films. Directed, produced and written by Mira Hamermesh; cinematography by Jacek Mieroslawski.

The Maelstrom: A Family Chronicle (Netherlands, 1997, b&w and colour, 60 minutes). Directed and produced by Péter Forgács.

The Man In The Glass Booth (USA, 1975, colour, 117 minutes) American Film Theatre Picture Corporation/Ely Landau Organisation/Cinevision. Directed by Arthur Hiller; written by Edward Anhalt (from the play by Robert Shaw); main cast includes Maximilian Schell, Lois Nettleton, Luther Adler, Lawrence Pressman.

Man – One Family (GB, 1946, b&w, 16 minutes) Ealing Studios (Sponsored by the Ministry of Information). Directed by Ivor Montagu; produced by Sidney Cole; written by Ivor Montagu; edited by Sidney Cole, assisted by Seth Holt; music by Van Phillips; scientific advisers Professor J. B. S. Haldane and Doctor Julian Huxley; commentary by Doctor Julian Huxley. Held in the IWM Film and Video Archive as CVN 246.

Max and Helen (GB/USA, 1990, colour, 100 minutes) Citadel Entertainment. Directed by Philip Savile; produced by Steve McGlothen; written by Corey Blechman (from Simon Wiesenthal's book); main cast includes Treat Williams, Alice Krige, Martin Landau.

Memory of the Camps (GB, 1945 [revised 1985], b&w, 55 minutes) SHAEF/Frontline. Edited by Stewart McAllister and Peter Tanner; produced by Sidney Bernstein; draft treatment and commentary by Colin Wills and Richard Crossman; consultants include Alfred Hitchcock and Solly Zuckerman; revised version narrated by Trevor Howard. The abandoned mute SHAEF (British) documentary on German concentration camp atrocities, intended for screening to German audiences. Original footage held in the IWM Film and Video Archive as A70 515; the revised version was specially completed, and voiced by Trevor Howard, for US television broadcast on 7 May 1985. This is also held in the IWM Film and Video Archive, as MGH 3320A.

Mr Emmanuel (GB, 1944, b&w, 97 minutes) Two Cities Films. Directed by Harold French; produced by William Sistrom; script by Gordon Wellesley and Norman Ginsburg; main cast includes Felix Aylmer, Greta Gynt, Walter Rilla.

Music Box (USA, 1989, colour, 126 minutes) Guild/Carolco. Directed by [Constantin] Costa-Gavras; produced by Irwin Winkler; written by Joe Eszterhas; main cast includes Armin Mueller-Stahl, Jessica Lange, Frederic Forrest, Donald Moffat, Lukas Haas.

A Napfény Íze (Sunshine) (Austria/Hungary/Canada/Germany, 1999, colour, 173 minutes). Directed by István Szabó; produced by Andras Hamori and Robert Lantos; written by István Szabó and Israel Horovitz; main cast includes Ralph Fiennes, Rosemary Harris, Rachel Weisz, Jennifer Ehle, Deborah Kara Unger.

Nazi Concentration Camps (USA, 1945, b&w, 59 minutes) US Army Signal Corps (Sponsored by the US Council for the Prosecution of Axis Criminality). Directed by George Stevens.

The Nazi Plan aka *The Rise of the NSDAP* (USA, 1945, b&w, 161 minutes) (Sponsored by the US Chief of Counsel, Nuremberg Tribunal). Compiled by Commander E. P. Kellogg (USNR). Held in the IWM Film and Video Archive as FOY 3.

The Nazis: A Warning From History (GB, 1997, colour, 350 minutes total) BBC. Directed by Laurence Rees and Tilman Remme; produced and written by Laurence Rees; narrated by Samuel West.

The Negro Soldier (USA, 1944, b&w, 45 minutes) War Department Special Service Division Army Service Forces with the cooperation of the US Army Signal Corps (Sponsored by the War Department). Directed by Stuart Heisler; produced by Frank Capra; written by Carlton Moss; music performed by Army Air Force Orchestra; featuring Carlton Moss. Held in the IWM Film and Video Archive as USA 2.

The Night Porter (Il Portiere di Notte) (Italy, 1973, colour, 118 minutes) Lotar Films. Directed by Liliana Cavani; produced by Robert Gordon Edwards and Esa Simone; written by Liliana Cavani and Italo Moscati; main cast includes Dirk Bogarde, Charlotte Rampling, Philippe Leroy.

The Nightmare Years (USA, 1989, colour, 384 minutes) Turner Home Entertainment. Directed by Anthony

Page; produced by Graham Ford; written by Ian Curteis (from a screen story by Christian Williams, Bob Woodward and Ian Curteis, based on books by William L. Schirer); main cast includes Sam Waterston, Marthe Keller, Kurtwood Smith.

None Shall Escape (USA, 1943, b&w, 85 minutes) Columbia Pictures. Directed by Andre de Toth; produced by Samuel Bischoff; written by Lester Cole; main cast includes Alexander Knox, Marsha Hunt, Henry Travers, Dorothy Knox.

Nuit et Brouillard (*Night and Fog*) (France, 1955, colour [part b&w], 31 minutes) Argos/Como. Directed by Alain Resnais; music by Hanns Eisler; written by Jean Cayrol.

Obchod na korze (*The Shop on Main Street* aka *A Shop on the High Street*) (Czechoslovakia, 1965, b&w, 128 minutes) Filmové Studio Barrandov. Directed by Ján Kadár and Elmar Klos; written by Ján Kadár, Elmar Klos and Ladislav Grosman; main cast includes Ida Kaminska, Jozef Kroner, Hana Slivková, Martin Hollý, Adám Matejka.

L'Oro di Roma (*The Gold of Rome*) (Italy/France, 1961, b&w , 105 minutes) Ager Film/Sancro Film/CIRAC/Lux Film. Directed by Carlo Lizzani; produced by Henryk Chrosicki and Giuliani G. De Negri; written by Luca Battistrada, Giuliani G. De Negri and Carlo Lizzani; main cast includes Anna Maria Ferrero, Jean Sorel, Gérard Blain, Andrea Cecchi.

Ostatni etap (*The Last Stage* aka *The Last Stop*) (Poland, 1948, b&w, 120 minutes) Film Polski. Directed and produced by Wanda Jakubowska; written by Wanda Jakubowska and Gerda Schneider; main cast includes Barbara Drapinska, Tatiana Górecka, Antonina Górecka, Wanda Bartówna, Huguette Faget.

Panorama: Journey Into Darkness (GB, 1994, colour, ca 50 minutes) BBC. Directed by David Harrison; produced by David Harrison and Rizu Hamid; camera by Glenn Middleton; reporter Fergal Keane.

Panorama: Killers (GB, 2004, colour, 58 minutes). BBC. Produced by Darren Kemp; edited by Mike Robinson; camera by Fred Scott; film editor Peter Norrey; reporter Fergal Keane.

Pasażerka (*The Passenger*) (Poland, 1961–63, b&w, 63 minutes) Zespoly Filmowe. Directed by Andrzej Munk and Witold Lesiewicz; written by Andrzej Munk, Zofia Posmysz-Piasecka; cinematography by Krzysztof Winiewicz; music by Tadeusz Baird; main cast includes Aleksandra Slaska, Anna Ciepielewska. Held in the IWM Film and Video Archive as FEA 37. Director Andrzej Munk was killed in a car accident in 1961, leaving the film unfinished; it was later completed (using still photography in lieu of the missing footage) by Witold Lesiewicz.

Pasqualino Settebellezze (*Seven Beauties*) (Italy, 1975, colour, 115 minutes) Medusa Produzione. Directed and written by Lina Wertmüller; produced by Lina Wertmüller, Giancarlo Giannini and Arrigo Colombo; main cast includes Giancarlo Giannini, Fernando Rey, Shirley Stoler, Piero di Iorio.

Pastor Hall (GB, 1940, b&w, 97 minutes) Charter Film Productions. Directed by Roy Boulting; produced by John Boulting; script by Leslie Arliss, Haworth Bromley and Anna Reiner; main cast includes Wilfrid Lawson, Nova Pilbeam, Seymour Hicks, Marius Goring.

...a pátý jezdec je strach (*...and the fifth horseman is fear*) (Czechoslovakia, 1964, b&w, 100 minutes) Filmové Studio Barrandov. Directed by Zbyněk Brynych; written by Hana Belohradska, Zbyněk Brynych, Ota Koval and Ester Krumbachová (based on *Bez krásy, bez límce* by Hana Belohradska); main cast includes Jiří Adamíra, Miroslav Machacek, Josef Vinklar, Jana Brezková.

The Pawnbroker (USA, 1965, b&w, 114 minutes) Landau-Unger. Directed by Sidney Lumet; produced by Worthington Miner; written by David Friedkin and Morton Fine (from the novel by Edward Lewis Wallant); main cast includes Rod Steiger, Brock Peters, Geraldine Fitzgerald, Jaime Sanchez.

The People's Century: Master Race (GB/USA, 1998, colour, 60 minutes) BBC/WGBH Boston. Directed and produced by Jonathan Lewis; produced by David Espar, Zvi Dor-Ner (WGBH) and Peter Pagnamenta (BBC); narrated by Alfre Woodard.

The Pianist (Poland/France/GB/Germany/Netherlands, 2002, colour, 150 minutes) A Focus Features presentation. Directed by Roman Polański; produced by Roman Polański, Robert Benmussa and Alain Sarde; written by Ronald Harwood (from Władysław Szpilman's book); main cast includes Adrien Brody, Thomas Kretschmann, Frank Finlay, Maureen Lipman, Emilia Fox.

Prisoners of Conscience (GB, 1987–92, colour, season of short documentaries 5 minutes each) BBC. Produced by Rex Bloomstein.

The Producers (USA, 1968, colour, 88 minutes) MGM/Springtime Productions/Crossbow Productions. Directed and written by Mel Brooks; produced by Sidney Glazier; main cast includes Zero Mostel, Gene Wilder, Kenneth Mars, Estelle Winwood, Dick Shawn.

The Roots of Evil (GB, 1997, colour, 150 minutes total) Channel 4. Produced by Rex Bloomstein.

Die Rothschilds aka *Die Rothschilds: Aktien auf Waterloo* (*The Rothschilds: Shares at Waterloo*) (Germany, 1940, b&w, 92 minutes) Ufa. Directed by Erich Waschneck; produced by C. M. Köhn; written by C. M. Köhn and G. T. Buchholz; main cast includes Michael Bohnen, Ursula Deinert, Walter Franck.

Scenes in the Concentration Camp at Belsen, Germany, After its Liberation by 8th Corps (allocated title)

(GB, 4/1945; b&w, ca 40 minutes total) Army Film and Photographic Unit. Original unedited footage shot by AFPU cameramen Sergeant C. M. Lewis and Sergeant William Lawrie. Held in the IWM Film and Video Archive as A70 304-1 to 4 and A70 308-3 to 4.

Scenes of the Release of Prisoners From Concentration Camp in Southern Italy (allocated title) (GB, 29/9/1943, b&w, ca 4 minutes) Army Film and Photographic Unit. Cameraman Sergeant Hopkinson (AFPU). Footage shot near Cosenza, Italy. Held in the IWM Film and Video Archive as AYY 556/1-3.

Schindler's List (USA, 1993, b&w [part colour], 195 minutes) Universal Pictures/Amblin Entertainment. Directed by Steven Spielberg; produced by Steven Spielberg, Gerald R. Molen and Branko Lustig; written by Steven Zaillian (from the novel *Schindler's Ark* by Thomas Keneally); main cast includes Liam Neeson, Ralph Fiennes, Ben Kingsley, Embeth Davitz, Caroline Goodall.

The Seventh Cross (USA, 1944, b&w, 112 minutes) Directed by Fred Zinnemann; produced by Pandro S. Bergman; written by Helen Deutch (from the novel by Anna Seghers); main cast includes Spencer Tracy, Signe Hasso, Hume Cronyn, Jessica Tandy, Agnes Moorhead.

Ship of Fools (USA, 1965, b&w, 150 minutes) Columbia Pictures/Stanley Kramer Productions. Directed and produced by Stanley Kramer; written by Abby Mann (from the novel by Katherine Anne Porter); main cast includes Vivien Leigh, Simone Signoret, Oskar Werner, Heinz Ruhmann, Lee Marvin, Michael Dunn.

Shoah (France, 1985, colour, 566 minutes total [Part 1 274 minutes, Part 2 294 minutes]) Les Films Aleph. Directed by Claude Lanzmann; cinematography by Dominique Chapuis, Jimmy Glasberg and William Lubtchansky; edited by Ziva Postec and Anna Ruiz.

Silence (GB, 1998, colour, 10 minutes) Halo Productions. Directed and produced by Orly Yadin and Sylvie Bringas; music by Noa Ain; narrated by Tana Ross. Held in the IWM Film and Video Archive as MGH 4602.

Sobibor, 14 Octobre 1943, 16 Heures (France, 2001, colour, 95 minutes) France 2 Cinéma/Les Films Aleph/ Why Not Productions. Directed by Claude Lanzmann; featuring Yehuda Lerner.

Soldiers of 15th (Scottish) Division Capture Celle, Germany (Parts 1 and 2) (allocated title) (GB, 12/4/1945, b&w, ca 5 minutes) Army Film and Photographic Unit. Shot by AFPU cameramen Sergeant C. M. Lewis (Parts 1 and 2) and Sergeant William Lawrie (Parts 3 and 4). Held in the IWM Film and Video Archive as A70 297-3 and A70 297-4. Includes footage of the liberation of Stalag XIB.

Sophie's Choice (USA, 1982, colour, 157 minutes) Universal Pictures. Directed by Alan J. Pakula; written by Alan J. Pakula (from William Styron's novel); main cast includes Meryl Streep, Kevin Kline, Peter MacNicol, Rita Karin, Josh Mostel.

Take a Deep Breath (Poland, 1962, b&w, 15 minutes) Directed by Mira Hamermesh; adapted from a short story by Ryszard Palczynski.

These are the Men (GB, 1943, b&w, 12 minutes) Strand (Sponsored by the Ministry of Information). Produced by Donald Taylor; devised and compiled by Alan Osbiston and Dylan Thomas (from an idea by Robert Neumann); commentary by James McKechnie and Bryan Herbert. Held in the IWM Film and Video Archive as COI 230.

To Be or Not To Be (USA, 1942, b&w, 99 minutes) Directed by Ernst Lubitsch; produced by Alexander Korda and Ernst Lubitsch; written by Edwin Justus Mayer (from a story by Ernst Lubitsch and Melchior Lengyel); main cast includes Jack Benny, Carol Lombard, Robert Stack, Stanley Ridges, Lionel Atwill, Sig Rumann; remade in 1983 by Mel Brooks, featuring Mel Brooks, Anne Bancroft and Tim Matheson.

Die Todesmühlen (Death Mills) (USA/Germany [Allied Military Government], 1945, b&w, 22 minutes). Produced by the Office of War Information (Sponsored by the US Office of Military Government in Germany). Directed by Hanuš Burger; written by Oskar Seidlin; edited by Sam Winston; consultant Billy Wilder; commentary spoken by Anton Reimer. Held in the IWM Film and Video Archive as USA 78.

Train de vie (Train of Life/Trenul vietii) (France/Romania, 1999, colour, 103 minutes) Directed and written by Radu Mihaileanu; main cast includes Lionel Abelanski, Clement Harari, Rufus, Michel Muller, Agathe de la Fontaine.

Transport z ráje (Transport from Paradise) (Czechoslovakia, 1962, b&w, 94 minutes) Ceskoslovenský Státní Film/Filmové Studio Barrandov. Directed by Zbyněk Brynych; written by Zbyněk Brynych and Arnost Lustig (based on Lustig's novel *Night and Hope*); main cast includes Zdenek Stepánek, Ilja Prachar, Jiri Vrstála.

La Tregua (The Truce) (Italy, 1996, colour, 140 minutes) Directed by Francesco Rosi; produced by Guido De Laurentiis and Leo Pescarolo; written by Tonino Guerra, Sandro Petraglia, Francesco Rosi and Stefano Rulli (from Primo Levi's book); main cast includes John Turturro, Massimo Ghini, Rade Serbedzija, Teco Celio.

Triumph Des Willens (Triumph of the Will) (Germany, 1935, b&w, 107 minutes) Leni Riefenstahl Studio Film (Sponsored by the National Socialist German Workers' Party [NSDAP]). Directed by Leni Riefenstahl. Held in the IWM Film and Video Archive as GWY 533.

Triumph of the Spirit (USA, 1989, colour, 120 minutes) Guild/Nova International. Directed by Robert M.

Young; produced by Arnold Kopelson and Shimon Arama; written by Andrzej Krakowski and Laurence Heath (from a story by Shimon Arama and Zion Haen); main cast includes Willem Dafoe, Edward James Olmos, Robert Loggia, Wendy Gazelle.

The True Glory (GB/USA, 10/1945, b&w, 120 minutes) Sponsored by the GB Ministry of Information, US Office of War Information, and approved by the Joint Anglo-American Film Planning Committee. Directed by Carol Reed and Garson Kanin; written by Irwin Shaw; music composed by William Alwyn. Compiled using footage from combat cameramen of USA, Canada, France, Poland, Belgium, Netherlands, Czechoslovakia, Norway, the UK and Germany. Commentary spoken by many voices including Peter Ustinov, Richard Attenborough, Garson Kanin, Carol Reed, Sam Levine and Claude Dauphin. Held in the IWM Film and Video Archive as CVN 319.

Understanding the Holocaust (GB, 1997, colour, 50 minutes) Nucleus Productions. Produced by Rex Bloomstein and Robert Wistrich.

Urgent Action (GB, 1988, colour, documentaries 5 minutes each) BBC. Produced by Rex Bloomstein.

Vaghe Stelle Dell'orsa (*Sandra* aka *Sandra of a Thousand Delights*) (Italy, 1965, b&w, 100 minutes) Vides Cinematografica. Directed by Luchino Visconti; produced by Franco Cristaldi; written by Luchino Visconti, Suso Cecchi D'Amico and Enrico Medioli; main cast includes Claudia Cardinale, Jean Sorel, Michael Craig, Renzo Ricci.

Views of the Largest Concentration Camp in Holland South of s'Hertogenbosch, Just Outside Vught (allocated title) (GB, 31/10/1944, b&w, ca 1 minute) Army Film and Photographic Unit. Shot by Sergeant Gordon. Held in the IWM Film and Video Archive as A70 187-6.

La vita è bella (*Life is Beautiful*) (Italy, 1997, colour, 122 minutes) Melampo/Buena Vista. Directed by Roberto Benigni; produced by Elda Ferri and Gianluigi Braschi; written by Vincenzo Cerami and Roberto Benigni; main cast includes Roberto Benigni, Nicoletta Braschi, Giorgio Cantarini, Giustino Durano.

Un Vivant Qui Passe: Auschwitz 1943, Theresienstadt 1944 (*A Visitor from the Living*) (France/Germany, 1997, colour, 65 minutes) Le Sept-Arte/Les Films Aleph/MTM Cineteve. Directed and produced by Claude Lanzmann; featuring Maurice Rossel and Claude Lanzmann.

Les Voix de la Muette (*If the Walls Could Speak*) (France, 1998, colour, 52 minutes). Directed, produced, photographed and recorded by Daniela Zanzotto; edited by Dominique Lutier; associate producer Gary A. Holding; additional photography by Tinge Krishnan; additional sound by Sara Qualter.

Voyages (France/Poland/Belgium, 1999, colour, 110 minutes) Les Films du Poisson. Directed by Emmanuel Finkiel; produced by Yael Fogiel; written by Emmanuel Finkiel; main cast includes Shulamit Adar, Liliane Rovère and Esther Gorintin.

Wannseekonferenz (West Germany/Austria, 1984, colour, 85 minutes) Bavarian Broadcasting Corporation/Intrafilm/ORF. Directed by Heinz Schirk; produced by Siegfried B. Gloker; written by Paul Mommertz; main cast includes Gerd Böckmann, Dietrich Mattausch.

War and Remembrance (USA, 1988, colour, 900 minutes) ABC/Paramount Pictures Television/Dan Curtis Productions. Directed by Dan Curtis; produced by Barbara Steele, Dan Curtis and Branko Lustig; written by Earl W. Wallace, Dan Curtis and Herman Wouk (from Wouk's novel); main cast includes Robert Mitchum, Jane Seymour, Hart Bochner, Victoria Tennant, John Gielgud.

War Pictorial News No 190 (GB, 25/12/1944, b&w, 8 minutes) War Pictorial News (Sponsored by Ministry of Information, Middle East) Edited by Charles Martin; commentary by Rex Keating. Newsreel issue. Held in the IWM Film and Video Archive as WPN 190.

War Pictorial News No 210 (GB, 14/5/1945, b&w, 10 minutes) War Pictorial News (Sponsored by the Ministry of Information, Middle East) Edited by Charles Martin; commentary by Rex Keating. Newsreel issue. Held in the IWM Film and Video Archive as WPN 210.

Warwork News No 33 [Main] (GB, 1943, b&w, 11 minutes) British Paramount News (Sponsored by the Ministry of Supply). Held in the IWM Film and Video Archive as S15 33.

Welt Im Film Nr 5 [Main] (GB/Germany [Allied Military Government], 15/6/1945, b&w, 19 minutes). Also initially screened under the title *KZ*. Held in the IWM Film and Video Archive as WIF 5.

The Winds of War (USA, 1983, colour, 883 minutes total) Paramount Pictures Television/Dan Curtis Productions. Directed and produced by Dan Curtis; written by Herman Wouk (from his novel); main cast includes Robert Mitchum, Ali MacGraw, Jan Michael Vincent.

Women of Courage (GB, 1980, colour, 52 minutes each) Yorkshire Television. Directed by Peter Morley.

The World at War Episode 20: Genocide (GB, 1974, colour, 52 minutes) Produced by Jeremy Isaacs and Michael Darlow; written by Charles Bloomberg; music by Carl Davis; Chief Historical Adviser Dr Noble Frankland DFC; narrated by Laurence Olivier.

The Young Lions (USA, 1958, b&w, 167 minutes) Twentieth Century-Fox. Directed by Edward Dmytryk; produced by Al Lichtman; written by Edward Anhalt (from Irwin Shaw's novel); main cast includes Marlon Brando, Montgomery Clift, Dean Martin, Hope Lange, Barbara Rush, Maximilian Schell, Lee Van Cleef.

BIBLIOGRAPHY

Ackerman, John (ed.) (1995) *Dylan Thomas: The Film Scripts*. London: J. M. Dent.

Adorno, Theodor (1965) *Erziehung nach Auschwitz [Education After Auschwitz]*. Radio broadcast.

____ (1973) *Negative Dialectics*, trans. E. B. Ashton. New York: Seabury Press.

____ (1998) *Critical Models, Interventions and Catchwords*, trans. Henry W. Pickford. New York: Columbia University Press [contains a translation of *Education After Auschwitz*].

____ (2003) *Can One Live After Auschwitz?: A Philosophical Reader*. Stanford, CA: Stanford University Press.

Agel, Henri (1961) *Le cinéma et le Sacre*. Paris: Éditions du Cerf.

____ (1981) *Cinéma et nouvelle naissance*. Paris: Albin Michel.

____ (1987) *Un Art de la Celebration: Le cinéma a Flaherty de Rouch*. Paris: Éditions du Cerf.

Albrecht, Gerd (1969) *Nationalsozialistische Filmpolitik*. Stuttgart: Ferdinand Enke Verlag.

____ (1979) *Film im Dritten Reich: Eine Dokumentation*. Karlsruhe: DOKU-Verlag.

Améry, Jean (1980) *At the Mind's Limits : Contemplations by a Survivor on Auschwitz and Its Realities*, trans. Sidney Rosenfeld and Stella P. Rosenfeld. Bloomington, IN: Indiana University Press [translation of *Jenseits von Schuld und Sühne*, 1966].

Amishai-Maisels, Ziva (1993) *Depiction and Interpretation: The Influence of the Holocaust on the Visual Arts*. Oxford: Pergamon Press.

Anstey, Edgar (1943) 'These are the Men', *The Spectator*, 9 April, 338.

Arendt, Hannah (1951) *The Origins of Totalitarianism*. New York: Harcourt, Brace.

____ (1963) *Eichmann in Jerusalem: A Report on the Banality of Evil*. New York: Viking.

Army Film and Photographic Unit (undated) 'Notes for Instructors', AFPU Training Course, Pinewood Studios, held in Imperial War Museum, Department of Documents.

Ascherson, Neal (1990) 'La Controverse autour de *Shoah*', in Claude Lanzmann (ed.) *Au sujet de Shoah, le film de Claude Lanzmann*. Paris: Ouvrage collectif, Éditions Belin.

Avisar, Ilan (1985) 'Christian Ideology and Jewish Genocide in American Holocaust Movies', in Sanford Pinsker (ed.) *Holocaust Studies Annual, Vol. 3: Literature, the Arts, and the Holocaust*. Greenwood, FL: Penkevill, 21–42.

____ (1989) *Screening the Holocaust: Cinema's Images of the Unimaginable*. Bloomington, IN: University of Indiana Press.

____ (1997) 'Holocaust Movies and the Politics of Collective Memory', in Alvin H. Rosenfeld (ed.) *Thinking about the Holocaust: After Half a Century*. Bloomington, IN: Indiana University Press.

Baron, Lawrence (2002) 'Holocaust Iconography in American Feature Films About Neo-Nazis', in *Film & History*, 32, 2, 38–47.

Barta, Tony (1996) 'Consuming the Holocaust: Memory Production and Popular Film', in *Contention: Debates in Society, Culture and Science*, 5, 2, 161–75.

Bartov, Omer (1996) *Murder in our Midst: The Holocaust, Industrial Killing, and Representation*. New York: Oxford University Press.

Bassani, Giorgio (1977) *The Garden of the Finzi-Continis*, trans. William Weaver. New York: Harcourt, Brace, Jovanovich.

Baudrillard, Jean (1994) *Simulacra and Simulation*, trans. Sheila Faria Glaser. Ann Arbor: University of Michigan Press.

Bauer, Alfred (1950) *Deutsche Spielfilmalmanach 1929–1950* (second edition). Munich: Filmladen Christoph Winterberg.

Bauer, Yehuda (1978) *The Holocaust in Historical Perspective*. London: Sheldon Press.

____ (1982) *A History of the Holocaust*. New York: Franklin Watts.

Bauman, Zygmunt (1989) *Modernity and the Holocaust*. Ithaca, NY and London: Cornell University Press.

Beauvoir, Simone de (1990) Preface to Claude Lanzmann, *Shoah: The Complete Text of the Acclaimed Holocaust Film*. New York: Da Capo.

Belohradská, Hana (1962) *Bez krásy, bez límce*. Prague: Československý spisovatel.

Benigni, Robert and Vincenzo Cerami (1998) *Life is Beautiful* (*La vita è bella*), trans. Lisa Taruschio. New York: Hyperion.

Bensoussan, Georges (1998) *Auschwitz en Heritage? D'un bon usage de la mémorie*. Paris: Éditions des Mille et Une Nuits.

Berenbaum, Michael (1993) *The World Must Know: A History of the Holocaust as told in the United States Holocaust Memorial Museum*. New York: Little, Brown.

Berkley, George E. (1968) *Hitler's Gift: The Story of Theresienstadt*. Boston: Branden Books.

Berkman, Ted (1962) *Cast a Giant Shadow: The Story of Mickey Marcus Who Died to Save Jerusalem*. Garden City, NY: Doubleday and Co.

Bernard-Donals, Michael F. (2001) *Between Witness and Testimony : The Holocaust and the Limits of Representation*. Albany: State University of New York Press.

Bernstein, Sidney: Bernstein Collection, Imperial War Museum Department of Documents, Ref No. 65/17/1–12.

Boelcke, Willi A. (ed.) (1966) *Kriegspropaganda 1939–1941: Geheime Ministerkonferenzen im Reichspropagandaministerium*. Stuttgart: Deutsche Verlags-Anstalt.

_____ (ed.) (1970) *The Secret Conferences of Dr Goebbels, October 1939–March 1943*, trans. Ewald Osers. London: Weidenfeld and Nicolson.

Borowski, Tadeusz (1992) *This Way for the Gas, Ladies and Gentlemen*, trans. Michael Kandel. London: Penguin.

Brown, Nancy Thomas (2002) 'From Weimar to Hollywood: Christian Images and the Portrayal of the Jew', *Film & History*, 32, 2, 14–23.

Burrin, Philippe (1994) *Hitler and the Jews: The Genesis of the Holocaust*, trans. Patsy Southgate. London: Edward Arnold.

Carr, Steven Alan (2001) *Hollywood and Antisemitism: A Cultural History up to World War II*. Cambridge: Cambridge University Press.

Carruthers, Susan L. (2001) 'Compulsory Viewing: Concentration Camp Film and German Re-education', *Millennium: Journal of International Studies*, 30, 3, 733–59.

Caven, Hannah (2001) 'Horror in Our Time: Images of the Concentration Camps in the British Media, 1945', *Historical Journal of Film, Radio and Television*, 21, 3, 205–53.

Cayrol, Jean (1947) *Poèmes de la nuit et brouillard*. Paris: Éditions Pierre Seghers.

_____ (1950) *Lazare parmi nous*. Neuchatel: Éditions de la Baconnière.

_____ (1956) 'Nous avons conçu *Nuit et Brouillard* comme in dispositif d'alert' [We Conceived *Night and Fog* as a Warning], *Les Lettres Françaises*, 606, 9 February.

_____ (1995) *Poèmes de la Nuit et du Brouillard: Suivis, de Larmes Publiques*. Paris: Éditions du Seuil.

Celli, Carlo (2000) 'The Representation of Evil in Roberto Benigni's *Life is Beautiful*', *Journal of Popular Film and Television*, 28, 2, 74–9.

Chamberlin, Brewster S. (1981) '*Todesmühlen*, Ein früher Versuch zur Massen-"Umerzeihung" im besetzten Deutschland 1945–1946', in *Vierteljahrheft für Zeitgeschichte XXIX Heft*, 3 July, 420–36.

Chanan, Michael (2004) 'Documentary and Social Memory', *Journal of British Cinema and Television*, 1, 1, 61–77.

Chaplin, Charles (1978) *My Autobiography*. Harmondsworth: Penguin.

Chapman, James (1998) *The British at War: Cinema, State and Propaganda, 1939–1945*. London: I. B. Tauris.

Clay, Lucius D. (1950) *Decision in Germany*. New York: Country Life Press.

Clendinnan, Inga (1999) *Reading the Holocaust*. Cambridge: Cambridge University Press.

Clinefelter, Joan (2000) 'A Cinematic Construction of Nazi Antisemitism: The Documentary Der ewige Jude', in Robert C. Reimer (ed.) *Cultural History Through a Nazi Lens: Essays on the Cinema of the Third Reich*. Rochester, NY: Camden House, 133–54.

Cohen, Sarah Blacher (ed.) (1983) *From Hester Street to Hollywood*. Bloomington, IN: Indiana University Press.

Colombat, André Pierre (1993) *The Holocaust in French Film*. Metuchen, NJ and London: Scarecrow Press.

Committee for the History of the Second World War (1955) *Résistance – Libération – Déportation* [exhibition and catalogue]. Paris: Musée pédagogique.

Concentration Camp Film 1945–1946. The National Archives, Public Record Office, Kew, Ref. No. FO 939/72.

Coultass, Clive (1989a) 'The Ministry of Information and Documentary Film, 1939–45', in Imperial War Museum Review, No. 4, 103–11.

_____ (1989b) *Images for Battle: British Film and the Second World War, 1939–1945*. London: Associated University Press.

Culbert, David (1985) 'American Film Policy in the Re-education of Germany after 1945', in Nicholas Pronay and Keith Wilson (eds) *The Political Re-education of Germany and Her Allies After 1945*. London: Croom Helm, 173–202.

____ (2002) 'The Impact of Anti-Semitic Film Propaganda on German Audiences: *Jew Süss* and *The Wandering Jew*', in Richard A. Etlin (ed.) *Art, Culture and Media under the Third Reich*. Chicago: Chicago University Press, 139–57.

Daney, Serge (1992) 'Le Travelling de *Kapo*', *Trafic*, 4, 7, 11 [English translation by Laurent Kretzschmar 'The Tracking Shot in *Kapo*' can be found online on the *Senses of Cinema* website, at http://www.sensesofcinema.com/contents/04/30/kapo_daney.html (31 May 2005).

Davies, Fred (2000) *Film, History and the Holocaust*. Portland, OR and London: Vallentine-Mitchell.

Davies, Ian (ed.) (2000) *Teaching the Holocaust: Educational Dimensions, Principles and Practice*. New York: Continuum.

Davis, Todd F. and Kenneth Womack (2001) 'The List is Life: *Schindler's List* as Ethical Construct', in Todd F. Davis and Kenneth Womack (ed.) *Mapping the Ethical Turn: A Reader in Ethics, Culture and Literary Theory*. Charlottesville, VA: University Press of Virginia, 151–64.

Dawidowicz, Lucy S. (1975) *The War Against the Jews, 1933–1945*. New York: Holt, Rinehart and Winston.

____ (1978) 'Visualising the Warsaw Ghetto: Nazi Images of the Jews Refiltered by the BBC', *Shoah: a Review of Holocaust Studies and Commemorations*, 1, 1, 5–6; 17–18.

Deichmann, Thomas (1997) 'The Picture that Fooled the World', *Living Marxism*, February, 24–31.

Delage, Christian (2001) 'L'image comme preuve. L'expérience du procès de Nuremberg', *Vingtième siècle: Revue d'histoire*, 72, October–December, 63–78.

Deutsche Propagandaministerium (1940) *Illustrierte Film-Kurier 279/1940, November 27, 1940*. Programme booklet published to accompany the film *Der ewige Jude* [Translation by Stig Hornshøj-Møller online at http://www.holocaust-history.org/der-ewige-jude/program.shtml].

Dodd, Thomas J. (1945) 'Trials of the Major War Criminals Before the International Military Tribunal', Record Group 238, National Archives Collection of World War II War Crimes Records.

Doherty, Thomas (1987) 'Representing the Holocaust: Claude Lanzmann's *Shoah*', *Film & History*, 17, 1, 2–8.

Doneson, Judith E. (1978) 'The Jew as a Female Figure in Holocaust Film', *Shoah: a Review of Holocaust Studies and Commemorations*, 1, 1, 11–13.

____ (1989) 'History and Television, 1978–1988: A Survey of Dramatizations of the Holocaust', *Dimensions*, 4, 3, 23–7.

____ (1996) 'Holocaust Revisited: A Catalyst for Memory or Trivialization?', *The Annals of the American Academy of Political and Social Science*, November, 70–7.

____ (2002) *The Holocaust in American Film* (second edition). New York: Syracuse University Press.

Douglas, Lawrence (1995) 'Film as Witness: Screening Nazi Concentration Camps before the Nuremberg Tribunal', *Yale Law Journal*, 105, November, 449–81.

Drame, Claudine (1996) 'Representer l'irreprésentable: les camps nazis dans les actualités francaises de 1945', *Cinémathèque*, 10, Autumn, 12–27.

Eley, Geoff and Atina Grossman (1997) 'Watching *Schindler's List*', *New German Criticism*, 71, 41–62.

Ellerman, Anne Elizabeth (1897) *The Prince Minister of Württemberg*. London: William Anderson.

Elsaesser, Thomas (1993) 'Portrait of the Artist as a Young Woman', *Sight and Sound*, 3, 2, 15–18.

____ (1996) 'Subject Positions, Speaking Positions: From *Holocaust, Our Hitler* and *Heimat* to *Shoah* and *Schindler's List*', in Vivian Sobchack (ed.) *The Persistence of History: Cinema, Television and the Modern Event*. London: Routledge, 145–83.

____ with Michael Wedel (ed.) (1999) *The BFI Companion to German Film*. London: British Film Institute.

Epstein, Leslie (1989) 'Blue Skies: Reflections on Hollywood and the Holocaust', *Tikkun*, 4, 5, September–October, 11–22.

Erens, Patricia (1984) *The Jew in American Cinema*. Bloomington, IN: Indiana University Press.

Erhart, Julia (2000) 'From Nazi Whore to Good German Mother: Revisiting Resistance in the Holocaust Film', *Screen*, 41, 4, 388–403.

Etcherelli, Claire (1967) *Élise, ou la vraie vie*. Paris: Denoël.

Etlin, Richard A. (ed.) (2002) *Art, Culture and Media under the Third Reich*. Chicago: Chicago University Press.

Feingold, Henry (1978) 'Four Days in April: A Review of NBC's Dramatisation of the *Holocaust*', *Shoah: a Review of Holocaust Studies and Commemorations*, 1, 1, 15–17.

Felman, Shoshana (1990) 'A l'âge du témoignage', in Claude Lanzmann (ed.) *Au sujet de Shoah, le film de Claude Lanzmann*. Paris: Ouvrage collectif, Éditions Belin.

____ (1994) 'Film as Witness: Claude Lanzmann's *Shoah*', in Geoffrey H. Hartman (ed.) *Holocaust Remembrance: The Shapes of Memory*. Oxford: Blackwell, 90–103.

Feuchtwanger, Lion (1918) *Jud Süss*. Munich: G. Muller.

____ (1933) *Die Geschwister Oppermann*. Amsterdam: Querida Press.

Film & History, 32, 1 and 2, 2002 [two special issues covering the Holocaust in cinema].

Films for Liberated Territories: Investigation of War Atrocities – Factual Film Report on German Concentration Camps with Catalogue of Films for Liberated Territories (1945). The National Archives, Public Record Office, Kew, Ref. No. FO 1/636.

Flanzbaum, Hilene (ed.) (1999) *The Americanization of the Holocaust*. Baltimore: Johns Hopkins University Press.

____ (2001) '"But Wasn't It Terrific?"': A Defense of Liking *Life is Beautiful*', *Yale Journal of Criticism: Interpretation in the Humanities*, 14, 1, 273–86.

Forgács, Péter with Bill Nichols (2003) 'The Memory of Loss: Saga of Family Life and Social Hell', *Film Quarterly*, 56, 4, 4–6.

Frank, Anne (1947) *Het Achterhuis*. Amsterdam: Contact.

____ (1952) *The Diary of a Young Girl*, trans. B. M. Mooyart. London: Vallentine-Mitchell.

Friedländer, Saul (1984) *Reflections of Nazism: An Essay on Kitsch and Death*, trans. Thomas Weyr. New York: Harper and Row.

____ (ed.) (1992) *Probing the Limits of Representation: Nazism and the 'Final Solution'*. Cambridge, MA: Harvard University Press.

____ (1993) *Memory, History and the Extermination of the Jews of Europe*. Bloomington and Indianapolis, IN: Indiana University Press.

Friedman, Lester D. (1982) *Hollywood's Image of the Jew*. New York: Frederick Ungar.

____ (1987) *The Jewish Image in American Film*. Secaucus, NJ: Citadel Press.

Friedman, Regine Mihal (1983) *L'image et Son Juif: Le Juif Dans le Cinema Nazi*. Paris: Payot.

Fröhlich, Elke (ed.) (1987) *Die Tagebücher von Joseph Goebbels*. Munich: Saur.

Fuchs, Esther (1999) 'Images of Women in Holocaust Films', *Shofar: An Interdisciplinary Journal of Jewish Studies*, 17, 2, 49–56.

____ (2003) 'Gender and Holocaust Docudrama: Gentile Heroines in Rescue Films', *Shofar: An Interdisciplinary Journal of Jewish Studies*, 22, 1, 80–94.

Furhammer, Leif and Folke Isaksson (1971) *Politics and Film*. London: Studio Vista.

Garrard, Eve and Geoffrey Scarre (ed.) (2003) *Moral Philosophy and the Holocaust*. Aldershot: Ashgate.

Gary, Romain (1969) *The Dance of Genghis Cohn*. London: Jonathan Cape.

Geehr, Richard, John Heinemann and Gerald Herman (1985) 'Wien 1910, An Example of Nazi Anti-Semitism', *Film & History*, 15, 3, 50–65.

Gellately, Robert (1991) *The Gestapo and German Society: Enforcing Racial Policy*. Oxford: Clarendon Press.

Geller, Jay (2002) 'The Rites of Responsibility: The Cinematic Rhetoric of Claude Lanzmann's *Shoah*', *Film & History*, 32, 1, 30–7.

Gellert, Charles L. (1989) *The Holocaust, Israel, and the Jews: Motion Pictures in the National Archives*. Washington, DC: National Archives and Records Administration.

Gilbert, Martin (1981) *Auschwitz and the Allies*. London: Michael Joseph/George Rainbird.

____ (1986) *The Holocaust: The Jewish Tragedy*. London: Collins.

____ (2000) *Never Again: A History of the Holocaust*. London: HarperCollins/Imperial War Museum.

Gilman, Sandor L. (1998) '"Smart Jews": From *The Caine Mutiny* to *Schindler's List* and Beyond', in Tony Barta (ed.) *Screening the Past: Film and the Representation of History*. Westport, CT: Praeger, 63–81.

____ (2000) 'Is Life Beautiful? Can the Shoah Be Funny? Some Thoughts on Recent and Older Films', in *Critical Inquiry*, 26, 2, 279–308.

Glazar, Richard (1994) *Treblinka, Slovo Jak z Dětske Říkanky*. Praha: Ústav pro soudobé dějiny AV ČR.

Glock, Charles Y., Gertrude J. Selznick and Joe L. Spaeth (1966) *The Apathetic Majority: A Study Based on Public Responses to the Eichmann Trial*. New York: Harper and Row.

Golding, Louis (1939) *Mr Emmanuel*. London: Rich and Cowan.

Green, Gerald (1969) *The Artists of Terezin*. New York: Hawthorn Books.

____ (1978) *Holocaust*. New York: Bantam Books.

Grobman, Alex (1983) 'Hollywood on the Holocaust', *Shoah: a Review of Holocaust Studies and Commemorations*, Fall/Winter, 6–10.

____ and Daniel J. Landes (1983) *Genocide: Critical Issues of the Holocaust*. Los Angeles: Simon Wiesenthal Center.

Gross, Jan Tomasz (2001) *Neighbours: The Destruction of the Jewish Community in Jedwabne*. Princeton, NJ: Princeton University Press.

Guerin, Frances (2002) 'Reframing the Photographer and his Photographs: *Photographer* (1995)' *Film & History*, 32, 1, 43–54.

Gutman, Israel (1990) *Encyclopaedia of the Holocaust*, 4 vols. London: Macmillan.

Haase, Christine (2002) 'Theodore Kotulla's *Excerpts from a German Life* (*Aus einem deutschen Leben*, 1977) or The Inability to Speak: Cinematic Holocaust Representation in Germany', *Film & History*, 32, 2, 48–61.

Haasis, Helmut (1998) *Joseph Süss Oppenheimer, Genannt Jud Süss, Finanzier, Freidenker, Justizopfer*. Reinbek bei Hamburg: Rowolt Taschenbuch.

Hamdorf, Wolfgang Martin (1995) 'Der Holocaust im Film', *Film-dienst*, 48, 20, 36–39.

Hansen, Miriam Bratu (2001) '*Schindler's List* is not *Shoah*: Second Commandment, Popular Modernism and Public Memory', in Barbie Zelizer (ed.) *Visual Culture and the Holocaust*. New Brunswick, NJ: Rutgers University Press, 147–51.

Hardy, Forsyth (ed.) (1946) *Grierson on Documentary*. London: Collins.

Harlan, Veit (undated) *Jud Süss: ein historische Film*. Archiv der Stiftung Deutsche Kinemathek, Berlin.

_____ (1966) *Im Schatten meiner Filme: Selbstbiographie, hrsg. und mit einem Nachwort versehen von H. C. Opfermann*. Gütersloh: Sigbert Mohn.

Harrison, David (1981) *The White Tribes of Africa*. London: BBC Publications.

Hart, Kitty (1962) *I Am Alive*. London and New York: Abelard-Schuman.

_____ (1981) *Return to Auschwitz*. London: Sidgwick and Jackson.

Hartman, Jan (1998) Interview, Imperial War Museum Sound Archive, Accession No. 18557.

Hartwell, Geoffrey H. (ed.) (1994) *Holocaust Remembrance: The Shapes of Memory*. Oxford: Blackwell.

Harwood, Ronald (2003) *The Pianist/Taking Sides*. London: Faber and Faber.

Haskell, Molly (1978) 'A Failure to Connect', *New York Magazine*, 15 May 1979, 79–80.

Hauff, Wilhelm (1962) *Jud Süss*. Stuttgart: J. G. Cotta'sche Buchhandlung Nachf.

Havel, Václav (1976) 'Alfred Radok: an obituary', in Jarka M. Burian, *Leading Creators of Twentieth-Century Czech Theatre*. London: Routledge, 59–76.

Hector, Susan (2000) 'Teaching the Holocaust in England', in Ian Davies (ed.) *Teaching the Holocaust: Educational Dimensions, Principles and Practice*. New York: Continuum, 105–15.

Heinrich, André (1994) '*Nuit et Brouillard* au-delà de la censure', radio broadcast, *France Culture*, 6 August 1994.

Herman, Felicia (2001) 'Hollywood, Nazism, and the Jews, 1933–1941', *American Jewish History*, 89, 1, 61–89.

Herzstein, Robert Edwin (1985) 'The Jew in Wartime Nazi Film: An Interpretation of Goebbels' Role in the Holocaust', in Sanford Pinsker (ed.) *Holocaust Studies Annual, Vol. 3: Literature, the Arts, and the Holocaust*. Greenwood, FL: Penkevill, 177–88.

Hilberg, Raul (1961) *The Destruction of the European Jews*. London: W. H. Allen.

_____ (1996) *The Politics of Memory: The Journey of a Holocaust Historian*. Chicago: Ivan R. Dee.

Hine, Lewis (1909) 'Social Photography, How the Camera May Help in the Social Uplift', in *Proceedings, National Conference of Charities and Corrections, June 1909*, reprinted in Alan Trachtenberg (1980) *Classic Essays on Photography*. New Haven: Leete's Island Books.

Hippler, Fritz (1942) *Betrachtungen zum Filmschaffen*. Berlin: Max Hesses.

Hirsch, Joshua Francis (2002) 'Post-traumatic Cinema and the Holocaust Documentary', *Film & History*, 32, 1, 9–21.

_____ (2004) *Afterimage: Film, Trauma and the Holocaust*. Philadelphia: Temple University Press.

Hoberman, J. (1994) '*Schindler's List*: Myth, Movie and Memory', *The Village Voice*, 29 March, 24–31.

_____ (1996) '*Shoah*: Witness to Annihilation', in Kevin MacDonald and Mark Cousins (eds) *Imagining Reality: The Faber Book of Documentary*. London: Faber & Faber, 316–24 [originally published in *The Village Voice*, 29 October 1985].

Hollstein, Dorothea (1983) *Jud Süss und die Deutschen*. Frankfurt: Ullstein.

Horak, Jan-Christopher (1984) 'Zionist Film Propaganda in Nazi Germany', in *Historical Journal of Film, Radio and Television*, 4, 1, 49–58.

Hornshøj-Møller, Stig (1997) '*Der ewige Jude*: A Source-Critical Evaluation of an Important Film Document' paper given at the Imperial War Museum, London, 17 November. Online at http://holocaust-info.dk/shm/london.htm.

_____ (1999) Stig Hornshøj-Møller on *Der ewige Jude*. Online at http://www.holocaust-history.org/der-ewige-jude.

Hornshøj-Møller, Stig and David Culbert (1992) '*Der ewige Jude* (1940): Joseph Goebbels' Unequaled Monument to Antisemitism', *Historical Journal of Film, Radio and Television*, 12, 1, 41–67.

Hull, David Stewart (1969) *Film in the Third Reich*. Berkeley, CA: University of California Press.

Hutchings, Peter J. (1997) 'Modern Forensics: Photography and Other Suspects', *Cardozo Studies in Law and Literature*, 9, 2, 229–43.

Huyssen, Andreas (1980) 'The Politics of Identification: Holocaust and West Germany', *New German Critique*, 19, 117–36.

Ignatieff, Michael (1994) *Blood and Belonging: Journeys into the New Nationalism*. London: Vintage.
____ (1999) *The Warrior's Honor: Ethnic War and the Modern Conscience*. London: Vintage.
____ (2000) *The Virtual War: Kosovo and Beyond*. London: Chatto and Windus.
Insdorf, Annette (2003) *Indelible Shadows: Film and the Holocaust* (third edition). Cambridge: Cambridge University Press.
Information Services Control: Germany and Austria 1945. The National Archives, Public Record Office, Kew, Ref. No. FO 945/905
International Journal of Political Education, 4, 1–2, May 1981 [special issue on the impact of the television series *Holocaust*].
Iordanova, Dina (2001) *Cinema of Flames: Balkan Culture and the Media*. London: British Film Institute.
Isaac, Dan (1980) 'Film and the Holocaust', *Centerpoint*, 4, 1, 137–40 [nb: The entire issue is devoted to the topic of the Holocaust].
Jackson, Robert H. (1946) 'Final Report of the Chief of Counsel for the United States, Submitted to the President, October 7 1946', in Record Group 238, National Archives Collection of World War II War Crimes Records.
Jaspers, Karl (1956) *The Origin and Goal of History*, trans. Michael Bullock. London: Routledge & Kegan Paul.
Jewish Black Book Committee (1946) *The Black Book: The Nazi Crime Against the Jewish People*. New York: Duell, Sloan and Pearce.
Johnson, Eric A. (1999) *Nazi Terror: The Gestapo, Jews and Ordinary Germans*. London: John Murray.
Kaes, Anton (1989) *From Hitler to Heimat: The Return of History as Film*. Cambridge, MA: Harvard University Press.
Kalinowska, Iza (2002) 'Być synem Szpilmana', *Kino*, 9, 14.
Kemp, Paul (1991) *The Relief of Belsen, April 1945: Eyewitness Accounts*. London: Imperial War Museum.
Keneally, Thomas (1982) *Schindler's Ark*. London: Hodder and Stoughton.
Klarsfeld, Serge (1994) *Memorial to the Jews Deported from France, 1942–1943*. Paris: Fils et Filles des des Déportés Juifs de France (FFDJF).
Knilli, Friedrich (1983) 'Die Gemeinsamkeit von Faschisten und Antifaschisten gegenüber dem NS-Film Jud Süss', in Friedrich Knilli, Thomas Maurer, Thomas Radevagen and Siegfried Zielinski (eds) *Jud Süss, Filmprotokoll, Programmheft und Einzelanalysen*. Berlin: Volker Spiess.
Knilli, Friedrich, Thomas Maurer, Thomas Radevagen and Siegfried Zielinski (eds) *Jud Süss, Filmprotokoll, Programmheft und Einzelanalysen*. Berlin: Volker Spiess.
Koch, Gertrud (1989) 'The Aesthetic Transformation of the Image of the Unimaginable: Notes on Claude Lanzmann's *Shoah*', *October*, 38, 14–24.
____ (1991) 'The Angel of Forgetfulness and the Black Box of Facticity: Trauma and Memory in Claude Lanzmann's *Shoah*', *History and Memory*, 3, 1, 119–34.
Kolb, Eberhard (2002) *Bergen-Belsen: From 'Detention Camp' to Concentration Camp, 1943–1945*. Göttingen: Vandenhoeck & Ruprecht.
Kolbert, Jack (2001) *The Worlds of Elie Wiesel: An Overview of His Career and His Major Themes*. London: Associated University Press.
Koestler, Arthur (1943) 'A Challenge to Knights in Rusty Armor', *New York Times*, 14 February. Online at http://partners.nytimes.com/books/00/01/02/specials/koestler-challenge.html)
____ (1981) Interview, Imperial War Museum Sound Archive, Accession No. 5393.
Kohler, Eric D. (1985) 'Hollywood and Holocaust: A Discourse on the Politics of Rescue', in Sanford Pinsker (ed.) *Holocaust Studies Annual, Vol. 3: Literature, the Arts, and the Holocaust*. Greenwood, FL: Penkevill, 79–93.
Koppes, Clayton R. and Gregory D. Black (1986) 'Blacks, Loyalty and Motion Picture Propaganda in World War II', *Journal of American History*, 73, 2, 383–406.
Kracauer, Siegfried (1974) *From Caligari to Hitler: A Psychological History of the German Film*. Princeton, NJ: Princeton University Press.
Kramer, Naomi (2001) 'The Transformation of the Shoah in Film', in Peter M. Daly (ed.) *Building History: The Shoah in Art, Memory, and Myth*. New York: Peter Lang, 143–48.
Krantz, Charles K. (1985) 'Alain Resnais' *Nuit et Brouillard*: A Historical and Cultural Analysis', in Sanford Pinsker (ed.) *Holocaust Studies Annual, Vol. 3: Literature, the Arts, and the Holocaust*. Greenwood, FL: Penkevill, 107–20.
Kraus, Dita (2002) Interview, Imperial War Museum Sound Archive, Accession No. 23090.
Krauss, Werner (1958) *Das Schauspiel meines Lebens*. Stuttgart: Henry Goverts.
Kuper, Leo (1981) *Genocide*. London: Penguin.
Kushner, Tony (1989) *The Persistence of Prejudice: Antisemitism in British Society During the Second World*

War. Manchester: Manchester University Press.

_____ (1994) *The Holocaust and the Liberal Imagination: A Social and Cultural History*. Oxford: Blackwell.

LaCapra, Dominick (1994) *Representing the Holocaust: History, Theory, Trauma*. Ithaca, NY and London: Cornell University Press.

_____ (1997) 'Lanzmann's *Shoah*: "Here, There is No Why"', *Critical Inquiry*, 23, 231–69 [originally presented as a paper at *History and the Limits of Interpretation, A Symposium*, at the Center for the Study of Cultures, Rice University, March 1996].

_____ (1998) *History and Memory After Auschwitz*. Ithaca, NY and London: Cornell University Press.

Lagrou, Pieter (2000) *The Legacy of Nazi Occupation: Patriotic Memory and National Recovery in Western Europe, 1945–1965*. Cambridge: Cambridge University Press.

Landau, Ronnie (1998) *Studying the Holocaust: Issues, Reading and Documents*. London: Routledge.

Landes, Daniel J. (1985) 'Modesty and Self-Dignity in Holocaust Films', in Alex Grobman and Daniel J. Landes (eds) *Genocide: Critical Issues of the Holocaust*. Los Angeles: Simon Wiesenthal Center, 11–13.

Lang, Berel (2001) *Holocaust Representation: Art Within the Limits of History and Ethics*. Baltimore: Johns Hopkins University Press.

Langer, Lawrence (1983) 'The Americanisation of the Holocaust on Stage and Screen', in Sarah Blacher Cohen (ed.) *From Hester Street to Hollywood*. Bloomington, IN: Indiana University Press, 213–30.

Langford, Barry (1999) '"You Cannot Look At This": Thresholds of Unrepresentability in Holocaust Film', *Journal of Holocaust Education*, 8, 3, 23–40.

Lanzmann, Claude (1979) 'From the Holocaust to the Holocaust', *Telos*, 42, 137–43.

_____ (1984) 'Holocaust, la représentation impossible', *Le Monde*, 3 March.

_____ (1990a) 'Les Non-lieux de la mémoire', in Claude Lanzmann (ed.) *Au sujet de Shoah, le film de Claude Lanzmann*. Paris: Ouvrage collectif, Éditions Belin.

_____ (1990b) *Shoah: The Complete Text of the Acclaimed Holocaust Film*. New York: Da Capo.

_____ (ed.) (1990c) *Au sujet de Shoah, le film de Claude Lanzmann*. Paris: Ouvrage collectif, Éditions Belin.

_____ (1994) 'Why Spielberg Has Distorted the Truth', *Guardian Weekly*, 3 April, 14 [originally published in *Le Monde*].

Lawrie, William F. (1984) Interview, Imperial War Museum Sound Archive, Accession No. 7481.

Leff, Leonard J. (1996) 'Hollywood and the Holocaust: Remembering *The Pawnbroker*', *American Jewish History*, 84, 4, 353–76.

Leiser, Erwin (1974) *Nazi Cinema*, trans. Gertrud Mander and David Wilson. London: Secker & Warburg.

Lennon, Helen (1995) 'Creating a Witness: Film as Evidence in International War Crimes Tribunals', PhD thesis, Department of Comparative Literature, Yale University.

Lentin, Ronit (2004) *Re-presenting the Shoah for the Twenty-First Century*. New York: Berghahn Books.

Levi, Primo (1960) *If This is a Man*, trans. Stuart Woolf. London: Orion.

_____ (1961) *Survival in Auschwitz*, trans. Stuart Woolf. New York: Macmillan.

_____ (1965) *The Truce: A Survivor's Journey Home from Auschwitz*, trans. Stuart Woolf. London: Bodley Head.

_____ (1988) *The Drowned and the Saved*, trans. Richard Rosenthal. London: Michael Joseph.

Levi, Trude (1996) *A Cat Called Adolf*. London: Vallentine-Mitchell.

Levin, Nora (1968) *The Holocaust: The Destruction of European Jewry*. New York: Schocken.

Lewis, Mike (1981) Interview, Imperial War Museum Sound Archive, Accession No. 4833.

Lewis, Stephen (1984) *Art Out of Agony: The Holocaust Theme in Literature, Sculpture and Film*. Montreal: CBC Enterprises.

Liebman, Stuart and Leonard Quart (1996) 'Czech Films of the Holocaust', *Cineaste*, 22, 1, 49–51.

Linenthal, Edward (1995) *Preserving Memory: The Struggle to Create America's Holocaust Museum*. New York: Viking Books.

Liotard, L. (2001) 'Le Travelling est-il une affaire du morale? Le cinéma d'Alain Resnais de *Van Gogh* è *Hiroshima Mon Amour* (1948–1959)', Masters thesis, University of Paris.

Liss, Andrea (1998) *Trespassing Through Shadows: Memory, Photography and the Holocaust*. Minneapolis: University of Minnesota Press.

Loiperdinger, Martin and David Culbert (1988) 'Leni Riefenstahl, the SA, and the Nazi Party Rally Films, Nuremberg 1933–34: *Sieg des Glaubens* and *Triumph des Willens*', *Historical Journal of Film, Radio and Television*, 8, 1, 3–38.

Longerich, Peter (1998) *Politik der Vernichtung, Eine Gesamtdarstellung der nationalsozialistischen Judenverfolgung*. Munich: Piper.

_____ (1999/2000) *The Wannsee Conference in the Development of the 'Final Solution' (Holocaust Educational Trust Research Papers 1, No 2 1999-2000)*, trans. Ian Gronbach and Donald Bloxham. London: Holocaust Educational Trust.

Loshitzky, Yosefa (ed.) (1997) *Spielberg's Holocaust: Critical Perspectives on Schindler's List*. Bloomington, IN: Indiana University Press.

____ (1997) 'Holocaust Others: Spielberg's *Schindler's List* versus Lanzmann's *Shoah*', in *Spielberg's Holocaust: Critical Perspectives on Schindler's List*. Bloomington, IN: Indiana University Press, 104–18.

Lubelski, Tadeusz (1992) *Strategie autorskie w polskim filmie fabularnym lat 1945–1961*. Kraków: Wydawnictwo Uniwersytetu Jagiellońskiego.

Lustig, Arnost (1959) *Démanty Noci*. Prague: Praha.

____ (1989) *Diamonds of the Night*. trans. Jeanne Nemcova. London: Quartet Books.

Mackenzie, Scott (2000) 'Lists and Chain Letters: Ethnic Cleansing, Holocaust Allegories and the Limits of Representation', *Canadian Journal of Film Studies*, 9, 2, 23–42.

Manchel, Frank (1995) 'A Reel Witness: Steven Spielberg's Representation of the Holocaust in *Schindler's List*', *Journal of Modern History*, 67, 1, 83–100.

____ (1998) 'Mishegoss: *Schindler's List*, Holocaust Representation and Film History', *Historical Journal of Film, Radio and Television*, 18, 3, 431–37.

Mann, Abby (2002) *Judgment at Nuremberg: A Play*. New York: New Directions.

Makarova, Elena, Serge Makarov and Victor Kuperman (2000) *University Over the Abyss*. Jerusalem: Verba.

Margry, Karel (1992) 'Theresienstadt (1944–45): The Nazi Propaganda Film Depicting the Concentration Camp as Paradise', *Historical Journal of Film, Radio and Television*, 12, 2, 145–62.

____ (1996) 'Das Konzentrationslager als Idylle', in Fritz Bauer Institut, Auschwitz Geschichte, Rezeption und Wirkung, Jahrbuch 1996 zur Geschichte und Wirkung des Holocaust. Frankfurt/New York: Campus.

____ (1999) 'The First Theresienstadt Film (1942)', *Historical Journal of Film, Radio and Television*, 19, 3, 309–37.

Marrus, Michael R. (1987) *The Holocaust in History*. Toronto: Lester & Orpen Dennys.

Mass Observation Archive. University of Sussex Special Collections Library. Online at http://www.sussex. ac.uk/library/speccoll/collection_descriptions/massobs.html.

Mazierska, Ewa (2000) 'Non-Jewish Jews, good Poles and historical truth in films of Andrzej Wajda', *Historical Journal of Film, Radio and Television*, 20, 2, 213–26.

____ (2001) 'Wanda Jakubowska's cinema of commitment', *European Journal of Women Studies*, 8, 2, 221–38.

Mazzetti, Lorenza (1962) *The Sky Falls [Il Cielo Cade]*, trans. Marguerite Waldman. London: The Bodley Head.

McBride, Joseph (1992) *Frank Capra: The Catastrophe of Success*. London: Faber & Faber.

Michel, Henri and Olga Wormser (ed.) (1954) *Tragédie de la déportation 1940–1945*. Témoignages de survivants des camps de concentration allemands. Paris: Hachette.

Miccichè, Lino (1985) *Cinema Italiano: gli anni '60 e oltre*. Venice: Marsilio.

Miller, Arthur (1992) *Homely Girl: A Life*. New York: Peter Blum.

Milton, Sybil (1985) 'Sensitive Issues about Holocaust Films', in Alex Grobman and Daniel J. Landes (eds) *Genocide: Critical Issues of the Holocaust*. Los Angeles: Simon Wiesenthal Center, 11–13.

Mintz, Alan L. (2001) *Popular Culture and the Shaping of Holocaust Memory in America*. Seattle and London: University of Washington Press.

Monaco, James (1979) *Alain Resnais*. New York: Oxford University Press.

Moorehead, Caroline (1984) *Sidney Bernstein: A Biography*. London: Jonathan Cape.

Morrow, Lance (1978) 'Television and the Holocaust', *Time*, 1 May 1978.

Mruklik, Barbara (1985) 'Wierność sobie: Rozmowa z Wanda Jakubowska', *Kino*, 6, 5–9; 20–1.

Muffs, Judith H. and Dennis B. Klein (1986) *The Holocaust in Books and Films: A Selected, Annotated List*. New York: Hippocrene books.

Neufeld, Amos (1992) 'Claude Lanzmann's *Shoah*', in David Platt (ed.) *Celluloid Power: Social Film Criticism From The Birth of a Nation to Judgment at Nuremberg*. Metuchen, NJ and London: Scarecrow Press, 457–66.

Niv, Kobi (2005) *Life is Beautiful, But Not for Jews: Another View of the Film by Benigni*, trans. Jonathan Beyrak Lev. Lanham: Scarecrow Press.

Novick, Peter (1999) *The Holocaust and Collective Memory: The American Experience*. London: Bloomsbury.

Nurckzyńska-Fidelska, Ewelina (1982) *Andrzej Munk*. Krakow: Wydawnictwo Literackie.

Oakes, Harry (1999) Interview, Imperial War Museum Sound Archive, Accession No. 19888.

Oberski, Jona (1978) *Kinderjaren*. s'Gravenhage: BZZTôH.

Ochman, Ewa (2003) 'Jedwabne and the Power Struggle in Poland: Remembering the Polish-Jewish Pact a Decade after the Collapse of Communism', *Perspectives on European Politics and Society*, 4, 2, 171–89.

____ (2004) 'Remembering the Polish-Jewish Pact a Decade after the Collapse of Communism', PhD thesis, European Studies Research Institute, University of Salford.

Olin, Margaret (1997) 'Lanzmann's Shoah and the Topography of the Holocaust Film', *Representations*, 57,

1–23.

Ophuls, Marcel (1972) *The Sorrow and the Pity*, trans. Mirielle Johnston. New York: Outerbridge and Lazard.
_____ (1985) 'Closely Watched Trains', *American Film*, 11, 16–7.

Palowski, Franciszek (1999) *Witness: The Making of Schindler's List*, trans. Anna and Robert G. Ware. London: Orion Books.

Patterson, James T. (1996) *Grand Expectations: The United States, 1945–74*. New York and Oxford: Oxford University Press.

Peck, Robert E. (2000) 'Misinformation, Missing Information, and Conjecture: Titanic and Historiography of Third Reich Cinema', *Media History*, 6, 1, 59–73.

Picart, Caroline Joan (Kay) (ed.) (2004) *The Holocaust Film Sourcebook*. Westport, CT: Praeger.

Planning Committee – papers circulated, 1940–1942. The National Archives, Public Record Office, Kew, Ref. No. INF 1/251.

Platt, David (ed.) (1992) *Celluloid Power: Social Film Criticism From The Birth of a Nation to Judgment at Nuremberg*. Metuchen, NJ and London: Scarecrow Press.

Płażewska, Jerzy (2002) 'Zeznanie przed trybunałem historii', *Kino*, 9, 15–16.

Porter, Katherine Anne (1962) *Ship of Fools*. Boston: Little, Brown.

Poxton, Robert O. (2001) *Vichy France: Old Guard and New Order, 1940–44*. New York: Columbia University Press.

Pritchard, R. John (annotated, compiled and edited) (1998) *The Tokyo Major War Crimes Trial: Transcripts of the Court Proceedings of the International Military Tribunal for the Far East*. Lewiston: Edwin Mellen Press.

Quart, Leonard (2000) 'A Second Look: *The Pawnbroker*', *Cineaste*, 25, 2, 48–50.

Rabinowitz, Paula (1994) *They Must Be Represented: The Politics of Documentary*. New York: Verso.

Radziwill, Anna (1989) 'The Teaching of the History of the Jews in Secondary Schools in the Polish People's Republic 1949–88', *POLIN: A Journal of Polish-Jewish Studies*, Vol. 4. Oxford: Blackwell, 402–24.

Rapaport, Lynn (2002) 'Hollywood's Holocaust: *Schindler's List* and the Construction of Memory', *Film & History*, 32, 1, 55–65.

Raphael, Marc Lee (ed.) (2003) *The Representation of the Holocaust in Literature and Film*. Williamsburg, VA: Department of Religion of the College of William and Mary.

Rashke, Richard (1983) *Escape from Sobibor*. London: Michael Joseph.

Raskin, Richard (1987) *Alain Resnais' Nuit et Brouillard: On the Making, Reception and Functions of a Major Documentary Film. Including a New Interview with Alain Resnais and the Original Shooting Script*. Åarhus: Åarhus University Press.

Rawlinson, Mark (1999) 'Adapting the Holocaust: *Schindler's List*, intellectuals and public knowledge', in Deborah Cartmell and Imelda Whelehan (eds) *Adaptations: From Text to Screen, Screen to Text*. London: Routledge, 113–27.

Reading, Anna (2002) *The Social Inheritance of the Holocaust: Gender, Culture and Memory*. Basingstoke: Palgrave Macmillan.

Records of Allied Operational and Occupation Headquarters, World War II. National Archives, Record Group 331, National Archives and Records Administration (NARA), Washington, DC.

Rees, Laurence (2002) *The Nazis: A Warning from History*. London: BBC Worldwide.

Reilly, Jo (1997) 'Cleaner, Carer, Occasional Dance Partner? Writing Women Back into the Liberation of Bergen-Belsen', in Jo Reilly, David Cesarani, Tony Kushner and Colin Richmond (eds) *Belsen in History and Memory*. London: Frank Cass, 149–61.
_____ (1998) *Belsen: The Liberation of a Concentration Camp*. London: Routledge.

Reilly, Jo, David Cesarani, Tony Kushner and Colin Richmond (eds) (1997) *Belsen in History and Memory*. London: Frank Cass.

Reimann, Viktor (1977) *The Man Who Created Hitler: Joseph Goebbels*. London: William Kimber.

Reitlinger, Gerald R. (1971) *The Final Solution: The Attempt to Exterminate the Jews of Europe, 1939–1945*. London: Sphere Books.

Renov, Michael (2000) 'Historical Discourses of the Unimaginable: Péter Forgács' *The Maelstrom*', conference paper delivered at *Visible Evidence VIII*, Utrecht.

Rentschler, Eric (1996) *The Ministry of Illusion: Nazi Cinema and its Afterlife*. Cambridge, MA: Harvard University Press.

Resnais, Alain (2000) Interview with Antoine de Baecque and Claire Vassé, *Cahiers du cinéma*, special issue 'Le siècle du cinéma', November, 73–4.

Reuth, Ralf Georg (1993) *Goebbels*. London: Constable.

Rice, Louisa (2002) 'The Voice of Silence: Alain Resnais' *Night and Fog* and Collective Memory in Post-Holocaust France', *Film & History*, 32, 1, 22–29.

Rich, Frank (1994) 'Schindler's Dissed', *New York Times*, 6 February, D–17.

Richards, Jeffrey (1982) 'British Board of Film Censors and Content Control in the 1930s: Foreign Affairs', *Historical Journal of Film, Radio and Television*, 2, 1, 39–48.

Richmond, Thomas (1996) 'The Perpetrators' Testimony in *Shoah*', *Journal of Holocaust Education*, 5, 1, 61–83.

Riefenstahl, Leni (1992) *The Sieve of Time: The Memoirs of Leni Riefenstahl*. London: Quartet Books.

Rosenfeld, Alvin H. (1983) 'The Holocaust in American Popular Culture', *Midstream*, June/July, 53–9.

_____ (1995) 'The Americanization of the Holocaust', *Commentary*, 99, 6, 35–40.

_____ (ed.) (1997) *Thinking about the Holocaust: After Half a Century*. Bloomington, IN: Indiana University Press.

Rosenstone, Robert (1995) *Visions of the Past: The Challenge of Film to our Idea of History*. Cambridge, MA: Harvard University Press.

Rothberg, Michael (2000) *Traumatic Realism: The Demands of Holocaust Representation*. Minneapolis: University of Minnesota Press.

Rousso, Henry (1987) *Le Syndrome du Vichy, 1944–1948*. Paris: Éditions du Seuil.

_____ (1991) *The Vichy Syndrome: History and Memory in France Since 1944*, trans. Arthur Goldhammer. Cambridge, MA: Harvard University Press.

_____ (1998) *La Hantise du passé*. Paris: Textuel.

Salmons, Paul (2001) 'Moral Dilemmas: History Teaching and the Holocaust', *Teaching History*, 104, September 2001. Online at http://www.iwm.org.uk/upload/pdf/teachinghistory_20040521104915.pdf.

Salomon, Charlotte (1981) *Charlotte Salomon: Life or Theater? An Autobiographical Play*, trans. Leila Vennewitz, with an introduction by Judith Herzberg. New York: Viking.

Scharf, Rafael (1993) Interview, Imperial War Museum Sound Archive, Accession No. 13378.

Scheel, Wolfgang (ed.) (2002) *Bergen-Belsen: Explanatory Notes on the Exhibition*. Hanover: Niedersächsische Landeszentrale für Politische Bildung.

Scheffer, David (2002) 'The Future of Atrocity Law', *Suffolk Transnational Law Review*, 25, 389–432.

Schulte-Sasse, Linda (1996) *Entertaining the Third Reich: Illusions of Wholeness in Nazi Cinema*. Durham, NC and London: Duke University Press.

Seghers, Anna (1943) *The Seventh Cross*, trans. James A. Galston. London: Hamish Hamilton.

Shandler, Jeffrey (1999) *While America Watches: Televising the Holocaust*. New York: Oxford University Press.

Shavelson, Melville (1971) *How to Make a Jewish Movie*. Englewood Cliffs, NJ: Prentice-Hall.

Shaw, Irwin (1948) *The Young Lions*. New York: Random House.

Shaw, Robert (1967) *The Man in the Glass Booth*. London: Chatto and Windus.

Sherman, Jodi (2002) 'Humor, Resistance, and the Abject: Roberto Benigni's *Life is Beautiful* and Charlie Chaplin's *The Great Dictator*', Film & History, 32, 2, 72–3.

Shirer, William (1941) *Berlin Diary: The Journal of a Foreign Correspondent 1934–1941*. New York: Alfred A. Knopf.

_____ (1960) *The Rise and Fall of the Third Reich*. New York: Simon and Schuster.

Sington, Derrick and Arthur Weidenfeld (1942) *The Goebbels Experiment*. London: John Murray.

Skirball, Sheba F. (1990) *Films of the Holocaust: An Annotated Filmography of Collections in Israel*. New York: Garland.

Smith, Helmut Walser (ed.) (2002) *Holocaust and Other Genocides: History, Representation, Ethics*. Nashville: Vanderbilt University Press.

Sobchack, Vivian (ed.) (1996) *The Persistence of History: Cinema, Television and the Modern Event*. London: Routledge.

Sontag, Susan (1977) *On Photography*. New York: Farrar, Straus and Giroux.

Sorlin, Pierre (1980) *Film in History: Restaging the Past*. Oxford: Blackwell.

Speer, Albert (1970) *Inside the Third Reich: Memoirs [Erinnerungen]*, trans. Richard and Clara Winston. London: Weidenfeld and Nicolson.

Steiner, George (1985 [1965]) 'A Kind of Survivor', in *Language and Silence: Essays 1958–1966*. London: Faber & Faber, 117–32.

Sterling, Eric (2002) 'All Rules Barred: A Defense of Speilberg's *Schlindler's List*', Film & History, 32, 2, 62–70.

Stern, Selma (1929) *Jud Süss*. Berlin: Akademie Verlag.

Stevens, Matthew (ed.) (1992) *Jewish Film Directory: A Guide to More than 1200 Films of Jewish Interest from 32 Countries Over 85 Years*. Westport, CT: Greenwood Press.

Stewart, Hugh (Lieutenant-Colonel) (1979) Interview, Imperial War Museum Sound Archive, Accession No. 4579.

Stier, Oren Baruch (2003) *Committed to Memory: Cultural Mediations of the Holocaust*. Amherst: University of Massachusetts Press.

Struk, Janina (2004) *Photographing the Holocaust: Interpretations of the Evidence*. London: I.B. Tauris, in association with the European Jewish Publication Association.

Styron, William (1979) *Sophie's Choice*. New York: Random House.

Sussex, Elizabeth (1984) 'The Fate of F3080', *Sight and Sound*, 53, 2, 92–7.

Szpilman, Władysław (1999) *The Pianist: The Extraordinary Story of One Man's Survival in Warsaw 1939–1945*, trans. Anthea Bell. London: Gollancz.

Tanner, Adam (2000) 'Nazi hate film maker looks back with some regrets', Reuters interview with Fritz Hippler, 11 December.

Tanner, Peter (1983) Interview, Imperial War Museum Sound Archive, Accession No. 7379.

Taylor, Fred (trans. and ed.) (1982) *The Goebbels Diaries 1939–1941*. London: Hamish Hamilton.

Tegel, Susan (1995) 'The Politics of Censorship: Britain's *Jew Süss* (1934) in London, New York and Vienna', *Historical Journal of Film, Radio and Television*, 15, 2, 219–44.

_____ (1996a) *Jew Suss, Jud Süss*. Trowbridge: Flicks Books.

_____ (1996b) 'Veit Harlan and the Origins of Jud Süss 1938-39: Opportunism in the Creation of Nazi Antisemitic Film Propaganda', *Historical Journal of Film, Radio and Television*, 16, 4, 515–31.

_____ (2000) '"The Demonic Effect": Veit Harlan's Use of Jewish Extras in *Jud Süss* (1940)', *Holocaust and Genocide Studies*, 14, 2, 215–41.

Themerson, Stefan and Franczika. Information at The Themerson Archive, London. Online at http://www.themersonarchive.com.

Thompson, David (2003) '*The Pianist*', *Sight and Sound*, February, 55–6. Online at http://www.bfi.org.uk/sightandsound/2003_02/review02_pianist.html.

Thorpe, Frances and Nicholas Pronay (1980) *British Official Films in the Second World War: A Descriptive Catalogue*. Oxford: Clio Press.

Totten, Samuel (1988) 'The Literature, Art and Film of the Holocaust', in Israel W. Charny (ed.) *Genocide: A Critical Bibliographic Review*. London: Mansell, 209–19.

Toll, Nelly (1998) *When Memory Speaks: The Holocaust in Art*. Westport, CT: Praeger.

Traba, Elzbieta and Robert Traba (eds) (1999) Tematy Żydowskiem. Olsztyn: Wspólnota Kulturowa Borussia.

Trachtenberg, Alan (1980) *Classic Essays on Photography*. New Haven: Leete's Island Books.

Tritton, Ronald (c. 1945) *War Diary* (unpublished), held in Imperial War Museum, Department of Documents.

United Nations, International Criminal Tribunal for Rwanda. Online at http://www.ictr.org.

_____ International Criminal Tribunal for the former Yugoslavia. Online at http://www.un.org/icty.

United States Holocaust Memorial Museum, 'Frequently Asked Questions'. Online at http://www.ushmm.org/research/library/index.php?content=faq.

Uris, Leon (1958) *Exodus*. Garden City, NY: Doubleday.

Various (1956a) 'The German Concentration Camp System (1940–1944)', special issue, *Revue d'histoire de la deuxième guerre mondiale*, 15–16, July–September.

_____ (1956b) 'The Condition of the Jews', special issue, *Revue d'histoire de la deuxième guerre mondiale*, 24, October.

Vaughan, Dai (1983) *Portrait of an Invisible Man: The Working Life of Stewart McAllister, Film Editor*. London: British Film Institute.

Veale, Eddie (1997) 'Evading the Charges', *Living Marxism*, March, 16–20.

Viano, Maurizio (1999) '*Life is Beautiful*: Reception, Allegory and Holocaust Laughter', *Film Quarterly*, 53, 1, 26–34.

Vietor-Engländer, Deborah (1996) 'Theater and Film as a Medium for Presenting the Experiences of Shoah Survivors Today', *European Legacy*, 1, 3, 1254–9.

Walker, Gila (1980) 'An Analysis of *Der ewige Jude*: Its Relationship to Nazi Antisemitic Ideas and Policies', *Wide Angle*, 3, 4, 48–53.

Wall, Ian (1996) *Schindler's List Study Guide*. London: Film Education. Online at http://www.filmeducation.org/filmlib/schindler.pdf.

_____ (1998) *Screening Histories*. London: Film Education.

_____ (2003) *The Pianist* [CD-ROM]. London: Film Education.

Wallant, Edward Lewis (1961) *The Pawnbroker*. New York: Harcourt, Brace and World.

Weinrich, Max (1999) *Hitler's Professors*. London: Yale University Press.

Weisman, Gary (2004) *Fantasies of Witnessing: Postwar Efforts to Experience the Holocaust*. Ithaca, NY and London: Cornell University Press.

Welch, David (1983) *Propaganda and the German Cinema, 1933–1945*. Oxford: Clarendon Press.

_____ (1992) '"Jews Out!" Antisemitic Film Propaganda in Nazi Germany and the "Jewish Question"', *British*

Journal of Holocaust Education, 1, 1, 55–73.

Wiedmer, Caroline (1999) *The Claims of Memory: Representations of the Holocaust in Contemporary Germany and France*. Ithaca, NY and London: Cornell University Press.

Wiesel, Elie (1960) *Night*, trans. Stella Rodway. London: MacGibbon & Kee.

____ (1978a) *A Jew Today*, trans. Marion Wiesel. New York: Vintage.

____ (1978b) 'Trivialising the Holocaust: Semi-Fact and Semi-Fiction', *New York Times*, 16 April.

____ (1985) 'A Survivor Remembers Other Survivors of the Shoah', *New York Times*, 3 November.

____ (2003) Preface to Annette Insdorf, *Indelible Shadows: Film and the Holocaust* (third edition). Cambridge: Cambridge University Press.

Wiesenthal, Simon (1982) *Max and Helen*. New York: Morrow.

Wieviorka, Annette (1987) 'Un lieu de mémoire et d'histoire: le Mémorial du martyr juif inconnu', *Revue de l'Université de Bruxelles*, 1–2, 107–32.

____ (1992) *Déportation et genocide. Entre la mémoire et l'oubli*. Paris: Plon.

Wilcox, Larry (2002) 'Special Focus: The Holocaust on Film', *Film & History*, 32, 1 and 2.

Williams, William R. (1995) Interview, Imperial War Museum Sound Archive, Accession No. 15437.

Winston, Brian (1981) 'Was Hitler There? Reconsidering *Triumph of the Will*', *Sight and Sound*, 50, 2, 103–7.

Wistrich, Robert (1992) *Antisemitism: The Longest Hatred*. London: Mandarin.

____ (1997) *Lessons of the Holocaust Educational Pack*. London: Holocaust Education Trust and London Jewish Cultural Centre.

Wolfgram, Mark A. (2002) 'West German and Unified German Cinema's Difficult Encounter with the Holocaust', *Film & History*, 32, 2, 24–37.

Wright, Basil C. (1945) Diary (unpublished) kept while making the film *A Defeated People*. Photocopy, Imperial War Museum Department of Documents, Ref. No. 83/10/1.

Wright, Melanie J. (2000) '"Don't Touch My Holocaust": Responding to *Life is Beautiful*', *Journal of Holocaust Education*, 9, 1, 19–32.

Wróbel, Piotr (1997) 'Double Memory: Poles and Jews After the Holocaust', *East European Politics and Societies*, 11, 3, 560–74.

Wrong, Michaela (2005) *I Didn't Do It For You: How the World Betrayed a Small African Nation*. London: Fourth Estate.

Wulf, Josef (1983) *Theater und Film im Dritten Reich*. Gütersloh: Sigbert Mohn.

Young, James E. (1988) *Writing and Rewriting the Holocaust: Narrative and the Consequences of Interpretation*. Bloomington, IN: Indiana University Press.

____ (1993) *Holocaust Memorials and Meaning: The Texture of Memory*. New Haven: Yale University Press.

____ (2000) *At Memory's Edge: After-images of the Holocaust in Contemporary Art and Architecture*. New Haven, CT: Yale University Press.

Zelizer, Barbie (ed.) (2000) *Remembering to Forget: Holocaust Memory through the Camera's Eye*. New Brunswick, NJ: Rutgers University Press.

____ (2001) *Visual Culture and the Holocaust*. New Brunswick, NJ: Rutgers University Press.

Zeman, Scott C. and Mark Chasins Samuels (2002) '"The Truth of a Mad Man": Collective Memory and Representation of the Holocaust in *The Partisans of Vilna* (1986) and the Documentary Genre', *Film & History*, 32, 1, 38–42.

Zielinski, Siegfried (1986) 'History as Entertainment and Provocation: The TV Series *Holocaust* in West Germany', in Anson Rabinbach and Jack Zipes (eds) *Germans and Jews Since the Holocaust: The Changing Situation*. New York: Holmes and Meier, 258–83.

Žižek, Slavoj (2000) 'Camp Comedy', *Sight and Sound*, 10, 4, 26–9.

Zuccotti, Susan (1987) *The Italians and the Holocaust: Persecution, Rescue, and Survival*. New York: Basic Books.

INDEX